SERIAL KILLERS:
UP CLOSE AND PERSONAL

SERIAL KILLERS:
UP CLOSE AND PERSONAL

INSIDE THE WORLD OF TORTURERS, PSYCHOPATHS, AND MURDERERS

Christopher Berry-Dee

Ulysses Press

Published in the United States by
ULYSSES PRESS
P.O. Box 3440
Berkeley, CA 94703
www.ulyssespress.com

First published in the U.K. in 2002 as *Talking with Serial Killers* and *Talking with Serial Killers 2* by John Blake Publishing

ISBN13: 978-1-56975-619-5
Library of Congress Catalog Number: 2007933420

Printed and bound in Canada by Marquis Book Printing

7 9 10 8 6

Acquisitions: Nick Denton-Brown
U.S. Proofreaders: Ruth Marcus, Amy Hough, Lauren Harrison
Production: Judith Metzener, Lisa Kester
Cover design: what!design @ whatweb.com
Cover photo: © istockphoto.com/Niilo Tippler

Dedicated to my lovely wife Tatiana,
and the memory of Leanna Williams
(died August 23, 1994), a two-year-old victim of her stepfather,
Santiago Margarito Rangel Varelas.

Contents

Contents

Acknowledgments

As Professor Elliott Leyton, the world's most widely consulted expert on serial killing, and former FBI Special Agent, Robert Ressler, the world's most renowned offender profiler both agree, unless you are a police officer or a psychiatrist, both of whom have unique access to the penal system, it is almost impossible to gain access to interview a single serial murderer, let alone two such creatures. I have interviewed, at length, over thirty.

Apart from the financial outlay, which may cost many thousands of dollars only for the offender to change his or her mind at the last minute as you arrive at the prison gate, one has to build up a relationship with a killer over many years of correspondence before they begin to trust you. But, this is only a fraction of the work involved.

Even to begin to understand the subject under study, one has to research their history back to birth. Meet with their parents, relations, friends, schoolteachers, work colleagues, the victim's next-of-kin, the police, attorneys, judges, psychiatrists and psychologists, even the correctional staff who are charged with their welfare while in custody, often on Death Row. Then, like the razor wire that forms an unpenetrable barrier around the prisons, one has to negotiate a way through the red tape that wraps up our killers. Without the permission of the Department of Corrections, you go nowhere. Only when each of the above has been "checked off" do you get to meet them—the most dangerous human predators on Earth.

As Sondra London says in her excellent book *Knockin' on Joe*, "Getting involved with these people is a dangerous matter, because when you concentrate deeply on any personality for an extended time, you find yourself drawn into their world ... And while you are in their cages studying them, they are studying you."

I have often had cause to contemplate the words of Friedrich Nietzsche: "Whoever fights monsters should see to it that in the process he does not become a monster. And when you look into the abyss, the abyss also looks into you."

Non-fiction is not possible without a collective effort by many people, and the study of violent crime on a first-hand basis can be, at once, rewarding, exciting and distressing. But at the end of the road, the time comes to reflect on that journey and to remember all those individuals and organizations who, in their various capacities, helped to make this book possible and, hopefully, worthwhile.

Many of their names already appear in the main text. Others do not, but they were equally important in the development, research and writing.

I would particularly like to thank, where appropriate, the victims' next-of-kin. The killers featured in this book have taken their revenge on society and there is no adequate measure for the agony they have wrought. Death is tangible, grief less so. Yet, despite the tragic losses of loved ones, those left behind have shown compassion for the killers of their children. Without their help, without their anguish, without their indelible pain, this book could not have struck the emotional balance it is hoped it has achieved.

I also thank the many Departments of Corrections for allowing unrestricted access to their penal systems and the offenders who were interviewed. Numerous law enforcement officers, attorneys and judges who have honorably discharged their professional duties, not only in bringing the offenders to justice, but in assisting, where they could, in the detailed research for this book. And, strange as this may seem, thanks are also due to the serial killers and mass murderers who allowed me into their dark worlds, for if society is to learn anything about how these beasts tick, we must, however abhorrent it may seem, listen to their words, their truths and lies.

As always, I am indebted to my close friend, Robin Odell. A superb writer and editor in any event, Robin knows this subject better than most. He has taken much of my raw manuscript, and has helped to polish it into the completed work sitting before you now.

For their personal support, perhaps now is the moment to thank a few of those who were patient enough to listen to my thoughts on serial homicide for months on end. Therefore, I extend much gratitude to my father and mother, Patrick and May. Great friends, Jackie Clay, Graham Williams, David "Elvis" Murphy, Ace Francis, Bob Noyce, Phil Simpson, Barbara Pearman, and Tony Brown, who kept my spirits up when they were low. My television producer, Frazer Ashford, Steve Morris, and my staff at *The New Criminologist.*

Special thanks to Phillip Simpson, Kirstie McCallum, Sarah Brown, Ruth Sands, Simon Beal (webmaster of TNC), and Martin Balaam.

Much gratitude is also extended to all of the professionals who have assisted me in the writing of this book.

For John Wayne Gacy: Joseph R. Kozenczak, former Chief of Police, Des Plaines PD, Judge Louis B. Garippo and attorney William Kunkle.

For Kenneth Bianchi: Frances Piccione (Bianchi's adoptive mother). Kenneth Bianchi, Veronica "VerLyn" Compton, Professor Donald T. Lunde, MA, MD, Professor David Canter, Professor Elliot Leyton, Judge Roger Boren, Bellingham PD, LAPD Homicide, Captain Lynde Johnston, Rochester PD Homicide, Det. Richard Crotsley LAPD Homicide, Agent Robert Beams FBI, Katherine Yronwode, Whatcom Security Agency, former SOCO Bellingham PD Robert Knudsen, the staff at Western Washington Correctional Center for Women (WWCCW) and the Washington State Penitentiary (WSP) Walla Walla.

A very special thanks with much love to my special PJ, because it did work out all right for you in the end, and I will always miss your company, and Alyona Minenok from Novosibirsk, Russia. The late night talks with you helped me immensely.

Finally, my publisher John Blake and Lucian Randall, along with the many thousands of readers.

Christopher Berry-Dee
Southsea, Hampshire

Introduction

With 5 percent of the world's population, the United States produces more serial killers than the rest of the world, accounting for 76 percent of the total. Europe produces the second-highest number of serial killers at 17 percent. England leads with 28 percent of the European total, followed by Germany with 27 percent.

California has the highest serial homicide rate in the United States, followed by New York, Texas and Illinois, while Maine has the lowest.

Over 90 percent of serial killers are white males, usually from low- to middle-class backgrounds; these men are usually intelligent but, as students, have generally had difficulty in focusing. Most have experienced a traumatic childhood, often having been abused psychologically, physically or sexually. Typically, they may have been raised in unstable families, often with criminal, psychiatric and alcoholic histories. As a result, children raised in such families often spend a great deal of time on their own with many of them indulging in animal cruelty at a very young age.

Most people who suffer as children grow out of it and become upstanding, decent human beings. But serial killers such as Kenneth Bianchi and John Gacy, who all suffered as children, repeat the same mistakes over the course of their lives. They cannot make their transition into adulthood; they have trouble making the transition in middle age and, at the very time they feel they should be reaching the pinnacle of success, they find they are sliding downhill fast. They want to feel important, they want to feel special; they crave the sense of power, dominance and control. But they simply cannot achieve it in any respectable way, so they kill, torture, sodomize and dismember, and this makes them feel good about themselves.

The typical sado-serial killer appears extraordinarily ordinary. He's a white, middle-aged man who has an insatiable appetite for power, control and dominance, and he kills not for money, nor for revenge, but because it makes him feel good. He does it because he enjoys trawling for prey, entrapping them, restraining and torturing them; he has fun killing, because he likes the thrill, the excitement and the exhilaration that he gets from squeezing the last gasp of breath from his dying victim's body.

Killers such as John Wayne Gacy, Kenneth Bianchi, and most of those who appear in this book enjoy the suffering on the part of the victim, and they try to make it slow and painful. It makes them feel superior to the extent that it makes their victims feel inferior.

Sixty-five percent of serial homicide victims are women. In the United States, there are, at most, 200 victims of sexual serial killers a year. That number, although very large, pales into insignificance compared with almost 18,000 single-victim murders in the U.S. on a yearly basis. The problem is not serial murder, it is domestic violence, or workplace homicide, or two guys going into a bar, where one takes out a gun and shoots the other.

The problem, on the other hand, is that serial murderers amass a large body count—a small number of men who do a lot of damage. They may kill five, ten or even twenty or more. Some of them have killed hundreds, and that is enough to terrify anyone.

HARVEY LOUIS CARIGNAN

"The guy's the fuckin' devil. They should have fried him years ago, period, an' they would have lined up to pull the switch. When he was dead, they should have driven a stake through his heart and buried him, digging him up a week later to ram another stake in, just to make sure he was fuckin' dead."

RUSSELL J. KRUGER
CHIEF INVESTIGATOR, MINNEAPOLIS POLICE DEPARTMENT

t was September 24, 1974, and early morning in Minneapolis. The sun was up and patrolmen Robert Nelson and Robert Thompson were cruising along 1841 E. 38th Street when they spotted the 1968 black-over-pea-green Chevrolet Caprice. It was parked across the road from a diner. Thompson made a slow circuit of the block, while his partner checked the police bulletin details issued the day before.

"That's it," said Nelson. "That looks like the car. All we gotta do is find the driver. He's a big guy and, according to this, he's built like a gorilla."

The two officers peered through the Caprice's window and scrutinized the interior. Sure enough, there was the red plaid car rug, pornographic magazines, and a bible. By the gearshift, they noticed several packs of Marlborough cigarettes; all items that had been detailed by a previous rape victim of the man the police were searching for.

While Nelson telephoned his precinct, requesting assistance, Thompson wandered into the diner, asking the owner if he knew who had been driving the car.

"Yeah, sure," came the suspicious reply. "He just saw you guys and high-tailed it out back."

Minutes later, Harvey Louis Carignan was stopped, briefly questioned then arrested. He was taken downtown, read his Miranda rights, and booked on charges of homicide and rape.

With up to 50 kills, one of America's most vicious serial murderers would never use his hammer again.

* * *

Even now, it sometimes seems my childhood was short, only a few days long. There is nothing about it I cling to and nothing to look fondly backwards toward. From where I sat then, and sit now, it was, and is, truly a pit of despair.

CARIGNAN, IN A LETTER TO THE AUTHOR, APRIL 14, 1993

Born on the wrong side of the tracks at Fargo, North Dakota, on May 18, 1927, like so many serial killers, Harvey was an illegitimate child who never knew his genetic father. His 20-year-old mother, Mary, was ill-equipped to care for her sickly boy who failed to thrive and, in 1930, during the lowest point of the Great Depression, she started farming him out to anyone who would look after him. Thereafter, the youngster was moved from place to place, and school to school, unable to form family roots or enjoy a solid education.

Very early in his formative years, Harvey developed a facial twitch. He suffered from bed-wetting until he was 13 years old. He also suffered Saint Vitus' Dance—or childhood chorea—a disease which manifests itself with uncontrollable spasmodic jerking movements.

At the age of 12, he was sent to a reform school at Mandan, North Dakota, where, according to his FBI "Rap Sheet," he remained for seven years. During this time, he alleges that he was constantly bullied and sexually abused by a female teacher. In a letter dated June 12, 1993, he writes:

… I had a teacher who used to sit at my desk and we would write dirty notes back and forth. I was either 13 or 14 at the time—and just show me a 14-year-old boy anywhere who wouldn't willingly and happily sit in a schoolroom and exchange porno notes with his teacher. I never got to lay a hand on her without getting slapped, but she would keep me after school and make me stand before her while she masturbated and called me names and told me what she was going to make me do—none of her threats she ever kept, damn it! The bitch wouldn't even let me masturbate with her! I took my penis out and she beat the living shit out of me! She had enormously large breasts. She was truly a cruel woman …

Harvey Carignan stayed at the Mandan reform school throughout his teenage years, then in 1948, at the age of 21, he joined the Army, who

3

welcomed him with open arms. Harvey was no longer the weedy little runt who, allegedly, had suffered mental and sexual abuse since the age of four. The high-carbohydrate and well-balanced diet at Mandan had helped him grow into a strapping, well-nourished and immensely powerful young man.

Carignan began his murderous career in 1949 when, during the early evening of Sunday, July 31, he killed 57-year-old Laura Showalter following an attempted rape in a small park at Anchorage, Alaska. Death came swiftly after he smashed her head, causing terrible brain injuries. The victim's face had been virtually destroyed from chin to forehead, bone and tissue crushed to a pulp under a battering from his massive fists.

"This killer was so strong," said a police officer, "with one punch he blasted a hole through her skull like a rocket slamming into a tank."

On Friday, September 16, 1949, Carignan attempted to rape a young woman called Dorcas Callen who managed to escape his assault. The soldier, who was clearly drunk, although it was only 11:00 a.m., had confronted her near a tavern in Anchorage Street. When the man asked Dorcas to take a ride with him, she refused and turned away.

"Hey," he shouted, "I think I know you … maybe."

"Please go away," Dorcas pleaded. "You don't know me."

She was now very scared. She knew that a woman had been bludgeoned to death in the neighborhood only weeks before. But the big soldier confronting her was angered by her refusal, and she could not get away from him. Before she could move, the man grabbed her and began to drag her away from the street. They fell into a ditch beside the road, and he was all over her, tearing at her clothes, his hands touching her breasts, and between her legs. In moments he could rape her.

Dorcas fought frantically to find a handhold in the soft dirt walls of the ditch. He was very strong, almost inhumanly strong. Screaming, she managed to clamber out of the ditch and ran across the street to the tavern where she called the police.

In the hospital, she relived the terror of the attack in detail through a bloody mask of bruised and bloodied facial skin. "He turned into something from Hell. His fury came out of nowhere, like he was suddenly switched on with evil," she said through swollen lips.

It was her description of her attacker that led to the arrest of Carignan later the same day. He stood trial for the first-degree murder of Laura Showalter in 1950 in the District Court for the Territory of Alaska, Third Division, Justice George W. Folta presiding. The prosecution held, as their ace card, a confession to murder given to Marshal Herring. Harvey Carignan was found guilty and sentenced to hang. At the subsequent appeal in the Supreme Court of the United States, Justices Reed, Douglas, Black and Frankfurter agreed that Harvey Carignan's conviction had come about because of a breach of the McNabb rule. This held that confessions should be excluded if obtained during an illegal detention due to failure to carry a prisoner promptly before a committing magistrate. Because this rule had been violated, the Justices ruled Carignan's confession as inadmissible. Thus Harvey escaped the hangman's noose but forfeited his freedom with a 15-year sentence. Prisoner #22072 was transferred from the Seward Jail in Alaska to the U.S. Penitentiary at McNeil Island, Washington State.

During his interview with the author, Carignan stated, "Laura Showalter ... Dorcas Callen? Those names mean nothin' to me."

* * *

Carignan was transferred to the U.S. Prison Alcatraz, in California, on September 13, 1951, where he spent the next nine years. On April 2, 1960, at the age of 32, he was paroled. Except for his few years in the Army, he had not been at liberty since he was a child of 11.

After landing at San Francisco's waterfront jetty wearing a cheap prison-issue suit, with his bag of belongings at his feet, he watched as the small prison launch chugged its way back across the bay to "The Rock," as Alacatraz is universally known, then he boarded a train for Duluth, Minnesota. There he moved in with one of his three half-brothers but, on August 4,1960, just four months after his release, he was arrested for third-degree burglary and assault with intent to commit rape.

Fortunately for Carignan, the rape charge was dropped through lack of evidence. If the rape charge had been proven, he would have returned to prison, never to be released again. However, as a parole violator, he was sentenced to 2,086 days in the Federal Prison at Leavenworth, Kansas.

Carignan was back in the community in 1964, and moved swiftly to Seattle, where, on March 2, he registered as a parole convict C-5073. On November 22 that year, he was arrested by the Sheriff of King County for traffic vagrancy and second-degree burglary.

April 20, 1965, saw him in the dock once again when he was sentenced to 15 years in the Washington State Penitentiary at Walla Walla, one of the tristate cities comprising of Richland and Kennewick, on the southeast border of Washington and Oregon.

Now locked up in one of the oldest and most notorious prisons in the United States, Carignan applied his mind to making up for his earlier lack of education. He obtained a high school diploma, took many college courses in sociology and psychology, and submitted papers on sexual psychopathy, the paranoid personality, and the well-adjusted individual. He read constantly, gained top grades, and studied journalism—all of which impressed his tutors. But there was a darker side that surfaced when he was alone. When talking with his fellow inmates, Harvey fantasized about nubile, young girls and he had a fixation about young flesh. He has often stated, and maintains even today, that young girls have to be his ultimate choice, which for a man now aged 74, is a very unhealthy desire indeed.

* * *

Middle-aged, and an ex-convict with unappealing physical characteristics, Harvey's chances of dating a teenager following his release from prison were remote, so he met and married Sheila Moran, a divorcée with three children. She had her own house in Ballard, the Scandinavian district of Seattle, where they made a home together. Coming from a decent upbringing, Sheila was soon left under no illusions about the personality of her new husband who hung around with a bunch of villains. He was always out until the late hours, tearing around in his car at breakneck speeds. Then, following Carignan's vicious assault on her aged uncle, she decided to pack up her things and take her children. She would simply run away. For his part, Harvey decided to kill her, and waited in vain for an entire night with a hammer clutched in his hand, but, fortunately, Sheila did not return home.

Harvey married again on April 14, 1972. Alice Johnson, a somewhat dim-witted, plain woman in her 30s fell for him. This naïve and gullible cleaning woman with few friends thought she'd met a hard-working, decent man. Alice had been married before and had a son, Billy, aged 11, and a pretty daughter, Georgia, aged 14, whom Harvey was soon lusting after.

By this time, Carignan had managed to lease a Sav-Mor gas station from the Time Oil Company, and it came to Alice's attention that he always had a string of young girls working the pumps. But no sooner had one started, she left, to be replaced by another girl just as young and pretty. While this behavior aroused her suspicions, gossip led her to the confirmation that her husband was totally obsessed by teenage girls. He would approach any girl he saw, with obscene suggestions and remarks, and when Alice confronted him with reprimands, he screamed and shouted at her, beat her son, and skulked away throwing lurid glances at Georgia, which made his stepdaughter feel decidedly uncomfortable.

Not surprisingly, the marriage collapsed soon afterward.

On October 15, 1972, Carignan raped and killed a teenager named Laura Brock, near Mount Vernon, Washington State.

* * *

A want ad placed in the *Seattle Times* on May 1, 1973, provided the first link in a chain of gruesome events. Help was required at a local gas station and the notice caught the eye of 15-year-old Kathy Sue Miller. She wasn't looking for a job for herself, but for her boyfriend, Mark Walker. The next morning, however, when she dialed the contact number advertised, Kathy was intrigued when the man who answered said he was looking for girls. She gave him her address and telephone number and agreed to meet him after school. They arranged that he would pick her up in his car outside the Sears building in Seattle, then drive her over to the gas station to fill out a job application form.

Kathy's mother was worried. She did not like the fact that her daughter had given her number to a stranger and she felt uneasy about the way the interview had been arranged. In particular, she disliked the thought of Kathy getting into a car with someone she had never met. Running through her mind was a recent news article about Laura Brock, who had been raped and murdered while hitchhiking.

"I mean it, Kathy," Mary warned her daughter. "Don't even think about meeting him."

Impatiently, Kathy promised not to and left for her classes, a stack of schoolbooks under her arm.

Mother and daughter shared the same bus that morning and Kathy got off first near Roosevelt High School. Mary watched through the grimy window as her beautiful daughter hurried away, turning once with a smile to wave back.

That afternoon, Kathy disobeyed her mother's orders and met Carignan as arranged. He had been waiting with growing impatience and his heart skipped a beat when he saw a tall, strong, athletic girl walking in his direction. Her blonde hair was darkened to a burnished butterscotch color and fell to the middle of her back in thick waves. Kathy had green eyes, and just the faintest suggestion of freckles sprinkling over her fair skin. She stopped opposite Carignan's car to cross the road, and he watched as the young woman, wearing a blue-and-white jumper, a navy-blue blouse and blue-tinged nylons waved in his direction.

Carignan leant across the front passenger seat and pushed the door open. However, Kathy walked to his side of the car and spoke to him through the window. Her first sight of Carignan was somewhat unedifying. He was an unattractive man with a peculiarly domed forehead. He had a receding chin and a deep scar over one eye. In fact, Carignan looked years older than his true age of 46, with his skin deeply lined, and bags and wrinkles beneath his eyes. His usual expression was a glowering frown, and to smile, he had to make a concentrated effort. But, this time, he turned on all the charm at his disposal.

"Hi! You must be Kathy," he asked, with a broad smile beaming across his face.

Kathy noticed the dimple on his chin, then smiled back. "Sure, that's me."

Motioning her to get into the car, he said, "We need to fill in the application forms and they are back at my office, just hop in. I'll drop you off home when we've finished."

Kathy felt uncomfortable. "My mom isn't too happy about this," she explained, and Harvey moved up a gear.

"Can't say that I blame her. I've got children of my own. Married, too. Nice house, lovely woman. Yep, we can't blame your mom for being careful."

Kathy was almost convinced by the man's reassurance. "You sure this is OK?" she asked.

"Absolutely. Tell ya what, I'll even introduce myself to your mom when I drop you off. Everything will be fine then."

Kathy Sue Miller was never seen alive again. Carignan, whose violent record was known to the police, was questioned at length and his movements watched for 24 hours a day, but there was insufficient evidence to charge him with abduction, let alone murder. Then, on Sunday, June 3, two 16-year-old boys driving their motorbikes through Tulalip Reservation, just north of Everett, found Kathy's body. It was wrapped in black plastic and was naked. It had decayed so badly it was initially impossible even to tell its gender. When the autopsy was carried out, it was found that the teeth matched Kathy's dental records. From the damage to the skull, it was clear that death had resulted from a severe battering.

Even with the discovery of the body, "Harv the Hammer" still managed to escape the clutches of the police. He moved first to Colorado and later to Minneapolis, Minnesota, where he murdered Eileen Hunley on August 4, 1974. Her body was found on September 18, in Sherburne County. In response to the murder, Carignan commented, "She was my common-law wife an' I thought she was seeing a black man so I stopped her in the street … I ran her head into a lamp pole, and stamped her face on to a drain cover until she was dead. Then I tried to feed her to some pigs."

* * *

A string of sexual assaults on hitchhikers in the states of Colorado and Minnesota in the latter part of 1974 bore Carignan's stamp. They were mostly carried out by a large man broadly matching his description wielding a hammer as his assault weapon. At least seven died and the remainder were scarred mentally and physically for life.

On September 8, 1974, a female hitchhiker was picked up by Carignan, driven to a rural area near Mora, and was sexually assaulted. She was then beaten about the head with a hammer and sexually assaulted with the hammer handle. The victim was left in a field to die, but survived. She was subsequently able to give a description of the assailant and the vehicle he was driving.

On September 14, 1974, Carignan picked up a woman named Roxanne Wesley, who was having car problems in a south Minneapolis parking lot. On the pretext that he was going to drive her to get help, he took her instead to a rural area in Carver County, sexually assaulted her several times, including forcing a hammer handle into her vagina, and also beat her about the head with the hammer and left her in a field to die. This victim also survived and was able to crawl to a road for help. She was also able to give a description of her assailant and his vehicle, including other distinguishing features of the car's contents.

Two teenage female hitchhikers reported on September 19, 1974, that they had been picked up by a man and driven into the country where he threatened to rape and kill them. One of the girls was struck in the mouth by Carignan, breaking a front tooth. Both were eventually able to escape by jumping out of his car when he stopped at a road junction. Again, their descriptions of the man and the vehicle, matched the descriptions given by the previous victims.

The next day, Minneapolis Police received a complaint from two other teenagers who said they had been approached by a man who offered them $25 each to assist him in picking up a car in northern Minnesota and driving it back to Minneapolis for him. The two girls said that they were driven to a rural wooded area where the man asked one of them to follow him into the woods, presumably to get the other vehicle he had talked about. He took a gas can and a screwdriver with him. A short time later, the girl who remained in the car heard screams so she ran to a nearby house to call the Sheriff. Subsequently, the other girl was found unconscious with severe head wounds as a result of hammer blows to the head. Their description of the attacker matched Carignan in every respect.

On September 21, another report of a similar assault in which the victim survived was received and, a few days later, Carignan was arrested.

* * *

What follows is part of a charge relating to five counts regarding offences committed on a 13-year-old girl. The name has been deleted to protect the victim's identity, and the document has been supplied courtesy of the Minneapolis and Hennepin County Prosecutors.

<u>Aggravated Assault. Aggravated Sodomy. Indecent Liberties.</u>
<u>Sodomy upon or with a child. Aggravated Sodomy.</u>

The said ——————, was hitchhiking in Minneapolis when the defendant, driving a truck-camper, stopped, picked her up, engaged her in conversation as to where she was going, stated that he would take her to her destination directly, forced her to commit oral sodomy upon him with the threat of hitting her with a hammer which he picked up from a compartment between the seats of his truck, compelled her to remove her clothing by threatening to "put a hammer through your head," attempted to shove the handle of the hammer up into her vagina, struck her several times in the area of her buttocks with the hammer when she resisted the advances of the defendant, again compelled her to commit oral sodomy on him, drove to a corn field where he compelled her to lie on her stomach where he attempted to have intercourse with her through the rectum, then, for the third time, again compelled her to commit oral sodomy on him. That the defendant then permitted the victim to dress and drove her to home of a friend situated at 5644 Lakeland Avenue, Crystal, Hennepin County, [Minnesota], where he allowed the victim to get out of the truck-camper; that in addition to the foregoing, the defendant told the victim that his first name was "Paul" and that his last name was "Harvey".

In separate trials conducted in 1975 and 1976, Carignan was convicted of just two of the murders and a number of other offences. He was given prison sentences amounting to 100 years plus life. In truth, he may serve only 40 years.

* * *

"I know where your house is. I know you have a young, pretty, dark-haired wife and two kids.

You have a silver Mercedes car. But I will make sure nothing an' no one hurts you or your family as I have friends in your country who look after me."

HARVEY CARIGNAN'S CHILLING WELCOME WHEN THE AUTHOR,
CHRISTOPHER BERRY-DEE, VISITED HIM IN PRISON.

Harvey Louis Carignan, known variously as "Harv the Hammer," or "The Want-ad Killer," currently resides behind the grim walls of the Minnesota Correctional Facility, Stillwater, which is on the Minnesota–Wisconsin border. An industrial prison, it is now the state's largest, close-security, level five institution for adult felons, and the population is currently around 1,320.

For five years, I corresponded with Harvey, and finally interviewed him during a "full-contact visit" in March 1995. This was the first and only interview granted by "The Hammer" since he was arrested for multiple rape and homicide on September 24, 1974.

Because individuals like Harvey have traversed such extremes, their souls have become like locked rooms hiding mysterious secrets. It therefore takes a certain sensibility to draw them out. For each case, I take an in-depth approach, spending an enormous amount of time getting to know the unique qualities of each individual, rather than depersonalising them with generalities based on their crimes. While I develop an empathy for my subject, I always take care not actually to sympathize to the extent that their dramas start playing in the theater of my own mind. It is a constant balancing act between identification and analysis.

To learn from a person, you must put yourself in their place, follow their train of thought and feel their emotions; however, while you follow the often dysfunctional thinking of your subject to some extent, you never become like them. You remain yourself. You may draw close for a while, close enough to get a sense of these often foreign ideas and emotions, but you must always pull back to restore the integrity of your own moral and mental boundaries.

And what was it that Carignan's psychiatrist had told me? Yes, that was it, "You'll get to interview Harvey, or something living inside his head. You'll get to interview him, and evil will get to interview you."

Harvey was called to the interview by his personal pager, and my first impression of this homicidal maniac is of a lumbering hulk of a man, standing well over 6 feet tall. He weighs 252 pounds and has an ape-like appearance. He has massive frame, a Neanderthal-like balding dome, and huge hands attached to over-long, gangly arms which hang from immensely powerful, sloping shoulders. Carignan has piercing blue eyes, and talks in a low, husky voice. At face value, his overall persona portrays a gentle, even understanding, giant of a man; however, we all know that such appearances can be deceptive. The Hammer is, in fact, one of America's most evil and notorious serial murderers, who even today, aged 74, can still do one-arm pull-ups for 15 minutes at a stretch without so much as a grimace.

Five minutes dragged past agonizingly without either of us saying a word, while all the time his dangerous eyes stared into my face. It was as if some alien creature, an insidious force even, was gently probing into my mind using long, squirming tentacles of enquiring thought, exploring, touching, sensing with taste and smell. Then, a secret but twisted smile started to play around Harvey's mouth. His lips, moistened by saliva, were slightly open, but otherwise his face was without expression.

This stone-cold serial killer was insidiously fascinating to observe at such close quarters, for he is the wolf in sheep's clothing, part-human, part-Antichrist and the stuff of our children's worst nightmares. Then he spoke for the first time.

"Ya, know, Chris, never did I commit a crime then commit another to keep it quiet. I committed murders to ensure that false accusations of rape would not occur."

The ice was broken, and my previous belief, that Harvey lives in a continual state of denial—a world where he admits some guilt, but not total responsibility for his brutal and heinous crimes—was confirmed.

As the interview continued, when he did admit he raped and killed a young woman, it was, so he claimed, as the result of their provocation. He said that it was always the victim who brought up the subject of sex when he offered them a ride in his car.

Nowhere can this better be illustrated than in his account of a lift he gave to a woman, a perfectly respectable 20-year-old nurse, whose car had broken down.

The truth is that he offered to fix her car, but beforehand he explained that he needed to fetch his tools. He forced her into his car and drove her into the country where he brutally raped and attempted to kill her by smashing into her head with a wheel wrench.

Carignan's account is of course something different, for he argues that she got into his car of her own free will. His story contains a smattering of the truth and a bucketful of lies. It is at once disturbing and disgusting, yet offers a fascinating account from the mind of a homicidal sexual psychopath and fully-emerged serial killer who, it is believed, may have slaughtered up to 50 women. What follows is not for the faint-hearted:

She got in and may have been somewhat nervous, but she did not seem afraid. During the ride we talked about another girl I used to see, one who had left because I had not given her $30 I had been giving her each and every week. It was not payment for anything, but a gift. The girl riding with me said she would never exchange sex for $30—making it seem she believed the other woman had and that herself despised her for what the first woman had done. I tried to enlighten her thinking, but she was adamant in her statement that she would not have sex for $30 because those were in her words and not that she would not have sex for money, which was my thought at the time.

It was then that I got the drift; that she thought I was offering her the same amount for sex and she was turning down the offer— but I am not saying she wanted money to have sex at all. The way the conversation went it could have been either, that she would not have sex for $30 or she would not have sex for any amount of money. It was no big deal to me at the time, so the conversation had no special meaning to me until much later when I tried to remember everything that was talked about and how it was said.

When we got to my friend's place where the tools were supposed to be, I stopped the car, turned around, and immediately drove away. My friend had told me if his pick up, a 1973 three-quarter ton Chevrolet, was not in the yard, to not hang around because his sons did not like me. This was a surprise because I did not know his boys. I had never met any of them. [Carignan did not have any so-called friends.] Anyway, I drove away and stopped the car just before driving on to the main road. I put my arm around her and, although she hesitated, she did move over closer to me when I *indicated with arm pressure that is what I wanted. It was not a pressure that forced her to move, not a hold that would have moved her had she declined. Instead, it was an indication of what I would like her to do, and she complied. I can remember my thoughts as plain as if it was yesterday, "She wants it!" This is spite of the fact that I wondered why she had been so adamant in denying she would have sex for $30, which in mind could have been any amount at the time. I slid my arm behind her head, put a slight, almost gentle pressure on her neck, and she bent down—not because of the pressure but with her own strength—unbuttoned my pants, took out my penis, and stroked it while we kissed, until I indicated with the same kind of pressure that I wanted her to suck it. She did.*

When she finished, I told her, "Spit that damned stuff out," when I saw her sitting there holding the semen in her mouth. She did—but I did hold on to her in case she wanted to jump out and run away. I was not satisfied that she was not going to say I had forced her to do what she had done. She looked at me, giving me a strange smile—like I was a fool for thinking she would run—closed the door, and I drove on.

While we were starting out I told her, "I want to fuck you. I know a place we can go!"

She asked, "How long will we be gone? I must be back by one o'clock." It was then about 10:30.

I did have a place in mind but it was miles away. So I drove along and pulled in next to a lake. When I stopped I saw a house in the midst of some trees and a man walking our way from another direction. I turned around and drove away. During this, the girl did not make any attempt to open the car door or get out.

Directly across the road from the lake a road led into a glen. It was about 500–622 feet from the main road. When we got there, I went to the trunk and took out a blue blanket [subsequently recovered by the police] and threw it on to the ground, and I told her, "Get ready!" I was not happy with her for some reason, but she was a very sexy woman, about 20 years old, and I wanted to have sex with her, especially since we already had after a manner of speaking. She took off my jeans and her panties and laid down on her back with her feet in my direction. The whole of her pudendum was pointing towards me—and it was beautiful, as was herself, a very pretty woman. Now, I do not know what other men look for or how they act, but I generally always look at the vulva, play with it. The prettier she looks in her genital area, the more I want sex.

Now, I only stopped to help the girl get her car started. When she climbed in, I only had it in mind to get the tools to fix it. Sex was not on my mind, and I did not kidnap her. Everyone assumes these women and girls as innocents. They generally are not. Each and everyone of them wanted something from me, either money, to drive one of my cars, or something they would not divulge. I never kidnapped them, or forced them to come with me. She is no different from the others. I am not a rapist, and the word itself is so revolting it turns my stomach.

Despite what anyone says, we had a delightful time in that clearing until she accused me of taking money from her purse, and then I thought, "Here we go again." I became much more angry than the moment called for and acted out within the content of that anger rather than against the accusation which called for no more than an explanation that I had not taken her money. The right rear tire on my car had gone flat and I was changing it when she screamed out at me. She kept screaming the money was not hers and almost insanely demanding I return it. Then, in a wink, her tone changed and she told me how she wanted to trade her car for another. That I should give her $200 for the trade or she was going to say I had raped her. Until that instant, I had gone on with the *business of replacing the lug bolts on the hub; but in that instant when she made that threat, I became what I see as being uncontrollably angry and I hit her with the lug wrench—and not with the hammer as she later testified, and what is generally believed. She was fully dressed and I can see it now as plain as it was happening even now. She fell to the ground as if she had been pole-axed and she slid slowly down a 12–14 feet incline into a ditch, feet first, with her brown sweater rolling up until was under her armpits. I did not panic, but put the lug wrench in the trunk and the remaining lug bolt in my pocket, got into my car, and drove away. At about 15–20 minutes down the road, maybe 15–20 miles, I realized I could not leave the woman there to die if she was only wounded, and I had to know, so I turned around and went back. As I drove by, there were several cars and a tractor with a wagon behind it stopped beside the road, and all of the people were bending over someone that I knew was her, so I kept on driving.*

When Harvey had finished talking, I confronted him about the reality of the attack. I reminded this man that in fact he had left the young nurse for dead in that ditch but she regained consciousness several hours later lying in a pool of her own blood and suffering from almost lethal head injuries. It was practically nightfall and, in dreadful pain, she crawled over a mile through ploughed fields to a road where the farmer found her, and summoned help in the morning.

Carignan later passed the ambulance as he was returning to the scene of the attack, not to save his victim's life, but concerned that she might survive and be able to describe him and his vehicle. He returned intending to finish her off but, by then, she had crawled to safety. The only thing that kept the young woman alive was the news that her sister had given her the previous day, that she was expecting a child and she was determined to see the baby.

Harvey claims he had been sexually abused by just about every female he came across, including his relations, babysitters, and his teacher at the reform school. And, while we are all too aware that, during the last three decades, child abuse has become exposed as a social blight, there is absolutely not a shred of solid evidence to confirm that Harvey was abused on the scale he continually asserts.

What we can say with a degree of certainty is that he grew up with a grudge against women in general, perhaps directed toward his negligent mother and her family and friends. But, maybe this is all the evidence we need, for in a literal way, people don't grow up to hate women, or men, for no reason, so perhaps Carignan is telling the truth after all.

Recently, Carignan said, "I hate women with a passion … They always played mind games with my head." Nevertheless, his account of sexual abuse may offer something else of value to us, as we look into his past. Those few lines in his letters are full of contradictions and without any doubt, this may be fantasy-fuelled. It is an account tailored to suit him, being abused by a domineering "truly cruel woman," while he, the poor young boy was helpless, yet at the same moment, apparently enjoying a situation in which he revelled.

As with so many killers, when Harvey Carignan came into this world he was immediately burdened by childhood problems. He carried the social stigma of being a bastard; a weak, nervous child; a bed-wetter who suffered from Saint Vitus's dance; and, like the British serial killer, Peter Sutcliffe, was bullied throughout his formative years.

He claims that women sexually abused him as a child, although these allegations are unsupported by fact. There is little doubt, though, that his mother and other female relations, including his aunts and grandmother, treated him with contempt. The psychological damage this caused may explain in large measure the passionate hatred that Harvey holds for women. He believes they all "played mind-games" with his head, which perhaps accounts for his use of blunt instruments to mutilate and destroy the heads of his victims. His fury was such that he didn't just hit them once or twice. More often than not he smashed their skulls to an unrecognizable pulp using demoniacal and inhuman force.

Revenge—more particularly, revenge against women—played an important part in his motivation, and his modus operandi was always the same. But there is another side to this killer's motive, which is, on the face of it, bizarre. While he slaughtered older women, perhaps in the image maybe of his mother, aunts and grandmother (with a few exceptions) he often allowed his teenage victims to live, despite the horrific attacks committed upon them. In a few cases, he even drove them home or patched up their cuts and bruises. The reason for this contradictory behavior might be explained by his clearly-stated sexual attraction to younger girls. In this respect, there can be no doubt that Carignan was, and still is, fantasy driven. Those fantasies of sex with young girls always give him immense pleasure, while thoughts of older women generated intense hatred for Carignan.

Throughout my extensive period of correspondence with Harvey, he made much of what he calls his "string of pearls." In effect, he implies that these "pearls of wisdom" are priceless details which he releases only when he judges the time is appropriate for him.

"The truth is in my pearls of wisdom," he bluntly stated. "I am not going to reveal the pearls of this part of the truth at least for years," he added before clamming up and refusing to answer any more questions about the nature of his crimes.

Harvey "The Hammer" Carignan devoted the remainder of the interview to claiming that he is a man with much feeling. A man of great knowledge and, as he studies philosophy, he is worthy of having his words and thoughts considered by others. But within The Hammer, there is still a fatal flaw.

Despite having spent the better part of his worthless life behind bars, this monster, in every sense of the word, is totally unable to come to terms with his guilt. This is a trait he shares with many other serial murderers. Even with the evidence being consistent and overwhelming in every case of sexual assault, rape or murder, Carignan is psychologically compelled to transfer most of the blame for his crimes on to his luckless victims.

When he is exposed, and all of his excuses stare him straight back in the face as complete untruths, he has a fallback position. He retreats to the trench used by so many offenders, namely the refuge which blames the entire law enforcement and justice system for fitting him up.

If the gravity and number of offences were not so serious, one might be forgiven for thinking that his excuses are laughable. Some may even argue that his letters are the ramblings of a madman and, as such, should be dismissed or, at best, ignored. However, Harvey is not mad by any definition. What he refuses to say, or hides between the lines, or chooses to forget to say, can ultimately be of greater interest, for in his pathological self-denial sits the true nature of The Beast.

At the present time, Carignan is eligible for parole, for no matter how many murders he has committed, no one in the State of Minnesota can serve more than 45 years in prison.

Harvey has a current pen pal. Thirty-year-old Gloria Pearson was convicted of murdering her young son after a period of child abuse. They write to each other frequently and, in this respect, they are well suited.

This chapter is based on exclusive audiotape interviews between Christopher Berry-Dee and Harvey Louis Carignan within the Minnesota Correctional Facility, Minnesota, in 1996, and many years correspondence.

ARTHUR JOHN SHAWCROSS

For a moment, his eyes zeroed in. Just a moment
before, a rare smile had masked Shawcross's simmering
fury; now that mask of sanity had slipped for the first
time, and the fire of homicidal insanity flared in his
eyes as he struggled to overcome the murderous
emotions boiling within. The interview room went
quiet, deadly quiet.

SHAWCROSS'S REACTION TO BEING QUESTIONED
BY CHRISTOPHER BERRY-DEE ABOUT THE MURDER OF
TEN-YEAR-OLD JACK BLAKE.

D eep within the Sullivan Correctional Facility, Fallsburg, New York, breathes the state's most notorious serial murderer, and his name is Arthur John Shawcross, dubbed "The Monster of the Rivers" by the media. I asked him how he had acquired the title.

"Because," he replied, "that's where I killed' em. That's where the monster inside of me came out, an' he came out down by the river pretty often."

"Art" was a small baby, weighing just 5 pounds. The infant was born at 4:14 a.m. on Wednesday, June 6, 1945, at the U.S. Naval Hospital in Kittery, just across the Piscataqua River from Portsmouth, Maine.

The birth certificate records the father's name as Corporal Arthur Roy Shawcross, aged 21, and the baby's mother as Bessie Yerakes Shawcross, aged 18. His parents lived at Apartment 5, 28 Chapel Street, Portsmouth, Maine.

His father was no stranger to the police himself, being a bigamist who had served with the U.S. Marine Corps during World War II. He landed on Guadalcanal with an artillery regiment of the 1st Marine Division, and in doing so earned a number of battle star commendations and medals. In February 1943, after mopping up the action, he and his fellow marines were sent for rest and recuperation to Australia, where he met Thelma June at a dance. They were married Monday, June 14, that year in Melby, Australia, and Thelma later gave birth to a son whom they named Hartley after their illustrious British namesake.

Arthur Roy Shawcross was granted a furlough in July 1944 and returned to the United States where he bigamously married his now pregnant childhood sweetheart, Bessie Yerakes, on Thursday, November 23. Bessie, popularly referred to as "Betty," was the daughter of factory workers who lived in Somersworth, New Hampshire. Her father, James Yerakes, was born in Greece, and her mother, Violet Libby, is of unknown Mediterranean descent. A week after Bessie was discharged from hospital with baby Arthur, her husband sent them to

Watertown, upstate New York, where they lived with his sister while he completed his tour of duty in the Marines. Shortly after he was demobbed, the couple found a small place of their own in the picture postcard town of Brownville, the home of 1,200 lower-middle-class citizens, just a stone's throw from the Canadian border and Lake Ontario.

Young Arthur became the oldest of four children. His siblings were Jean, Donna and James and it would be fair to say that Arthur turned out to be the only rotten apple in a basket of otherwise good fruit. His education started normally enough at the Brownville-Glen Park Central School but personality problems soon surfaced. He resented his brother and sisters, with the exception of Jean, with whom he imagined having sex.

By the age of five, Art had created two imaginary friends. One was called "Paul," apparently a boy of Arthur's own age; the other "friend" was slightly younger, a blonde-haired girl with no name. During the months to follow, he carried on long conversations in baby talk with these imaginary friends, which gave fellow pupils and teachers the impression that he was talking to himself. "I had to have these friends," he told the author, "because I wanted someone to play with. No one else liked me."

Now called "Oddie" by his classmates, young Arthur became the subject of ridicule and bullying. He retreated into a twilight world of his own, often wandering from class to class in a dream. He was easy meat for the stronger children who tormented him at every opportunity, and when they did so, he screamed and shook his fists, or went home in a sulk to torment his younger brother and sisters by way of revenge.

Realizing that they had a problem child on their hands, the school welfare officers made inquiries, soon finding out that his parents spoiled Arthur. When he misbehaved, his mother would spank him lightly, or send him to his room. The school also reasoned that Arthur's father was excessively lenient with his boy.

Events took a more serious turn when Arthur ran away from home. Of course, he was quickly brought back, but then he took to traveling to school on a bus carrying a tire iron with which to hit the other children if they bothered him. The young Shawcross had learned that what he couldn't achieve with his fists, he could make up for using a weapon. Just before his eighth birthday, the school called for a mental health evaluation on Arthur. Psychologists from the Jefferson County Mental Health Clinic felt that Mrs. Shawcross was giving her "attractive, well-dressed, neat child," mixed emotional messages. It seemed that the mother–son relationship was very complex, for while she treated her son like a little doll on the one hand, she also punished him at the drop of a hat for no apparent reason, which left the boy feeling very confused.

Mrs. Shawcross had taught her son to be neat and tidy, and she and her former marine husband imposed what might be called old-fashioned values with echoes of military discipline. Arthur had to keep his room spotless, his clothes had to be neatly folded at all times and, for the slightest infraction, he was spanked or sent to his room. In return, and in attempts to curry favor, Arthur showered his parents with gifts, never forgetting a birthday or anniversary, yet still appeared to be confused. He developed a fear of unusual noises but, slowly, confusion gave way to resentment. He stole money from his mother to pay off the bullies at school. He had no friends, was mean to his younger brother, and it was very difficult to get the truth out of him because he always seemed afraid. Added to this, the psychiatrists thought that Arthur perceived his father as favoring the other children, and that his mother was rejecting him.

Arthur's interest in school now fell apart, his progress slipped and he began to regress, sliding to the bottom of his class. The teachers put this down to a bad attitude rather than lack of intelligence, but the larger boys still bullied and hounded him. About this time he developed a characteristic blink, which he still has today. He also started to make a noise like a bleating lamb, and often lapsed into baby talk. He began suffering from nightmares and wetting the bed, which he continued to do until his early teens. Then he ran away from home again, only to be dragged back, screaming and protesting. Although the date is uncertain, a pivotal event occurred in the Shawcross household which turned it upside-down with lasting consequences.

Arthur was aged nine when his grandmother, on his mother's side, received a letter from Thelma June in Australia. In it, Thelma claimed, quite correctly, that in fact Arthur Roy Shawcross was her husband, and that they had a son now aged ten. Understandably, when Bessie Shawcross saw the note she took a serious view of her husband's secret, and from that day on, she hated every moment she spent in his company. Indeed, she decided to make his life a misery. Already an oversensitive and confused boy, Arthur now kept away from home as much as possible. He was ashamed of his father and he could not stand the constant feuding that had become part-and-parcel of his parents' lives.

He ran away again to spend hours on end with his grandmother whom he adored. Although basically a very thoughtful and kind boy, he had now developed a much darker side. In effect, his mind was splitting in two, and he was mirroring the behavior of his mother who exhibited two sets of opposing attitudes and emotion.

By 1960, real behavioral problems began to emerge when young Arthur was in the seventh grade at the General Brown High School. In his spare time he started to torture small animals, skinning fish alive and toying with their bodies. He watched them suffer and saw how long it took them to die. He snared rabbits, taking his time to break their necks. He caught bats, putting them inside parked cars and watching as the drivers panicked. He tied cats together, pounded squirrels and chipmunks flat, shot darts at frogs nailed to his dartboard, and scraped the feathers from live chicks. On one occasion, he carried a sack to a nearby lake, and tossed it in the water. "Who says cats can't swim?" he said to another schoolboy. When the terrified animal escaped and swam to shore, he picked it up and threw it even further. After four attempts to reach safety, the kitten drowned.

During this period of juvenile sadism, Shawcross learned that killing animals had one drawback; they made a noise and the excrement and urine leaking from their bodies soiled his clothing. To prevent this, he resorted to stuffing leaves and other debris into their body apertures, a bizarre practice which he later included in his modus operandi when he took to murdering women and children. By the age of 15, the worm had really turned and Arthur became the scourge of his neighborhood, especially where other children were concerned. He knew no fear, was very strong, and often discharged his .22 caliber air rifle at anyone he came across. If another teenager upset him, he would mercilessly pound them with a baseball bat, or beat them unconscious with his fists.

Arthur was now uncontrollable and any attempts by his tutors to discipline him resulted in him storming out of class, shouting, "Shove this room up your fuckin' ass," and similar obscenities. Aged 17, and much to the relief of his teachers, he dropped out of school. Now, with time on his hands, he took to petty theft, stealing anything that wasn't nailed down. He burgled the locality, looted summer cottages, and stole money from the cash register of a gas station, where he worked for a short time. He broke into local stores, taking food and cash, and shoplifted on an almost daily basis.

One Sunday night in December 1963, he broke into the basement of a Sears Roebuck store, and was arrested by the police after he triggered an alarm. The judge, however, was lenient, sentencing Arthur to 18 months' probation as a minor offender. His excuse, which appeared to find favor with the judge, was that he was stealing in order to buy Christmas presents, which was true.

By now, the teenage sadist, thug and burglar was exhibiting stranger behavioral characteristics, which included speaking in a childish, duck-like, high-pitched voice. Arthur also developed a weird habit of walking "cross-lots," covering long distances at a fast pace, over-swinging his arms, holding his body erect and rigid like a one-man band, and walking in the straightest line over any obstacle that blocked his path. A cousin recalled Arthur doing this, and said, "He'd tear his pants on a wire fence rather than use a gate several feet away. He'd walk into a swamp and have a hell of a time getting out. He really was nuts in those days."

Aged 20 and already known to the police, Shawcross was charged with attacking a 13-year-old boy following a snowball fight. It seemed that he preferred the company of children much younger than himself, and he was often spotted secretively playing with children's' toys. The budding killer was also accident-prone. Apart from occasional blackouts, he knocked himself unconscious while pole-vaulting, suffered a hairline fracture of the skull when he was hit by a discus, took an electric shock from a faulty electrical switch, was hit by a sledge-hammer, fell from the top of a 40 foot ladder, and was hospitalized for the fifth time when he was struck down by a passing truck.

Around this time, although the date is not known, Arthur met Sarah Louise Chatteron. They were married in September 1964 at the Sandy Creek Baptist Chapel, and they had a son whom they named Michael. But blissful wedlock soon ended in acrimony. Sarah would later go on the record as saying, "Arthur was very immature, and always faking illness or injury to miss out on work. Sex with him was lousy. He just couldn't keep it up." The couple separated in August 1966, with Shawcross blaming Sarah for the break-up. He complained that she refused to give him oral sex, which was his favorite, but neither of them mentioned his constant acts of adultery.

Single once again, Shawcross hit the fast food joints and dance halls. He wrecked his souped-up Pontiac, and then he met Linda Ruth Neary whom he started to date, but on Friday, April 7, 1967, he was drafted into the Army. If anything could sort out Arthur's psychological problems, surely the Army could, and so 22-year-old Private 52967041, Arthur John Shawcross, started his training at Fort Lee, Virginia.

The rookie soldier's first taste of military justice occurred when a sergeant criticized him for "goofing off." Official army records show that Shawcross responded, "What do you think I'm doing, pulling my pud?" He was fined $27 for his insolence. He completed his basic training at Fort Benning, Georgia, and was designated a supply and parts specialist. When he failed to show up for a work detail, he was fined $11 and restricted to the post for 14 days. After that, he accepted army discipline, and his service record shows no subsequent charges. On various intelligence tests, he scored from subnormal to slightly above. His efficiency ratings ranged through "fair" and "good," but were mostly "excellent." This was an early example of his improved behavior in structured settings.

While on leave, he married Linda Neary in October 1967, after which he was flown in a C-130 transport to South Vietnam where he served a somewhat indifferent 12-month tour of duty with the Supply and Transport Company of the 4th Infantry Division based at the South Vietnamese city of Pleiku. At this time, South Vietnam was suffering the Tet Offensive when the VC/NVA launched coordinated attacks on virtually all the major cities and towns. With seemingly no end to the war in sight, U.S. forces were stretched to the limit, needing every serviceman they could muster for duty.

An examination of Arthur's service record reveals that he saw no action apart from dodging the occasional incoming shell. But he tells an entirely different story, claiming that he was based in the Central Highlands, and was a Rambo-type, one-man, first-strike weapon, fighting in the heat of the action. In one of his letters to the author, he wrote enthusiastically:

Another time I went on patrol and shot a kid chained up into a tree. He killed one GI, with an M1 our own weapon, too. That made three. Again on petrol [sic] I killed two women in a river, after they had killed two GI's. They had a map of base camp, plus AK47 rifles

and ammo, food and $280,000 in money belts. I split the money
with some guys, smashed the AK's and ammo, took everything else
back to camp. We let the bodies drift in the current downstream.

In another handwritten account, this erstwhile Rambo described how
he allegedly committed other atrocities. These are disgusting accounts
which must be taken with a grain of salt:

I shot one woman who was hiding some ammo in a tree. She didn't
die right off. I tied her up, gaged her [sic], then search the area [sic].
Found the hut with another girl inside of the age about 16. Knocked
her out with the butt of the gun and carried her to where the other
girl was. There was a lot of rice, ammo and other stuff in the hut. I
tied the young girl to a tree, still gaged, tied her legs too. They didn't
say anything to me at all. I had a machete that was very sharp. I cut
the girl's throat. Then took off her head and placed it on the pole in
front of that hut.

That girl at the tree peed then fainted. I stripped her then ...
First I gave her oral sex. She couldn't understand what I was doing
but her body did! I untied her, then retied her to two other small
trees ... She fainted several times. I cut her slightly from the neck to
crotch. She screamed and shit herself. I took my M16, pulled on a
nipple then put the gun to her forehead and pulled the trigger. Cut
off her head and placed it on a pole where they got water.

On reassignment furlough in Oklahoma, Specialist Fourth Class
Shawcross repaired weapons and made reluctant visits to the camp
psychiatrist. He was honorably discharged in the spring of 1969, and
moved with his wife to Clayton, on the St. Lawrence River. He promptly
put in a disability claim for war injuries and, although a Veterans
Administration examiner found no substance to Arthur's claim, the
former soldier's constant badgering won him a $73-a-month disability

pension for leaving the examiner in peace.

Seven months after leaving the Army, Arthur Shawcross was divorced again and soon in trouble with the police. He had found employment at a paper factory, the city's largest employer, and he repaid the firm for giving him a job by setting fire to the place, causing $28,000 worth of damage. Within three months a hay barn mysteriously caught fire, and it was Arthur who raised the alarm. Three days later, he set fire to a milk bottling plant. This was the city's second-largest employer and, this time our community-minded Arthur was at least considerate enough to telephone the fire brigade, then stand back admiring the red vehicles as his handiwork reduced the building to ashes.

Shortly after melting the milk depot, he bungled a robbery at a gas station. The proprietor, who knew Shawcross by sight, called the Sheriff and he was arrested, confessing to all of his crimes, which included the arson attacks. Hauled before the Court, Jefferson County Judge Milton Wiltse, who was an irate old judge from the whip 'em and hang 'em school, sentenced Arthur to five years imprisonment in Attica.

* * *

At the start of his prison sentence, Shawcross was subjected to a psychological evaluation. He was assessed as "an immature adolescent with a schizoid personality who decompensated [disintegrated or broke down] in ego functioning under the influence of unemployment stress, employment stress, rejection by wife. He should be viewed as a schizoid arsonist who requires supervision, emotional support and immediate referral to a mental clinic on parole later projected homicidal attempt of at least two of his arsons should not be underestimated. He is a fair parole risk … will require psychiatric treatment plus close supervision."

Shawcross was paroled on Monday, October 18, 1971, after serving just 22 months in prison. At first, he worked with Frink Sno-Plows in

Clayton but he was laid off four days later when it was learned that he was a thief and arsonist with a criminal record. Just after Christmas, the Watertown Public Works Department hired him under the Federal Emergency Employment Program. A supervisor assigned him to a far corner of the 60-acre landfill at the end of Water Street. As it transpired, his first murder victim lived a mile away.

Early in 1972, Shawcross attacked and raped a 16-year-old girl in an underground room of Watertown's old railroad station but, luckily for him, the victim failed to report the incident to the police. Then he met an old school friend called Penny Nichol Sherbino. She was a short woman with a good figure, lively brown eyes, tawny hair and a rural vivacity that took the form of a ready laugh and a giggle. They dated for a short while before taking their wedding vows on Wednesday, April 22, 1972, and setting up home in a neat, two-story apartment at 233 Cloverdale Apartments on Clover Street.

On Sunday, May 7, 15 days after the wedding, Arthur was shuffling along Clover Street with the intention of fishing Kelsey Creek. Set into a triangle of woods and marshland bordered by Interstate Highway 81 and State Routes 37 and 12 East, the creek was just a mile from his home. It was about mid-morning when 10-year-old Jack Blake rushed up to him asking if he wanted any worms as bait. Jack went out fishing that day with Shawcross and was never seen alive again.

The Blakes were a rough family, but they loved their children, and Mary Blake had warned her impressionable son not to associate with Arthur Shawcross. She didn't like the cut of the man who was always boasting about his service in Vietnam, and showing the boy photographs of naked women. "He was a weird sort of guy," she said. "He rode around on a white, woman's bike."

When Jack didn't return home later that day, Mary reported to the police that her son was missing, explaining that Jack had wanted to go fishing with Shawcross and, despite her warning, had probably gone against her wishes.

Suspicion, therefore, fell upon Shawcross from the outset. He denied being with Jack that day, and with no other evidence to suggest otherwise, Shawcross was released following two interviews with police who now thought that Jack was a runaway from home.

On Friday, May 26, Shawcross was again in trouble with the police. This time he was caught stuffing grass cuttings down the shirt and shorts of a six-year-old boy, and spanking him. For this offence, Shawcross received a $10 fine and a reprimand from the Court.

Tragedy struck Watertown again on Wednesday, September 2, 1972, when Shawcross raped and strangled eight-year-old Karen Hill. The blonde-haired child had been staying with family friends in Pearl Street because her parent's home, had, ironically, been destroyed by fire.

The chances against any American citizen falling into the clutches of a predatory homicidal sexual psychopath are about 350 million to 1. However, Karen's chances increased considerably when such a monster came on the scene as she played on her front lawn during this beautifully clear Sunday.

At about 3:30 p.m., a man meeting Shawcross's description was spotted by children leading Karen across the iron Pearl Street Bridge over the Black River, just a short downhill walk from where Karen had been staying. Although the children didn't know the man by name, they, and specifically a teenage girl, recognized his distinctive white bike with its brown mudguards and a basket, which he had leaned against the south wall. From a distance, the curious children watched as the man lifted Karen over the railings and gingerly led her down the precipitous bank ostensibly to show her the fish.

When the alarm was raised that Karen was missing, the children came forward to tell the cops what they had seen. At 10:00 p.m., search officers equipped with flashlights discovered a crumpled body. It was covered by a slab of concrete and laying face down, crammed into a sewerage outfall pipe on the south bank of the bridge.

Police dogs were called for. They tracked a scent up Pearl Street to Starbuck Avenue, and eagerly tugged their handlers left into Clover Street, straight to the stoop of Arthur's front door. He was arrested immediately. At the autopsy, the medical examiner discovered that Karen had been raped vaginally and anally. She had died as a result of suffocation under a mound of silt. Apart from those particularly disturbing aspects of this homicide, Shawcross had also stuffed weed and debris into the child's nose, mouth, vagina and rectum.

But what about Jack Blake? During his interrogation for the murder of Karen Hill, Shawcross hinted at the disappearance of the young boy, although he made no admissions. Nevertheless, this hint was enough to prompt the police into renewing their searches. Their efforts were rewarded on Wednesday, September 6, following their first sweep of Kelsey Creek which took four hours. Detective Gordon Spinner, along with Under-Sheriff John Griffith, noticed that long strips of bark had been peeled from a tree and neatly laid over a mound of spongy earth. Easing the bark away with his boot, Spinner recoiled in disgust as bluebottle flies rose from a lump of rotting flesh. The almost skeletal corpse was unclothed and a scrap of blonde hair was attached to the skull. Several of the bones were out of position, which indicated that animals had been feasting on the gruesome remains. Police also found a broken tooth, and Jack's clothing in the woods. His blue overalls, black sneakers, green jacket with its arms tied together in a knot, and a T-shirt marked "Blake" with a pen, with the slogan "I act different because I am different," were all neatly folded some 30 feet from the shallow grave.

Shawcross had never admitted this murder until he was interviewed in prison by the author. Piecing together what information is now available, the following scenario emerges of what happened on that fateful date.

Jack accompanied his killer to Kelsey Creek to go fishing. They walked across a railway track and into the marsh and trees nearby. Suddenly, the monster in Shawcross surfaced and he ordered Jack to strip naked. Reluctantly, and in fear of his life, Jack did as he was told, but then the terrified boy made a run for it. What happened next must have amounted to a cat and mouse chase through this remote marshy area.

Jack proved to be no match for the agile ex-soldier. Barefoot, the boy made it to the railway line—cinders were found embedded in the soles of his feet—and in a frantic attempt to climb over a four-strand barbed wire fence, he fell back into Shawcross's grabbing hands. Now, the boy was doomed. He was punched in the face and beaten unconscious. Shawcross says he raped Jack, cut off his penis and testicles, then ate them. He has since told psychiatrist, Dr. Richard Theordore Kraus, that he had cut out the heart and eaten part of that, too. There is no evidence to confirm that he was being truthful or otherwise.

On Tuesday, October 17, 1972, Shawcross pleaded guilty to the lesser charge of first-degree manslaughter and, after proceedings, which lasted 20 minutes, he was sentenced to the maximum term of 2 to 25 years for the murder of Karen Hill by a disgusted Judge Wiltse, who had had the misfortune of having had Shawcross in front of him before.

* * *

Shawcross served fourteen and a half years in prison where he experienced a rough time from the other inmates whose brotherly admiration for each other's crimes did not extend to the rape and murder of children. The beatings and abuse started for Shawcross on his admission to Attica, and this treatment followed him through the penal system until he arrived at the notoriously tough Greenhaven Correctional Facility, at Stormville, New York.

Set into rugged hill country between the Hudson River and the Connecticut border, some 40 miles north of New York City, this prison houses many of the State's most evil criminals where 742 prisoners (33 percent of population) are rapists and murderers. For Shawcross, a convicted pedophile murderer, this was simply not the safest place to be. The prison psychiatrists diagnosed him as, "a dangerous schizo-phrenic pedophile, suffering from an intermittent explosive person-ality," and it was noted that "he heard voices when he was depressed, and engaged in fantasy as a source of satisfaction. He also has an oral-erotic fixation for the need of maternal protection."

Placed in the A-1 protective segregation unit for his own good, Shawcross was a troublesome inmate in a unit of 41 men. For the greater part of his sentence, he continually faked illness or psychiatric problems to gain attention. However, Shawcross was no one's fool and, like thousands of convicted felons, he soon learned that the probable key to early parole lay in sucking up to the welfare officers, the prison shrink and the Church. Consequently, Shawcross started to behave himself and he became a model prisoner. He earned his high school equivalency certificate, and qualified in carpentry.

Now well into his sentence, Arthur was found exhibiting all the welcome behavioral traits of a "reformed" man. He figured that it was better to accept responsibility for the murder of Karen Hill, if only for the benefit of the psychiatrists and, apart from attending the religious services, he wheedled his way into a counsellor's job in the jail's mental health unit. While there, he learned the language of psychiatry and psychology and, in doing so, he eventually conned the support of a three-man State Parole Panel, who granted his freedom.

Arthur Shawcross walked out of the gates of Greenhaven on Tues-day, April 28, 1987. Although, he had been receiving excellent evaluations from one group of experts, their high opinion of his pro-gress was not shared by everyone. A report from senior parole officer, Robert T. Kent, noted, "At the risk of sounding dramatic, this man could be possibly the most dangerous individual to have been released to this community in years." Dr. Kent's assessment was much nearer the mark, but what was the real reason for the release of such a dangerous man as Shawcross? The probable answer lies in politics, and the overcrowding of the entire U.S. penal system.

Policy dictates that if there is the slightest chance that an inmate is "reformed," then the authorities want him out of prison as soon as possible. With his low ranking in the criminal pecking order as a mere first-degree manslaughter felon, Shawcross was simply an innocuous number in the system and was released merely to make room for another of the tens of thousands of new arrivals each year.

* * *

Shawcross, now 42 years old, grey-haired and bulky, had undergone a dramatic transformation from the strapping ex-serviceman who had entered the penal system 14 and a half years previously. Divorced for the third time, he walked straight out of the gates into the arms of a pen pal, Rose Marie Walley.

His attempts to settle down in a number of communities were thwarted because his murderous reputation dogged his every step. Local law enforcement agencies and the press were quick to advise their citizens that a murderous pedophile was walking the streets. Eventually, Rose and Arthur settled in Rochester, a cautious, conservative city, sometimes dubbed Smugtown, U.S.A. Rochester owes its existence to the fast flowing Genesee River, which Nathaniel Rochester harnessed to power his flour mills in the early nineteenth century. Despite the effects of industrial pollution, the gorge still provides a leafy sanctuary for anglers and lovers. Arthur Shawcross was one of those attracted by its charms; he chose it as an ideal place to fish.

After staying in a hostel for a short while, Shawcross and Rose Walley set themselves up at 241 Alexander Street, a brownstone and brick, bubble-fronted apartment just two blocks from Monroe Avenue, one of the city's busiest thoroughfares. To pay the rent, Rose enrolled as a nurse at the local hospital, while Arthur found work with Fred and Tony Brognia Produce, a vegetable and fruit wholesaler based in the public market, to the south of the city.

Despite the fact that Arthur was a "bullshitter," he proved to be a good employee. Always on time, or even early for work, he would ride an hour each way on a ladies-style, blue Schwinn Suburban bike, which had a shallow basket, the Stars and Stripes flag on the handlebars, and two deep baskets straddling the rear wheel, in which to stow his fishing gear. His weekday working hours were between 7:00 a.m. and 3:30 p.m. which left him the evenings to pursue his hobbies and recreation.

Around this time, Shawcross resumed his old philandering ways. He was enjoying an affair with Clara Neal, a 58-year-old woman who had 10 children and 17 grandchildren. On occasions, he would borrow her cars, either a small, metallic-blue Dodge Omni, or a grey Chevrolet, using them for day outings or to go fishing, yet he still found time to marry Rose.

The Brognia brothers soon learned from Arthur that he was a former convict, for he had told Tony that he had served time for murdering a man who had allegedly killed his wife in a hit-and-run accident. Meanwhile, he told Fred that he had been a Mafia hit man in New York. When the brothers conferred, they quickly realized that their employee's stories just did not add up. After speaking with a local police officer, who informed them of Arthur's real criminal past, the Brognia brothers engineered Arthur's release from their employment.

He next turned to selling hot dogs on Main Street before landing a permanent job as a salad maker for G & G Food Services which provided catering services to hospitals and schools. Arthur worked nights, being paid $6.25 an hour, and this nocturnal employment regime seemed to be the cue for the onset of Rochester's reign of terror.

* * *

Dorothy "Dotise" Blackburn was the 27-year-old mother of a six-month-old boy and two older children. She was a small-boned woman, with a slender figure, brown eyes and long brown hair. Petite and dainty, she was streetwise, with two convictions for loitering in 1985. She was last seen alive on Tuesday, March 15, 1988, after lunching with her sister at Runcone's Grill on Lyell Avenue.

Dotsie's body was found during the morning of Tuesday, March 24, floating face-down in Salmon Creek, a stream that meanders through farmland and woods on Rochester's eastern fringe. A crew of laborers clearing debris and garbage that had clogged a culvert thought they had found a mannequin covered with a layer of silt. They soon realized, however, that they were looking at a woman's frozen body.

Her face had distinctive heavy eyebrows, full lips, slightly irregular teeth, and her left eye was shut. She had long, dark hair and wore jeans, a hooded sweatshirt and a single white "Soda Pops" brand sneaker. Her navy top was pulled up from the belt line showing a bare midriff. At the autopsy, the medical examiner determined that she had died as the result of manual strangulation and noted that she had been bitten several times around the clitoris and on the vagina.

During his interview with me, Shawcross claimed that he had been driving Clara Neal's Omni, and he admitted that he had killed Dotise at Northampton Park because she had bitten his penis during fellatio.

"She was laughing at me," he said, "cause' I couldn't get my pecker up ... I slapped her around the head, an' she bit me. I got madder than Hell. That's what made me kill her. Then I dumped her clothes in a trash can, cleaned the blood from the seat, and drove home."

* * *

Anna Marie Steffen, aged 27, was an emaciated prostitute who took to the streets to support a drug habit after her paralyzed sister died. She was last seen alive walking along Lyell Avenue on Saturday, July 9. Shawcross met her by the Princess Restaurant on Lake Avenue, and he walked with her to the back of the YMCA. Afterward, he drove her down to the Driving Park and, during oral sex, he grabbed her throat and strangled her before rolling her body over the edge of the Genesee River gorge.

Her body was found on Sunday, September 11, 1988, by Hector Maldonado, while he was searching for returnable bottles so that he could buy cigarettes. The victim was lying on her left side curled in a semi-fetal position. A pair of Calvin Klein jeans were pulled down around the ankles and turned inside out. A white tank top with red shoulder straps was wrapped around the right wrist. Police found a pair of blue flip-flops nearby. A hank of hair had been ripped from the skull, and the eyes were missing from their sockets.

* * *

Dorothy Keeler was a drifter with an alcohol problem. Despite her distrust of strangers and dislike of men, Dorothy allowed herself to be befriended by Shawcross. She visited his apartment where he employed her as a cleaner and, on Friday, July 29, 1989, with the lie that he wanted to take her fishing, he lured her down to the brushy, five-acre Seth Green Island, where they stripped naked for sex. Afterward, he accused her of stealing from his home. When she protested and threatened to tell Rose Walley about their affair, Shawcross beat her to death with a piece of wood.

Three salmon fishermen discovered the body on Saturday, October 21, describing it as "a bunch 'a bones in clothes." The corpse lay in the fetal position. The jeans were unzipped and pulled down. Three pullovers covered an assortment of upper body bones and a rib was fractured. The head was missing because Shawcross had returned to the murder scene to masturbate over the corpse. He had hacked the head from the body and had thrown it into the Genesee River. "It floated for a bit," he said, "sort of swirled around in the current, then it disappeared. Just as I was walking away, it come up again. It sort of looked at me and smiled. Then it was gone."

* * *

Patricia Ives, also known as "Crazy Patty" was a 25-year-old drug-dependent school dropout with a baby boy who had been placed into foster care. The once-attractive woman, who used to bear more than a resemblance to film star Julia Roberts, was now a walking skeleton. A known prostitute with a ragged and unkempt demeanor, she had long, dirty hair, a sliced-bread complexion, and ragged needle marks from her elbows to the backs of her fingers. It was thought that she had AIDS and perhaps herpes.

A witness who was driving past the corner of Lake and Driving Park at about 7:30 p.m. on Friday, September 29, 1989, was the last person to see her alive. Later, he told police that he knew her, and that she had been in the company of a white male who was riding a bike with balloon tires. There were fishing rods protruding from the bicycle's rear baskets. The witness also added that he had watched as the couple climbed through a hole in the fence behind the tennis court of the YMCA.

Patty was reported missing the following day by her pimp and local burglar boyfriend who delighted in the name "Ratface Billy." Patty's body was found by children who were hunting for a lost baseball on Friday, October 27. They saw a foot sticking out from a pile of flattened cardboard lying under a large maple tree near the lip of the gorge. The corpse, clothed in black pants and a heavy sweatshirt, lay face up. A wedding ring was missing from her finger, there were no shoes or socks, and maggots had devoured most of her flesh.

Shawcross said that he had killed her because she went through his wallet. "There were children playing nearby," he said. "I put my hand over her mouth and held her nose. She didn't struggle, didn't holler, and didn't fight."

* * *

June Stott was the youngest of eight children and slightly retarded. She was a shy, homeless woman who heard mysterious voices in her head and had taken to sleeping rough on Lyell Avenue. Aged 30, June wasn't a hooker or a drug addict, she was just a lost and lonely soul who thought that evil sprits were always chasing her. Shawcross knew her because she had visited his home for dinner a number of times. On Monday, October 23, 1989, he saw her sitting on a bench between Dewey Avenue and Saratosa. He suggested that they go fishing together on the banks of the Genesee River and she accepted.

Down by the water's edge, he tried to have sex with her and, when she refused, telling him that she was going to report him to the police, he strangled her. After removing her clothes and dropping them into the river, he drove Clara's dodge Omni back to her house where he picked up his bicycle to ride home. Two days later, he returned to the body and dragged it down into the swaying cattails, where, using a knife he had found in her pocket, he cut open her body from the neck to the anus. Then he gutted her like a large fish, throwing the entrails into the swirling waters.

On Thursday, November 23, Mark Stetzel was walking his dog in the northern Rochester suburb of Charlotte and, among the beached, rusting river barges, he noticed an ice-covered object that had been dragged into the reeds. It was a piece of frozen carpet, under which was the badly decomposed body of June Stott. A few feet away was a bloodstained Handi-Wipe. The corpse was face down, but lividity staining showed that she had been rolled over long after death had supervened. The right leg was bent inward at the knee, elevating the buttocks, and thus suggested the possibility of anal intercourse, probably after death. The body was slashed from breastbone to crotch, the vagina was clotted with blood, and the genital lips were missing.

Shawcross said, "I cut the vagina out and ate it. Then I covered her up with the rug, picked up all the excess stuff that was there and threw it in the river, and left."

When I asked him why he hadn't disposed of the body in the river as well, he replied, "Well, I kinda liked her."

* * *

Maria Welch had a five-month-old son named Brad, and the 22-year-old woman was described as 5 foot 2 inches in height, weighing about 100 pounds, with a light complexion, brown eyes and brown hair which she often dyed blonde. She was last seen alive by another hooker near Lyell Avenue, at midnight on Sunday, November 5, 1989. She was reported as missing by her 60-year-old boyfriend, Jim Miller, the following day. He told police that she had been wearing white sneakers, a thigh-length blue jacket, jeans, a purple T-shirt, and she would have had a gold chain around her neck. Her body was tattooed with a unicorn on her forearm, a marijuana leaf and a rose on her left ankle to cover up the name "Leo"; a leaf on her right leg near the ankle; and "L-O-V-E" over the knuckles of her left hand.

Maria's body was not found until Shawcross was arrested. He told the author that he had picked up Maria at the Marques Restaurant in Lake Avenue.

"We went down that area and parked," he said. "We sat and talked, for she was cold. Had the heater on high. Gave her $30. She took off her shoes, socks and jeans. Then took off the rest of her clothes. I only unzipped. I asked her if she was on the rag, and she said 'No.' But when I put my hand in her, I felt a Cotex and blood. I've never done it that way. I asked for my money back, and she told me to go fuck myself. I choked her until she passed out. Had some rope in the car and tied her hands behind her, plus her feet to her hands. I had to take out that Cotex and pushed in a bar towel. She came to, and asked me what I did to her. Then she wanted me to untie her. I was sweating like crazy. Kept wiping my head and face off. I pulled out that bar towel and it was almost clean. Then I mounted her. My sweat dripping into her face. That was when she said 'I love you.' I kissed her, then I killed her."

* * *

Francis "Franny" Brown was a 22-year-old drug addict. A mother at 18 with a baby girl, she had been talking with a neighbor shortly before she disappeared on Saturday, November 11, 1989, from the red light district of Lyell Avenue.

A fisherman walking down Seth Green Drive found her body at 3:00 a.m., on Wednesday, November 15th. In the early morning light, he thought he had found a tailor's mannequin. The corpse was naked, except for a pair of white go-go boots. Shoulder-length hair framed her once-attractive face and her buttocks bore the home-made tattoo "KISS OFF." Her body was decorated with other tattoos including a cross on the right ankle, a wing on the left shoulder, and a butterfly around one wrist. She was in a slightly off-center kneeling position, and she appeared to be clutching a cement block. The police thought that she may have been thrown over the top of the gorge and had come to rest against a small tree on the ledge.

Shawcross explained that they "... had sex, 69 oral. She asked me to deep-throat her so I did, but she got carried away. I didn't pull out so she could breathe. She peed in my mouth and I kept pushing. Uncontrolled reaction to doing it that way. She suffocated. I used her also then while she was still warm. Even to kissing her and sucking her tongue and breast. Didn't have an orgasm. I put my on my clothes and got out of the car. Opened her door and rolled her over the cliff."

* * *

Kimberley Logan, a slightly retarded 30-year-old black mute, was last seen talking to a man of Arthur's description near her home on Friday, November 15th. Later in the day, a man called Jimmie James literally stepped on her naked, battered and bruised body, which was partially pushed under his parked RV trailer in a yard in Megis Street. Kim had been strangled to death. Leaves and other matter had been forced into her nose and mouth. Her clothes were neatly folded nearby.

Shawcross has always denied this murder. However, following my interview with Shawcross, this case has now been closed to the satisfaction of the Rochester Police Department.

* * *

During the period of the Rochester murders, it must have seemed like a crime profiler's dream come true; clues ran through the homicidal matrix like steel wire. Most of the victims were prostitutes who worked the red light district of Lake and Lyell Avenues. The women were either strangled or beaten to death, and each was disposed of naked, or partially clothed, around the city, and close to, or immersed in icy cold water. The majority of the victims had vegetation debris stuffed into their ears, nose, anus and vagina. Their clothes were often found neatly folded and close to the corpses, which ranged in decomposition from skeletal to well preserved. In several instances, the body exhibited signs of having been partially eaten by wild animals, or cannibalized by the killer himself.

Recognizing these patterns, and the obvious fact that a serial murderer was at large in the community, the Rochester police doubled the size of its Physical Crimes Unit. Around-the-clock surveillance by the entire Rochester PD Tactical Unit focused attention on the red light district where many of the victims had last been seen alive. Hundreds of hookers were questioned by the police. Indeed, later in the investigation, June Cicero, who had been warned to be extra careful, sadly ignored the advice and was killed by Shawcross within minutes of speaking with Vice Squad detectives. Investigators were reminded of the paramount importance of keeping crime scenes intact and of not jeopardizing the search for trace evidence by overzealousness. Thousands of dollars worth of new equipment was purchased for use by the police evidence technicians. NYSP/HALT, and FBI/VICAP forms were completed, and the services of both FBI and New York State Police profilers were called upon to complete a psychological profile of the serial killer. But all this proved of little use, for the killings continued unabated.

* * *

Elizabeth Gibson, a one-time beauty queen, married the day she left school. A bright young woman, she turned to cocaine and she started passing bad checks to feed her habit. She ended up a common prostitute who was last seen plying for tricks on Lyell Avenue on Saturday, November 25. Her body was found two days later by a deer hunter walking through woods ten miles to the east of Rochester. She had been suffocated. Police discovered tire impressions in the muddy ground, and blue paint chips where a vehicle had scraped a tree. This paint was later matched to Clara's blue Dodge Omni, the car Shawcross often borrowed.

Down by the Genesee River, a familiar encounter had taken place. Shawcross had accused Elizabeth of stealing money from his wallet. She put up a fight, grabbing at his eyes and digging her fingernails into his face. During the struggle, she kicked out and snapped the gearshift of the car. Shawcross said, "I tried to revive her. I wept a little." Then, after dumping her body in the woods, he drove back to the city, dropping her clothes off en route.

* * *

Darlene Trippi, aged 32, was a petite brunette who knew Shawcross well enough for them to exchange gifts at Christmas. In fact, just a few days before she went missing, Shawcross had visited her home carrying a joint of venison; indeed, over coffee, they even discussed the murders that were plaguing Rochester at the time.

Much loved by her family, who chose not to dwell on their daughter's career as a prostitute, she was last seen alive by her married sister on Friday, December 15, when she was cruising for business on a street corner. Shawcross came on the scene and took the unwitting woman down to the Genesee River, where, he says she accused him of being hopeless after an aborted sex session. "I got mad, then I choked her," he said. After his arrest, Shawcross directed police to Darlene's frozen body. It was lying in a culvert, five miles beyond Salmon Creek.

* * *

Shawcross's penultimate victim was June Cicero, aged 34, a strong character with a drug habit. She had arrived in Rochester from Brooklyn, New York, in 1973, and she had been well known on the streets of Rochester for 16 years where she was regarded as something of a mother figure to many of the younger hookers who operated in the red light district. Streetwise, and considered something of a wildcat by vice officers, June suddenly vanished without trace from the "City Mattress," the local name for the red light area, during the late evening of Sunday, December 17, 1989.

A police helicopter crew spotted her frozen corpse lying in the icy Salmon Creek on Wednesday, January 3, 1990. The body was naked except for a white sweater, white socks, and a single small earring with a distinctive pink stone.

Shawcross was seen standing on the nearby bridge parapet by the helicopter observer, and he was seen to drop something into the creek before driving off. It was this incident which led to his arrest. During a search of the scene, evidence technicians deployed a Luma-lite 2000A. This specially designed lamp casts a phosphorescent beam which illuminates trace evidence that would otherwise go undetected using normal procedures. Bathed in an eerie glow, small flecks in the snow proved to be human tissue. "It was like human sawdust," said a scenes-of crime-officer.

Shawcross explained that he had taken June down to the river, where she called him a "wimp."

"I smacked her in the mouth," he said. "I strangled her because she was going to call the cops."

With the dead body in the trunk of Clara's car, he drove along Route 31 to Northampton Park. He then stopped and heaved the mutilated corpse into the frozen Salmon Creek which runs directly through a viaduct under the road. En route, he stopped at a Dunkin' Donuts stall where he had a cup of coffee while passing the time with local cops who were discussing the string of murders.

* * *

Felicia Stephens was described as a small woman, five foot five, about 115 pounds, with black hair, brown skin, and brown eyes. She worked as a prostitute and had the misfortune to climb into Shawcross's car on Lyell Avenue, during the late evening of Thursday, December 28, 1989. Three days later, a guard in Northampton Park spotted a pair of ice-encrusted, black denim jeans in the snow. Identification found in the pockets identified the wearer as Felicia Stephens.

Later, during a more thorough search, police found her pleated grey boots and assumed she was buried close by. A deer hunter called 911 on Sunday, December 31, after he had discovered the woman's body in a derelict farmhouse about 300 yards from where her clothes had been found.

Shawcross later claimed that, apart from wearing a fur coat and boots, Felicia was wearing nothing else when she stuck her head through his open car window on Lyell Avenue. "She was running away from her pimp," he said. "I sorta got real scared and pushed the window button. I dragged her several blocks, then stopped, an' she just got in the car and asked about sex. I took her down to the river, and strangled her, too."

* * *

The successful capture and subsequent trial of Arthur Shawcross was due to a combination of good luck and dogged police work in equal measure. Ultimately, though, it was the "mind set" of this psychopath that sealed his fate for, on Thursday, January 4, 1990, Shawcross offered himself up and, in doing so, brought about his own arrest.

During that afternoon, a New York State Police helicopter was flying over the east corner of Northampton Park, some two and a half miles from where June Cicero's clothing had been found just days beforehand. Senior Investigator John P. McCaffrey was one of two observers in the aircraft. He spotted what he thought was a body frozen in the ice of Salmon Creek. At almost the same moment, the other observer's attention was drawn to a portly white male, who appeared to be urinating, or masturbating, over the bridge parapet.

The man stopped, looked skyward and threw a plastic bottle into the creek before driving off in a grey Chevrolet sedan. The vehicle was soon traced to a nursing home in Spencerport, and the trail led to Arthur Shawcross.

Upon learning of their suspect's criminal past, the police questioned Shawcross at his home. He vehemently denied any involvement in the murders, and the decision was made to leave him alone overnight pending further inquiries. In the meantime, his house was kept under observation by a static police unit until morning. Early the next day, Detectives Lenny Boriello and Dennis Blythe took him in for a quiet chat in the police station. Within hours, Shawcross confessed and he is now serving two sentences of 250 years to run concurrently. The only way Arthur will leave prison this time is in a pine box.

* * *

From the time he was incarcerated, Arthur Shawcross consistently refused to be interviewed and it took several years of spasmodic correspondence before he changed his mind. When he did, the confirmation came in the form of a blunt, handwritten note, which said simply, "I will see you."

As part of the preparation for the interview, I set about talking to everyone who had been involved with Arthur's life and crimes, particularly Clara Neal, who, in her wisdom, feels that Art should be released.

"I will keep him on tablets so he won't murder again," she promised. "Besides, we are getting married soon. I really love him. He is such a wonderfully gentle man."

At 10:15 a.m., Monday, December 19, 1994, the first interview started at the Sullivan Correctional Facility. Before being admitted into the serial killer's presence, the guards explained to me that Shawcross was still considered a highly dangerous and formidable killing machine.

"He can revert to type within a microsecond," they said. "If his features whiten, then tighten up, or if he breaks into a sweat, then get out of his way as fast as you can. He is strong enough to rip your head right off."

Weighing in at around 280 pounds, Arthur Shawcross is 5 foot 11 inches tall. With a potato-shaped head topped with thin, silvery hair, a bulbous nose and small, black, ever-watery, pig-like eyes set close together, he is quite an intimidating sight. Massive arms hang from immensely strong sloping shoulders, his chest merging into a potbelly which hangs over his belt. From his waist down, the shape of Shawcross is reversed. From the rolls of fat that circumnavigate his middle, he has short, stumpy legs that terminate in very small feet. All in all, one gets the impression that he is top heavy and could topple over at any moment.

For the first of four interviews, we came face to face in a small locked cell. No one else was present while Shawcross was engrossed with eating his lunch. He greedily stuffed the food into his mouth, and his eyes were furtive, darting around as if someone was about to snatch his food away.

After he wiped the grease and food particles from his mouth, he was asked why he had eaten the body parts of many of his victims. Shawcross smiled, and said, "Yes, sir, I have. The human meat, well, ah, it tastes like pork. I eat meat, uncooked meat, and it's like that. I eat hamburgers raw. I eat steak raw, an' I eat pork raw. I don't know why I ate parts of people, but I just did. Period."

For a long moment, Shawcross fell silent. His pudgy fingers fiddled nervously with a Styrofoam cup. His eyes scanned the ceiling as if he was searching for an invisible fly, then he added, "Yeah, an' I ate another one with the bone. I just remembered that."

God, I thought. How can someone "just remember that"?

Although the truth of the matter is that Shawcross never fired a gun in anger while serving in Vietnam, he nevertheless wanted to boast about his service career during this period. Talking about his favorite subject was a good way of gaining his confidence and, true to form, Shawcross came up with the goods. He explained that he had killed up to 50 people while out on what he called "search and destroy missions." He claimed that he was tasked to destroy any living human he came across.

Despite the improbability of these gruesome acts, Arthur obviously enjoyed talking about them if only to cause shock waves. When pressed, this intellectual pygmy came up with a multitude of often conflicting reasons in his efforts to mitigate his heinous behavior. These ranged from various types of child abuse, especially incest, to his self-perceived Rambo-type activities carried out in Vietnam. "The Army taught me how to kill. but it didn't teach me how not to kill. I have been a god unto myself. I've been the judge, the jury and the executioner. I have murdered, butchered and totally destroyed 53 human beings in my lifetime. I just wanna know why."

Arthur's excuse for murdering prostitutes was equally bizarre. At first, he stated that he was ordered by God to murder them because they all had AIDS. When questioned about the obvious fact that he had also raped and killed two young children, and two quite decent women, he clammed up and could not provide an answer. And, as the interviews progressed, he tripped himself up at every turn.

He admitted that he had murdered many of the women after having had sex with them. But, then, he changed his excuse once again: "I went out with 80 to 100 women, including hookers. I was trying to find out why I was impotent, something like that."

Then Arthur argued that he was suffering from a rare genetic disorder, and this was why he turned to serial homicide, changing tack almost immediately to blame his four wives for denying him sex so that he had to go out and find hookers to kill. Finally, he said that bright lights give him terrible headaches, and this is the cause of his problems.

In an effort to tap into the black abyss of Shawcross's mind, I questioned him about the emotions he experienced prior to, and during the acts of murder. True to form, he did not disappoint with his answer.

"It was a combination of the quietness of the area, the starlight, an' I got sweating an' stuff. I can't control that. I strangled most of them, an' it ain't like on TV where they just drop dead. In real life, they can hold their breath for three minutes, and up to seven minutes before they susscumm [*sic*]. One woman, well, just as I was strangling her, she said, 'I know who you are.' Then she went limp an' she didn't feel nothing. She just went limp."

Asked why some of his victims' bodies bore multiple bruising, while some had been disembowelled and others had had vegetation debris forced into their body orifices, he started to become agitated. His fingers and hands constantly fidgeted, and his eyes darted around the room.

After a few moments, he regained his composure, replying, "Yes, sir. Some of the bodies, yeah, they had bruises on them. That's where I knelt over them with my body weight, or I dragged 'em into the rushes down by the water's edge. I cut 'em open so's they'd rot a lot quicker that way. Kinda gutted 'em like fish an' stuff. The other stuff. Well, I just don't need to talk with you about this just yet."

Then he had the gall to ask me to be the best man at his forthcoming marriage to Clara Neal!

* * *

Lynde M. Johnston, Captain of Detectives of the Rochester Police Department, took considerable interest in the progress of my interviews with Shawcross, who is also suspected of murdering 30-year-old Kimberly Logan, a black girl whom he had befriended. Now behind bars, Arthur is smug enough to refuse to answer police questions and, with the case still open for investigation, the police needed all the help they could get.

The Rochester PD allowed me access to the Logan file as part of the research for this book. It was apparent from the crime scene photographs and the autopsy reports that there were disturbing similarities between the Logan murder and the confirmed kills committed by Arthur Shawcross.

Special interest focused on several witnesses' references to a suspect who matched Shawcross's description. This man had been wearing a red T-shirt around Megis Street at the time in question. At the time of his arrest, Shawcross denied ever knowing Kimberley Logan, and he rejected the assertion that he ever owned a red T-shirt. With the police unable to find such a garment when they searched Shawcross's home, this item proved to be the missing link because no other evidence, forensic or otherwise, was found.

Kimberly was a trusting, yet slightly retarded, young mute, and the sort of person who could make friends with anyone, including Arthur. For his part, Shawcross had established the set pattern of a serial murderer by the time of Kimberley's death; indeed, her demise was sandwiched between the murder of Frances Brown on November 11, 1989 and that of Elizabeth Gibson on November 25, 1989. Moreover, Kimberley's murder was distinguished by several hallmarks of Shawcross's modus operandi—battery, strangulation, no evidential signs of rape, heavy bruising, nose and mouth stuffed with vegetation debris, clothes found neatly folded near to the corpse, and an attempt to cover the body to prevent premature discovery. Of course, these attempts to hide the bodies did not always pay off, but Arthur knew that the longer the victims were exposed to the elements and the ravages of animals, the faster forensic evidence would deteriorate. In other words, he was "forensically aware."

With Shawcross in the frame, so to speak, it was perhaps more by luck than good detective work that brought to light a photograph of Shawcross wearing a red T-shirt. The bearer of such a piece of good fortune was none other than Arthur's fiancée, Clara Neal, who in her genuine efforts to prove that Arthur was a "loving and caring man," produced a photo album containing pictures of Arthur taken around the time of his homicidal spree. Flipping through the pages I saw a Polaroid photo of her man wearing a bright red T-shirt, a garment he has denied owning, and one that fitted the witnesses' descriptions. When the photograph was shown to Shawcross, he responded by declaring, "That's fuckin' bullshit. I ain't never had one of them, and now you're getting' on my fuckin' nerves."

With this point-blank denial recorded on audiotape and effectively in the bag, the Rochester police were able to close the Logan file.

As it turned out, this particular matter raised more questions than it solved. Why, when he had admitted to all of the other Rochester murders, did Shawcross deny murdering Kimberley Logan? The Rochester police had never released the gruesome details of the Logan murder to the media, so the chances of a copycat crime being committed with an identical M.O. at the same time in the same city, were millions-to-one against. It was a puzzle indeed.

The answer to this riddle rests with the fact that Shawcross is a racist. Time and again over the years, he has expressed hatred for the black population. He has said that to have sex with a black woman is repugnant to him, but, suddenly confronted with the red T-shirt, Shawcross back-tracked and, in one of his letters, he explained:

I had sex—good sex—with 5 black ladies and they are all alive today. [Notwithstanding the fact that he murdered Felicia Stephens who was black-skinned]. Some may get stoned, but what the hell, it's their choise [sic]. I do not hate blacks, only some of them, whites as well plus Spanish! You can tell the Rochester police to kiss what the sun does not shine [sic]. Kimberley Logan did not enter my life. I've never seen her or met her in real life. I'll grant a polygraph test to anyone on this subject and talk to the cops. She is not my victim or body.

When I offered Shawcross the facilities of a lie-detector test along with the opportunity to speak to the police, he flatly refused. Nevertheless, having completely contradicted himself all over again, he then went on to write another letter:

None of the women and girls did I mess with near where I lived. I went with about 6 to eight ladies near home and never killed them. <u>Mostly with the mute. I felt sorry for this one. We got along as friends</u>. [Author's underline.]

Even a cursory examination of this categorical statement shows that Shawcross is lying again. In reality, he murdered 30-year-old Dorothy Keeler who cleaned his apartment. Darlene Trippi knew Shawcross well enough to exchange small gifts. And no one has ever told Shawcross that Kimberley Logan was a mute, the fact being that she was the only mute killed.

From the outset, Shawcross had made it perfectly clear that he would not, under any circumstances, discuss the 1972 murder of Jack Blake. Arthur is by no means an intelligent man, but he possesses a certain animal cunning, and has the instinct to smell a rat a mile away, so broaching the subject was not a simple task. But it needed to be done for, although Mrs. Blake has been confronted with incontrovertible proof that her son was dead, she still believes that, one day, Jack will return home.

"They say Shawcross killed my boy," she sobbed during a sensitive interview at her home. "I believe in God, I am a good woman, Christopher, and I will only rest if I hear the truth from Mr. Shawcross. Then I can sleep."

During a third interview with Shawcross, reference was made to the 14-and-a-half years he had previously spent in prison. I put it to him that to document his life thoroughly, as indeed he wished, just rubbing those years out, as if they didn't exist, was not good enough. What follows is taken verbatim from this audiotaped interview, and it makes for disturbing reading.

AS: So, whaddaya wanna know about it?

CBD: Fourteen years jail time, Art. How do we deal with this?

AS: We don't. You ain't taking me there, so don't fuckin' try. DON'T FUCKIN' GO THERE.

CBD: OK. So, I take out an eraser and out goes 14 years?

AS: Yes, sir.

CBD: What about Jack Blake?

By asking this question, I knew that I was treading on unsafe ground because if the prison population heard that in the past Shawcross had raped and killed two little children, then his problems with other inmates, who would kill him at the drop of a hat, could surface all over again.

Within the blink of the eye, Shawcross's expression changed. His skin tightened and a curious paleness washed over his face. Beads of perspiration formed across his brow, running in glistening rivulets to stain the collar of his prison-issue shirt. Then, in anger, he suddenly reached out and grabbed my arm in a vice-like grip.

"You don't know who ya dealing with, fuckface," he snarled. "You don't know WHO I am, or WHAT I am."

'You don't need to do this," I replied. "Okay, you have a problem with Jack, and now you have a problem with me. You mess this interview up and Clara will climb the wall, pal."

At the very mention of Clara's name, it was as if someone had flicked a switch inside his head. Shawcross's expression reverted to normal and he relaxed his grip, letting his hand fall away. Now, he looked confused as he shook his head negatively from side to side. The killer's eyes started to moisten, and he began to mouth a mumbled form of apology, his voice shaking.

AS: OK, yeah, I killed him, okay. I told him to go home, and he wouldn't. An' then I got kinda mad at him. Yeah, I killed him, an' I buried his body under the dirt, and went fishin.' It was his fault he died. It ain't got nuthin' to do with me…I'm sorry.

CBD: And, the clothes. What about Jack's clothes?

AS: He took 'em off, an' I told him to just fold 'em up, an' stuff.

CBD: Why?

AS: Dunno. Maybe to keep him shut up, ya know. Let him think he's gonna put 'em again. Stuff like that. I dunno. Just went back and did stuff to him the next day.

Asked if his parents made him fold his clothes up when he took them off as a child, Arthur replied that it was one of the rules of the house.

I then returned to Jack Blake.

CBD: What did you do to his body, Art?

AS: I ain't going there.

CBD: Why?

Again I reminded him that if I walked out of the interview, Clara would be furious with him because she was expecting him to be totally honest during the interviews.

CBD: What about little Karen Hill. Why did you murder her?

AS: Same reason, ya know. She kinda wanted it, ya know. Sex, an' stuff like that. Then, I get started, an' she starts cryin' and wants her mom, so I suffocated her. Not with my hands. Covered her mouth with dirt and stuff.

CBD: But you did have sex with her. Vaginally and anally, Arthur.

AS: Yeah. But that was after she was dead. Then I went home.

Then came the final question.

CBD: Art, how come you stuffed leaves and twigs into your victims' ears and noses. Things like that?

AS: I dunno, really, I dunno. Just don't want to make a mess, I s'pose.

With that, the interviews were completed. Shawcross rose slowly to his feet and shook my hand for the last time. Meekly, he allowed himself to be bodysearched by the guards after his "full contact visit" with the outside world. Then "The Monster of the Rivers" was led shuffling back into the depths of the prison. He never looked back and didn't say goodbye.

* * *

At the root of this evil is Arthur Shawcross, for without his antisocial behavior, the world would have been a much safer place. Having apprehended Shawcross and placed him in custody for the murders of Karen Hill and Jack Blake, the responsibility for his welfare, and society's common good, fell upon the shoulders of others.

The trial judge for the Rochester homicides was His Honor Donald J. Wisner. During a meeting with him during a court recess, he said, upon reflection, that the prosecution should have pressed a first degree murder charge against Shawcross for the two earlier murders when they had had the opportunity. Indeed, the prosecution could have gone even further and pressed for an aggravated charge, which would have ensured that he would never have been released again.

"He most certainly would have received a natural life sentence, had that been the case," said the judge. "Instead, in an effort to save the state the expense of such a case, they opted for a lesser charge and, in doing so, they behaved like Monday morning quarterbacks."

The State Prosecutor for the Rochester murders felt much the same way, supporting Judge Wisner's sentiments to the hilt. Charles "Chuck" Siragusa—later a Justice of the New York State Supreme Court, was, and still is, disgusted that Shawcross was released after 14 and a half years to kill again and again. Perhaps the most damning indictment of the entire episode came from the pursed lips of Edwin Elwin, the Director of the State Division of Paroles. On learning of Shawcross's murderous spree of terror after his release from prison, Elwin casually stated that "he [Shawcross] did a comfortable adjustment to parole. We simply hate it when one of our people goes sour."

Greenhaven Prison psychiatrist, Dr. Robert Kent, had formed the opinion that "Shawcross was possibly the most dangerous individual to have been released to the community for years," and this evaluation was supported by Dr. Y. A. Haveiwala, another of Greenhaven's psychiatrists who had completed several evaluations on the killer. Shawcross, who had refused group therapy sessions, could not tell Dr. Haveiwala why he had murdered the children and raped Karen after she was dead; more to the point, Shawcross even expressed his concerns that he might kill again when he was released. Dr. Haveiwala had concluded that Shawcross was "a grave parole risk with an antisocial personality disorder [sociopath] and schizoid personality disorder with psychosexual conflicts." Unfortunately, Dr. Kent and Dr. Haveiwala's colleagues thought they knew better.

Shawcross's prison psychiatric records show a hodgepodge of so-called professional interpretations laced with educated and uneducated guesswork with just the one inconsistency: that he might, or might not, murder again. Yet, still this monster was released ten years before his full 25 five year sentence had expired.

Today, Arthur Shawcross repairs locks for the prison, cooks for fellow inmates and he has, once again, wheedled his way into the psychiatric unit, where he counsels other prisoners. Currently, he claims to be suffering from what he calls, "a rare genetic disorder," and first impressions of this claim may lead us to believe that this is simply one more convenient peg to hang his hat of rationalization upon. But is it? This claim, which is substantiated by many of America's leading authorities in the field who subscribe to the theory that XYY abnormalities may be the cause of violent and homicidal behavior, is that Shawcross is certainly suffering from an extremely rare biochemical imbalance linked to a rare XYY genetic disorder. It is contended that this mix could be the cause of at least part of the reason why he turned to commit such antisocial acts of violence.

Looking back to his formative years, there is well-documented evidence, even then, to show that Shawcross was showing signs of antisocial behavior. We know he was bullied before the worm finally turned and he became a bully and sadist himself. The roots of his evil had already been planted at this time. Indeed, this genetic disorder was within his at conception, and might account for his being the only member of his immediate family to turn to such extreme practices.

The prison authority medical officer, when approached on this issue, declined to confirm that Shawcross has any such problem. But Dr. Kraus, who spent months evaluating Shawcross, found solid evidence that he has an XYY disorder. Approaches to several of the world's leading authorities, seeking clarification on the XYY phenomenon linked to antisocial behavior, not surprisingly, brought no clear answer. There are two camps, each with its own strongly felt views. With our present level of knowledge, it seems that chromosomal abnormality can only have a bearing on a minute fraction of the criminal population. It is necessary to consider the millions of people throughout the world who have an XYY abnormality and who exhibit no antisocial tendencies whatever. Consequently, while an XYY disorder might partly account for Shawcross's behavior, it cannot provide the total picture.

There are a hundred million brain cells in the average person, and the presence of one extra chromosome in each cell equates to the presence of an additional one hundred million chromosomes in the XYY male, which are not present in the normal XY male. Geneticist Dr. Arthur Robinson once screened 40,000 newborns for XYY, and he has claimed that about 2,000 XYY males are born in the United States each year. His research shows that two-thirds are thin, tall and awkward, with an IQ range of 80 to 140. Robinson says, "These people are excitable, easily distracted, hyperactive and intolerant of frustration. Fifty percent are learning-disabled (compared to 2 to 8 percent in the general population) and most suffer delays in speech development." Many of these personality characteristics uncannily match Shawcross's profile.

Dr. Kraus has commented, "Studies report that the XYY male has a 10- to 20-fold increase in his lifetime risk, as compared to their incidence in the population, of being institutionalised in a mental hospital or prison—a risk that is not trivial. XYY males have a much higher average rate of learning disability and are described as 'problem children' who cause serious behavioral and management problems at home and school. Studies describe how 'at least some XYY boys show behavioral disability that makes them not only a great problem in family management, but also quite disparate from other family members in their behavior altogether.'"

This is a finding consistent with the early life history of Arthur Shawcross and his own frequently reported belief that he was "different" from all of his family members. Personality characteristics associated with these children also include descriptions of them as drifters or loners, disposed to running away from home, who, as they grow up, are frequently agitated, experiencing pedophilic urges, committing arson, threatening to kill others, molesting children, stealing and exhibiting moments of sudden violence and aggression. These are all the personality traits well documented in Shawcross's life.

So, it seems that, at the very least, an XYY chromosome disorder is part of Shawcross's problems. But what of the biochemical imbalance? In searching for a diagnosis in Shawcross's case, Dr. Kraus turned his attention to blood and urine testing where he hit upon a little known chemical called kryptopyrrole. So little was known about kryptopyrrole that half of the authorities Dr. Kraus spoke to for advice had never heard of it, and the biochemistry laboratory at the University of Rochester didn't know how to spell the word, replying, "… it sounds like something out of a *Superman* movie, doesn't it."

During laboratory examination of Shawcross's bodily fluids, Dr. Kraus found that Kryptopyrrole showed "H 200.66mcg/100cc" against an expected value 0–20. The "H" was laboratory shorthand for "High." The chemical structure of Kryptopyrrole resembles other chemicals known to be toxic to brain function, such as LSD and can be considered a biochemical marker of psychiatric dysfunction, much like the reading of an elevated clinical thermometer. This is normally present in humans in either very low amounts, or not at all, and it can be detected in the urine, which may have a mauve-colored appearance.

Feeling now that he was finally on to something, the indefatigable Dr. Klaus burned even more midnight oil, and, in doing so, learned that any kryptopyrrole reading of 20mcg/100cc was a cause for concern. Kryptopyrrole is also related to bile, and when excessive amounts are present, can combine with vitamin B6 and zinc to cause a metabolic defect called "pyroluria." This proved to be another clue to understanding Shawcross, for pyrolurics function well in controlled settings of low stress, proper diet and predictability. Apart from the initial settling down periods, which are common to all prison inductees, Shawcross has always been quite at home within the structured prison system where he enjoys a balanced diet. Conversely, pyrolurics appear to suffer poorly outside controlled conditions. Unable to control anger once provoked, they have mood swings, cannot tolerate sudden, loud noises, are sensitive to bright lights, and tend to be "night people." They usually skip breakfast, have trouble recalling night dreams, and they suffer poor short-term memory, so they make bad liars. Sometimes, they lack pigment in the skin, and are, therefore, pale. The hair is prematurely grey, and they have a diminished ability to handle stress. As such, they may be very dangerous and constitute a risk to the public.

All of this shows Shawcross's personality and behavior in an interesting light. Dr. Kraus argues that the symptoms manifested by Arthur Shawcross correlate in every way with one suffering from the abnormally elevated levels of this toxic chemical invasion.

* * *

There seems little doubt that Shawcross was born handicapped, certainly in the genetic and biochemical sense. The 47 XYY chromosome disorder, linked to the abnormally high levels of kryptopyrrole, had formed a human time bomb upon conception. For the first 25 years of his life, his sexual history highlights an inclination towards children far younger than himself. He certainly enjoyed sexual fantasies about making love to his sister, Jean, and with his inbred predisposition towards violence, perhaps it was inevitable that pedophiliac behavior leading to rape and homicide was pre-programed into him like a faulty computer chip. Murdering Jack Blake and Karen Ann Hill serve as grim testimony to that.

A sexual inadequate throughout his life, Shawcross blamed his wives for letting him down in that department. Millions of men use prostitutes for one reason or the other, so perhaps on his release from prison, Shawcross graduated to the seedier side of prostitution to fulfill this need, too.

There is also evidence suggesting that people with the genetic and chemical disorders ascribed to Shawcross can metamorphose into extremely dangerous individuals who thrive during the hours of darkness. "The Monster of the Rivers" came out at night and, when the beast surfaced, it was the prostitute population that suffered its homicidal wrath. Looking back with all the gifts of hindsight, couldn't it be argued that Shawcross's rationale and modus operandi were predictable?

Clothing—not only his, but that of his victims—was important to him. Garments subconsciously obsessed him, and he always mentioned clothing in his police statements and in letters and during interviews. Maybe we will never know why clothing was so important to this man, but the folding up of the garments was an indelible hallmark of his crimes, perhaps for the reason he gave during one of his interviews, "Fold the clothes up and they'd think they were going to get dressed again" was his calculated remark. As a young child, Arthur's mother demanded that he be neat and tidy, more especially with regard to his clothes, so this was possibly a legacy from childhood, and a trait that he carried through to form part of his modus operandi.

What is the explanation for his disgusting—yet quite unique—practice of forcing vegetation debris into the ears, nose, mouth, vagina and anuses of many of his victims? Again, this may be an echo from his early days when he indulged in torturing and killing small animals, fish and birds. Back then, as a child, he learned that by forcing material into his victims, he could not only prevent them from screaming out in pain, but also stop their urine and excrement from leaking out and spoiling his clothes. Shawcross murdered all of his victims near water, and this part of his M.O. is far easier to explain for he had been a keen angler since childhood, and during these isolated periods down by the rivers, he had ample time to fantasize about sex. Hence, Shawcross had an affinity with water. The riverbank was his territory, where he felt safe and secure.

Shawcross also returned more than once to the bodies of his victims. Often, he would sit with the rotting corpses and discuss his life with the remains. He told them how his wives disgusted him. He explained that he did love children, and that it wasn't his fault that he killed little Jack Blake or, for that matter, Karen Hill.

On at least two occasions, Shawcross cut open his victims and ate their most intimate body parts. With June Cicero, his penultimate victim, he returned three times, the second time to cut into the frozen corpse, as it lay in a creek, to take his gruesome trophy.

"It took some getting out," he explained. "I hacked it some, then I thawed it under the car heater as I drove along. I ate it raw. I wanted to show the police where the bone was, but they didn't want to know."

Shawcross feels no remorse for his crimes; he always, without exception, lays the blame for his antisocial acts at the feet of others—his wives, God, the Army and, more recently, what he feels is his genetic and biochemical abnormality. In shifting blame in this manner, he is able to justify his behavior to the extreme point of grand appraisement, which finds him standing on a pedestal in the serial killers' hall of fame, arguing that he is a very special human being and, as such, he is worthy of scientific study. He may be right about that, if only for the possibility of examining more closely his genetic and biochemical makeup in the hope of furthering our understanding of what he is.

The following extract is taken from a letter written by Shawcross to the author. It is published here with his permission.

I have been asked, Did I kill? Yes, too many times for any one person to do so! It is said I have partaken of human flesh. Think back in history: You will see that man hunted man (still do in some remote parts of the world.) Think about the animal we call pig or boar. Why does it say in some books we can't eat this animal? Because it tastes just like human flesh. I have eaten flesh of man or woman …

So the next time any of you sit down to eat bacon, ham or a nice juicy pot roast or pork chop, think about the taste, the flavor of eating human flesh. But this only affected me when I got very angry—the hunger of the predator.

I have been a god unto myself. I've been the judge, the jury and the executioner. I dear people, have murdered, butchered and totally destroyed 53 human beings in my life time. Why?

Picture in your mind: I was taught to sit for hours at a time and not move; I was taught to seek out and destroy the enemy as I received them to be.

The prostitutes I am accused of killing were the enemy to me in their own fashion, because they can kill with social diseases and AIDS and get away with it! Do I regret it, I have been asked? My answer is, I very much regret it, to the point of wondering why I was chosen to carry out this assignment.

The United States government taught me how to kill; what it did not teach me was the desire not to so! I still get those feelings—but the pills I am now on dampen them to the point of calming me down. Why not before?

Why am I like I am? Study it—seek the answer before too many people get killed! I am like a predator, able to hunt and to wantonly destroy at any given time or moment … I have been pushed and threatened, but somehow the pills stop or slow down the desire to fight. I know that when I do fight there will be no control—I'll be the predator again.

Most people tell me I will die in prison! (So what.) Do, you have a choice of when and where you will die? … Many people believe that when they die they will go to heaven. Not so! Your soul waits to be called: Read your Bible if that is what you believe in. As for me, I will live again and go on to the next transition. I am a spiritualist … Death is but a transition of life. The people I have killed are in their next transition. They will live again, but in a much better way than the one they left behind! ... I have lived in many parts of the world, even in England, Kent to be exact. The fens were home to me 700 years ago.

What went on in the home I grew up in is better left unsaid, but I cannot do it! I, as a child, had no control on who my sex partner was! I cannot say I did not enjoy it, be it a cousin, sister or the old girl herself.

Every man, woman or child from 10 years of age and up is able to kill knowingly. How did I kill without the use of drugs or a struggle! Let me explain this further. The body has many pressure points: some to relax you, some to excite you and some to give pain or remove it. A few of them to stun you and, be that as it may, to kill you! Many of you humans portray me as mad-crazy. This is your free will. What you think may not be so.

Look to the heavens, I came from there! So did you but you wont admit it! My time is near in this transition. I will move on shortly, I feel what I feel. If every man, woman and child had the same as everyone else, then crime and war would be nonexistent.

Remember: watch the heavens, we are coming to rescue you from you.

I am, or am I?

SIGNED BY ARTHUR SHAWCROSS
SEPTEMBER 19, 1994

This chapter is based on exclusive television and audiotape interviews between Christopher Berry-Dee and Arthur John Shawcross within the Sullivan Correctional Facility, Fallsburg, New York State, on Monday, September 19 and Friday, September 30, 1994, and correspondence covering three years.

Shawcross welcomes correspondence, and his address is: Inmate # 91-B-0193, Sullivan Correctional Facility, P.O. Box 116, Fallsburg, NY 12733-0016.

MICHAEL BRUCE ROSS

"There was nothing they could have said or done.

They were dead as soon as I saw them.

I used them. I abused them, then I killed them.

I treated them like so much garbage.

What more do you want me to fucking say?"

MICHAEL ROSS IN AN INTERVIEW WITH THE AUTHOR

S uddenly, there he was, Connecticut's only convicted serial killer, shuffling along, surrounded by three immaculately-dressed prison officers wearing starched shirts, knife-edge creased trousers, and spit-and-polished boots. He was handcuffed and shackled at the legs, his loose-fitting prison uniform covering a plumpish physique. Michael Ross stands around 5 feet 10 inches, and weighs about 140 pounds. He appears bookish, with his glasses perched high on the bridge of his nose, and is polite.

Michael has the intellect. He has a bright intelligence and, with an IQ of 150, became an Ivy League student at Cornell University. He has a fresh complexion, with a chubby face, a cheeky smile and mischievous eyes, giving the impression of a stereotypical "All-American," home-grown boy. At face value, Michael is very much the boy next door, the type a father might approve of his daughter dating. But, as all fathers know, appearances can be deceptive. In real life, he is a sexual sadist and serial murderer who raped six precious daughters before killing them.

During the course of several interviews, he added to his murderous record by confessing, for the first time, to raping and killing two other girls, and having anal intercourse with the dead body of another.

* * *

Michael Ross was born in Brooklyn, Connecticut, on July 26, 1961. He was the first of Daniel and Patricia Ross's four children, the others being Donna, Kenneth and Tina. The marriage was a stormy one, and Patricia, a borderline schizophrenic, who would, later, twice run away from her husband, never hid the fact that she was forced to get married because she became pregnant with Michael. From the outset, her baby was an unwanted child.

Family and friends have described Patricia as a woman who could be charming one minute, and cold and calculating the next. She had spent time in the state mental hospital at Norwich. A number of people who knew her had witnessed at first hand a volatile, manipulative woman who would take out her resentments on her family, especially Michael, whom she blamed for ruining her life.

Michael remembers his mother's mood swings, which all of the children feared. They couldn't understand how she could laugh after making them ill by feeding them bad meat. Or why she would ruin her two daughters' clothes with a box of dye. Spiteful, vicious and sadistic, Patricia tried to trick young Michael into shooting his pet dog, after convincing him that it was suffering from a short illness. She even set his mattress on fire on the front lawn because she had caught him masturbating. So, by all accounts, Patricia was "The Mother from Hell."

Yet the four kids loved their mother, simply because she was their mom. They grew to accept her mood swings, and learned to keep out of her way when she was angry. Like unwanted pets, which return even meager scraps of affection with devotion and loyalty, the children had to love her just to survive.

Michael Ross explained this in an audiotaped interview, and the authenticity of his account has been verified by one of his sisters:

We had what we called "Mom drills." The first person up in the morning would go downstairs while the rest of us kids would wait and be real quiet and listen to what type of reception we'd get from our mother. And, if we got one kind of reception, we'd know how to act. An' I'll give you an example. See, one day my sister, Tina, was setting the table, and, uh, there was six of us in the family, you know. So, she opened up the dishwasher to get six glasses, three in each hand. You know how you do it. You know, the glasses clink together. My mother went off. She was screaming and yellin,' so we knew that was a bad day coming. You just knew how she was but we loved her.

The Ross children had little time for fun and games, and they were even discouraged from having any friends, or participating in after-school activities. With these restrictions in place, they had bonded into a tight-knit group, for self-preservation and mutual support, although Michael was alienated because his brother and sisters erroneously believed that he was favored as a "mama's boy."

For his part, young Michael was very proud of his father, and the family egg farm business in Brooklyn, Connecticut. Eggs Inc. would become the most important part of Michael's formative years. Indeed, by the age of ten, he had his own set of chores, which included wringing the necks of sick and deformed chicks. Michael was a hard worker, a mixed-up kid who desperately wanted to live up to his father's high expectations of him, while, at the same time, he was very much seeking the approval of his schizoid mother, and constantly vying for her rare affection. When asked if he was physically abused as a child, he had this to say:

It's hard for me to tell you what was wrong with my family because I don't know anything different. That's how I was raised. I was beaten sometimes but I don't think that was it. It was more emotional abuse, an' like I mean with my dad when we were beaten, we would have to go out an' pick up a stick out of the garage where we had a wood pile. An' what you would do was to go out and you couldn't pick one that broke 'cause if it broke he'd get pretty mad. But, you didn't pick yourself a club. You know, you didn't want to get the hell beaten outa you. An', so I had my own stick put away, hidden away in the back so that people coming in to get firewood wouldn't inadvertently take it. But, I mean there is something wrong there when a kid goes to the wood house and picks up his stick, his own special stick for getting beaten. And, he hides it so no one accidentally takes it. And, you know if you got beat you didn't scream because my father just got madder.

Michael loved his parents despite the physical and psychological abuse they handed out, but the effects of such treatment on the developing mind are often irreparable unless drastic counter-measures are taken to remedy the problems.

Many psychiatrists and psychologists now generally agree that if contact and interaction with others in a peer group are restricted during the early stages of infant development, the ability to interact successfully at a later stage in life is retarded. That is, the infant and child must experience love and feel valued, or the limbic nuclei in the brain will not develop normally and gross mental abnormalities may result. Children will lose the ability to form emotional attachments with others, or, any attachment that does come about may only be superficial, and this abnormality may last for the rest of their lives.

Michael Ross certainly had this problem, and it is not surprising to learn that, during an FBI study of serial sexual murderers, 53 percent of the subjects' families had a history of psychiatric problems, 42 percent of the subjects had been subjected to physical abuse, and 74 percent had a psychological abuse history.

* * *

In September 1977, after a period of schooling at the ironically named Killingly High School, Michael's future looked decidedly bright as he drove his car on to the Cornell University campus in Ithaca, New York. He had overcome long odds and was justifiably proud of himself, as only 10 percent of Killingly High's vocational agricultural (vo-ag) students went on to college. Fewer still attended Ivy League schools.

At Cornell, Ross enrolled as an animal science major, and he started a course of study that would well suit his ambition to become the third generation to run the family poultry business. This was an obsession with Michael and, for a time, his fraternity brothers even called him "The Egg King."

Michael joined AgPAC, the Agricultural Student Union Council, and attended the Collegiate Future Farmers of America. He was a student teacher, counsellor, researcher teaching assistant, and a study group leader around this time. Alpha Zeta, one of the two campus fraternities dedicated to agricultural activity, recruited Ross, and he pledged to them in 1977. He lived in the fraternity house, throughout his sophomore and junior years. His brothers, who were mostly young men, had small-town farming backgrounds.

Since his incarceration for serial murder, a number of Michael's old Cornell friends have said that he enjoyed the house, its social life, and the chance to share common interests. His classmates, though, also recall that Michael was a loner, aloof and somewhat arrogant at times.

The student body of Cornell was three times larger than the entire population of his hometown of Brooklyn, and the campus became a large playground for Michael Ross. Now free from his mother's unpredictable influence, he could do whatever he wanted, without fear of reprisal. He literally went crazy with all the fun he was having, plunging headlong into the party life to the extent that he started taking Ritalin three times a day to control his hyperactivity. He would continue to use this drug for a further six years. He drank heavily and he started to experiment with sex, often sleeping with different girls four nights a week.

During his first year at Cornell, Michael met his first true love, a pretty girl called Connie Young. They met at a party, and he walked her home through the moonlight, and they kissed as they watched a team of divers swimming in the shimmering silver water of Beebe Lake. They strolled to the statues of the college's founding fathers, and he explained how they were supposed to move together and shake hands when a virgin passed between them. On this occasion, the statues apparently did not move, for "Connie was hotter than a kitchen stove," Michael recalled.

Connie remembers Michael as a "go-getter," and a guy who always liked to be "the center of attention." At first she accommodated this behavior because he seemed a worthwhile prospect. She certainly overlooked his arrogance and constant boasting about his father's egg farm. In Connie's eyes, he was handsome, if just a little nerdy. He was articulate, took her dancing and dined her out. She remembers that he always had money when he needed it and, for his part, he enjoyed taking her to places to show her off. To everyone who knew them, they seemed the perfect couple, and most were thrilled when they became engaged to be married.

For a short period, Connie shared his bed, and then the arguments started. Michael's fraternity brothers threw him out of the house because he was breaking the rules by sharing his room with a female. As a result of this, the couple rented a small apartment where Michael withdrew into himself. The schooling pressure and the demands made by the close relationship with Connie had started to take their effect. Added to this were his parents' escalating marital problems, and these were clouding his judgement over the future, as home issues were never far from his mind.

Connie's distress over her lover's change of attitude came to a head when he started to miss classes. She was a dedicated student, trying to cram four years of education into three, but Michael Ross seemed to have lost interest, and he started to hang around their apartment all day, watching television and reading pornographic magazines. He changed his major to Agricultural Economics, and his grades plummeted. He became extremely lazy, expecting Connie to do all the housework and cooking and, despite the fact that she was exhausted after studying, he demanded sex with her at least four times a day.

Initially, Connie complied with Michael's demands, for fear of rejection. She loved him deeply, and even allowed him to have rough sex with her, although it hurt her badly. Then, as the day-to-day events became even more unpleasant, she now started to wonder if marrying

Michael was such a good idea at all. He was, she now believed, sex crazy, and getting worse. With his graduation approaching in the spring of 1981, Michael could not face the prospect of leaving Connie behind at Cornell, and he became even more restless and agitated, withdrawing for much longer periods into a fantasy dream world of his own.

Even as a preteen, he had experienced constant fantasies about women in which he would take them to what he called "a special, under-ground place," where he hid them, and kept them so that they could fall in love with him. From juvenile criminal records, it is known that, at the age of 15, he molested several neighborhood girls. Now an adult, Michael's fantasies grew more sexually extreme and progressively more violent. During these fantasies, he says that he was always the assailant and, by the time of his graduation, Connie had joined his faceless dream victims. He terrorized his fantasy girls and humiliated them by forcing them to undress and drop to their knees in front of him. Michael gained enormous sexual pleasure and relief from raping his fantasy victims. He savored the sense of domination that accompanied their fear, and he reasoned that he had control over real women, too, even though these bizarre thoughts were still locked away inside his mind.

Whatever dreadful thought patterns were developing inside Michael's head during that period in his life, it seemed that there was a meeting between his distorted subconscious thinking and the bland reality of everyday life. This is where the two roads met, for not only did Ross overlay the beautiful face of Connie on to his fantasy victims, his demands for kinkier sex from her began to spiral out of all control. Added to this, he masturbated himself raw. Although he did not know it, he was suffering from hypersexuality, a disorder of the sex drive.

More and more, Michael found himself wandering aimlessly around the campus. He became titillated by stalking female co-eds, staying just far enough behind them to remain undetected. He explained, "This turned me on so much I always had a hard on." To release this almost uncontrollable compulsion, he had to masturbate ever more frequently, or else tip right over the edge, and act out his fantasies in reality.

Michael Ross crossed that threshold in April 1981, when he found himself running up behind a co-ed, grabbing her and dragging her into a small copse where he forced her to act out his fantasy of stripping naked before him and giving him oral sex. After he ejaculated, he ran off into the night, swearing to himself that he would never do such a terrible thing again.

Just three nights later, he was revisited by the same uncontrollable demons and, overcome with sexual compulsion, he attacked a second girl. During this assault, he slipped a rope around the student's neck, enjoying the heightened power this form of restraint bestowed on him. The terrified co-ed was like an animal he could control with a quick tug of his hand. Fortunately, someone approached the scene before he raped her and he fled into the shadows, his sexual frustrations still boiling inside him.

Michael has said that he firmly believed that these outrageous acts would cease after he left Cornell, and that he prayed that he could last out the final month without attacking anyone else. At the same time, he says he also felt cheated of the ultimate sexual satisfaction, which had been denied him during the previous attacks. Weighing up the pros and cons on his mental balance sheet, he said he was compelled to satisfy himself fully, at least once before he graduated, but he promised himself that this would have to be the final attack, after which he would never hurt a woman again.

* * *

On Tuesday, May 12, 1981, Ross stalked a pretty 25-year-old student called Dzung Ngoc Tu. He followed the delicate young woman from her class, and raped her in a secluded area of the campus. During the attack, she recognized her assailant and, when she told him this, she effectively signed her death warrant. To avoid arrest, Michael now had no option other than to kill her, so he strangled her before throwing the body over a bridge and into Beebe Lake.

A chilling fact of this murder was that, during the autopsy, the medical examiner determined that the cause of death was by drowning, indicating that Dzung had been alive when she plunged into the icy water. Although Ross has always been suspected of committing this murder, he has never allowed himself to be interviewed by the police. The case was finally cleared up when he admitted to the murder, during one of the interviews which form the basis of this chapter.

* * *

Michael believed that his parents attended his graduation ceremony only for appearance's sake and he decided, from that moment, not to return to the family farm. By a stroke of good fortune, despite his poor grades, he managed to land an enviable job in June 1981 with Cargill Inc., of Minnetonka, on the outskirts of Minneapolis.

Cargill is an international agricultural business best known for grain sales, and Ross was employed at one of the company's more modest operations in Louisburg, a country town about 30 miles northeast of Raleigh, North Carolina. As a production-management trainee in the poultry products division, Michael was taught how to supervise the care and management of a quarter of a million laying hens. It was a job well suited to him and, by all accounts, his career prospects with Cargill were excellent.

During the transitional period between graduation and full-time employment, Michael tried to convince Connie to transfer to the North Carolina University, where, he suggested, she could complete her studies. Over the preceding months, their relationship had so deteriorated that he was now paranoid about the separation and feared that she would soon be gone for good. Nevertheless, he was secretly hopeful they would marry one day. Connie had ideas of her own, and marriage was no longer one of them; besides, she was now dating someone else.

Then a bomb dropped on Michael's world when he learned over the phone that his mother and father had separated for the third time, with Mr. Ross leaving the family home and business to their own devices. Patricia flew to Louisburg, and Michael was pleased, if not surprised, to see his mother so quickly after learning the bad news. Mistakenly, Michael thought this visit was a sign that his relationship with his parents might improve. At the very least, he wanted to believe that his mother could keep the egg farm going until he returned home to take charge, if only for his father's sake. This thought was the furthest thing from Mrs. Ross's devious mind, for she had, in fact, come to visit her son for one reason only. She needed Michael to sign over his shares in Eggs Inc so that she could dispose of the company, while becoming rich into the bargain.

Having been duped into signing the share transfer, and soon after learning of the true reason behind his mother's impromptu visit, Michael felt that he had betrayed not only his father but himself.

Then life was made even worse when Connie flew to North Carolina with more bad news. For her, the trip was a short one. She explained that she didn't like Michael's parents, and even if he did end up running the egg business, this wasn't exactly her idea of a future. The finality of the relationship hit home on Tuesday, August 25, 1981 when, at Raleigh Durham airport, the couple fell into each other's arms, sobbing their farewells. Michael could not bring himself to believe that his relationship with Connie was finished, so he was understandably distraught as he drove back down Highway 401 to Louisburg.

At around 6:30 p.m., he passed through the small town of Rolesville where he spotted a young woman pushing her seven-month-old child, in a buggy, along Main Street. Within milliseconds, his uncontrollable sexual urges surfaced again and, after parking his car, Ross ran up to the woman and offered to carry her groceries.

Rolesville was a friendly place, with just 353 residents, and violent crime was virtually unknown until Ross drove down Main Street. The young mother, used to such a secure environment, did not hesitate when this helpful and decent young man approached her. She thanked Ross for his offer and passed over the heavy bags. They walked to her home several blocks away and, as they entered the backyard, Ross suddenly dropped the bags, whipped off his leather belt, and threw it over the woman's head. He dragged her into a nearby soy bean field, while threatening to smash the baby's head against a tree if it didn't stop crying.

This innocent woman now became a repository for the months of Ross's pent-up anger and sexual frustrations. He smashed his fists into her face, and he choked her with the belt, forcing her to her knees to beg for mercy. Then, with his hands tightly clasped around her neck, he ejaculated.

After regaining his breath, Ross sat back on the ground with his victim squirming around in front of him. Somehow he felt cheated, for he had wanted to satisfy his perversions by ejaculating as she died, not beforehand. Enraged, acting like a wild animal, he ripped off the woman's clothes, beating her again and again before strangling her with his bare hands while the baby screamed close by. And, as suddenly as he had appeared, Michael Ross vanished. It was over an hour before the woman regained consciousness. Painfully, she crawled across the street to a neighbor who summoned the local police chief, Nelson S. Ross. Officers arrived almost immediately and roadblocks were set up to the county line, but Michael was long gone. He was not charged with this offence until he was arrested in Connecticut, three years later.

When asked if he recalled the Rolesville attack, Michael said, "I don't really remember her, or any of my victims for that matter. It's like an old, black and white movie, a collage of strange faces, that's all. Nope, I couldn't remember this woman if you had showed me her photograph the next day. There was nothing she, or any of them, could have done when I zeroed in on them. They were dead. All over. That this one lived ain't got nothing to do with me. That she lived? Well, that was purely an act of God."

When I asked him if the Rolesville victim fought back, and tried to escape, Ross said, "Nothing. She could have got away or something, but it never happened. I can't remember. I can't remember any kind of struggling with her or anything like that. I can't remember, uh, any kind of fighting at all. I do recall, with the Rolesville victim, saying that I would smash the baby's head into a tree or a wall. So, I would imagine I probably said things equally horrible to, uh, the other ones that would make them stop and think not to do anything."

Ross simply carried on his daily existence as if nothing untoward had happened at Rolesville. Then, on Tuesday, September 17, 1981, his parents filed divorce papers at the Windham County Superior Court. A week later, Michael's employer, Cargill, sent him on a field trip to Illinois, where he would visit the Chicago Commodities Exchange. Before this trip was over, Ross would be arrested for the first time.

He decided on Monday, September 28th, to look over the Cargill operation in La Salle, which is about 11 miles southwest of Chicago. He rented a car at Chicago's O'Hare International Airport, and headed west across the flat, central Illinois farm country. Just before 11:00 p.m., an attractive 16-year-old La Salle girl was walking along a road that threaded through a cluster of houses, when she noticed a car slowly creeping past her. She had noted the vehicle several times beforehand, and she was now becoming frightened for her safety.

Without warning, the teenager was suddenly grabbed from behind and a handkerchief was stuffed into her mouth. She was dragged into nearby woods where the attacker wrapped a belt around her neck and asked her for money. She gave him the 22 cents she had and, when he loosened his belt, she screamed. She was now moments from a terrifying rape when salvation arrived. A woman living nearby had just switched off her television with the intention of having an early night when she heard a noise that made her blood chill. Opening her kitchen window, she heard a gurgling sound and rustling noises in nearby bushes, so she called the police. Luck was now on the teenager's side, even more so because a patrol car was only 100 yards away, and it arrived at the scene in a flash. When Ross saw the beams of police flashlights illuminating the woods, he hurried back to his car but, this time, his luck deserted him.

Sergeant Lewis of the La Salle Police explained how Ross got himself arrested. "What happened is, when we took the girl home, Ross had his car parked on the same street she lived on. And, on the way home, she saw the car, and said, 'That's the car, that's the car.' And, so pretty soon we were looking at the car, and he comes up and says, 'What's the problem?'"

After Michael's arrest, for "unlawful restraint," Sergeant Lewis said that he was puzzled by the contradiction, between Ross's demeanor, and what he had done.

"He was real humble," Lewis recalled. "He wouldn't look you in the eyes when you talked with him. He was a very educated and a talented kid. He didn't appear to be the kind of guy who would go out to other towns and do this kind of stuff. He more or less kept his mouth shut, and he was subdued and spiritless when we took him in."

The downside of the La Salle attack was that Ross was fined $500 after pleading guilty and on Tuesday, October 8, he was fired from his job. On the upside, and with no alternative, he returned to Brooklyn where he attempted a reconciliation with Connie. Indeed, he was very pleased when she invited him to spend Christmas with her at her parents' home in Vermont. He was even more delighted that they had also been invited to share the New Year with his mother in Brooklyn.

Unfortunately, the visit to Mrs. Ross was an unmitigated disaster. His mother could not stand the sight of such a beautiful young woman in her house, and Michael was very upset by the fact that his father had been reduced to living in a run-down shed nearby. The hoped for rekindling of his relationship with Connie failed, for the second time, and she went off to Ithaca, New York, to visit a "friend." This was the catalyst that precipitated Ross into rape and murder again.

* * *

Seventeen-year-old Tammy Lee Williams lived with her family on Prince Hill Road, Brooklyn, which was only a mile or so from the Ross's egg farm. That Christmas, among the gifts from her parents, she received a pocketbook. A free-spirited young woman, who had quit high school, she came and went as she pleased, and it wasn't unusual for her walk along Route 6 to visit her boyfriend who lived in Danielson, about three miles away.

At 10:15 a.m., on Monday, January 4, 1982, Tammy left her boyfriend's apartment and started to walk home, after first promising him that she would telephone him to let him know that she had arrived safely. She did not fulfill this promise because she encountered Michael Ross on her journey. He was surprised to see the young woman walking along a busy road on such a bitterly cold day. Seizing the moment, which distinguishes the opportunist killer, he parked his car and ran up to Tammy offering her a lift. When she declined, he dragged her screaming and struggling into nearby woods, where he forced her to strip and get to her knees. He raped and strangled her before hiding the body, under a pile of rocks and brush, in a swamp. He said it took him all of eight minutes to throttle her to death, because he kept getting cramps in his hands. Each time this happened, he had to release his grip and massage his fingers before finally throttling the life out of her.

Tammy's father reported his daughter missing the next day and, on January 6th a motorist found Tammy's pocketbook, lying along Route 6, at the junction of Brickyard Road. Michael Ross explained that he had thrown the item out of his car moments before arriving back at his mother's place, shortly after the murder.

On Saturday, June 30, 1984, he guided police officers to the decomposed corpse of Tammy Williams, and said later that she had recognized him and that she pretended to enjoy the violent rape to avoid being killed. He also said that he returned to the corpse several times, during the weeks following the murder, in order to masturbate over the body.

During January and February, 1982, Ross's thoughts continually returned to Connie. Acting on impulse, he decided to drive to Ithaca to visit her, without prior warning of his intentions. On arrival, he found Connie in bed with another man. He stormed out in a rage and headed south in search of a victim to kill.

* * *

May Day fell on a Monday, in 1982, and Paula Perrera left Valley Central High School early because she didn't feel well. With no money for a bus fare, she started hitchhiking, and she was last seen alive near the Montgomery Auto Shop, on Route 211, during the early afternoon. Paula's mother, Christine Canavan, reported her 16-year-old missing to the Crystal Run Police later that day.

Although Ross has always been the prime suspect in the Perrera killing, there has never been enough evidence available to charge him with her murder, a situation exacerbated by the fact that Ross has refused to be interviewed by the police investigators. This changed when Ross was subsequently interviewed in prison as part of the research for this book. Confronted by me with police documents and a newspaper article, Ross made a full confession on videotape, giving details of the murder that only Paula's killer could have known. The case is now classified as solved.

He said that he had seen her walking along Route 211, and had offered her a ride home. At a spot near a marshy wooded area, and close to a rest stop, he pulled over and raped his victim before strangling her. He hid the body near a low stone wall, and then drove home. His confession closed the file on this murder inquiry. Asked during the interview what Paula had been wearing, he said he could not recall the details and tossed the documents to the floor, saying, "Well, it's just another murder, isn't it?"

* * *

Ross started work at Croton Egg Farms on Friday, March 5, 1982. The world's largest poultry operation, based in the small town of Croton, northeast of Columbus, Ohio, hired him as a co-supervisor for 30 employees. He was also responsible for 14 henhouses and over one million birds.

A fellow supervisor, Donald Harvey, remembered Ross, saying, "He was a disaster in the job, and we were planning to fire the guy pretty soon. He was very bossy. And he just didn't relate to you in giving an order. He just didn't know how to come across. He wanted everyone to know that his education was much higher than theirs, and they were hourly workers and high school drop-outs."

On Sunday, April 25, 1982, Ross spotted Susan Aldrich in a laundromat in Johnstown, a town close to Croton, and followed her home. She was completely unaware that she was being stalked and he was completely unaware that she was an off-duty police officer. He knocked on her door and told her that his car had broken down and asked if he could use her telephone. As soon as Susan turned her back, he reached over her shoulder, cupped his hand over her mouth to prevent her screaming, and forced her to the floor. She struggled, and managed to shout out, saying that her husband was a policeman, and that he would be home at any moment. After giving her a severe beating, Ross ran back to his car, ripped a parking ticket from the windshield and drove off.

Ross's car had been parked close to the laundromat, and it was there that he got the ticket. Police also found a witness who saw him running from the direction of Susan Aldrich's home towards his vehicle, so they put two and two together and traced the owner through the Vehicle Licensing Office. In an act of poetic justice, it was Susan's husband who arrested her attacker.

Ross was fired from Croton Egg Farms on May 3rd, and bailed to his mother's home before sentencing. While there, he visited a psychiatrist, at the Learning Clinic in Brooklyn. He was trying to win a little sympathy from the doctor, who might have influence with the Ohio court.

The following month was another disaster for Michael Ross, for, although he had returned a number of photographs to Connie, she still had his engagement ring and he wanted it back. However, the day before he turned up to collect it, she set off across country to marry her new boyfriend. When Ross learned of this, he went crazy with anger. But, if that slap across the face was hard to take, a family development enraged him even further.

Financially, his mother's divorce had paid off handsomely. When Patricia flaunted her new lover before speeding off in her flashy new Cadillac, it was too much for Michael. These emotional setbacks coming so close together were sufficient to set him off on the murder trail again.

* * *

The last time anyone could recollect seeing 23-year-old Debra Smith Taylor alive was around midnight on Tuesday, June 15, 1982. She was driving home with her husband when their car ran out of gas, on Highway 6, near Hampton, just eight miles east of Mrs. Ross's home. A state trooper came across the stationary car, and drove the couple to a service station in Danielson, where the boyfriend of one of Ross's earlier victims, Tammy Williams, had lived. The trooper recalled that the Taylors were arguing, and that Debra was so annoyed that she said that she would find her own way home. After leaving her husband to his own devices, she walked across Danielson town green, to the bandstand, where she gratefully accepted the offer of a ride home from a bespectacled young man who had walked up and spoken to her.

Two hunters discovered the skeleton of Debra Taylor on Saturday, October 30th, in one of the large tracts of woodland east of Route 169, in Canterbury. The spot was less than ten miles from the Ross's farm. The body was so decomposed that identification was only possible by means of dental records and items of jewelry.

* * *

During the first week of August 1982, Ross returned to Ohio for sentencing over the assault he had committed four months previously. The psychiatrist who had examined him earlier said that Michael was an "over achiever," and had "too much spare time on his hands." In his report, the psychiatrist also suggested that he should find a hobby, such as learning how to fly an airplane. The judge nevertheless packed Ross off to the Licking County Jail, where he would serve a six-month jail term for the assault on Susan Aldrich. He was ordered to pay a $1,000 fine. Daniel collected his son from prison on Wednesday, December 22nd, drove him back to Connecticut, and offered him a place to stay.

Michael Ross had misrepresented himself when he applied for work at Croton Egg Farms by declaring that he had never been in trouble with the police, and he did exactly the same thing again in May 1983,

89

when he applied for a job with the Prudential Insurance Company of America. He would become one of the 40 agents selling health, life, automotive, property, casualty insurance and securities, from the company's office in Norwich, Connecticut. With steady money in his pocket, Ross rented an apartment at 58 North Main Street, in Jewett City. He settled in, and his landlady remembers him as a decent, smart and extremely affable young man, whom she enjoyed having around her large, Victorian-style house.

Ross's female work colleagues also took an immediate liking to him. They thought of him as sweet, and inexperienced in romance. He dated when the opportunity arose, and when he met recently-divorced Debbie Wallace, while out canvassing for business, he reasoned that his past problems were well behind him.

During this relationship, Ross says he spent a great deal of time masturbating, fantasising and stalking women. Some he followed at random. With others he set out to learn their daily schedules. He slipped into apartments, just to watch women undress and get into bed. And he raped once during this time, allowing to his victim to run away.

Although he was often out until all hours of the morning, Debbie Wallace was totally ignorant of Michael's perverted behavior. She believed that he would make a good father for her three children; however, like Connie, Debbie was stubborn, independent and strong willed. She was a spitfire, full of energy, and sex with Michael was excellent. Their relationship was volatile, too, and their frequent arguments often ended in physical violence. During Thanksgiving 1983, the couple had a furious fight over dinner arrangements.

From the outset, Patricia Ross had never liked Connie, and she didn't approve of Debbie either, so she invited her son for a meal but refused to extend the invitation to Debbie. Ross did not know what to do. He felt torn between the two women, so he and Debbie fought and the outcome was that he spent the vacation alone.

Around the time Ross was learning the insurance business—giving a new meaning to the term "The Man from the Pru"—19-year-old Robin Dawn Stavinsky was moving from Columbia to Norwich, where she hoped to find a job that paid enough that would allow her to go to college.

In August 1983, she took a job as a switchboard operator at DPM Enterprises. At 9:30 p.m. on Wednesday, November 16, 1983, she disappeared after apparently arguing with her boss. Although it was cold and dark, Robin refused a ride from a workmate and, in what proved to be a fateful mistake, decided to walk to her boyfriend's house.

That evening, Ross was driving along Route 52 between New London and Norwich, when he saw Robin storming along the roadside. He stopped, climbed out of his car and approached her with the offer of a lift. When she rebuffed him, he became angry and dragged her struggling into a patch of dense woodland just a few hundred yards from the office of the Connecticut State Police Major Crime Squad. Ross had started to strangle Robin as soon as he grabbed her, and by the time he was ready to rape the young woman, she was barely conscious. Ross recalled that by now he was longer excited by the idea of sex, and his satisfaction came about only from the act of killing, and by reliving the moment, occasionally driving by the murder scene and masturbating, until the body was discovered eight days later.

A jogger, running through the grounds of the Uncas-on-Thames Hospital in Norwich, found the partially-clothed corpse of Robin Stavinsky under a pile of leaves. Police retrieved the remainder of the dead woman's clothing, from a river, after Ross's arrest.

The brutal murder of Robin Stavinsky was to prove a dreadful watershed in Ross's killing career. Previously, he had murdered out of the fear of recognition if his victims survived. However, he had always hoped that one day he would achieve his ultimate sexual thrill, that of ejaculation as his victim's death supervened. So far, the murders had provided him with only part-realization of this fantasy. The overwhelming emotions, topped up with feelings of power, domination and the act of murder were there, but he reasoned that Robin Stavinsky had short-changed him. She had provided him with none of the sickening criteria because she had collapsed limp and helpless as he dragged her into the scrub. Nevertheless, he strangled her and raped her after death. He said later, "I was surprised, ya know. It was a pretty good thrill, but not the best."

* * *

Two more young women, both 14, disappeared in eastern Connecticut on Easter Sunday, 1984. Leslie Shelley and April Brunais, inseparable friends and neighbors in Griswold, had decided to walk into Jewett City. Both girls were aware that their parents would not permit them to walk back during the hours of darkness, so each said that the other's parents had agreed to drive them home. It was this childish deception that would cost them their lives.

As darkness fell, the girls called their homes; both were ordered to walk back as punishment. At 10:30 p.m., when neither girl had returned, their distraught parents called the police who made the initial mistake of listing the youngsters as "runaways."

The exact time Ross stopped and offered the girls a lift is unknown. It is known, however, that April, who was the more assertive of the two, climbed into the front passenger seat, while the petite and fragile Leslie sat behind. Both were understandably startled when Ross drove right past the end of their street, and despite their protests that he had missed their turning, he wouldn't stop. April pulled out a small pocketknife, with which to threaten their abductor, but Ross easily disarmed her. Driving east out on Highway 138, he headed for Voluntown, and the nearby Beach Pond, a vast expanse of water with a dam holding back the Pachaus River, which separates the states of Rhode Island and Connecticut.

Parking up at a still undetermined location, Ross tore off April's jeans, cutting them into strips which he used to bind his victims' hands and feet. He shut Leslie into the trunk of his car, and then dragged April a few yards and forced her to her knees. There can be no doubt that the terrified Leslie overheard her friend arguing with Ross. April put up a spirited fight for her life before he raped and strangled her to death.

Ross now turned his attention to Leslie. He said later that the girl made a great impact on him.

"She [Leslie Shelley] was delicate with wispy blonde hair," he stated. "She was calm as I talked to her in the car. I told her I didn't want to kill her, and she cried when she found out that her friend was already dead. Yes, I suppose she started shaking and appeared resigned to her fate when I rolled her over. This is the murder that bothers me. I can't remember how I strangled her, but her death was the most real and hardest to deny. With the others, it was like someone else did it, and I watched from afar through a fog of unreality. This was real but somehow not real. It was fantasy but not really fantasy. Her death? Leslie? It wasn't someone else and for the first time I saw it was me. I watched myself do those things and I couldn't stop it. It was like an invisible barrier was between us. I didn't want to kill her."

At this point during his interview with me, Ross showed the first signs of stress and remorse. He stopped talking, lowered his head, and sucked in a lungful of stale prison air. When he resumed his sickening account of the murder of Leslie Shelley, there were crocodile tears in his eyes: "I couldn't do anything but watch as I murdered her, and you want to know something outrageous? Well, I cried afterward. You know something else? Well, ah, I don't know but nobody knows this. Well, I wanted to have sex with her straight after I raped and killed April, but I couldn't get it up. So, I had to sit back with Leslie for an hour, just talkin' an' stuff. Then, because she started crying, saying that she would be in trouble for being late home, I had to kill her. But, I anally raped her, after death, to release the tension. You see, nobody has been told this before."

Then he smiled sheepishly before adding, "You know, they call me a serial killer, right? Well, I've only killed eight women. Big deal. There are a lot more guys you could meet and they've killed dozens more than me. An' in that context, I'm a nice guy. I'm such a nice guy really."

With that, he burst into an uncontrollable fit of laughter, before explaining that he had dumped the bodies of April and Leslie at another location near Beach Pond, occasionally revisiting the site to masturbate over their remains.

"I'd just sit there, just to look at their decomposing bodies. Like my childhood fantasies, they were there for me and they gave me pleasure when I needed it."

Ross took police to the bodies of April Brunais and Lesley Shelley shortly after his arrest on Tuesday, June 28, 1984, although the precise location of the murder scene was never established. This was put down as an "oversight" by the Connecticut State Police, and later proved in court to be a deliberate attempt by them to avoid a jurisdictional boundary dispute with the Rhode Island law enforcement agencies who had to foot the bill for this murder inquiry.

* * *

Ross was now nearing the end of his run, he was mentally out of control, and his work at the Prudential Insurance Company was suffering as a result. Faced with the prospect of dismissal, as he was failing to bring in new business, Michael was also coping with his turbulent relationship with Debbie Wallace which had taken a more active turn. Debbie's father had died while she and Michael were on vacation and, after the funeral, on the return journey home, they had argued. A major rift followed and, once again, he felt alone and rejected.

* * *

For 17-year-old Wendy Baribeault, Friday, June 15, 1984 was the final day of examinations at Norwich Free Academy where she was a junior. She stopped at her mother's home after school before catching a bus back to Jewett City to visit a convenience store. It was a fine afternoon, so she decided to walk back and, at around 4:30 p.m., she was seen, by a passing motorist, walking along the fairly busy Route 12. But she was not alone, for other witnesses later came forward to say that she was being followed rapidly by a man on foot. He was about 6 feet tall, white, clean-shaven, of medium build and had dark hair. Other witnesses saw this man get out of a blue, compact car with a rear window wiper, and they recalled that he walked briskly off in the direction of the young woman who answered Wendy's description.

When Wendy failed to return home, her mother reported her missing the following day. Hundreds of police and local residents launched a search of the immediate area, and, two days later, her body was found by a fireman. The corpse was in dense woods and hidden in an ancient stone wall just a quarter of a mile from her home. She had been raped and strangled.

Ross explained later that he had intended to go to work that day, but had cut himself while shaving, and blood seeped on to the collar of his only clean shirt. After phoning in with the excuse that he was ill, he dressed himself in smart, casual clothes, and hung around his apartment, reading pornographic material and masturbating. At around 2:00 p.m., he went for a drive, and later on he saw Wendy walking along the road towards her home.

After swinging his car around and parking up at the entrance of a gravel track, he dashed across the road and asked Wendy if she would like to go to a barbecue that night. When she turned him down, Ross her dragged into a clearing in nearby woods, where he rolled her over on to her stomach before strangling her. He ejaculated almost imme-diately, so he throttled her again. She struggled and kicked, and her body twitched. Michael had cramp in his hands as he fought to strangle the life out of his victim. When he stopped to massage his fingers, she heaved and squirmed under him until reapplied his grip. Finally, a kick of her legs told him she was dead.

* * *

Known for disarming suspects, using his boyish smile and supportive manner, State Police Detective Mike Malchik has used his investigative skills to crack even the toughest of homicide inquiries, including 40 or more which were considered "unsolvable" by his colleagues. A legendry figure in Connecticut, the fair, blue-eyed cop often worked alone and unpaid on these jobs, such was his dedication to law enforcement. The case of Wendy Baribeault was no exception.

Mike had already found solid links between the murders of Debra Taylor and Tammy Williams, and when he placed Robin Stavinsky and Wendy Baribeault into the equation, he knew he was looking for a sexual psychopath and serial killer who would not stop murdering until he was arrested and brought to justice.

Mike Malchik's experience in homicide cases was such that he did not need to consult the FBI for advice, but, to confirm his belief, he spoke to a colleague at the National Center for the Analysis of Violent Crime in Quantico, Virginia. Malchik already knew what type of suspect he was looking for. He would be a young, dark-haired Caucasian male in his late twenties or early thirties. He would be of the "white-collar" type, who worked in Norwich yet lived further south, and this man would frequently travel along Route 12 between his place of work and his home. Griswold was a good bet for the suspect's locus and now there was the extra bonus of knowing that the man drove a blue, foreign make of sedan car.

Using what Mike calls "basic common sense," he reasoned that whoever had murdered Wendy Baribeault would want to flee the crime scene and get home as quickly as possible, so he reasoned that his target was a local man. He called the Vehicle Licensing Department and asked them for a printout of all vehicles, and their owners, in the locality. For this service, the VLD charged the police department $12, which proved to be a cheap investigative tool. When the list rolled out of his fax machine, Malchik started looking for a blue, foreign make of car. At number 27 on the list was the vehicle owned by one Michael Bruce Ross who lived in Jewett City.

Ross seemed intrigued when Malchik arrived on his doorstep on Thursday, June 28th, to question him. He invited the detective in for a cup of coffee and enjoyed the attention of the police. For his part, Mike actually felt that the personable young Ross could not have been a serial killer. As he was about to leave to rejoin his colleague, Detective Frank Griffen, outside in their car, Malchik was asked a question. Ross wondered if such a murderer would be declared insane, and escape the electric chair, if he was convicted? It was such a pointed question that it prompted Malchik to return to Ross's sitting room.

The sleuth knew that the description of a blue car didn't exactly match that of Ross's vehicle, which was parked outside. The cop was looking for a hatchback with rear wipers and, while Ross certainly had a blue Toyota, it was a sedan and had no rear wiper blades. After a few more minutes of general conversation, Malchik got up to leave, for the second time. He had only walked a few yards before a gut instinct prompted him to turn around and ask Ross a question of his own. "What were your movements on Friday, June 15th, the day Miss Baribeault went missing?"

Amazingly, thought Malchik, Ross immediately reeled off his movements for that day almost to the minute, with the exception of the hour encompassing 4:30 p.m. This was the time when witnesses had seen Wendy walking along the road, with Ross following her. Malchik thought it remarkable that anyone could recall his or her exact whereabouts, along with solid timings, two weeks after an event, so he reckoned that June 15th must have been a special day for Ross. He then asked him what he had been doing on the two days either side of this crucial date. Ross couldn't remember a thing and the detective was stunned, for the implication was now obvious. Ross had tried to alibi himself for the day of the murder, and in doing so had proved himself too clever for his own good.

Malchik then asked his suspect to accompany him to the nearby murder incident room, which had been set up in the Lisbon Town Hall. Ross thought that a ride in an unmarked police car would be "fun," so he changed into a white, short-sleeved shirt, and dark, lightweight slacks for the ten-minute journey, the very same clothes that he had worn when he killed Wendy Baribeault.

Once he was seated in the police interview room, Ross was soon rambling about his life to the amiable cop. By now, Malchik was privately convinced that he had a serial killer sitting in front of him. But in the bustling confines of the command post, obtaining a full confession was another matter entirely. At one point, just as Ross was about to make some serious admissions, a cleaner burst into the room and started to mop the floor. This unexpected intrusion broke the spell and Malchik had to begin coaxing his suspect again.

Suddenly, Ross asked, "Mike, do you think I killed Wendy?"

Malchik said that he believed so, and with that, Ross admitted 11 sexual assaults and 6 murders.

Recalling that first meeting, during a subsequent prison interview, Ross said, "I remember the detective coming to the door. He was looking for a blue hatchback with wipers, and I didn't have a blue hatchback. I had a blue sedan with no wipers. And, uh, he was getting ready to leave, and I told him something. I don't remember exactly what I said, but something that made him pause. And he said he had better ask me a few more questions and then afterward he was getting ready to go. An' I said something else, so I guess I didn't really want him to leave."

Remembering the interview with Mike Malchik, Ross explained, "You know, it's not exactly the easiest thing in the world to do. You know, 'Hello, Mr. Police Officer, I killed a load of people.' You know, it was hard for me. If you actually listened to the audiotape confessions, ah, it was very difficult for me to admit that I did it, and then I had one got out. Then, he would have to kinda get the next one out. Then I could talk about that one. Yes, it was hard at first saying I killed this one, or that one. I mean I told 'em about two they didn't know about. I mean they didn't even question me about them 'cause they thought they were runaways."

When I asked Ross why he had confessed to the murders of April Brunais and Lesley Shelley, when he hadn't even been asked about them, the killer complained, "Well, the police said that there was something wrong with me, and there was a place called Whiting for insane criminals. Yeah, I fell for that one, an' I thought I was going to get the help I needed and that's what I wanted to hear. "'Hey, you know you have got something wrong with you and we are going to do something about it 'cause the murders have stopped.'" Yeah, Malchik said all the right things, so I thought, What the hell, and I gave 'em everything."

To be fair to Mike Malchik, he did honor his promise to Ross, for the murders did stop, and the law eventually did something about Ross's problem. They executed him.

* * *

Wyndham County prosecutor, Harry Gaucher, only charged Ross with the 1982 murders of Tammy Williams and Debra Smith Taylor. Whether it was because of lack of physical evidence to support the rape portion of an aggravated capital felony charge, which carried the death sentence, or Gaucher's anxiety about losing his case at trial, he allowed Ross to plead guilty solely to murder.

Sitting on Saturday, December 13, 1986, the trial judge sentenced Ross to two consecutive life terms. He would serve no less than 120 years behind bars. However, the murders of Wendy Baribeault, Robin Stavinsky, April Brunais and Lesley Shelly fell under the jurisdiction of a more tenacious prosecutor. New London County State's Attorney, C. Robert "Bulldog" Satti, of the "hang 'em and whip 'em" brigade, wanted to be the first prosecutor for decades to send a murderer to Connecticut's electric chair.

Satti also knew that he was up against a death penalty statute that tipped the balance in favor of life imprisonment. But the counsel stuck to his guns, for he strongly believed that if ever there was a man worthy of the chair, it had to be Michael Bruce Ross. Apart from the morality of executing a man in liberal Connecticut, there was another cost to consider. "Old Sparky" had not been used since Joseph "Mad Dog" Taborsky had been electrocuted in it on Tuesday, May 17, 1960, since which time it had fallen into disrepair. If they wanted to kill Michael Ross, the state would have to pay out at least $30,000 to make the chair serviceable, and redecorate the witness viewing area and death house suite.

For their part, the defense attorneys had to convince a jury that Ross was not legally responsible for the crimes to which he had confessed. Making their job tougher was the fact that Ross didn't qualify for an insanity defense. Moreover, the case had received so much pretrial publicity that, in the summer of 1987, the venue was moved to Bridgeport, where the prosecution would argue that Ross was a rapist, a cold blooded, calculating monster, who had planned his assaults and murdered his victims, simply to stay out of prison.

In June 1987, after four weeks of testimony, the eight men and four women of the jury took just 87 minutes to convict Ross of capital felony murder. At the penalty phase, three weeks later, it took them under four hours to prove that Connecticut's death sentence could be imposed. On Monday, July 6, 20 days before his twenty-eighth birthday, Ross was condemned to death. Under Connecticut law, he would have been spared this sentence if the court had found even one redeeming factor or quality, that the jurors believed to indicate remorse or mitigation. They could not, for Ross, it seemed, did not have a conscience and didn't give a damn.

* * *

Ross explained to me that he was not afraid of dying in the electric chair. He said that living is too good for him, but he is worried that, if that fateful day does arrive, he will say the wrong thing, or show weakness in the face of death. He was also afraid of something he says is worse than death.

"I've always felt that I had to be in control of myself and, even to this day, I feel the need to be in control. What scares me the most isn't life in prison, or the death penalty, but insanity. I'm scared of losing touch with reality. Sometimes I feel I'm slipping away and I'm losing control. If you are in control you can handle anything, but if you lose it, you are nothing."

When asked if he had any feelings or remorse for his crimes, he replied bluntly, "Nope! I don't feel anything for them. I really wish I did. I don't feel anything. I feel really bad for the families. I mean, I feel lots of times. Like I can see Mrs. Shelley, the mother of one of them girls I killed, on the witness stand crying. And, then there's Mrs., ah, I can't remember her name, but I can think of another one on the stand describing her daughter. She went to the morgue and saw her at the morgue. But the girls themselves I feel nothing for, and I never have."

Ross then explained why he hadn't turned himself in to the police when he started to commit his earlier offences, way back at Cornell University, when he knew he needed help.

"I made myself believe that it would never happen again. And, I know it sounds hard, but looking back, I can't understand how I did it. It was a fluke because I really didn't do those things. Even sitting here now, I know if I was released I'd kill again. There's no reason to think otherwise. But, I can't, as I sit here now, picture myself wanting to do that. I can't really see myself doing it. I mean, it's like being on different levels."

When asked if he had any detailed memories of the murders, Ross chuckled, and then said, "Yes and no. I used to fantasize over the crimes every day and every night. I would masturbate to the point of, um, actually having raw spots on myself from the masturbation. I would bleed. It's weird. I get a lot of pleasure from it. It is really a pleasurable experience. But, when it's all over, it's a very short-term thing. I guess it's like getting high. You know I've never used drugs, but you can get high, then you come down and crash. That's almost how it is. It's just not any easy thing to live with."

An inevitable question was to ask him what had been going through his mind when he was raping and killing his tragic victims. His reply was, "Nothin'." But, after a moment's reflection, he added, "That's what's so weird about this thing. Everybody seems to think, you know, the State's theory that I'm a rapist and I kill them so they can't identify me. Look, most of the time it's broad daylight. I mean, I'm not a stupid person. As sure as hell, if I was going to do something like that, I sure as hell wouldn't do it that way. There was nothing going through my mind until they were already dead.

"And then it was like stepping through a doorway. And, uh, I remember the very first feeling I had, was my heart beating. I mean really pounding. The second feeling I had was that my hands hurt where I always strangled them with my hands. And, the third feeling was, I guess, fear, and the kind of reality set in that there was this dead body in front of me.

"And, again, I don't want to mislead you because I knew what was going on, but it was like a different level. I mean it was like watching it. And, after it was all over, you know, it kinds of sets in, an' that's when I would get frightened and stuff. I would hide the bodies and cover them up, or something."

Ross lived in his death row cell which is truly an ancient dungeon painted a muddy brown color. "Death Row" is stamped in white stencil on the steel door leading to the tier which houses Connecticut's seven condemned men. On my final visit to the prison, only Ross and Robert Breton were at home. Sedrick Cobb, Ivo Colon, Richard Reynolds, Todd Rizzo and Daniel Webb were enjoying fresh air in the exercise yard, and taking in a little sun.

Ross was proud of his cell. It was piled high with books and writing materials; indeed, he boasted about the fact that he had been allocated a second cell, where even more of his books were stored. Michael also bragged about the dozens of pretty young women who court his attentions, one of whom is as pretty as a starlet and has even signed her photograph "With Love." Her letters show that she would marry him in a flash, but he would probably kill her in an instant.

Michael Ross is not unique among the serial killer breed but, to his credit, he was struggling to understand why he was driven to commit such terrible crimes on young women. Indeed, he strove to understand the forces that propelled him into such severe antisocial behavior in the first place. To this end, he volunteered for a series of treatment, which includes chemical and surgical castration, the latter being refused by the State.

Many acknowledged experts seem to believe that this treatment could separate the beast from the decent Michael Ross and, for an extended period, he was prescribed Depo-Provera to reduce his enormous sex drive. At the same time as he was taking this drug, he was being prescribed Prozac, a powerful antidepressant, and this cocktail certainly reduced his abnormal sexual desires. Unfortunately, excessive use of Depo-Provera ballooned his weight by around 30 pounds and, as a result, he suffered pathological changes in liver function and hormone levels and his depression reappeared.

Before these drugs were prescribed, Ross claims he masturbated constantly. Occasionally, when in the company of a female correctional officer, he experienced an overwhelming desire to kill her. The Depo-Provera reduced his sex drive, and Michael said, "You know that everybody has had a tune playing over and over again inside their heads. And, if you have this tune that plays all day, over and over, it can drive you nuts. An' just imagine having thoughts of rape an' murder, an' you can't get rid of it. Well, just like the tune, it'll be driving you nuts. No matter what you do to get rid of that tune, it's going to stay in your head. And that's how I am. I don't want these thoughts."

Asked if he thought this tune was, in reality, the monster, he replied, "No, I think he's separate. He goes to sleep for a while and, uh, you never know where he's gone, and that's very true. I mean, sometimes he's there, and especially with the Depo-Provera, I can feel him back here. [Ross touched the back of his head.] I don't know how anybody is going to understand this, but he used to be always in front of my mind, and always intruding, like an obnoxious roommate, always butting into your business and you can't get rid of him."

In a letter, Ross described what happened to him when he became used to the drugs:

I would do anything to clear my mind. The medication gave me some relief but my body has adjusted to it now, and the thoughts and urges have returned. Now, my obnoxious roommate has moved back in and things seem worse because now I saw what it was like without him. Today, I feel like a blind man from birth who was given eyesight as a gift, but was taken away a month later. It's really hard to understand what is normal for everybody else if you've never had it yourself.

It is a rare thing for defense and prosecution psychiatric experts to agree on both a diagnosis and its ramifications, but the Ross case was unusual and, in this instance, there was a consensus that he was suffering from sexual sadism, a mental disease that resulted in a compulsion in Ross to "perpetrate violent sexual activity in a repetitive way." Unknown to the members of his trial jury, forensic psychiatrists from both sides had also agreed that the crimes committed by Ross were a direct result of the uncontrollable sexual aggressive impulses to which he was prey. But the State, aware of the damage that could be caused by their own psychiatrist, effectively giving evidence against them by concurring with the defense team, presented no psychiatric witness at all. Hence, the jury were kept in the dark as to a probable mitigating factor which would have removed the threat of the death penalty from Michael Ross.

Contrary to this line of argument, the State successfully argued that Ross was sane, and therefore totally responsible for his crimes. Their suggestion to the jury was that Ross had been examined by a psychiatrist who had found him not to be suffering from a mitigating psychopathology, which was patently untrue. Amazingly, the defense failed to ask why the State's expert was not made available to testify. Had they done so, it would have become apparent that he had withdrawn from the case, a damaging admission for the prosecution. This amounted to constructed deceit, for the jury had been led to believe that there was a difference of opinion between the State and defense psychiatrists, when there was not. This resulted in rulings that improperly excluded evidence, disingenuous summations, and instructions that allowed the jury to draw inferences that were insupportable.

But what had happened to the State's psychiatrist? Again, unknown to the jury, Dr. Robert B. Miller had concurred with the defense expert's assessment and, in his report to the State's attorney a year prior to the trial, had concluded, "Were a specific diagnosis to be attached to Mr.

Ross's condition at the time of his offences, it would be, in DSM-III, 302.84, Sexual Sadism." He added that, notwithstanding this diagnosis, he believed that Ross could still conform his behavior to the requirements of the law.

Some time later, Dr. Miller explained that he had suffered sleepless nights, having been influenced by the media reports of the case, and the awfulness of the crimes. This, he claimed, had colored and tainted his otherwise professional opinion. His conscience now weighed heavily on him, for his diagnosis could help a man into the electric chair. This was something the doctor said he could not live with, and if the State had its way, they might as well be using him to push the switch.

To rectify his error of judgement and to clear his conscience, just days before the trial, Dr. Miller wrote a letter to the judge explaining his reason for having to withdraw from the case. In due course, this distasteful issue was brought before the State of Connecticut's Supreme Court for a ruling, and the prosecution came in for a roasting. In their summation, the justices ruled in Ross's favor, to the effect that his illness, that of sexual sadism, was a mitigating factor after all. "The State" they said, "was able to seize upon inflammatory connotations of the sexual sadism diagnosis to turn a legally mitigating factor into an aggravating factor ... and the judgment of the court is reversed."

So, Ross had won the day, and with no experts to disagree with the defense, the law now pronounced he had been suffering from overpowering, uncontrollable, sexual urges, and that all of the rapes and murders were one continuous act.

Of course, Ross claimed successfully that he was not only unable to control his sexual desires, but also the need to inflict suffering. In other words, he was a walking time-bomb—99 percent unstable for most of the time, requiring the slightest jolt to set him off. But was there any real substance to his claims that the problem is like an intrusive roommate who lived inside his head?

The hypothalamic region of the limbic system is the most primitive and important part of the brain. It appears to act rather like an on/off sensor, on the one hand seeking or maintaining the experience of pleasure and, on the other, escaping or avoiding unpleasant, noxious conditions. Hence, feelings elicited by this part of the brain are very short-lived; it cannot bear a grudge, and the feelings generated may disappear completely after just a few seconds. This is much the way Ross described his thoughts.

So the limbic system can reward or punish the entire brain, and thus the individual. If, for example, the hypothalamus experiences pleasure, be it from satisfying a craving for chocolate, drugs or sex—even the need for sadistic sex and murder—it will switch on "reward" feelings so that the person continues engaging in the activity desired. If it begins to feel displeasure, it will turn off the reward switch. But, if the switch jams half-way, so to speak, the limbic needs go unmet, and the individual will experience depression, anger or even homicidal rage.

Even in perfectly normal people, emotions elicited by the hypothalamus are often triggered reflexively and without concern or an understanding of the consequences. The hypothalamus seeks pleasure and satisfaction, and whether the stimulus is thirst or sexual hunger, the basic message from the hypothalamus is "I WANT IT, NOW!" There is no consideration of the long term consequences of its acts because it has no sense of morals, danger, values, logic or right and wrong.

If the limbic system is physically damaged, feelings of love, hate, affection and even sexual responsiveness and desire may be abolished, or become severely abnormal. It is not necessary to suffer physical damage to this area to experience these types of altered responses, for electrical stimulation of the limbic center can also cause feelings of violence, which can lead to murder. Moreover, if certain regions in the limbic system (such as the amygdala) are damaged, heightened and indiscriminate sexual activity can result, including excessive and the almost constant need for masturbation. It is interesting to note that the FBI found that 81 percent of the serial murderers they interviewed indulged in compulsive masturbation.

Imagine a complete amateur building a complex computer without any previous experience and little understanding of the complicated instruction manual. Inevitably in such a case, there will be a pile of chips, nuts, bolts and wiring left over, and when the computer is switched on it is bound to malfunction, and continue to produce erroneous calculations, no matter what inputs are entered via the keyboard. While the machine might appear quite normal from the outside, the electromechanical switching systems inside are inherently flawed. For basic functions, it might even work quite well for some of the time, but it will break down when more complicated calculations are required of it. This illustrates what happened to Michael Ross.

* * *

In 1998, Ross began to move away from appeals against his death sentence. While his family protested on his behalf and protests swelled across liberal New England against the unpopular sentence, Ross remained obstinately focused upon relieving his victims' families of any further pain. After the collapse of an appeal in 2004, Ross said, "I owe these people. I killed their daughters. If I could stop the pain, I have to do that. This is my right. I don't think there's anything crazy or incompetent about that."

On May 13, 2005, Ross finally got his wish. His refusal to appeal made him a so-called volunteer for execution—up until his final moment, he could have halted the proceedings by simply asking for another trial. He made no such request. Nor did he ask for a special last meal, but dined on the prison's standard fare of turkey with rice, mixed vegetables and white bread. While as many as 300 protestors gathered outside Somers, Connecticut's Osborn Correctional Institution, Ross was led to the execution chamber. He made no final statement to the 20 witnesses, who included nine relatives of Ross's victims and the two police detectives who first brought their suspect to justice.

At 2:25 a.m., Michael Bruce Ross was put to death by lethal injection.

This chapter is based on video and audiotape death row interviews between Christopher Berry-Dee and Michael Bruce Ross within the Osborn Correctional Institute, Somers, Connecticut, commencing 10:15 a.m., Monday, September 26, 1994, and several years correspondence.

RONALD JOSEPH "BUTCH" DEFEO JR.

"I've been fuckin' waiting for two hours for you.

Who'd do ya think I am? I got better things to do."

RONALD DEFEO'S LESS-THAN-WELCOMING GREETING
ON FRIDAY, SEPTEMBER 23, 1994, PRIOR TO HIS INTERVIEW
WITH CHRISTOPHER BERRY-DEE AT THE GREENHAVEN
CORRECTIONAL FACILITY, STORMVILLE, NEW YORK

I f it were not for a sensational best-selling book and a subsequent motion picture called *The Amityville Horror*, along with several sequels, the village of Amityville, Long Island, and the story of the slaughter that occurred at the DeFeo house, would hardly evoke any public interest. As it is, Amityville has become identified with what was marketed as an outstanding true horror story but which, in the final analysis, is only a well publicized, run-of-the-mill haunted house story with overtones of mass murder. Did the evil spirit of a dead Indian chief haunt the house? Was the property built on the site of an ancient Indian burial ground? Did green slime ooze from the walls and blood pour from taps? Is Ronald DeFeo Jr. the son of Satan?

Because of the horrific events that took place in Amityville during the night of November 13, 1974, one thing is certain—Amityville will never be the same again, so I set out on an equally terrifying journey to find out why.

My journey started in the sleepy Long Island village of Amityville, then I went on to call upon several of the drug-crazed friends of Ronnie DeFeo. I met with a bunch of crooked and brutal cops, a biased "whip 'em and hang 'em" judge, and I examined vital evidence that the police had "lost," then mysteriously found. Finally, I met the monster they call "The Amityville Horror," behind the grim walls of his prison in upstate New York. This is the true story of "The Amityville Horror" and you can believe every word.

* * *

Ronald Joseph DeFeo Jr. was born on September 26, 1951, at the Adelphi Hospital in Brooklyn, New York. He was the first of five children and, his father, Ronald Sr., then a textile worker, was 20 years old. His mother, Louise, was still a teenager.

A short and porky child, Ronald Jr.'s classmates nicknamed him

"Butch," a soubriquet that has stayed with him until the present day. He was a sullen, troublesome and lazy pupil who caused trouble, not only to his teachers, but also to other students with whom he was always fighting. He was always coming home bruised black-and-blue and, on one occasion, he suffered a superficial stab wound in the back when another boy attacked him with a knife.

In the early '70s, Ronald Sr. started working for his father-in-law, and appears to have been well paid for his labors. Deciding that their Brooklyn apartment was now too small, and with Louise expecting her fifth child, they moved out to the more affluent surroundings of Long Island and, after a little house hunting, they chose the sleepy waterside village of Amityville.

The name "Amityville" suggests peace and contentment and, at the very least, friendship. The township is home to around 11,000 residents, many of whom commute daily to New York, 35 miles to the west. Amityville straddles the Great South Bay on Long Island, and is a popular boating center because its proximity to ocean beaches attracts a large influx of summer residents. "Until the DeFeo massacre," said one resident, "about the only crimes were when vandals ripped small boats from their moorings in the bay nearby."

On July 28, 1965, Ronald DeFeo Sr. attained a trophy-sized piece of the American dream when he purchased a two and a half story, Dutch Colonial style house at 112 Ocean Avenue, with a swimming pool and private dock backing into a protected canal. Initially, the family was overwhelmed with the house and its amenities but they soon began to find their feet in their new surroundings and grew accustomed to life in suburbia. But not everyone in Amityville was happy that the loud and flashy DeFeos had chosen to live in their quiet community, and gossip was rife that the family had links with organized crime.

Symbolizing his family's new life, Mr. DeFeo placed a sign in their front yard that read "HIGH HOPES." To distinguish themselves even further, he commissioned an artist to create life size portraits of the family, which eventually hung on the walls of the staircase. In one, father and son, Ronald Sr. and Butch, sit side by side, smiling at the artist, while father pours a glass of wine for his son. In another, the two daughters pose on a love seat, half-smiles on their faces. In a third painting, the two young brothers pose with Mark's arm on John's shoulder. Appropriately perhaps for such a paternalistic family, there was no portrait of the mother, Louise.

The interior of the house was made even more explicit, with its expensive furnishings, crystal chandelier and alabaster fireplace. All of this gave solid substance to the DeFeo's middle-class family life. But if the façade the family presented to the outside world was a "tasteful" expression of middle-class family values, the actual relationships within the family were quite the opposite.

Ronald DeFeo Sr. was the son of Rocco and Antoinette DeFeo. According to those who knew him, Ronald was a physically imposing man who ruled his family with an iron fist and demanded respect. He would change from a civil person into a savage animal at the slightest infraction, and everyone in the household knew that nothing could stop the man when he lost his temper.

Louise DeFeo was the youngest daughter of Michael and Angela Brigante. She was a gentle person, and loyal to her husband. He did not share these warm feelings, believing that his wife was enjoying a string of affairs, including a dalliance with the painter who had produced the family portraits. Although there was no evidence of adultery, mere suspicion seemed to merit beatings, and she experienced these on a regular basis.

Beneath the veneer of success and happiness, then, Ronald DeFeo Sr. was a hot-tempered man, given to bouts of rage and violence. There were stormy fights between him and Louise, and he loomed before his children as a demanding authority figure. As the eldest child, young

Ronald bore the brunt of his father's temper and attempts to impose discipline. Bullied at school, his father encouraged him to stick up for himself. While this advice pertained to school problems, it did not apply to the way Ronald was being treated at home. DeFeo had no tolerance for backtalk and disobedience, keeping his eldest son on a short leash, and refusing to let him stand up for himself in the way he was commanded to at school.

After moving to Long Island, Ronald's first school was the Junior High in Riverhead. As he matured into adolescence, he gained size and became less of a sitting duck for his father's abuse. There were frequent shouting episodes which often degenerated into boxing matches as father and son came to blows with little provocation. While DeFeo Sr. was not highly skilled in the art of interpersonal relations, he was astute enough to realize that his son's bouts of temper and violence were highly irregular, and of a different kind to his own. After Butch seriously beat up his sister, Dawn, he and his wife arranged for him to visit a psychiatrist. This was to no avail because Butch simply employed a passive-aggressive stance with his therapist and rejected any notion that he needed help.

In the absence of any solution, his parents employed a time-honored strategy for placating unruly children by buying Butch anything he wanted and giving him money. His father presented his 14-year-old son with a $14,000 speedboat to cruise the Amityville River. Whenever Butch wanted money, all he had to do was ask, and if he wasn't in the mood to ask, he just took what was lying around.

When this strategy failed, Butch was packed off to St. Francis Prep in Brooklyn, where he was thrown out at the end of his ninth grade. Finally, he attended the Amityville High School and, at the age of 17, left the school system for good. On the same day, his father bought him a car.

By this time, he had begun using drugs, such as heroin and LSD, and had also started dabbling in schemes involving petty theft. His behavior was becoming increasingly psychotic as well, and not confined to outbursts within his home.

One afternoon, while out on a hunting trip with a few friends, he pointed a loaded rifle at one member of the party, a young man he had known for years. He watched with a stony expression as the young man's face turned white before his fear made him take flight. At this point, Butch calmly lowered his gun and when they caught up with each other later that afternoon, Butch asked, sneeringly, why his friend had left so soon.

At the age of 18, Butch was given a job at his father's car dealership which was a sole agency for Buick. By his own account it was an easy job, where little was expected of him. Regardless of whether he showed up for work or not, he received a cash allowance from his father at the end of each week, which sometimes amounted to $500. This he used to run his car, and buy alcohol and drugs.

In January 1971, Butch DeFeo met a young woman named Geraldine in the Ninth Bar in New York City. They dated for quite a while, then, in December 1973, she found out that she was pregnant. His father started hounding the couple to get married, and after their daughter Stephanie was born, they married on October 17, 1974, at the Garfield Grant Hotel in Long Branch, New Jersey.

Altercations with his father were growing ever more frequent and progressively more violent. One evening, a fight broke out between Butch's father and mother. In order to settle the matter, Butch grabbed a 12-gauge shotgun from his room, loaded a shell into the chamber, and charged downstairs to the scene of the fight. Without hesitation or calling out to the participants to break up the argument, Butch pointed the barrel at his father's face, yelling, "Leave that woman alone. I'm going to kill you, you fat fuck! This is it."

He pulled the trigger, but the gun mysteriously did not discharge. Ronald Sr. froze where he stood and watched in grim amazement as his own son lowered the weapon and simply walked out of the room, with casual indifference to the fact that he had almost killed his own father. While that particular fight was over, Butch's actions foreshadowed the violence he would soon unleash, not only upon his father, but also his entire family.

This incident with the shotgun seems to have inspired in Ronald Sr. something akin to a religious conversion. He became a devout Catholic, and built several religious shrines amid the manicured grounds of High Hopes, and neighbors often saw him saying his rosary in front of a shrine of St Joseph and the Christ child that he had built on his front lawn.

* * *

In the weeks before the Amityville slayings, relations between Butch DeFeo and his father reached breaking point. Apparently dissatisfied with the money he "earned" working for his father, Butch devised a scheme to defraud his family further. Two weeks before the massacre, he was sent on an errand by one of the staff at the Buick dealership, charged with the responsibility of depositing $1,800 in cash and $20,000 in checks at the bank. Accompanied by a fellow worker from the dealership, they departed for the bank at 12:30 p.m. They were gone for two hours. When they finally returned, it was to report that they had been robbed at gunpoint while waiting at a red light. Ronald Sr. exploded with rage, berating the staff member who had sent his son in the first place.

The police were called and naturally asked to speak to Butch. In reality, he and his accomplice had kept the money and split it two ways. Instead of engaging in at least a pretense of cooperation, he concocted a description of the fictional robber, becoming tense and irritable with detectives. As the officers began to suspect that he was lying and focused their questions on the two hours he was away, his behavior became aggressive.

"Wouldn't you have rushed back to the dealership once you had been robbed of so much money?" asked the police. "Where had you been during that time?"

In response to their questions, Butch began to curse at them, banging on the hood of a car to emphasize his rage. The police backed off for a moment, but his father had already come to the conclusion that his son was lying and had stolen the money himself.

On the Friday prior to the murders at High Hopes, Butch had been asked by the police to examine some mug shots in the possibility that he might be able to recognize the robber. Initially he agreed, but pulled out at the last moment. When Ronald DeFeo Sr. heard of this, he cornered his son at work, demanding to know why he wouldn't cooperate with the police.

"You've got the devil on your back," his father screamed at him.

This time Butch did not hesitate. "You fat prick," he screamed, "I'll kill you."

Then he ran to his car and sped off. While this incident had not resulted in an exchange of blows, a final confrontation was clearly imminent.

* * *

The still shroud of night blanketed the village of Amityville in the early hours of Wednesday, November 14, 1974. Stray house pets and the occasional passing car were the only signs of life as families and neighbors slumbered. But hatred and savagery were brewing beneath the seeming calm at High Hopes on Ocean Avenue. The entire DeFeo family had retired to bed, with the exception of Butch. He sat in the quiet of his room, brooding on what he wanted to do, which was to ensure that his father and family would trouble him no more.

Butch was the only member of the family with his own room. His violent disposition and the fact that he was the eldest had afforded him this small luxury. It also provided him with a private storage place for a number of weapons he collected and sometimes sold. On this particular night, he withdrew a .35 caliber Marlin martini-action rifle from his closet. He set off, stealthily but resolutely, towards the door of his parents' master bedroom. Quietly pushing the door open, he stood, momentarily observing them as they slept, totally oblivious to the horror that was about to engulf them. Then, without hesitation, Butch raised the rifle to his shoulder and pulled the trigger. The first of eight fatal shots fired that night, slammed into his father's back.

Just after 3:00 a.m., Butch DeFeo completed the annihilation of his family. Each defenseless member had been brutally slain in cold blood. The family dog, Shaggy, tied up outside the boathouse, was barking furiously in reaction to the sporadic bursts of violence emanating from the house. The animal's barking did not distract Butch in the least. Aware that he had completed the task he had set out to do, he now turned his attention to cleaning himself up and establishing an alibi to throw off the inevitable police investigation that would ensue.

First, he showered, and trimmed his beard. Then, dressed in jeans and leather work boots, he collected up his bloodied clothing, the rifle with its scabbard, and retrieved one of the expended cartridge cases from the floor. Stuffing everything into a pillowcase, he drove off into the pre-dawn light. His first stop was at the end of Ocean Avenue, where he threw the rifle into the dock. From there, he drove to Brooklyn and disposed of the pillowcase and its contents by throwing them into a sewer. Then he reported for work, at his late father's dealership, as if nothing had happened. For him, it was 6:00 a.m. and business as usual.

Butch did not remain at work for long. He called home several times and, when his father failed to show up, he acted as though he were bored with nothing to do and left around noon. He called his girlfriend, Mindy

Weiss, to let her know that he would be at her place early from work, and that he wanted to stop by and see her. On his way, he passed a friend, Robert Kelske, and recalled the incident later during a prison interview,

"In my drugged stupor, I was driving down the road in Amityville and Robert Kelske, a junkie strung out on heroin, pulled up alongside of my car and started asking off-the-wall questions. This didn't register then because Kelske was a junkie and a thief who had previously burglarized both of my neighbor's homes, so I paid his questions no mind."

DeFeo reached his girlfriend's house at around 1:30 p.m. Mindy was 19 years old, an attractive and popular waitress at Longfellow's Bar. He casually mentioned on arrival that he had tried to call home several times and, although there were cars in the driveway, there was no response. To make the point, he called his home from Mindy's apartment with the same predictable result.

Acting as though he was puzzled but unconcerned, Butch took Mindy shopping during the afternoon. From the mall in Massapequa, they drove to see Patricia and Robert Geiger, where DeFeo bought five $10 bags of heroin and shot them up. He said, "I was out of it and actually forgot about what had happened at my house ... I sort of blacked out."

Just after 6:00 p.m., Butch arrived at Henry's Bar in Amityville, where he met Robert Kelske. Once again, he feigned concern over his inability to reach anyone at home.

"I'm going to have to go home and break a window to get in," he said.

"Well, do what you have to do," his friend replied blithely.

Ronald left the bar on his supposed journey of discovery, only to return within minutes in a state of agitation and dismay.

"Bob, you gotta help me," he implored. "Someone shot my mother and father!'

The two friends were joined by a small group of patrons, and they all piled into Butch's car, driving off with Kelske at the wheel. Approximately 15 hours had elapsed since the murders were committed. Within moments of arriving at the house, Kelske had entered the front door and raced upstairs into the master bedroom. He retraced his steps to find Butch distraught with grief and dismay. Joe Yeswit found a telephone in the kitchen and called the police.

At precisely 6:40 p.m. on November 13, 1974, Patrolman Kenneth J. Greguski of the Amityville Village Police Department based at Greene Lane, received a call from his control room to provide help at 112 Ocean Avenue, where there had been a report of a shooting. As he drove up to the house, he saw a group of young men standing in the driveway, and one of them tearfully introduced himself as Ronald DeFeo. He said, "My mother and father are dead."

"I went into the house and climbed the stairs," said the officer. "In the master bedroom, I found a white male lying on his stomach, and he had been shot dead. Next to him was a white female in the same position, and she had been shot to death. I proceeded to a second bedroom where I discovered two young boys in separate beds. They were lying on their stomachs and they had been shot dead. I came downstairs and used the dining room telephone to call my headquarters and informed them that there were four bodies in the house, and they should notify the First Squad Detectives."

Continuing his account, the policeman added, "Almost immediately, Ronald DeFeo told me that he had two sisters. Evidently he had heard me talking over the telephone, and with that, I ran back upstairs and checked a bedroom door that had been closed. I found a young girl's body there. She was lying, like the others, spread-eagled on her stomach. She was shot dead, too. And I seen a staircase, that I thought led to an attic, which actually led to another bedroom upstairs on the third floor, and I found another female body there. I immediately came back downstairs, re-called my headquarters and advised them I had two more bodies. After that call I went into the kitchen. I stood there with

Ronald DeFeo and his friend Robert Kelske, and I put my hand on his shoulder and just told him to take it easy. I stood there and waited until Detective Sergeant Cammaroto and Lieutenant Edward Lowe turned up. They just checked the scene and they came back downstairs, too, and it was shortly thereafter that the homicide detectives arrived. It was a scene that I'll never forget, and it haunts me to this day."

At the autopsy, the medical examiner, Dr. Howard Aldeman, determined that, Ronald DeFeo Sr., aged 43, had been shot twice in the lower back. The bullets went through the kidney and spine. One stopped in the neck and the other ploughed through the body and on to the mattress. Death was most likely instantaneous since he had stayed on the mattress and did not crawl out of bed.

Louise DeFeo, aged 42, had been shot twice. The gunfire that had killed her husband seems to have awakened Butch's mother, and she was turning in her bed towards the doorway. The first bullet entered her back, exited through her chest, re-entered her left breast and wrist before landing in the mattress. The second bullet destroyed her right lung, diaphragm and liver. Death most likely occurred in a matter of seconds, since she never put up a struggle.

Mark DeFeo, aged 12, and John DeFeo, aged 7, had been shot once. From the evidence, the medical examiner determined that their killer stood less than two feet from the boys when he discharged the gun. Bullets penetrated the heart, lungs, diaphragm and liver of each victim. In addition, John's spinal cord was severed, causing involuntary movements of his lower body.

Allison DeFeo, aged 13, had been shot once. Like her mother, she had awakened and turned her head towards the doorway. The bullet smashed upward from her left cheek to her right ear, entering the brain and skull. The bullet exited, hitting the wall and bounced on the floor where it came to rest. Death was instantaneous, and powder burns on Allison's eyes indicated that she was awake at the time of her murder and staring down the barrel of a gun.

Dawn DeFeo, aged 18, had been shot once. Her killer had stood less than three feet away and fired at the back of her neck. The bullet entered the left ear and collapsed the left side of her face. Brain particles soaked the pillow and the sheets were covered with menstrual blood.

In Dr. Aldeman's opinion, it appeared from the evidence that this was a gangland-style execution, and that at least three or four people had been involved with the control of the victims and their murders.

* * *

From the outset, Ronald Defeo was known to have a police record. He was a drug user, currently on probation for stealing an outboard motor. He was first interviewed at the scene of the shootings at 6:55 p.m. by Detective Gaspar Randazzo, who had been working with the First Squad Detectives for eight years. Randazzo asked the sole survivor to account for his movements that day. DeFeo replied, "I went to work and, upon coming home, I found the door locked. I figured there might have been something wrong because the doors were locked and I saw my parents' cars outside the house. I went back to the bar and spoke to Robert Kelske. I went back to the house, forced a window, and found the bodies of my family. I was scared, so I ran out and drove back to the bar for help. Then we all drove back and Joe called the police."

Shortly after the interview began, Reverend McNamara arrived to administer last rites to the victims.

At 7:15 p.m., Detectives Gozaloff, Napolitano, Shirvell, Grieco, Harrison, Reichert and Detective Sergeant Barylski, all of the First Homicide Squad, arrived on the scene. They obtained permission to use the house next door, home to the Ireland family, as a command post. DeFeo was asked to leave the scene, and he was escorted next door where Detective Gozaloff spoke to him.

Asked who might have shot his family, Butch told the detective that a man named Louis Falini had a grudge against his folks. He was a Mafia hit man, and he could be the murderer.

"I had an argument with Falini," he said. "I called him a cocksucker and that caused problems between him and my father."

DeFeo pledged his full cooperation and agreed to go to the First Precinct, calling beforehand at the Amityville Police Station to complete the paperwork that relieved the Amityville Police of jurisdiction over the murders.

On arrival at the First Precinct, Detective Gozaloff interviewed DeFeo in more depth. Butch explained that he worked for his father, who was the Service Manager of Karl-Brigante Buick in Brooklyn, and that his grandfather, Mike Brigante, was the owner.

He described the layout of his home in some detail. That night, he said that he was up late watching a film called *Castle Keep*. He fell asleep watching the television around 2:00 a.m., and awoke at 4:00 a.m. with stomach pains. He remembered walking past the upstairs bathroom, and noticed that his brother's wheelchair was in front of the door. Mark could only walk on crutches following an injury playing football, Butch explained. He also claimed to have heard the toilet flush. Since he couldn't get back to sleep, he decided to go to work early, and went on to describe what he had been doing until the time he discovered the bodies.

After Butch submitted his signed statement, the detectives continued to question him about his family and the suggestion that Falini might be the killer. Butch replied that Falini had lived with them for a period of time, during which he had helped Butch and his father carve out a hiding place in the basement where Ronald Sr. kept a stash of gems and cash. His argument with Falini had stemmed from an incident during which Falini criticized some work Butch had done at the auto dealership. Butch also voluntarily confessed to being a casual user of heroin, and admitted that he had set one of his father's boats on fire so that an insurance claim could be made rather than paying for the motor, which Butch had originally blown up. The detectives finished their questioning at around 3:00 a.m. and Butch went to sleep on a cot in a filing room at the back of the police station. DeFeo had given every appearance of a cooperative witness and, so far, the detectives had no reason to hold him under suspicion of murder.

The circumstances began to change, though, as investigators intensified their examination of physical evidence, both at the crime scene and in the police laboratory. A crucial discovery was made at around 2:30 a.m. on November 15th, when Detective John Shirvell conducted a last sweep through the DeFeo bedrooms. The rooms where the murders had taken place had been scoured thoroughly, while Ronald's room had, up to that point, been given only a cursory once-over. But, on closer scrutiny, Detective Shirvell spotted a pair of empty rectangular boxes, each with labels describing their contents as .22 and .35 Marlin rifles. Shirvell was unaware that a .35 caliber Marlin had been the murder weapon, but he took the boxes anyway in the event that they may become important evidence. Indeed, they were!

Shortly after returning to the police headquarters with the boxes, he learned exactly what make of weapon had been used in the shootings, because a firearms examiner had identified the caliber of the murder weapon. Detective Sergeant Della Penna had wasted no time in examining the spent shell casings and the bullets used to kill the DeFeo family. He had determined that powder residue found at the scene was partially burned particles of nitrocellulose gunpowder. The spent, lead jacketed bullets were of .35 caliber Remington Arms manufacture, and were originally components of Western Co .35 caliber cartridge cases.

Detectives leading the murder investigation now began to consider the possibility that Butch had been lying to them and, indeed, that he may be their prime suspect, knowing far more about the killings than he had so far told them. At 8:45 a.m., Detectives George Harrison and

Napolitano shook DeFeo awake.

"Did you find Falini yet?" was his first question. As he quickly found out, the officers were not there to answer Butch's questions, but to read him his rights. Butch protested that he had been trying to cooperate all along, and that it wasn't necessary to read him his rights. He went so far as to waive his right to counsel, all to prove that he was an innocent witness with nothing to hide.

By this time, Gozaloff and Napolitano were due to go off duty and two other officers, Lt. Robert Dunn and Detective Dennis Rafferty, took over. They meant business and, in the years following the Amityville shootings, both would be heavily criticized by a New York Commission of Investigation for using illegal practices to gain verbal confessions from suspects. Rafferty began by reading Defeo his rights, and proceeded to question him about his activities and whereabouts over the prior two days. Suddenly, Rafferty zeroed in on the time of the murders. Butch had written in his statement that he was up as early as 4:00 a.m., and that he heard his brother in the bathroom at that time.

"Butch, the whole family was found lying dead in their bedclothes," said Rafferty. "That indicates to me that it didn't happen at, like, one o'clock in the afternoon after you had gone to work."

Rafferty continued to press until he was able to pry Butch away from his earlier account of when the crime took place, establishing that the murders actually occurred between 2:00 a.m. and 4:00 a.m.

With this slight fissure, DeFeo's crudely constructed story began to crumble. Dunn and Rafferty hammered at the discrepancies between Butch's stated version of the events and what the crime scene evidence indicated had actually happened. Once the time of the murder was established, Butch was implicated by his own statement, which confirmed his presence in the house at the crucial time. His response to this predicament was a desperate attempt to lead the detectives up the garden path. But they were not accepting the bait.

"Butch, it's incredible," said Rafferty. "It's almost unbelievable. You know we have a .35 caliber gun box from your room. Every one of the victims has been shot with a .35 caliber. And you've seen the whole thing. There has to be more to it. It's your gun that was used, so where's the fuckin' gun?" he shouted, just inches from Butch's face.

His desperation growing by the minute, DeFeo continued to lie, even though his lies sucked him in more squarely to the commission of the murders. He told his interrogators that at 3:30 a.m. Louis Falini woke him up and put a revolver to his head. Another man was present in the room, he said but, upon further questioning, he could not provide any kind of physical description to help the police. According to his new version of events, Falini and his companion led Butch from room to room, murdering each one of his family members.

The police allowed DeFeo plenty of rope and, as he continued talking, he eventually implicated himself with his account of how he gathered up and removed the evidence from the scene.

"Wait a minute," said Rafferty. "Why did you pick up the cartridge if you had nothing to do with it? You didn't know it was your gun that was used."

Perhaps sensing that his position was deteriorating rapidly, Butch did not immediately respond to the question. The detectives played a waiting game and allowed him to keep talking. They had already obtained a good deal of evidence implicating DeFeo, particularly the absurd pretence that Falini and his accomplice had taken him along on their killing spree while sparing his life alone. Once they had been given a solid description of how, according to Butch, the murders had taken place, Dunn went in for the kill.

"They must have made you a piece of it," he said. "They must have made you shoot at least one of them—or some of them." Butch tripped on the snare and the trap was sprung.

"It didn't happen that way, did it?" asked Rafferty.

"Give me a minute," DeFeo replied, putting his head in his hands.

"Butch, they never were there, were they? Falini and the other guy were never there."

At last came the confession. "No," said Butch, "It all started so fast. Once I started, I just couldn't stop. It went so fast."

On Wednesday, November 19, 1975, a year and five days after the murders, the presiding judge instructed the jury in the deliberation chamber to return to the court with a verdict. On Friday, November 21, 1975, Ronald DeFeo Jr. was found guilty of six counts of second-degree murder. Two weeks later, he was sentenced to 25 years to life in prison on all six counts. He became eligible for parole in 1999 and insists that he is an innocent man.

* * *

Around the time of the Amityville murders, Suffolk County, covering the eastern portion of Long Island, beginning approximately 45 miles east of Manhattan and adjacent to suburban Nassau County, had a population of well over 666,500. It has one of the largest police departments in New York State after the New York City Police Department, the New York State Police and the Nassau County Police. Suffolk also ranks as one of the highest-paid police departments in the country. This police force also has something else to be proud of, for it enjoys the highest confession and oral admission rate of probably anywhere in the world.

In April 1989, a State of New York Commission of Investigation published its report on an *Investigation into the Suffolk County District Attorney's Office and Police Department*. In various sub-reports, the Commission unearthed a number of serious problems, which included misconduct and deficiencies in homicide investigations and prosecutions, misconduct and deficiencies in narcotics investigations and prosecutions, illegal wiretaps, failure by the District Attorney's Office to investigate and punish misconduct by agency employees and law enforcement personnel, deficiencies in the oversight of police personnel, and a whole host of other issues including corruption, the unlawful gaining of confessions by over-zealous police officers, police brutality, and "precinct jumping," an unlawful police practice, used to stonewall lawyers trying to gain access to their clients. As a result of the Commission's damning findings, one senior police officer committed suicide and dozens of other ranks "retired."

From December 7 to 11, 1986, *Newsday* published a lengthy five-part series on deficiencies and misconduct in Suffolk County homicide prosecutions stretching back to the early '70s. The series included a statement that 94 percent of Suffolk homicide prosecutions involved confessions or verbal admissions. This figure was confirmed to the commission by the former commanding officer of Suffolk County Homicide, none other than Detective Lieutenant Robert Dunn, one of the two detectives who had obtained a confession from Ronald DeFeo.

This was an astonishingly high figure compared to other jurisdictions; so high, in fact, that it provoked scepticism regarding the police agency's use of confessions. For example, in *Newsday*'s study, which compared 361 Suffolk homicide defendants, from 1975 to 1985, to seven hundred cases from six other large suburban counties, Suffolk's 94 percent confession rate far exceeded the 55 percent to 73 percent rate in the six other jurisdictions. The national average was 48 percent.

There is no doubt that DeFeo had been "precinct jumped," as two attorneys, Richard Wyslling and Richard Hartman, who had tried to see him were given a thorough run-around by the Suffolk County Police. Ronald DeFeo also says that his confession was "beaten out of him" by Detective Lt. Robert Dunn and Detective Dennis Rafferty, who hit him with a telephone book. To verify this claim, it is only necessary to go back to the first day, when DeFeo appeared before District Judge Signorelli. The judge was so shocked at the defendant's appearance that he ordered a medical examination. The next day, a doctor reported that he had found black-and-blue bruises over different parts of the defendant's body and legs, a cut lip, and a great deal of swelling on his face. These injuries were not present when DeFeo was taken into police custody. During an interview for this book which took place at the Yaphank Police Headquarters on September 27, 1994, a smiling Dennis Rafferty said, "Sure, of course we did a good job on him … what do you expect?"

Ronald DeFeo Jr. was not the only one to receive a good beating from the police. Robert Kelske, Chuck Tweskbury and Barry Springer also say that they were seriously assaulted and ordered to sign confessions for murder. Patricia and Robert Geiger were even accused of murder.

On November 16, 1974, DeFeo received a visit from Reverend McNamara, the priest who had given the dead family their last rights. Within hours of McNamara's departure, jail records show that Butch's uncle, Vincent Procita, paid Butch a visit. Rocco DeFeo, Butch's grandfather, and his brother Peter, both members of the organized crime circuit, had asked Procita to get Ronald to sign a document making Rocco administrator of his late father's estate. Butch was told that if he refused, he would be killed in prison. He deferred to his relatives and signed.

The following day, DeFeo received a visit from the FBI and was questioned for two hours about the DeFeo and Brigante families' links with the Mafia. Agent Robert Sweeney explained that his own daughter had been acquainted with Dawn DeFeo. He went on to say that the FBI had placed a legal wiretap on Michael Brigante's telephone. One of the conversations they recorded was between Brigante and Peter Defeo, who said that Butch knew too much, and they were going to have him killed. Sweeney offered Butch the witness protection program if he told them what he knew; he refused.

Jail records show that on November 19th, DeFeo received a visit from two more attorneys. Alexander Hesterberg and Jacob Sigfried told him that Michael Brigante wanted him to sign another document, this time making him the administrator for the late Mrs. DeFeo's estate. Butch told them about the visit from the FBI, and Jacob Sigfried said, "That's all the more reason to sign, then." He was also told that his aunt, Phyllis Procita, was working for the District Attorney's office, which she was, and, unless he agreed to allow Sigfried to represent him with an insanity defense, he wouldn't get out of prison alive. Realizing that his life was now in great peril, DeFeo agreed to both suggestions.

At his second court appearance, Sigfried failed to turn up. When the Judge asked DeFeo where his lawyer was, he told him about the prison visits and the Judge remarked, "Even Stevie Wonder could see through this." Events took an even more sinister turn, a few weeks later, when the Judge appointed William E. Weber as DeFeo's defense attorney. Weber, who had never represented anyone in a murder case before, was also running as the Judge's campaign manager in the forthcoming surrogate court elections.

Weber collected a fat retainer from the DeFeo and Brigante families and moved on to prepare an insanity defense. Indeed, he started off with honorable intentions by employing the services of Herman Race, acknowledged as one of the most experienced investigators on Long Island. He had been a homicide detective for 20 years, and his first job was to examine the firearm and ballistic evidence on behalf of his client. He quickly discovered traces of "backfire" on Dawn DeFeo's nightdress caused by unburned gunpowder blowing back on to her clothing. The only conclusion that can be drawn from this is that Dawn had fired the rifle, at least once, on that fateful night. Armed with this information, an excited William Weber was quick to inform DeFeo's relatives, who were not pleased.

The next afternoon, while the attorney was pulling up outside his home, two police officers stopped him and asked questions about unpaid parking tickets. They searched his car and, in the glove compartment, they found an unlicensed handgun and arrested him. Later, under the influence of the Brigante family, the police decided to drop the charge. Weber was left in no doubt that the matter of the nightgown should not be raised again.

With Butch protesting that he was not insane, William Weber, nevertheless, was carrying out his instructions from his client's family who were, as DeFeo said, "calling the shots." Counsel retained the services of a psychiatrist, Dr. Daniel Swartz, for a fee of $8,000 and a professional opinion that was tantamount to saying that Ronald DeFeo, Jr. was insane.

Shortly before the trial started, the prosecutor, Assistant District Attorney Gerald Sullivan, asked Judge Signorelli to remove himself from the case, which he did. In turn, and quite illegally, Sullivan picked Judge Thomas M. Stark, a tough, no-nonsense man whom the prosecution could rely on to bat for their side. Judge Stark later dismissed this matter with a wave of his hand.

"In hindsight," he said, "this was quite wrong, but things were different back then."

With a psychiatrist in their pocket, the defense team now started to trawl elsewhere for people who knew DeFeo, and tried to coerce them to testify that they thought that Butch was insane. William Davidge was approached, and in a sworn affidavit before Esther B. Hopkins, Notary Public for the State of Florida, dated October 6, 1988, he had this to say:

"I was a defense witness at the request of Attorney William Weber, defense counsel for DeFeo in Suffolk County, State of New York. Weber told me during consultations that DeFeo was guilty, but told me he would get DeFeo declared insane by fabricating a defense of insanity. Weber had me state facts to back up his defense. I was uncooperative with Weber over matters he stated to me about my personal friendship with DeFeo and his family that were not true.

"Weber startled me, because he was an officer of the Court and represented DeFeo. I wanted to help DeFeo by telling the truth. I was directed through Weber to describe Ronald DeFeo as insane, by testifying to acts to support the defense of insanity.

"The acts described were purposely directed to me while testifying, by Weber's cross-examination at the DeFeo trial, in an attempt to place DeFeo in a mental hospital, and exonerate DeFeo from all criminal acts alleged in the indictment and proceedings. Weber advised me and ordered me to testify at his will, to support his insanity defense, and he refused to allow me to testify in any other manner, other than directed by him. At the time of my testimony, I did not know that I was violating any laws, nor could I appreciate a violation of any laws being violated, as I was completely unaware. I can also say that my brother, Frank Davidge, informed me that he and William Weber made a deal in a 'back-room' discussion in 1975."

If William Weber was reluctantly breaking almost every rule in the book, the District Attorney had no compunction in breaking them all. Having schemed at standing down one judge, and illegally engineering the appointment of another, more "suitable" judge to try the case, Gerald Sullivan now needed to find a motive for the defendant's crimes. He thought he had hit the jackpot when he learned that the DeFeos had a substantial horde of valuable jewellery in the house, which was now missing from the secret recess in the basement. He reasoned, therefore, that the accused had stolen it and, when his father had discovered the theft, Butch killed him and the rest of the family as well. Unfortunately, from Sullivan's point of view, the jewellery had recently been placed in a safety deposit box at the European Savings Bank in Amityville.

In a desperate and quite illegal move to save the day, Sullivan called on the services of none other than Detective Rafferty who was told to visit a number of DeFeo's friends, including Lin and Roger Nonnewitz. After speaking to them over some quite spurious matter, the detective asked them to testify that the DeFeos had other jewellery, and that Butch had stolen it. Not only did the Nonnewitzes expose this in court, but they also signed sworn affidavits explaining that the prosecution had asked them to commit perjury. Judge Stark dealt with this serious issue with his usual air of casual indifference and that was the end of it.

There is no doubt that a confession had been beaten out of DeFeo by the Suffolk County Police, and it had done him no good trying to implicate the alleged hit man, Louis Falini, who was able to provide a solid alibi for the time of the murders. There was also no doubt that Ronald DeFeo was in the house when the murders were committed. But with the absence of motive, what was his reason for killing his family? The answer is that he did not have one, whereas his sister, Dawn, had a very strong motive indeed. After considerable research, it has been possible to disentangle the web of lies spun by DeFeo surrounding the murders, and arrive at something nearer the truth.

During the evening before the murders, DeFeo had been visiting his estranged wife, Geraldine. At around 8:00 p.m., she received a phone call from Mrs. DeFeo, who was in a distressed state and crying. She asked to speak to her son who came to the telephone, and then informed everyone else present that there was trouble between Dawn and her father. "The fuckin' bitch," he said, "she's started again."

Dawn was not the neatest person in the world, and had often left food to spoil in her room, which subsequently attracted a plague of flies all over the house. Now aged 18, she was attending the Katherine Gibbs Secretarial School, at her parents' request. She was in love with her boyfriend, William Davidge, who was moving to Florida, and she wanted to join him. Her parents were strongly against this idea and, according to friends and relatives, she had started experimenting with drugs as an escape from her situation at home and, when aroused, she, like her father and eldest brother, had a terrifying temper that knew no bounds.

In his sworn affidavit before Theodore Yurak, Notary Public for the State of New York, dated July 27, 1990, William Davidge affirmed that he knew that Dawn wanted to follow him to Florida, that she was using drugs such as LSD and Mescaline, and that she had a "bad temper that got out of hand at times." Davidge also said that Dawn had a deep hatred for her parents and her eldest brother, whom she used for cash handouts.

Immediately after receiving the telephone call from his mother, DeFeo, and Geraldine's brother, Richard Romondoe, departed for "High Hopes." When they arrived, Butch gave Dawn the keys to his car and told her to take a long drive until she cooled off. Apparently, she followed his advice. Under the influence of drink and drugs, Butch and Richard went down to the basement, leaving the door open so that they could hear what was going on upstairs. They turned the television down low and began to play pool. Time seemed to pass very quickly for the two men, when, to their shock, they heard a "loud roar."

Rushing upstairs, they located the bodies of the DeFeos with the exception of Dawn, whom they found in her third-floor bedroom, dressed in a nightgown, and cradling the .35 caliber Marlin rifle. Butch made a grab for the gun and, in the struggle that followed, his sister was shot in the head. Butch and Richard disposed of the weapon and the other incriminating evidence in the manner later explained to the police.

Geraldine DeFeo recalled that during the early morning of the murders, Butch had woken her up and had told her what had happened. He then left the house and that was the last she saw of him until his trial. She also recalled that her brother had confirmed the story, saying, "I have got to leave and get away otherwise I am going to get fitted up for something I didn't do."

Richard, who now lives under an assumed name in Florida, has since got married and has a son. "I know what I saw," he told the author, "and what Ronnie says is the truth. Problem is that my wife knows nothing about this, and I don't trust the police."

Geraldine DeFeo has since been threatened, pushed to the ground, arrested and released by the police for conspiracy in the Amityville slayings. The officer involved was Detective Dennis Rafferty.

If DeFeo's claims of innocence were to stand up, it was vital that two forensic issues were resolved. First and foremost was the matter of DeFeo's clothing that was contaminated with a small trace of blood. Detective Rafferty claimed that this was Dawn's blood, an assumption he had arrived at solely because the suspect had said he had picked up a blood-covered cartridge case and wiped it on his shirt and jeans. For his part, DeFeo says, "This was an outright lie by Rafferty. The blood on my clothes was mine from the several beatings given to me by the Suffolk County Police. DNA testing can easily prove this because they still have the clothing."

For many years, DeFeo has argued that it was his sister who killed the family, and that he shot Dawn, during the struggle, when he tried to retrieve the weapon, so the second issue revolves around Dawn's nightgown and the traces it bore of unburned gunpowder, indicating that she must have fired the .35 caliber Marlin rifle at least once that fateful night.

At the autopsy, it was proved that the single bullet that had killed her had been fired at a distance of about three feet. This discounts any possibility that Dawn had shot herself, which leaves only one outstanding question: which member, or members, of the family did she shoot dead?

In June 1992, DeFeo's request for a motion for discovery and reexamination of the nightdress was heard before Judge Stark who said that if DeFeo could fund the tests, and if the clothing was still in existence, he would order further forensic examinations.

Gerald L. Lotto, acting for DeFeo, had received $10,000 from his client's grandmother, Angela Brigante, for DNA and gunpowder analysis. This money was now in an escrow account and, therefore, satisfied the first part of the Judge's ruling. Lotto's task was now to ascertain the whereabouts of Dawn's nightdress. In reply, Assistant District Attorney Karen Petterson twice told the court, under the penalty of perjury, that the garments had been destroyed. Perhaps her deceit weighed heavily on her, for several days later, her colleague, Barbara Rose, wrote a letter to the Judge that significantly watered down Petterson's claim. Again, under penalty of perjury, Assistant DA Rose said, "The clothing is no longer in the possession of the Suffolk County District Attorney's Office, nor the Suffolk County Police Department."

On August 21, 1991, an investigator working on another case had reason to visit the Suffolk County Police Property Evidence Bureau at Yaphank. While rummaging around, and quite by accident, Dennis O'Doherty discovered two boxes marked "DeFeo." They contained Dawn's nightdress, a bag of bullets and DeFeo's clothing, comprising a pair of black and blue socks, construction boots, brown work uniform, pair of blue jeans, plaid shirt, three printed pillow cases and one blood-stained pillow case.

Several days after this discovery, Karen Petterson wrote to Judge Stark, apologizing, and explaining, "... the clothing was found due to the ongoing efforts of the DA's office and the police department," which was yet another distortion of the truth. With the funding for tests in place, and the clothing rediscovered, Judge Stark was legally obliged to honor his ruling, except that he chose not to.

The evidence in question is still in existence today and, when interviewed during the research for this book, Dennis Rafferty said, "Not a chance in Hell. This stuff [the clothing] will never be looked at again. We'll make sure of that."

* * *

In reality, Ronald DeFeo Jr. is a short, insignificant little man with a blood-drenched reputation. Ferret-faced, with a good physique, he angrily argued his case of innocence for two hours, during his interview as part of the research for this book, but doubts that he will ever be released from prison. So what do we understand about Ronald DeFeo?

We know that he was, and still is, an illiterate and bullying thug, characteristics which he shares with many individuals who are not criminals. We know that he was addicted to heroin; again, hardly an unusual occurrence in today's society. We know that telling lies was routine, commonplace behavior for him. He manufactured countless versions of the crimes, in a manner so characteristic of serial killers and mass murderers. Yet none of these qualities necessarily makes a multiple murderer. The main problem is that DeFeo cried "wolf" too many times, so who would believe a word he says today? He is a liar through and through.

More recently, Butch argued that he did not throw the rifle into the dock. "I did not throw the .35 Marlin rifle in the water," he wrote in a letter, "nor did I realize that he [Richard] threw it there." When shown the map of the dock and the drawings made by the police, which were initialled by him, I asked Butch how the police diver managed to locate the exact location of the rifle so quickly, when no one had told them where it was? He contradicted himself saying, "I told them it was behind my house because I didn't want to be beat up any more."

When pressed about the diagrams, he changed his story again: "The Marlin rifle was found after I was in the Suffolk County Jail, so there is no way I told the police. I never knew where the gun was thrown and that's the truth. And I never signed any diagrams. I initialled blank pieces of yellow paper only."

What do we know about the trial and surrounding circus? If we know nothing else, we know that many questions, possibly of grave importance, were both unasked and unanswered. Even today, the issues raised by the bloodstained clothing and unburned powder found on Dawn's nightdress, which could so easily be resolved, remain in the realms of mystery.

We know about the strange conversation between Butch's grandfather and another thug. This was recorded on tape by the police, and included references, among other unsavory topics, to the murder of Butch in prison. We know that the police investigation and the resultant convictions were concluded in a very untidy manner, clearly just to get the job done. Yet none of these qualities necessarily makes a false conviction.

With the exception of any startling new evidence which might appear to dispel public anxieties about the behavior of those in authority, it is clear that at least some of the police, lawyers and one judge involved in the case, acted unethically, if not illegally. To assume otherwise would blind oneself to the true nature of the American judicial system. Disturbing though this may be, it does not necessarily entail a false conviction. Nevertheless, William E. Weber seemed to do very well for himself out of the DeFeo case.

Over a few bottles of wine, during the evening after Butch was sentenced on December 4, 1974, Weber and the new owners of "High Hopes," George and Kathleen Lutz, cooked up a story that shocked the world. The house was haunted, they said, possessed by the evil spirit of a long-dead Shinnecock Indian chief and, of course, had been built on an ancient Indian burial ground. It was this story that subsequently became the movie, *The Amityville Horror*. Once the Lutzs realized now much money was involved, they decided to cut Weber out of the deal. In turn, he filed a lawsuit in the U.S. District court in Brooklyn, presided over by Judge Jack B. Weinstein.

In his decision, the Judge stated, "… the canons and ethics of law prevent Mr. Weber from being involved in Mr. DeFeo's criminal case and his appeals, while at the same time being involved in movie deals, books etc …"

As a result of this ruling, Weber had to settle for a small amount of money out of court but it did not prevent him taking $20,000 from DeFeo's relatives for appeals of the conviction. Nor did it stop him from finding other ways to profit from the Amityville tragedy. He teamed up with Professor Hans Holzer, a ghost-hunter from England. Together, they wrote a book called, *Murder in Amityville*, which, subsequently became the motion picture, *Amityville II—The Possession*.

Was one of Butch's stories true and, if so, which account can we believe? Did he stumble upon some kind of gangland execution in progress? This is feasible to the extent that the medical examiner was convinced that at least three people had been involved with the subduing and shooting of the victims. But if this was the case, is it not likely that Butch would have been shot along with the rest of his family? Who else, incidentally, knew about the .35 caliber Marlin lever-action rifle that belonged to him? Were there conspirators who wanted a pawn, someone trained to passivity and dependence, who would take the blame for them? Why, then, the long silence from Butch and his friends until 20 or so years after the crimes were committed?

An answer may lie in the fact that each and every one of Butch's close friends, including his estranged wife, were threatened, bullied and even assaulted by the police at the time. Many of these police officers, including Detective Lieutenant Robert Dunn and Detective Dennis Rafferty were still employed with the Suffolk County Police at the time this book was being researched. Perhaps these witnesses had every reason to fear reprisals from law officers who survived immense criticism, only to resurface, unscathed, many years later. Another factor is that DeFeo came from a family with strong links to organized crime and the Mafia. Is it any wonder that Richard Romondoe, for example, went into hiding and assumed a false identity?

* * *

George and Kathy Lutz moved into 112 Ocean Avenue on December 18. Twenty-eight days later, they fled in terror.

So begins Chapter One of Jay Anson's novel *The Amityville Horror*. Written as a work of non-fiction, the book purports to relate the day-to-day events that drove the new residents of "High Hopes" from their home in terror. The book became a runaway bestseller and was made into a popular movie starring Rod Steiger, Margot Kidder and James Brolin.

Their fantastic story, never disclosed in full detail, makes for an unforgettable book with all the shocks and gripping suspense of The Exorcist, The Omen or Rosemary's Baby, but with one vital difference ... the story is true ... reads the book's back cover. In truth, the entire book and subsequent movies were little more than fiction. Nevertheless, the Lutzes brief stay and claims of supernatural activity at High Hopes thrust Amityville and 112 Ocean Avenue into the world spotlight. For more than 30 years, the house has stood as an icon of terror, erasing the happier times that any family had enjoyed inside the charming Dutch colonial property. Eventually, the notoriety the Lutzes had heaped upon themselves paid them back. Pestered by sightseers, and turned into pariahs in their own decent community, they were forced to move out. On August 30, 1976, they returned their home to Columbia Savings and Loan, instead of returning to live in it, or selling it to another family in the normal way.

On March 18, 1977, Jim and Barbara Cromarty purchased the house for a mere $55,000, quite unaware of its infamous reputation. When they learned about its recent history, they were forced to change the address to 108, and add a fake window to the front of the building. Determined as they were to make their home part of the community again, the Cromartys were bombarded with hordes of tourists looking for ghosts and demons. Eventually, the fans proved unbearable and they put the house on the market and moved out.

The Cromartys left Frank Birch to tend to the property, and act as house-sitter while they were away. Neither Mr. Birch, nor the Cromartys ever reported supernatural occurrences in the house. The family eventually moved back in and took the house off the market. They remained there until 1987, when David Roskin, Barbara's son from a previous marriage, passed away unexpectedly.

On August 17, 1987, Peter and Jeanne O'Neill bought 108 Ocean Avenue for an unspecified amount. They lived happily there until 1997, when they were forced to sell the place because of the high taxes associated with it, which amounted to $7,000 a year. According to friends, they chose to spend the money on their children's college education, rather than give it to the tax collector.

On June 10, 1997, Brian Wilson purchased the house for $310,000. At the time of writing, he resides there with his wife and two children, who attend college. Mr. Wilson says that he is very happy with the house and has no complaints. In fact, he has invested in the property by restoring the boathouse and improving the accommodation. When I visited "High Hopes" I asked Brian Wilson whether perhaps, he might consider at some time in the future to replacing the spooky quarter-moon windows on the third floor?

He smiled and said, "Maybe."

This chapter is based on an exclusive videotaped interview with Christopher Berry-Dee and Ronald Joseph "Butch" DeFeo within the Greenhaven Correctional Facility, Stormville, New York, on Friday, 23 September 1974, and extensive correspondence.

Ronald DeFeo welcomes correspondence, and his address is: Inmate #75-A-4053, Great Meadow Correctional Facility, Box 51, Comstock, New York 12821.

AILEEN CAROL WUORNOS

"I've got respect for myself. Always did have.

Weird, right?"

AILEEN WUORNOS TO CHRISTOPHER BERRY-DEE

AILEEN CAROL WUORNOS

Aileen (Lee) Carol Wuornos arrived at the Broward Correctional Institute, Pembroke Pines, Florida, on January 31, 1992. Lying mid way between Fort Lauderdale and Miami, Broward is a prison for women at which death row is sited in a large grey building, trimmed in pink and bordered with tropical flowers. Here, Aileen Wuornos joined the State's five other women who live in cells that look like drum-tight submarine hatches, a shower room down the hall, a caged outdoor exercise yard with a basketball hoop, and additional cells for future residents. Also located on the "row" is a room designed as the "death-watch" cell where inmates are housed 24 hours prior to execution. Death is now delivered by lethal injection at the Florida State Prison, Starke.

At the time of writing, there are currently 47 women condemned to die in the United States. Working alone or with a partner, they have been convicted of killing their husbands, children, boyfriends and strangers. A large percentage have well-documented histories of physical or sexual abuse, as well as drug and alcohol addictions. More than half are white. Many are mothers with school-age children. Few have murdered for monetary gain. The majority live in specially-designed cell-blocks separated from the main prison population, and where their movement is greatly restricted.

Compared to their male counterparts, numbered in the hundreds throughout the penal system, women comprise only about 2 percent of the nation's felons who have been condemned to death. California, Florida and Oklahoma have the largest number of women on death row. A handful of other states, such as Idaho, have only one condemned woman and must grapple with a unique problem because most States are mandated by law to segregate women from the regular male prison population.

* * *

Aileen (Lee) Carol Wuornos was born in a leap year on February 29, 1956, in Clinton Hospital Detroit, Michigan, to teenage parents, Diane Wuornos, just 16 years old, and 19-year-old handyman, Leo Dale Pittman.

The marriage, which proved to be tumultuous, ended a few months before Lee was born, leaving the young Diane to raise the new baby and her older brother, Keith. Lee never knew her father, who was jailed on charges of kidnapping, rape and child molestation. He fashioned a noose from a bed sheet and hanged himself in prison. Lee was 15 years old at the time.

Diane soon found the responsibilities of single motherhood unbearable and, when Lee was six months old, her mother left home and never returned. Diane did, however, call her parents, asking them to pick up the children.

Laurie Wuornos, a Ford factory worker, and his wife, Eileen Britta, subsequently adopted both children. Their home was an unprepossessing one story building. Its wood cladding was a sad yellow color, sited amidst a cluster of trees, away from the roadside in suburban Troy, Michigan. Innocent looking and otherwise unremarkable, the house was nevertheless a place of secrets. Nearby neighbors who were never once invited to set foot inside, even for casual pleasantries, recall the curtains always being tightly drawn across the small windows of the Wuornos house. The outside world was held very much at arm's length.

Laurie and Britta raised Lee and Keith with their own children, but they did not reveal that they were, in fact, the children's grandparents.

Behind those shaded windows, frequent clashes of will took place between young Lee and her adoptive father. The omnipresent third party was a wide, brown leather belt, with Western-style tooling, that he kept hanging on a peg behind his bedroom door. At his bidding, this strap was cleaned, almost ritualistically, by Aileen with saddle soap and conditioner which were kept in the dresser drawer.

Stripped naked and forced to bend over the kitchen table, the petrified child was beaten frequently with the doubled-over belt. Sometimes she lay face down, spread-eagled naked on her bed to receive her whippings, while all the while her father screamed that she was worthless and should never have been born. "You ain't even worthy of the air you breathe," he shouted, as the belt lashed down again and again.

During her ninth year, a chemical explosion, which Lee and a friend accidentally set off, resulted in her sustaining severe burns on the face and arms. She was hospitalized for several days and confined for months afterward. The burns healed slowly, but Lee worried that she would be deformed and scarred for life. Today, faint scars on her forehead and her arms still bear grim testimony to the accident.

Around the age of 11, Lee learned that her parents were indeed her grandparents. She was already incorrigible, with a fearsome and socially unacceptable temper. Her volcanic explosions, which were unpredictable and seemingly unprovoked, inevitably drove a further wedge between her and her "parents."

When she was 14, she became pregnant and was sent to an unmarried mothers' home to await the birth of her child. The staff found her hostile, uncooperative and unable to get along with her peers. She gave birth to a baby boy, who was put up for adoption in January 1971.

In July of the same year, Britta Wuornos died. On hearing this news, Diane Wuornos invited Aileen and Keith to stay with her in Texas, but they declined. Lee then dropped out of school, left home, and took up hitchhiking and prostitution.

* * *

In March 1976, Lee, now aged 20, married multimillionaire Lewis Gratz Fell. By any measure, this was a curious match. Silver-haired Fell, with his reputable Philadelphia background, was 69 years old. He had picked up Lee when she was hitchhiking. They married in Kingsley, Georgia, less than two months after the death of her grandfather, Laurie, who had committed suicide at 65, younger than Lee's new husband.

Most of those who knew Lee viewed her marriage cynically, finding it impossible to judge it as anything other than a purely mercenary move. The unwitting Lewis Fell had no idea what he was letting himself in for, although some took the view that it was a mutually acceptable relationship. For his part, Fell had a pretty young woman on his arm, and Lee enjoyed the fruits of what his money could buy.

"The bottom line," said Lee to the author, "is that he was a cheap, flash, dirty old man who had money. Basically, he bought my sex. Wanted to keep me at home with him. Give me a break ... what else do you want to hear?"

Early in July, she and Lewis rolled into Michigan in a brand-new, cream-colored Cadillac and checked into a motel. Lee had sent a few friends newspaper clippings of their wedding announcement from the society pages of the *Daytona Press*, complete with a photograph of a man who looked old enough to be her grandfather, describing Fell as the president of a yacht club, with a private income derived from rail-road stocks and shares.

On July 13th, Lee went out on the town and ended up at Bernie's Club in Mancelona where she flaunted her body and started to hustle at the pool table. Some time after midnight, the barman and manager, Danny Moore, decided he had seen enough of her. She was drunk, rowdy, shouting obscenities, uttering threats to other patrons, and generally being objectionable. He casually walked over to the pool table and announced that the table was closing down. As he was gathering up the balls, he heard someone shout, "Duck!" He turned just in time to see Lee aim a ball at his head. It missed him only by inches, but had been hurled with such force that the missile became lodged in the wall.

When Deputy Jimmie Patrick of the Antrim County Sheriff's Department arrived, Lee was arrested for assault and battery and hauled off to jail. She was also charged on fugitive warrants from the

Troy Police Department, who had requested that she be picked up on charges for drinking alcohol in a car, unlawful use of a driver's licence, and for not having a Michigan driver's licence. She was bailed when a friend turned up with her purse containing $1,450. Three days later, her brother, Keith, aged 21, died of throat cancer.

As might be expected, the marriage between Lee and Fell was short lived. From the outset, she had been torn between her desire to get drunk and hang out in bars and the boredom of sitting around with her older husband in his plush, beachside condominium. When he refused to give her more money, she beat him up. He obtained a restraining order and an annulment of the marriage. He claimed she had squandered his money and beaten him with a walking cane.

The divorce papers stated, "Respondent has a violent and ungovernable temper and has threatened to do bodily harm to the Petitioner and from her past actions will injure Petitioner and his property ... unless the court enjoins and restrains said Respondent from assaulting ... or interfering with Petitioner or his property."

Lee's marriage officially ended on July 19th, with a divorce issued at the Volusia County courthouse in Florida. She pawned the expensive diamond engagement ring. Two days later, Keith was cremated at the same funeral home as Britta and Laurie Wuornos. Lee arrived late for the service.

Having rejected her son in life, but acknowledging him in death, Diane flew in from Texas for Keith's funeral. Other mourners were surprised to see her, apparently too distraught to sit through the service for the son she had abandoned and who had not long joined the Army.

On August 4th, Aileen pleaded guilty to the assault and battery charge, paying a fine and costs of $105. Then Keith's army life insurance paid up and, as next of kin, she received $10,000. The money was immediately put down as a deposit on a shiny black Pontiac (which was soon repossessed). She also bought a mixed bag of antiques and a massive stereo system although she had no home in which to put them. The money was gone within three months.

Adrift in the world once again, she embarked on a series of failed relationships and small-time forgery, theft and a rather ridiculous armed robbery that put her in prison for a spell. From time to time she turned tricks, but even as a prostitute working exit-to-exit on the interstate highway, she was not exactly sought after. When she met 24-year-old Tyria "Ty" Jolene Moore at a Daytona gay bar in 1986, Lee was lonely and angry. She was ready for something new.

After splitting with Fell, and like many millions of Americans, Lee went in search of a dream. She ended up in Daytona with all its sun-kissed mirages and promises and it was there, while drinking in a gay bar, that she met another lonely young woman. Tyria Moore would become the only true love of her life. Lee discovered that Tyria, unlike everyone else she had met, did not want anything from her. On the contrary, Tyria was not a materialistic person and demonstrated her love and respect by devoting most of her free time to be in Lee's company.

In an interview, Tyria said, "Lee was very pretty in those days. She dressed very provocatively and I considered her a real catch. We had some great times. She was a great lover. Very gentle and caring as if she needed my love in return. She was my best friend. But what I admired the most was her strength. She was very … er, over-protective of me. No one messed with me when Lee was around. I truly loved her, but I don't think anyone will understand this. Even when she was drunk, she was funny. It was a ball of laughs, you know."

* * *

Getting to Daytona Beach was easy for Aileen Wuornos. She had run away from home, and run away from her marriage. She had crossed State line after State line, hitched south on Interstate 95, and found what she thought was paradise. There was sunshine, jobs and cheap living. You could even drive your car on the firm white beach at Daytona. Sea, sex, prosperity and exhaust fumes. An American illusion served up on a beach so exploited it was more like a sandy parking lot.

For a while, it was great. Ty loved Lee and stayed close to her. She even quit her job as a motel maid for a while and allowed her girlfriend to support her with earnings from prostitution. In due course, perhaps predictably, their ardor cooled and money began to run short. Yet, still Ty stayed with Lee, following her like a puppy, from cheap motel to cheap motel, with stints in old barns in between.

Lee's market value as a hooker, never spectacular, fell even further. Their existence, meager though it was, became more difficult to maintain. Clearly something had to change, but getting out of Daytona was not easy. There was never enough money to get to Miami, and the two women now realized that jobs were scarcer than they had first thought. They had blown all of their money, and their dreams of good times had faded as quickly. Desperation crept in, and temptation was quick to follow. It was a formula that often leads to crime and, in Lee's case, it meant big-time crime.

People get murdered in Daytona, as in any city, for the usual reasons—money, revenge, sex and business—but Daytona Beach seems to provoke a unique end-of-the-line dementia. Looking at what the city has to offer, who is buying and what is the main product, it is always sex. The gritty beach town lies about 60 miles east of Orlando. A good bet for a cheap, working man's vacation. Redneck tourists from all over the southeast knew this, and so did 51-year-old Richard Mallory, from Clearwater, Florida, who disappeared on Thursday, November 30, 1989.

Richard Mallory was a private man, not very communicative, a mystery even to those who should have known him best. He lived alone in a multi-family apartment complex called "The Oaks." Few people came to know him on account of his erratic lifestyle and, at his television and video repair shop, Mallory Electronics, in the strip shopping mall in Palm Harbor, his absences were frequent and unexplained.

He was a good looking man with a full head of dark hair combed back from a high forehead. Standing at just under 6 feet tall, the neatly moustachioed Mallory surveyed the world through hazel eyes, behind wire-rimmed glasses. He cut a trim figure, tipping the scales at just less than 170 pounds, and he thought of himself as 51 years young.

A long-time divorcée, and recently separated from a girlfriend named Jackie Davis, he had always been drawn to the opposite sex. He loved to party in the carnal sense, a regular visitor to the kinds of establishment dedicated to catering to pleasures of the flesh. He liked the way women looked, the way they smelled and moved. He liked the way he felt when he was with them—powerful, controlling, sensuous. He was a sufficiently regular customer at the topless bars in the Tampa and Clearwater area that the strippers, go-go dancers and hookers mostly knew him by sight, if not by name, although no one knew that he had spent ten years in prison for sexual violence. But now, Richard Mallory's days, spent trawling for sex, were about to come to an abrupt end.

Mallory was also in dire financial straits. He owed $4,000 in rent arrears and his affairs were due to be audited by the Internal Revenue Service. He owned two vans, one white and the other maroon. But the night he disappeared, heading for a weekend in Daytona, he was driving his light beige, two-door, 1977 Cadillac Coupe de Ville, with its brown interior and tinted windows. It was a vehicle more suited to the pursuit of hard drinking and pleasure-seeking. In the early evening of Thursday, November 30th, he closed up his TV repair shop, drove home, threw a few bags into the back of his car and headed for Daytona.

A handful of northbound rides had deposited Lee Wuornos outside Tampa on Interstate Highway I-4, right at the point where it passes under I-17. It was raining heavily and she lingered under the overpass in order to avoid the downpour, until the weather improved. Mallory spotted her and slowed down, then reversed and offered her a lift. As they drove, they chatted amicably, and en route, stopped for a pack of beer. It was around 5:00 a.m. when Mallory broached the subject of sex. He pulled off the road and into nearby woods. Lee peeled off her clothes before he did, and they hugged and kissed for a while.

Suddenly, and apparently without being provoked, she produced a .22 caliber pistol and began firing at her companion. The first bullet struck his right arm and entered his body. Desperately, he tried to crawl out of the car when another bullet slammed into his torso, quickly followed by a third and a fourth. Mallory did not die immediately. The copper-coated, hollow-nose bullet, which struck him in the right side of his chest, had penetrated his left lung, passing through the organ before coming to rest in the chest cavity. During its passage, the bullet caused a massive and fatal hemorrhage. He struggled to cling on to life for a further 15 minutes as Lee Wuornos stood by and watched him die.

The following day, Mallory's car was found abandoned near John Anderson Drive in Ormond Beach. Deputy Bonnevier was out on a routine patrol when he stopped to examine the vehicle. He noticed bloodstains on the front backrest, behind the steering wheel, but there were no signs of either the driver or any passengers. The car keys were not in the ignition, but numerous items were found a short distance from the car. Partially buried in the sandy soil was a blue nylon wallet, containing Richard Mallory's Florida driving licence, miscellaneous papers, and two long-expired credit cards. There were also two plastic tumbler-type glasses and a half-empty bottle of vodka, along with several other items, suggesting that Mallory had not been alone. The driver's seat had been pulled as far forward as it would go, in a driving position which would have been extremely uncomfortable for a man of Mallory's size.

Two young men, out scavenging for scrap metal on Wednesday, December 13th, found Richard Mallory's corpse at a spot roughly five miles across the river from where his car had been found. Volusia County deputies, who answered the 911 call, saw a body which was skeletonized from the collarbone to the top of the head. It lay under a piece of cardboard with only the fingers showing. It was fully dressed in jeans and a pullover, the belt slightly askew. The pockets of the jeans had been turned inside out. The man's dentures lay on the ground next to the body.

Charles James Lau, an investigator with the Volusia County Sheriff's Department, oversaw an immediate autopsy of the unidentified body and recovered four bullets from its torso. The hands of the victim were removed and transported to the crime laboratory for latent print examination because, as Lau explained, "When we have an unidentified body, you can't roll the fingerprints because of the decomposition."

By the middle of May 1990, the murder of hapless Richard Mallory had been all but forgotten by the Volusia County Sheriff's Department. There was, seemingly, no reason to believe it was anything other than an isolated homicide.

* * *

As ex-husbands go, 47-year-old David Spears was a dream come true. Predictable, honest and hardworking, he was a man people counted on. He earned his living as a construction worker and lived in Winter Garden, near Orlando, traveling each day to Saratosa to work at Universal Concrete. A shy, soft-spoken giant of a man, 6 foot 4 inches tall, bearded, greying and weather-lined from his outdoor lifestyle, he cared enough about his former wife, Dee, to give her a regular portion of his monthly pay check.

Just before lunchtime on Friday, May 18, 1990, David called Dee and told her to expect him to call in somewhere between 2–2:30 p.m. the next day. On Saturday, he left work at about 2:10 p.m. in his cream pickup and he was not seen alive again.

He spotted Lee Wuornos, somewhere near the point where Route 27 intersects with I-4, about 36 miles from Winter Garden, and offered her a ride. She explained that she needed to get to Homosassa Springs. This was right out of his way; nevertheless, he agreed to take her, and they ended up pulling off the road on U.S. 19, close to Homosassa Springs, and then drove so deep into the woods that Spears was worried that his truck would get stuck.

David Spears' truck was found abandoned near County Road 318 and I-75 in Marion County on May 20. A blonde hair was found on the steering wheel and a ripped condom packet was found on the floor of the vehicle. All his personal property, including tools, clothing and a one-of-a-kind ceramic statue of a panther, which he had bought as a present for Dee, was missing. The driver's seat was pulled too close to the steering wheel for a man of his height, indicating to the police that someone else had driven the truck after Spears had been killed.

On June 1st, a man found the body of an unidentified male lying in a clearing amidst pine trees and palmettos. Mathew Cocking had just walked past an illegal dumping site on Fling Lane, a dirt road south of Chassahowitzka and running adjacent to U.S. 19.

When the police arrived, they found a badly decomposing body, naked except for a camouflage baseball cap which sat jauntily atop a ravaged head. On the ground near the body were a used Trojan condom, its torn black packet, and several empty cans of Busch and Budweiser beer. At first, because of the state of the body, the police were unable to determine the sex, age or likely cause of death. The corpse lay on its back, legs apart, arms outstretched, palms facing skywards. Lee Wuornos had stolen her victim's wages, his daughter's graduation money and a quantity of cash, which had been hidden in the truck for emergencies, amounting to about $600.

Dr. Janet Pillow carried out the autopsy on Monday, June 4th. The man, who weighed around 195 pounds in life, had been reduced to 40 pounds by the time his body was discovered. Six .22 caliber bullets were recovered from the remains. Two days later, another body was found in Marion County.

* * *

Forty-year-old Charles Carskaddon, a sometime road digger and rodeo rider, was on his way from his mother's home in Prairie, Missouri, to Tampa to pick up Peggy, his fiancée. He never arrived. His naked body was found off State Route 52, and I-75 in Pascoe County, on Wednesday, June 6th. The corpse was covered with grass and foliage and a green, electric blanket. He had been shot nine times in the chest with a .22-caliber handgun.

Carskaddon's brown 1975 Cadillac, a car he had lovingly restored, was found the next day near I-75 and County Road 484 in Marion County. Although the licence plate had been ripped off, the vehicle identification number (VIN) was still intact and revealed the owner's name. Carskaddon's mother, Florence, told police that when her only son left home he was carrying a blue steel .45 caliber pistol with a pearl handle, a Mexican blanket, stun gun, flip-top lighter, watch, tan suitcase, black T-shirt, and grey snakeskin cowboy boots. "He had removed the firing pin from the gun," she said, "because he was scared to use it." None of these items were found in his car.

* * *

Peter Siems was a 65-year-old retired merchant seaman, living near Jupiter, Florida. Early in the morning of June 7th, neighbors saw the part time missionary placing luggage and a stack of Bibles into his 1988 silver-grey Pontiac Sunbird. They assumed, correctly, that the balding, bespectacled man, was off on another of his "word-spreading" trips as a member of the "Christ Is the Answer" crusade. On his travels, he intended to visit relatives in Arkansas.

On July 4th, a silver-grey Pontiac Sunbird careered off State Road 315 near Orange Springs, Florida. The car smashed through a steel gate and a barbed-wire fence, shattering the windshield before coming to rest in the undergrowth. For a brief second, it appeared that it might roll over, but it righted itself, with steam hissing from the radiator.

Rhonda and Jim Bailey, who were sitting on their porch enjoying the sun, saw the spectacular accident happen. They observed two women clamber out of the car, noting that one was a short, heavy blonde (Lee Wuornos) and the other, a tall brunette (Tyria Moore). The blonde, whose arms were bleeding from the cuts sustained in the crash, started throwing beer cans into the woods and swearing at her fellow passenger, who said very little.

The bemused witnesses noted that the women grabbed a red-and-white beer cooler from the back seat and, still arguing, staggered off along the road. At the approach of other cars, they would dash into the woods and hide, only to reappear after the vehicles had passed. When the coast was clear, they returned to the car.

When Rhonda rushed over to offer what little assistance she could, the blonde begged her not to call the police, saying that her father lived just up the road. The two women climbed back into the car and, with some difficulty, managed to reverse it on to the road and drive off. Within minutes, a front tire went flat and, with the car now disabled, Wuornos and Moore had no other option other than to abandon it. They pulled off the rear licence plate and threw it, together with the car keys, into the woods and walked away.

A motorist, thinking that the women might need help, pulled over and offered assistance. He noticed that the blonde was not only bleeding but also very drunk. When she asked him for a lift, he thought better of it and refused, whereupon Lee became angry and abusive. The man drove away, but contacted the Orange Springs Fire Department, and told them about the injured woman.

Two emergency vehicles were despatched to the scene, but when they arrived, Lee Wuornos denied that they had been in the car. "I don't know anything about any accident," she snarled. "I want people to stop telling lies and leave us alone."

At 9:44 p.m. Trooper Rickey responded to the emergency call, and found the car. (It was not until almost two months later that detectives learned exactly where the Sunbird had first crashed, or heard the account given by Rhonda and Jim Bailey.) Marion County's Deputy Lawing was dispatched to investigate the abandoned, smashed up vehicle. The VIN was checked, identifying the missing Peter Siems as the owner. Latent bloody prints were found in the vehicle and there were bloodstains on the fabric of the seats and on the door handles. Items removed from the car by the police included Busch and Budweiser beer cans, as well as Marlboro cigarettes and two beverage cosies. Underneath the front passenger seat lay a bottle of Windex window spray with an Eckerd Drugs price label attached to it. This was easily traceable to a store on Gordon Street in Atlanta, Georgia.

By now, the police artist had drawn composites of the two women, based on descriptions given by witnesses of the incident with the Sunbird. Armed with these sketches and the bottle of Windex, the investigators traveled to Atlanta to question the manager of Eckerd Drugs. Viewing the pictures, he recalled the two women entering his store on a Friday night. "We are in a bad part of town in a predominantly black area and white people do not venture into this area after dark," he said. The manager remembered that the women purchased cosmetics and a black box of Trojan condoms, the same brand found near David Spear's body and inside the trunk of his car. A beverage cosy was also traceable to a Speedway store near to the entrance/exit ramps of I-75 in Wildwood.

Peter Siems and his wife were missionaries. They neither drank nor smoked, and relatives stated that the couple had never traveled to Atlanta. John Wisnieski of the Jupiter Police had been working on the case since Siems was reported missing. He sent out a nationwide Teletype containing descriptions of the two women, and he also sent a synopsis of the case, together with descriptions and sketches of the two women, to the Florida Criminal Activity Bulletin. Then he waited. He was not optimistic about finding Siems alive. The man's body had not been found, his credit cards had not been used, and money had not been withdrawn from his bank account.

* * *

Ever-smiling Eugene "Troy" Burress celebrated his fiftieth birthday in January 1990. With a natural gift of gab, he was employed as a part time salesman for the Gilchrist Sausage Company in Ocala, a resort town in northern Florida, where he lived. He also ran his own company, Troy's Pools, in Boca Raton.

On July 30, 1988, Burress set out on Gilchrist business, traveling the company's Daytona route, which took him to several customers throughout central Florida. His last planned stop was to have been Salt Springs, in Marion County. This was "Wuornos killing country," and he never arrived.

When he failed to report at his office after work, Gilchrist's manager, Mrs. Jonnie Mae Thompson, started calling around and discovered that Burress had failed to show up for his last delivery. She immediately went out in search of him and, at 2:00 a.m., he was reported missing by his wife. The police recorded her description of a slightly-built man around 5 foot 6 inches in height and weighing about 155 pounds, with blue eyes and blond hair.

This time there was a fast response and a quick, though tragic, outcome. At 4:00 a.m., Marion County deputies found the Gilchrist delivery van, distinctive with its black cab, white refrigerator back and company logo, on the shoulder of State Road 19, 20 miles east of Ocala. The vehicle was locked and the keys were missing, as was Troy Burress.

A family out for a picnic in the Ocala National Forest, found his body five days later. They chanced upon his body in a clearing, just off Highway 19, and about eight miles from his abandoned delivery van. Florida's heat and humidity had hastened decomposition, precluding identification at the scene. Identification was confirmed later by his wife by means of the wedding ring he was wearing. He had been killed with two shots from a .22 caliber handgun, one to the chest and one to the back. A clipboard with delivery details and receipts, which had been removed from the van, was found near the body, but the company's takings were missing.

* * *

Dick Humphreys, of Crystal River, Florida, never made it home from his last day of work at the Sumterville office of the Florida's Department of Health and Rehabilitation Services. An investigator specializing in protecting abused and injured children, he was about transfer to the department's office at Ocala. Aged 56, he was a man of some experience who had formerly served as a police chief in Alabama.

On September 11, 1990, he disappeared after picking up a blonde hitchhiker. The following evening, his body was found off County Road 484 near I-75 in Marion County. He had been shot seven times. Six .22 caliber bullets were recovered from his body but the seventh copper-jacketed round had passed through his wrist and was never found. His money and wallet were missing.

Humphrey's Firenza car was found on September 19th, some 70 miles to the north. It had been backed into a space behind an abandoned Banner service station at the intersection of I-10 and State Route 90, near Live Oak, in Suwannee County. The licence plate, keys and a bright yellow Highway Patrol Association bumper sticker had been removed from the car. During an initial examination of the vehicle, it was noted that everything which told the world it had belonged to Dick Humphreys was gone or trashed, just like his life. Missing items included his ice scrapers, his maps, his personal papers, business papers and warranties. His favorite pipe, in the newly-carved wooden tray up on the dashboard, was also gone. In return, Lee Wuornos left one can of Budweiser beer under the passenger seat.

Back at the police pound, a closer examination of the car's interior revealed a cash register receipt for beer or wine from EMRO store number 8237, a Speedway truck stop and convenience store located at State Route 44 and I-75 in Wildwood. The receipt was time-stamped 4:19 p.m. on September 11, 1990, the day that Dick had disappeared. The clerk who had been on duty at the time could not identify the man but did recognize the composite police sketches of Wuornos and Moore. From their body language, the clerk formed the impression they were hookers. When they left the store, she believed they had driven away and therefore did not call the police, as she was obliged to because prostitutes are banned from truck stops throughout Florida.

Most of the victim's personal effects, including his pipe, were found a month later in a wooded field off Boggy Marsh Road in southern Lake County near U.S. 27.

By now, a number of law enforcement officers, investigating the various murders, were starting to collate their evidence. Marion and Citrus detectives had compared notes on the Burress and Spears killings. Then they spoke to Tom Muck, in Pascoe County, after they read in the Florida Department Law Enforcement (FDLE) bulletin that Muck's victim might be linked to Spears. That made three, indicating that a serial killer was at large.

The crimes had a number of features in common, including the fact that the victims were all older men who had been robbed, and two of them had had their pockets turned inside out. All three killings had been carried out using a small caliber weapon. Bullets, recovered from the bodies, were .22 caliber, copper-coated, hollow-nosed, with rifling marks made by a 6-right twist firearm.

Another link emerged when the police exchanged the composite sketches made by their individual witnesses. They bore significant similarities, suggesting they were looking for the same short, blonde woman. If she was a sole killer, and not working with a man, the officers reasoned, then she might well use a small handgun as an "equalizer."

Captain Steve Binegar, commander of the Marion County Sheriff's Criminal Investigation Division, knew about the Citrus and Pascoe murders. Today, he is based at the county jail in Tallahassee, where he recalled that he could not ignore the similarities between the murders, and had begun to formulate a theory. His first job was to form a multi-agency task force, with representatives from counties where the bodies were found.

"No one stopped to pick up hitchhikers in those days," Captain Binegar explained. "So the perpetrator/s of those crimes had to be initially non-threatening to the victims. Specifically, when I learned that two women had walked away from Peter Siems's car, I looked at the Trojan brand of prophylactics. Then came the composites and the truck stop clerk who said that the two women looked like hookers. Then I said to the other guys, 'We gotta be looking for a highway hooker, period.'"

Binegar decided to turn to the press for help. In late November, Reuters ran a story about the killings, reporting that the police were looking for two women. Newspapers throughout Florida picked up the story and ran it, along with the sketches of the women in question.

* * *

Sixty-year-old Walter Antonio, from Cocoa, Florida, was driving to Alabama, in search of a job. Recently engaged, he wore a gold and silver diamond ring, a gift from his fiancée. On November 18th, a police officer, out hunting, found a man's body, naked except for a pair of tube socks, near the intersection of U.S. 19 and U.S. 27 in Dixie County. Walter Antonio had been shot four times, three times in the torso and once in the head, with a .22 caliber handgun.

His maroon Pontiac Grand Prix car was found on November 24th in a wooded area near I-95 and U.S. 1, in northern Brevard County. The licence plate and keys were missing and, like Humphrey's car, a bumper sticker had been removed. A piece of paper had been crudely pasted over the VIN, and the doors were locked. Empty Budweiser cans were found on the ground near the vehicle, which had been wiped clean of fingerprints.

Detectives learned that Antonio meticulously recorded every purchase he made of car fuel, retaining the filling station receipts on which he noted his mileage. From this methodical behavior, they were able to deduce that, in the week since his disappearance, his car had been driven for over 1,000 miles.

His fiancée gave the police a list of possessions that had been in his car, including handcuffs, a reserve deputy badge, police billy club, flashlight, a Timex wristwatch, a suitcase, a toolbox and a baseball cap. All of these items were missing.

Walter Antonio's personal identification and clothing were discovered in a wooded area in Taylor County, approximately 38 miles north of the body's location. The rest was never found.

In just over a year, Lee Wuornos had scattered a trail of middle-aged male corpses across the highways of central Florida.

* * *

Following Captain Steve Binegar's appeal for information through the newspapers, calls began to pour in and, by mid-December 1990, detectives had a number of firm leads involving the two women suspects. A man in Homosassa Springs, where Wuornos asked David Spears to drop her off, said that two women, who fitted the composites, had rented an RV mobile home from him about a year earlier. After searching through his records, he came up with the names of "Tyria Moore" and "Lee."

A witness in Tampa said two women had worked at her motel south of Ocala, close to where Troy Burress was murdered. Their names, she said, were Tyria Moore and Susan Blahovec and they let it be known they had bought an RV in Homosassa Springs. The informant remembered that the blonde, Blahovec, was the dominant of the duo and believed she was a truck stop prostitute. She also told the police that both were lesbians.

The information from these two callers rang immediate alarm bells with the task force—David Spears; Homosassa Springs; RV trailer; two women … Troy Burress; Ocala; RV trailer; the same two women. The investigation was starting to pay off as previously tenuous links started coming together.

Meanwhile, the composite sketches, published by the media, of the red lipped blonde with the stringy hair and her dark haired, moon-face companion in the baseball cap, began to haunt Moore day and night. This was her excuse to flee Daytona Beach and go home to Ohio for Thanksgiving. Tyria, who had never hurt anyone in her life, had a lot of serious thinking to do because, although she was emotionally attached to Lee, she could not believe that her lover was the serial killer for whom the State had launched a massive search operation.

The breakthrough for the investigators came from Port Orange near Daytona. Local police had picked up the trail of the two women and were able to provide a detailed account of the couple's movements from late September to mid-December. They had stayed, primarily, at the Fairview Motel, in Harbor Oaks, where Blahovec registered as Cammie Marsh Greene. They spent a short while living in a small apartment, behind a restaurant near the Fairview, but returned later to the motel. Then Wuornos—a.k.a. Blahovec, a.k.a. Greene—returned alone and stayed until December 10th.

A national police computer check gave driver's licence and criminal record information on Tyria Moore, Susan Blahovec and Cammie Marsh Greene. Moore had no record worth considering, having had breaking and entering charges against her dropped in 1983. Blahovec had one trespassing arrest, while Greene had no record at all. Additionally, the photograph on Blahovec's licence did not match the one for Greene.

The Greene ID was the one that finally paid off. Volusia officers checked area pawnshops and found that in Daytona, Cammie Marsh Greene had pawned a 35mm Minolta Freedom camera and a Micronta Road Patrol Radar Detector bought at Radio Shack (both of the type owned by Richard Mallory), at the OK Pawn Shop in Daytona Beach. Cammie got $30 for the trade, showed her driver's licence and duly left the obligatory thumbprint on the collection receipt. Few people even own a Radio Shack radar detector, let alone associated with a Minolta .35mm camera, so this combination sparked the detective's interest. In Ormond Beach, she had pawned a set of tools that matched the description of those taken from David Spears's truck, although the police failed to recover these.

The thumbprint proved to be the key. Jenny Ahearn of the FDLE's Automated Fingerprint Identification System found nothing on her initial computer search, but she visited Volusia County with colleagues where they began a hand-search of fingerprint records. Within an hour, she struck gold. The print showed up on a weapons charge and out-standing warrant against a Lori K. Grody. Her fingerprints matched a bloody palm print found in Peter Siems's Sunbird. All of this information was sent to the National Crime Information Center, and responses came from Michigan, Colorado and Florida, confirming that Lori K. Grody, Susan Blahovec and Cammie Marsh Greene were all aliases for one Aileen Carol Wuornos.

Posing as leather-clad bikers, two undercover detectives, Mike Joyner and Dick Martin, finally spotted Lee Wuornos at 9:19 p.m. on Tuesday, January 8, 1991, and kept her under surveillance. She was drinking at the Port Orange Pub, on Ridgewood Avenue, in Harbor Oaks, about half a mile north of her favorite bar, The Last Resort, one of the many bikers' bars that line Highway One. Suddenly, to the dismay of the undercover officers, two uniformed Port Orange police officers walked into the bar and took Wuornos outside. Joyner and Martin frantically telephoned their command post at the Pirate's Cove Motel where authorities from six jurisdictions had gathered to bring the investigation to a head. They concluded that this development was not a leak but simply a case of alert police officers doing their jobs. Bob Kelly of the Volusia County Sheriff's Office called the Port Orange Police Station and told them not to arrest Wuornos under any circumstances. The word was relayed to the officers in the nick of time, and Lee was allowed to return to the bar.

The action shifted back to the two undercover detectives, who struck up a conversation with her and bought her a few beers. She left the bar at around 10:00 p.m., carrying a leather suitcase and declining the offer of a lift. Once again, the cautious arrest was almost ruined when two Florida police officers pulled up behind Wuornos, following her with their lights off as she walked down Ridgewood Avenue. Police at the command post radioed the officers to back off, allowing Lee to proceed to The Last Resort.

Joyner and Martin met her at The Last Resort, drinking and chatting until midnight, when she left. But she did not go far. Lee Wuornos spent her last night of freedom sleeping on an old yellow vinyl car seat, under the tin roof overhang of the bar.

Surveillance was planned to continue throughout the following day, but when the police learned that a large number of bikers was expected for a party at the bar that evening, they decided further surveillance would be impossible. By simply donning a crash helmet, Lee could quite easily disappear among the hundreds of motorcyclists milling around at the party, and vanish for good. The decision was made at that point to go ahead with the arrest. Joyner and Martin asked her if she would like to use their motel room to clean up before the party. At first she was reluctant, but then changed her mind and left the bar with them.

Outside, on the steps leading to the bar, Larry Horzepa of the Marion County Sheriff's Office approached Lee and told her that she was being arrested on an outstanding warrant for Lori Grody. This related to the illegal possession of a firearm and no mention was made of the murders. The arrest was kept low key and no announcement was made to the media that a suspected serial killer had been arrested. Their caution was well advised for, as yet, the police had no murder weapon and no Tyria Moore.

Lee's companion was located on January 10th, living with her sister in Pittston, Pennsylvania. Jerry Thompson of Citrus County and Bruce Munster of Marion County flew to Scranton to interview her. She was informed of her rights but not charged with any offence. Munster made sure she knew what perjury was, swore her in, and sat back as she gave her statement.

Tyria said she had known about the murders since Lee had arrived home with Richard Mallory's Cadillac. Lee had openly confessed that she had killed a man that day, but Moore had advised her not to say anything else. "I told her I don't want to hear about it," she told the detectives. "And then any time she would come home after that and say certain things, telling me about where she got something, I'd say I don't want to hear it." Tyria had her suspicions, she admitted, but wanted to know as little as possible about Lee's business. The more she knew, she reasoned, the more compelled she would feel to report Lee to the authorities. She did not want to do that. "I was just scared," she said. "She always said she'd never hurt me, but then, you can't believe her, so I don't know what she would have done."

The next day, Tyria Moore accompanied Munster and Thompson on their return to Florida to assist in the investigation. A confession would make the case against Wuornos virtually airtight, and Munster and Thompson explained their plan to her on the flight. They would register her in a Daytona motel and have her make contact with Lee in jail, explaining that she had received money from her mother and had returned to collect the rest of her things. Their conversations would be taped. She was to tell Lee that authorities had been questioning her family, and that she thought the Florida murders would be mistakenly pinned on her. Munster and Thompson hoped that, out of loyalty to Tyria, Lee would confess.

Still under the impression that she was only in jail for the Lori Grody weapons violation, the first call came from Lee on January 14th. When Tyria voiced her suspicions, Lee reassured her. "I'm only here for that concealed weapons charge in '86 and a traffic ticket," she said, "and tell you what, man, I read the newspaper, and I wasn't one of those little suspects." She was aware, though, that the jailhouse phone she was using was being monitored, and made efforts to speak of the crimes in code words and to construct alibis. "I think somebody at work ... where you worked at ... said something that it looked like us," she said. "And it isn't us, see? It's a case of mistaken identity."

The calls continued for three days. Tyria Moore became even more insistent that the police were after her, and it became clear that Lee knew what was expected of her. She even voiced suspicion that Moore was not alone, that someone was taping their conversations. But, as time passed, she became less careful about what she said. She would not let Moore go down with her. "Just go ahead and let them know what you need to know … what they want to know or anything," she said, "and I will cover for you, because you are innocent. I'm not going to let you go to jail. Listen, if I have to confess, I will." And, on the morning of January 16th, she did just that.

During her confession to Larry Horzepa and Bruce Munster, Lee returned again and again to two themes. First, she wanted to make it clear that Tyria Moore was not involved in any of the murders. Secondly, she was emphatic in her assertion that nothing was her fault, neither the murders nor the circumstances that had shaped her life as a criminal. She claimed that all the killings were acts of self defense. Each victim had either assaulted, threatened or raped her. Her story seemed to evolve and take on a life of its own as she related it. When she thought she had said something that might be incriminating, she would back up and retell that part, revising the details to suit her own ends. Lee claimed to have been raped several times over the years and decided it was not going to happen again. In future, when a customer became aggressive, she killed out of fear. Several times, Michael O'Neill, an attorney from the Volusia County Public Defender's Office, advised her to stop talking, finally asking in exasperation, "Do you realize these guys are cops?" Wuornos answered, "I know. And they want to hang me. And that's cool, because maybe, man, I deserve it. I just want to get this over with."

News that the police had secured a female serial killer's confession soon leaked out to the public domain and an avalanche of book and movie deals poured in to detectives, to Moore and Wuornos and to the victims' relatives. Lee seemed to think she would make millions of dollars from her story, not yet realizing that Florida had a law against criminals profiting in such a manner. She commanded headlines in the local and national media. She felt famous, and continued to talk about the crimes with anyone who would listen, including Volusia County Jail employees. With each retelling, she refined her story a little further, seeking to cast herself in a better light each time.

On January 28, 1991, Lee Wuornos was indicted for the murder of Richard Mallory. The indictment read,

> In that Aileen Carol Wuornos, a.k.a. Susan Lynn Blahovec, a.k.a. Lori Kristine Grody, a.k.a. Cammie Marsh Greene, on or about the first day of December 1989, within Volusia County, did then and there unlawfully, from a premeditated design to effect the death of one Richard Mallory, a human being, while engaged in the perpetration of or attempt to perpetrate robbery, did kill and murder Richard Mallory by shooting him with a firearm, to wit: a handgun.

Counts two and three charged her with armed robbery and possession of a firearm and, by late February, she had been charged with the murders of David Spears, in Citrus County, and Charles Humphreys and Troy Burress in Marion County.

Lee's attorneys engineered a plea bargain, whereby she would plead guilty to six charges and receive six consecutive life terms. One State's attorney, however, thought she should receive the death penalty, so on January 14, 1992, she went to trial for the murder of Richard Mallory.

The evidence and testimony of witnesses were severely damaging. Dr. Arthur Botting, the medical examiner, who had carried out the autopsy on Mallory's body, stated that he had taken between ten and twenty agonizing minutes to die. Tyria Moore testified that Wuornos had not seemed overly upset, nervous or drunk when she told her about the Mallory killing. Twelve men went on to the witness stand to testify to their encounters with Lee along Florida's highways and byways over the years.

Florida has a law, known as the Williams rule, that allows evidence relating to other crimes to be admitted if it serves to show a pattern.

Because of the Williams rule, information regarding other killings, alleged to have been committed by Wuornos, was presented to the jury. Her claim of having killed in self defense would have been a lot more believable had the jury only known of Mallory. Now, with the jury being made aware of all the murders, self defense seemed the least plausible explanation. After the excerpts from her videotaped confession were played, the self defense claim simply looked ridiculous. Wuornos appeared on the tape and seemed not the least upset by the story she was telling. She made easy conversation with her interrogators and repeatedly told her attorney to be quiet. Her image on the screen allowed her to condemn herself out of her own mouth. "I took a life ... I am willing to give up my life because I killed people ... I deserve to die," she said.

Tricia Jenkins, one of Lee's public defenders, did not want her client to testify and told her so. But Wuornos overrode this advice, insisting on telling her story. By now, her account of Mallory's murder barely resembled the one she gave in her confession. Mallory had raped, sodomized and tortured her, she claimed.

On cross examination, prosecutor John Tanner obliterated any shred of credibility she may have had. As he brought to light all her lies and inconsistencies, she became agitated and angry. Her attorneys repeatedly advised her not to answer questions, and she invoked her Fifth Amendment right against self-incrimination 25 times. She was the defense's only witness, and when she left the stand, there was not much doubt about how her trial would end.

Judge Uriel "Bunky" Blount, Jr. charged the jury on January 27th. They returned their verdict 91 minutes later. Pamela Mills, a schoolteacher, had been elected Foreperson and she presented the verdict to the bailiff. He, in turn, handed it to the judge. The judge read it and passed it to the clerk who spoke the words that sealed Lee's fate. "We, the jury, find Aileen Wuornos guilty of premeditated felony murder in the first degree," she told an expectant assembly in the courtroom. As the jury filed out, their duty done, Lee exploded with rage, shouting, "I'm innocent! I was raped! I hope you get raped! Scumbags of America."

Her outburst was still fresh in the minds of jurors as the penalty phase of her trial began, the next day. Expert witnesses for the defense testified that Wuornos was mentally ill, that she suffered from a borderline personality disorder, and that her tumultuous upbringing had stunted and ruined her. Jenkins referred to her client as "a damaged, primitive child," as she tearfully pleaded with the jury to spare Lee's life. But the jurors neither forgot nor forgave the woman they had come to know during the trial. With a unanimous verdict, they recommended that Judge Blount sentence her to die in the electric chair. He confirmed the sentence on January 31st, first quoting his duty from a printed text.

> *Aileen Carol Wuornos, being brought before the court by her attorneys William Miller, Tricia Jenkins and Billy Nolas, having been tried and found guilty of count one, first-degree premeditated murder and first-degree felony murder of Richard Mallory, a capital felony; and count two, armed robbery with a firearm … hereby judged and found guilty of said offences … and the court having given the defendant an opportunity to be heard and to offer matters in mitigation of sentence … It is the sentence of this court that you, Aileen Carol Wuornos, be delivered by the Sheriff of Volusia County to the proper officer of the Department of Corrections of the State of Florida and by him safely kept until by warrant of the Governor of the State of Florida, you, Aileen Wuornos, be electrocuted until you are dead.*
>
> *And may God have mercy on your corpse.*

A collective gasp arose from the courtroom, diminishing the solemnity of the occasion. The sense of shock was less to do with the judge's sentiment than his choice of words. May God have mercy on your corpse? Did Judge Blount really say that? *Corpse?* Members of the media stopped, with pencils poised in midair. He had got it wrong. Surely, he should have said, "May God have mercy on your soul." Could they quote him, they whispered among themselves?

Aileen Wuornos did not stand trial again. On March 31, 1992, she pleaded no contest to the murders of Dick Humphreys, Troy Burress and David Spears, saying that she wanted to "get it right with God." In a rambling statement to the court, she said, "I wanted to confess to you that David Mallory did violently rape me as I've told you. But these others did not. [They] only began to start to." She ended her monologue by turning to Assistant State Attorney Ric Ridgeway, and hissing, "I hope your wife and children get raped in the ass!"

On May 15th, Judge Thomas Sawaya handed her three more death sentences. She made an obscene gesture and muttered, "Motherfucker."

For a time, there was speculation that Wuornos might receive a new trial for the murder of Richard Mallory. New evidence showed that Mallory had spent ten years in prison for sexual violence, and her attorneys felt that jurors would have seen the case differently had they been aware of this. No new trial was forthcoming and the State Supreme Court of Florida affirmed all six of her death sentences.

In 2001, Wournos began to refuse appeals and, in fact, to welcome the death penalty. In a letter to the Florida Supreme Court she threatened, "I'm one who seriously hates human life and would kill again." And so, at 9:47 a.m. on October 9, 2002, Aileen Carol Wournos was put to death by lethal injection at Florida State Prison in Starke. Her final words were, "I'd just like to say I'm sailing with the Rock and I'll be back like Independence Day with Jesus, June 6, like the movie, big mothership and all. I'll be back."

* * *

Aileen Carol Wuornos shared death row with several faces familiar to students of crime in the U.S. Judias "Judy" Buenonano, aged 48, and popularly known as "The Black Widow," had been on death row since 1985. Convicted of poisoning her husband, drowning her quadriplegic son by pushing him out of a canoe, and planting a bomb in her boyfriend's car, she had the distinction of being the first woman to die in Florida's electric chair on March 30, 1998.

Deirdre Hunt was sent to death row in 1993 and her sentence has since been commuted to life.

Andrea Hicks Jackson was sentenced to death for shooting a police officer in 1983, and has also had her sentence reversed. Like Hunt, she no longer lives on "The Row."

Virginia Gail Larzelere, aged 49, has recently been given the death penalty for murdering her husband at Edgewater, near Daytona Beach, on March 8, 1991.

Ana M. Cardona, aged 40, was sentenced to death for aggravated child abuse, and the first-degree murder of her three-year-old son, in Miami, on November 2, 1992.

At the time of writing, Aileen Wuornos was 46 years-old, but looked a decade older. The condemned woman, wearing an orange T-shirt and blue trousers, stood 5 feet 4 inches and weighed 133 pounds. The characteristic strawberry-blonde hair, described by witnesses, framed her face but her eyes were constantly bloodshot. Always looking washed out, her once attractive looks had been replaced with a face that life has not treated kindly. She had a scar between the eyes and burn scars on her forehead. Her body was marked with a long cut along her lower left arm and a crude appendectomy scar across the middle of her abdomen.

The cell in which Lee was confined measures 8 feet by10 feet. It was painted a dull-looking pink, and the ceiling was quite high, maybe 15 feet, which made the room seem larger and more airy than it really was. She had a black and white television, placed above the stainless steel toilet, on a varnished brown shelf. The furniture consisted of a grey metal footlocker that doubled as a desk, but no table and only a single chair. There was also a dirty, lime-green cupboard at the foot of a metal bed, which contained her clothes and personal possessions. Everything had to be locked away at bed inspection time, between 9:00 a.m. and 11:00 a.m. The only view she had of the outside world was a parking lot and a high fence, festooned with glittering razor wire. There were no bars at her cell window but a metal door with a small hatch separated her from the rest of the cell block. It cost the State of Florida $72.39 a day to keep Lee Wuornos incarcerated.

Describing her routine, she said, "The food ain't all bad. We're served three meals a day. At 5:00 a.m., 10:30 to 11:00 a.m., an' 4:00 p.m. to 4:30. They cook it in here. We get plates and spoons, nothing else. I can take a shower every other day, and we're counted at least once an hour. Everywhere we go, we wear cuffs except in the shower and exercise yard where I can talk to my cellmates. Lately, I like to be by myself. Apart from that, I am always locked up in my room. I can't even be with another inmate in the common room."

She spent the long, solitary hours reading books on spiritual growth and writing lengthy letters to her mother. Lee's lifestyle was spartan and monotonous—and the days and years rolled indistinguishably and uneventfully past her locked cell door. In the knowledge that 11.3 years is the average length of stay on death row, prior to execution, Lee knew that when her death came, it would be a painful experience.

Yet, knowing this, Lee appeared unfazed. "Death does not scare me. God will be beside me, taking me up with him when I leave this shell, I am sure of it. I have been forgiven and am certainly sound in Jesus' name."

On the highways and byways of Florida there are always crossroads, off- and on-ramps, where two lives can meet, with destructive results. One comes to an end, and the other takes a permanent detour. Lee Wuornos haunted those places like a deadly spider sitting at the center of its web. To all intents and purposes, she was a non-threatening woman hitching a ride. As she explained, "What I'm sayin' ... you want the truth. I want to tell it as it was. I'm telling you that I was always going somewhere, and most times I hitched a ride. There are thousands of guys and women out there who'll say they gave me a ride, and we got on just fine, ya know. They gave me no hassle. I'm a good person inside, but when I get drunk, I just don't know. It's just ... when I'm drunk it's don't mess the fuck with me. Ya know. That's the truth. I've got nothing to lose. That's the truth."

When asked who had initiated the subject of sex during the rides, Lee claimed, "I was always short of money, so I guess sometimes I brought up sex. Mallory wanted to fuck straight off. He was a mean motherfucker with a dirty mouth. He got drunk and it was a physical situation, so I popped him and watched the man die. Spears was made out to be a nice, decent guy. That's shit. He wanted a quick fuck. He bought a few beers and wanted a free fuck ... an' you wanna know about the third one [Carskaddon]. How do think he got undressed? Wise up. He wanted sex ... got undressed. Ask yourself, what's that all about if he didn't want a cheap fuck? 'Cause the cops didn't say about the others ... never found the johnnies. Yeah, OK, man. Look, you gotta understand that guys don't get nude with some broad if they don't want sex. The last one ... I can't remember his name [Walter Antonio] was ... Jesus Christ ... he was fucking engaged. He bought a six-pack. The dirty motherfucker. And, I do have one thing, though ... their families must know that no matter how they loved the people that I killed, they were bad 'cause they were going to hurt me. I suppose you think I really suck, right?"

Most killers are able to describe their crimes, and Lee Wuornos was more adept than some, telling and retelling her story with added layers of gloss to suit her own ends. But one aspect of her story remained constant. She swore that each of her victims wanted sex, and either raped her against her will, or intended to. For that very reason, she shot them dead, eliminating them with no more compassion than swatting a fly.

"You've gotta understand … I ain't so bad. I've been with hundreds and hundreds of men. I just ain't killed them all. I would make money but they wouldn't abuse me or nothin'. I'd just make my money out in the boonies, stick it in my wallet and go. Never hurt them, right? Then you get a few dirty old men who go radical on me. So you see what I'm sayin' … I kinda had to do what I had to do. What am I supposed to do? It was all their fault, and that's the God's honest truth."

Because the body of Peter Siems has never been found, Lee was asked where she had left the corpse. "Look. I can't remember their faces or their names, so don't shit me. How the fuck am I going to recall where he is? But I'm tellin' you that he's got to be seriously dead by now."

Asked if her grandfather had sexually abused her, Lee said, "Ya know, I have said different things about this over the years, but, the truth is, yeah. I was. He'd do stuff to me and give me pocket money to shut up. He'd finger me. I lost my virginity to his fuckin' finger when I was about seven. He'd beat the shit outa me, ya know. But he'd strip me naked beforehand … that's fuckin wrong … you understand? He made me what I am. He made me hate men like him. Dirty, cheap, no good motherfuckers like him. Look at me … I'm shaking all over even thinking about it. For fuck's sake, let's leave it. OK, Christopher? I'm sort of getting freaked out and I don't need this right now."

* * *

Knowing the enormity of the crimes committed by Lee Wuornos, it is easy just to follow the general line of thinking and dismiss her simply as another one in a long line of serial killers. While there have been many female mass murderers, there have been few female serial killers. By making a man suffer, she transformed herself from a victim to the victimizer, eagerly grabbing power for herself with both hands and with the aid of a handgun. She made herself unique in a gross kind of way.

Lee Wuornos had an antisocial personality disorder. Although one in twenty males suffer from such a disorder, meaning that their actions are not inhibited by guilt or moral boundaries, very few kill, and even fewer women kill. Even fewer are hookers who kill for money when selling their bodies; indeed, prostitutes are the all too familiar victims of male serial killers. Lee Wuornos may fairly be described as unique and, as such, she merits more than a passing study. She perhaps represents a reason why society should not, out of revenge, use the ultimate penalty of execution, which is usually carried out more for the sake of political expediency than for the sake of deterrence. If her life serves no other purpose, Lee Wuornos might just provide some valuable insights into a rare breed of killer.

Her life was a tangled thread of alcohol and loneliness, spent for the most part, rootless and penniless, roaming the highways of Florida. She hung around the haunts of bikers, but sought love from her female companion, Tyria Moore, hating men as the source of all her troubles and luring at least six of them to their deaths. But the question remains—what preceded Lee's dance of death? What finally made the bough break?

To answer the first question, it would be fair to say that she did not enjoy a healthy childhood. Her true father, a man she never met, was a sexual pervert who later hanged himself in prison. Her mother abandoned her when she was six months old, and she was adopted by an authoritarian grandfather and grandmother. Throughout her entire formative years, the young girl was humiliated, sexually abused, beaten and rejected, and her world was filled with pain, rage and alcoholism, all suffered behind the closed curtains of a house of secrets.

There are those who subscribe to the view that *all* serial killers enjoy using, abusing and controlling fellow human beings. This is why some observers have stated that Wuornos is a new type of breed of killer, leaping on the notion that she is a pioneer, a predatory hitchhiker, stalking the highways, from whom no man is safe. Conversely, it seems to be generally agreed that women rarely kill just for kicks.

Lee has always said that she was short of cash. That was a problem which could always be resolved with a trick here and there; besides, there is the undeniable fact that she hitched hundreds of rides from men, and only murdered six. There is no doubt that she had sex with many of those who offered her lifts and who were probably blissfully unaware that she always carried a gun.

So what was the murderous impulse that led her to homicidal violence? Captain Steve Binegar argued that "when she was picked up by men they usually lived, but when they went into the woods with her, they never came out alive." This is a simplification, as Captain Binegar later agreed. "Maybe I was generalizing," he said. "No guy is going to strip on the highway ... risk police seeing a parked car ... windows steamed up ... rocking up an' down. Perhaps I was wrong. I'm damned sure I wouldn't mess around like that on the highway."

In trying to understand what triggered Lee's impulse to kill, it is plausible and, indeed, likely that her "killing days," like those of Michael Ross, were precipitated by personal crisis or extra stresses in her life. As her feelings of powerlessness heightened, her mind tried to compensate by converting those feelings into a desire to exert control over another human being. Many serial killers, including most of those featured in this book, commonly admit that an argument with the opposite sex, a close partner or a parent, preceded the act of murder.

A study carried out by the FBI on male subjects showed that 59 percent specifically mentioned conflict with a woman. Lee had conflicts with Tyria Moore, her only love, at the time of the murders of Mallory, Spears, Carskaddon, Siems, Humphreys and Antonio. Either Tyria was threatening to leave, or the presence of a competing force for Tyria's affections had made Lee fear she might lose her.

Another attractive lesbian, Sandy Russell, had entered Tyria's life, just a few days before Lee murdered Richard Mallory. When another woman, Tracey, visited Tyria, Lee killed David Spears, Charles Carskaddon and Peter Siems. When Tyria was dismissed from employment at the Casa Del Mar restaurant, she talked about leaving Florida and, by implication, deserting Lee. This happened in the week before Richard Humphreys was murdered. Tyria had left for Ohio, for Thanksgiving, amid talk about making a break from Lee, when Walter Antonio was shot dead. There seems to be a pattern here and it takes no great stretch of the imagination to envisage a crisis in their relationship, at the end of July, which preceded the murder of Troy Burress.

If this line of reasoning is valid, the idea that Lee took the lives of her victims in the image of her abusive grandfather is erroneous. Despite the monstrous picture she has painted for herself, she has always been—and will continue to be—a lonely, scared woman who shares the fundamental human desire for love, respect, and attention. She was denied such fulfillment from the beginning of her life and when she found the one person she could really love, and whom she imagined, unequivocally, loved her, she cherished this relationship in her own particular way.

Alone, out on the wet highways, with her domestic problems in the forefront of her mind, Lee found "Murder Crossroads." Older men with sex on their minds, maybe in the image of her grandfather, crossed her path. Seemingly respectable men with money, wives and lovers, who were only too keen to buy six-packs of beer and booze in exchange for cheap sex in the sordid confines of a car on a lonely back road.

"I was really OK with these guys. That is the God's honest truth," said Lee Wuornos during an interview. "A few drinks, they thought I was cheap … started talking rough an' dirty like I'm shit, man. I've had that all my life … didn't need the shit … I'm a reasonable person. They wanted to fuck my ass … couldn't get that with their wives an' stuff. They wanted to abuse and humiliate me. Ya know, despite what you think, I've got respect for myself. Always did have. Weird, right!"

Giving a ride to Lee Wuornos, buying her a few cheap drinks, pulling off the highway and talking her down was a murderous cocktail, indeed.

This chapter is based on an interview between Lee Wuornos and Christopher Berry-Dee on death row, Pembroke Pines Correctional Institute, Florida, in 1996, and other research.

KENNETH ALLEN MCDUFF

"Killing a woman's like killing a chicken.

They both squawk."

KENNETH MCDUFF'S CHILLING APPRAISAL
TO HIS ACCOMPLICE ROY DALE GREEN

"He was out on parole when McDuff killed our kids.
We got three death sentences, and now he is out on
parole again. They are going to have blood on their
hands, those people who turned him loose."

BILL BRAND, FATHER OF ROBERT BRAND,
ONE OF MCDUFF'S 1966 VICTIMS

He didn't just kill his victims; he savaged them in unspeakable ways. He raped them with a sadism that made veteran police officers cringe. This killer blew off his victims' faces at point-blank range, he slashed and stabbed with knives, and bludgeoned with clubs. He crushed one victim's neck with a broomstick.

* * *

Tall, dour and icy-eyed, McDuff had scattered corpses around central Texas—estimates have ranged upward of 15—since he was a teenager, so who is this ogre who terrorized a whole state?

There is little recorded information on the early life of Kenneth McDuff. What we do know is that he was born on Sunday, March 3, 1946, at 201 Linden Street, in the small, central Texas hamlet of Rose-bud, Falls County. The saying, "All is rosy in Rosebud," suggests a cosy place untroubled by violence.

On the eastern edge of Rosebud, Linden Street heads south from Main Street toward a baseball field, carved out of surrounding farm-land. Small wooden houses, old but well kept, and shaded by large pecan trees, line the streets. On the east side of Linden, only the second building from Main, stands a premises that was once the Rosebud Laundromat. A small living area is connected to the rear of the laundro-mat, where the family of John Allen "J.A." McDuff lived. At least some of the McDuff's children, including two boys named Lonzo (Lonnie) and Kenneth, were born in far-off Paris, Texas, and no one seems to know why the McDuffs, who lived in the Blackland Prairie before moving to Rosebud, ended up in the area.

Kenneth was one of four children born to Addie L. and J.A. McDuff. J.A. did farm, masonry and concrete work. His wife was a hefty, domineering woman who ruled the roost. She was known locally as "The Pistol Packin' Momma," on account of her violent temper and her habit of toting a sidearm in her handbag. Ken was in trouble from the moment he could walk.

He grew up to be a bully, a sadistic child who roamed the neighborhood with a .22 caliber rifle, shooting any animal or bird that fell into his sights. The town's residents called him "the bad boy of Rosebud." People feared him even as a teenager and he beat up any youth who upset him, whether they were older or not.

Mrs. Martha Royal, McDuff's fifth-grade teacher, remembers him as intelligent youngster, but something of a loner. "Kenneth was the son of a mild-mannered, hard-working father who was in the building trade, and a permissive mother who was quick to excuse his misdeeds. His troubles began in junior high, and never stopped. He did not get along with the other children very well. He seemed to live in a world of his own. On several occasions, I tried to speak with him in private, to ask if he had any problems at home, and things like that. But he wouldn't say a word to me. He just stared straight into my face. From the age of five, he had murder in his eyes. It was quite disturbing, I can tell you that."

McDuff was always in trouble. In his teens, he was involved in robberies with his brother and, more than once, Sheriff Larry Pamplin said he tried to shoot their car tires out, but they always got away.

McDuff's documented criminal career began in 1964, when, aged 18, he was convicted of 12 counts of burglary and attempted burglary in Bell, Milam, and Falls County. He received 12 concurrent four year sentences for these crimes but achieved parole in Falls County in December 1965. Several months later, he got into a fracas and his parole was revoked. In 1966, he was released and, a short time later, he committed capital murder with an accomplice, a somewhat weak-willed 18-year-old, Roy Dale Green.

Green was employed as a carpenter's helper. He had previously lived with his mother but, after she remarried, he moved in with a friend named Richard Boyd. It was Boyd who introduced Green to McDuff and, at the time of the triple homicide, the two men had known each other only a month.

The two men seem to hit it off well. McDuff was a well-built, good-looking 20-year-old, who was proud of his criminal record. He was a tough, no-nonsense young man. He spoke his mind and he bragged about his sexual conquests, to the point that he said that he had raped two young women and killed them. Green, on the other hand, was a weedy individual with a speech impediment who looked up to his stronger companion. But, secretly, he put McDuff's murderous claims down as hogwash.

The two men spent Saturday, August 6th, pouring concrete for McDuff's father and, after completing their labors, decided to drive into Fort Worth for a few drinks. At around 5:00 p.m., they climbed into McDuff's brand new Dodge Coronet and rode around before buying a pack of beer from a 7-11 store. At 7:00 p.m., they visited Edith Turner, a mutual friend, and later they bought a hamburger.

Meanwhile, three teenagers—Robert Brand of Alvarado, aged 18; his cousin, 16-year-old Mark Dunman from Tarzana, California; and Robert's girlfriend, vivacious 16-year-old Edna Louise Sullivan, from Everman—spent the evening at a drive-in movie. When the show finished, they drove to a spot near a baseball field in Guadalupe County where they parked their 1957 Ford. At around 10:00 p.m., McDuff and Green came on the scene and the trio of teenagers became their randomly-selected quarry.

What took place is graphically described in the statement Green gave to Detective Grady Hight. This is dated Monday August 8, 1966, the day Green gave himself up:

We rode around the baseball park and wound up on a gravel road. He [McDuff] saw a car parked there, and we stopped about 150 yards in front of it. He got his gun and told me to get out. I thought it was all a joke. I just didn't believe what he said was going to happen. I went halfway to the car with him, and he went on. He told the kids in the car to get out or he would shoot them. I went on up there and he had put them in the trunk of their car. He drove his car back to their car, and he told me to get in his car and follow him. I did, and we drove for a while across the highway we had come in on, and he pulled into a field. I followed, and he said that the field wouldn't do, so we backed up and went to another field. He got out and told the girl to get out. He told me to put her in the trunk of his car. I opened the trunk and she climbed in. It was then that he said that we couldn't leave any witnesses, or something like that. He said, "I'm gonna have to knock 'em off," or something like that.

I got really scared. I still thought he was joking, but I wasn't sure. They were on their knees, begging him not to shoot them. They said, "We're not going to tell anybody." I turned towards him and he stuck the gun into the trunk of where the boys were and started shooting. I saw the fire come out of the gun on the first shot, and I covered my ears and looked away. He shot six times. He shot one twice in the head, and he shot the other boy four times in the head. A bullet went through a boy's arm as he tried to stop the fire. He tried to close the trunk, but it wouldn't close. He then told me to back up his car. By that time I was almost dying of fright, and I did what he said. He got in the boy's car and backed it into a fence, and he got out and told me to help him wipe off the fingerprints. I wasn't going to argue with him. I was expecting to be next so I helped him.

After a break in the interview, Detective Hight asked Green about the murder of Edna Sullivan, and what follows is again taken verbatim from Green's statement:

We wiped out the tire tracks and got into his car and drove off another mile and turned off on another road and he stopped, and he got the girl out of the trunk and put her in the back seat. He told me to get out of the car, and I waited until he told her to get undressed. He took off his clothes and then he screwed her. He asked me if I wanted to do it, and I told him no. He asked me why not, and I told him I just didn't want to. He leaned over, and I didn't see the gun but thought he would shoot me if I didn't, so I pulled my pants and shirt off and got in the back seat and screwed the girl. She didn't struggle or anything, and if she ever said anything I didn't hear her. All the time I was on top of the girl I kept my eye on him. After that he screwed her again.

After Edna Sullivan had been raped several times, the two men drove her a short distance then stopped. McDuff ordered Green out of the car and asked him if he had anything with which to strangle the girl. He offered McDuff his belt. Green then described the most brutal murder, which followed.

He told the girl to get out of the car. He made her sit down on the gravel road, and he took about a three-foot piece of broomstick from his car and forced her head back with it until it was on the ground. He started choking her with the piece of broomstick. He mashed down hard, and she started waving her arms and kicking her legs. He told me to grab her legs and I didn't want to, and he said, "It's gotta be done," and I grabbed her legs, and held them for a second or so, then let them go. He said, "Do it again," and I did, and this time was when she stopped struggling. He had me grab her hands and he grabbed her feet and we heaved her over a fence. We crossed the fence ourselves, then he dragged her a short ways and then he choked her some more. We put her in some kind of bushes there.

That night, the two men stopped at a Hillsboro gas station for Coca-Colas before returning to Green's house, where they slept in the same bed. The following morning, McDuff buried the revolver by the side of his accomplice's garage and they drove to a friend's house where Richard Boyd allowed McDuff to wash his car.

Later in the day, Green was so overcome with fear and remorse that he had to confide in Boyd whose parents called Green's mother, and she convinced her son to give himself up to the police.

In 1968, McDuff received three death sentences, while Roy Dale Green was sent to prison for 25 years. He served 13 years before being released on parole.

* * *

During his time behind bars, McDuff walked to the electric chair on two occasions and, each time, received last-minute stays of execution. Then, in 1972, the death statute was ruled "unconstitutional" by the United States Supreme Court, so McDuff's death sentence was commuted to life. He would serve just a handful of years before his mother bribed a parole board official to rubber-stamp his release. McDuff's death sentence was commuted to life and, on October 11, 1989, he was set free and paroled to Milam County.

The McDuff scandal was not simply limited to a corrupt parole board official. The seeds were sewn in 1972, when a federal court ruled that the Texas Department of Corrections was overcrowded. The State was faced with two choices: either build more prisons or lock up fewer prisoners in the existing ones.

Three successive governors—Dolph Briscoe, Bill Clements and Mark White—talked tough about crime, but did nothing to encourage the construction of new facilities because they were too expensive to build. By the end of Clement's second term in office, the system had just about broken down. With public pressure mounting by the day, the Governor was forced to reconsider, and plans were drawn up for several new jails. In addition, in order to reduce the overcrowding problems, parole considerations were relaxed. The order was to parole 750 of the lowest-risk inmates a week. Before long, there were not even 750 inmates left in the entire system of some 60,000 who met eligibility standards. At that point, the parole system cracked under the strain. It its haste to meet the quota, the board began rubber-stamping the applications almost as soon as it received them. Applications were rushed through without being read properly and, with McDuff being just another number among thousands, he became one of the 20 former death row inmates and 127 murderers to be released.

This shambles resulted from the fundamental problems with the system as it then operated, and Jim Parker, the Legislative Director for Governor Ann Richards, later made this point, "Some people put in prison were less dangerous than the people being released. We're jailing hot check writers and DWI's (driving without insurance), and letting out the Kenneth McDuffs. In our panic to make our streets safe again, we're imprisoning non-violent offenders; we're filling up the available space with people who belong in drug rehabilitation centers, or whose debt to society could be paid by doing community service."

Because the Board of Pardons and Paroles was not empowered to set policy about who achieved parole, they relied on a few assumptions and wild, speculative theories in determining who was safe to release and who was not. As one distinguished attorney put it, "This was as random as throwing darts in the dark."

Among the assumptions was the belief that, as most murders are committed in moments of rage or passion, such offenders are good parole risks because they are unlikely, to kill for a second time. The weakness of this concept was that it did not take into account those criminals who kill for pure enjoyment, one of whom was Kenneth McDuff.

Another ill-conceived theory was that a long time in prison breaks an inmate and "burns out" their meanness. This was certainly a parole consideration for McDuff when he was released after having served 23 years in jail. But, in the lottery of number crunching to which the parole system had been reduced, McDuff and his ilk were inevitably lumped together with the more benign killers who fitted the so-called category of "unlikely to kill again." The strange consequence of this, as Jim Parker explained, "isn't that we have just the one McDuff, it's that we don't have hundreds of McDuffs back on the streets."

* * *

Within days of being released in October 1989, McDuff murdered 31-year-old Sarafia Parker, whose body was found on October 14th by a pedestrian strolling the 1500 block of East Avenue, Temple, a small city 48 miles due south of Waco. She was black, about 5 feet 6 inches tall and weighed about 150 pounds. She had been beaten and strangled no more than 24 hours before her body was found.

She was quickly identified and Texas Ranger John Aycock later located and interviewed a witness who thought he could place Parker in a pick up truck, driven by McDuff, on or around October 12th. On that day, Kenneth McDuff had reported to his parole officer, who happened to work in Temple. No other connection between the murder of Sarafia Parker and McDuff has been established or made public.

McDuff was returned to prison for breaking his parole conditions after he made death threats against a black youth in Rosebud, and it was at this point that Addie McDuff stepped into the picture. She paid $1,500 to Huntsville attorney Bill Habern and his consulting partner, Helen Copitka, of Austin, plus a further $700 for her "expenses," to evaluate her son's new parole prospects.

Habern next spoke to James Granberry, the chairman of the parole board, a man known for his tendency to release convicted murderers from prison. It came as no surprise to learn that McDuff was back on the streets within a year, walking out of the prison gates on Tuesday, December 18, 1990. Subsequently, Granberry resigned, after coming under fire from a House investigation committee. He had the gall to set up his own parole consultancy firm which he was forced to close amid a storm of public protest.

* * *

Sometime during the evening of October 10, 1991, Brenda Thompson, a prostitute and drug addict, climbed into McDuff's red pick up truck in Waco. They drove south on Miller Street and encountered a Waco Police Department vehicle checkpoint on Faulkner Lane. McDuff stopped about 50 feet from the barrier and one of the officers walked to the pick up. As he did so, he shone his flashlight on himself so that the driver could see clearly he was a police officer.

Suddenly, Brenda began screaming and kicking. To the officer, it appeared as if her arms were tied behind her back and she was desperately trying to get out of the truck. She lay back and began kicking at the windshield with such force that it shattered on the passenger's side. She continued to kick vigorously, with her legs clad in a pair of red polyester pants, cracking the windshield more and more with each kick. McDuff immediately floored the accelerator and drove straight at the officers. According to the police report filed that day, three officers had to move quickly to avoid being hit. As the vehicle sped off, the patrolmen scrambled to their cars to give chase. McDuff raced south on Miller Street toward Waco Drive, turned off his lights and disappeared into the darkness, taking Brenda Thompson with him. He eluded police by going the wrong way on one-way streets. Eventually, he turned west on U.S. 84, and then north on Gholson Road for about eight miles until he arrived at a wooded area where, furious at the damage done to his prized pick up, he inflicted an excruciatingly torturous death on

Brenda. Her body was discovered near Gholson Road on October 3, 1998, just a month before McDuff's eventual execution.

* * *

On October 15, 1991, McDuff dated a 17-year-old hooker called Regenia DeAnne Moore. At around 11:30 p.m., the couple were seen arguing, outside a Waco motel, and a witness said they then drove away in a pick up truck. McDuff took Regenia to a remote area along Highway 6, north and east of Waco. At the site of a bridge traversing the Tehuacana Creek, McDuff pulled off the road on to a very steep embankment down to the edge of the creek, where he drove under the bridge. Passing motorists could not have seen his car. The road there is a freeway, and cars rushing over the bridge easily made enough noise to drown out any screams Regenia may have made.

A forensics team recovered Regenia's body, on Wednesday, September 29th, from a sinkhole near Tehuacana Creek. Her hands had been tied behind her back and her ankles were bound with stockings tied together in such a way as to allow her sufficient movement to hobble along. McDuff had apparently "marched" her to the spot where she was killed. The remains of her dress were wrapped around her pelvic area. She was found lying on her back with her legs bent. After being missing for seven years, Regenia was finally going home to her mother.

* * *

During the late afternoon of Sunday December 29, 1991, 28-year-old Colleen Reed, a native of Ville Platte, Louisiana, drove into Austin, Texas, where she deposited $200 at an ATM. She then went shopping, for a gallon of milk and a bottle of vitamins, at Whole Foods Market on North Lamar Boulevard and, afterward, drove to the carwash at West

Fifth Street. Witnesses recalled seeing a light-colored, late-model Ford Thunderbird, which was heading toward the carwash. They heard a short scream before the car's doors slammed shut and watched in amazement as the vehicle screeched away along Powell Street leaving a cloud of exhaust smoke in its wake.

Standing at 5 feet 3 inches, weighing 115 pounds, with dark-brown hair and brown eyes, Colleen was wearing gold-rimmed glasses, blue jeans, a T-shirt, and a black and white Nike jacket. Her body was found on October 6, 1998, after McDuff gave police the location of the grave. It was in a grassy area that had been a popular fishing and partying spot for McDuff when he was growing up.

By now, police suspected that he was a serial murderer, although he remained extremely elusive and almost impossible to track down. The best hope was that he would make a mistake. The pursuers' luck changed when Investigator Tim Steglich, of the Bell County Sheriff's Department, pulled in one of McDuff's known associates for questioning. What follows is the April 1992 statement of 34-year-old Alva Hank Worley, who was an accomplice of McDuff's in the abduction, rape and murder of Colleen Reed.

McDuff picked me up at 6 or 7 that night. We went to Love's Truck Stop near Temple, and he got gas. I don't know if he used a credit card or paid cash. We started to go towards Austin, and it was just kind of understood we were going to get some speed or coke, whatever we could find. We stopped at a Conoco truck stop on Interstate 35, on the northbound side of the highway, past Jarrell. I bought a six-pack of Budweiser Longnecks. We had already drunk a six-pack or better before that.

McDuff drove on to Austin, and I thought we were going down to the UT (University of Texas) campus to get the dope. But Mac drove downtown, and drove around because we had beer left. He would not let me get any more beer after the second six-pack. I don't know why. I know we went down Sixth Street and in that area. I remember we got a hamburger at Dairy Queen, I think on Congress. I remember the streets were real lit up at that time. We rode around and ate. Mac was just driving, and he pulled into a car wash, right into a bay, and I thought he was going to wash his car. I need to explain that we were in Mac's cream Ford Thunderbird. It was about 8:30, or 9 p.m. when we pulled into this wash.

Worley went on to explain that McDuff spotted the young woman, and within seconds he had her by the throat and was dragging her towards his car. "She was shouting like hell," Worley added, "She was screaming, 'Not me, not me. Please let me go.' '

"He took her to the driver's side and shoved her in the back seat. Her hands were tied behind her. I think she was saying, "Please let me go, please don't let this happen to me." I was stunned. I didn't know what to say. He got in the driver's seat and drove off, just fast enough to get away in a hurry."

Begging for her life, Colleen Reed was subjected to what can only be described as a ride of terror as the threesome headed north along Interstate 35 toward Round Rock, where McDuff pulled over and stopped the car. Climbing into the back with Colleen, McDuff ordered Worley to drive, and then the raping started.

I remember he told her to take her clothes off, so I don't know if he untied her. He was telling her, "All you have to do is fuck." He was trying to put it in her head that if she would just fuck, she would be turned loose. She was saying she would do what she was told. She was trying to buy time. That's what she was trying to do. Mac had his shirt off, and I believe he had his pants down. I do not know if the kid was facing up or down when he raped her. I remember he made her give him a blow job. I remember that because he almost choked her. Mac had hit her several times in the head when he first got in the back with her. He was forcing her head down on him, and she was choking.

I was just driving, and when I got to the Stillhouse Hollow exit, I decided to get out there to go to my sister's house. Mac was just sitting there at Stillhouse. I pulled over near the spillway, near the trailer houses there. I moved over to the passenger seat, and Mac got the keys out and popped the trunk. He pulled her out of the back seat, and put her in the trunk. She was quiet at that time and he had to force her into the trunk. That was the last time I saw that girl or heard anything about her. Mac drove to my sister's house.

After further questioning, Worley admitted that McDuff had asked to borrow his penknife and a shovel. He also said that McDuff had burned the woman, with a cigarette, on the vagina, but insisted that he did not know what happened to Colleen Reed after that. He said that he had not seen McDuff since.

The next day, Tim Steglich interviewed Worley for the second time. Under pressure from the intensive interrogation, he admitted that they had driven along a deserted track, just a mile from McDuff's parent's home at Temple.

"I did rape her," Worley finally conceded, "but Mac broke her neck after he tortured some more with the lighted cigarettes. He snapped her neck, and it sounded like a tree limb breaking, then he threw her, like a sack of potatoes, into the trunk of his car."

Frank Worley was charged with rape and murder, and he was held in the Travis County Jail, in lieu of $350,000 bail, while a manhunt for McDuff was launched. The body of Colleen Reed was recovered, shortly before McDuff's execution.

* * *

On Sunday, February 24, 1992, McDuff strangled a black, part-time prostitute and student called Valencia Joshua, while he was attending the Texas State Technical College in Waco. At the time, he was studying to become a machinist, and shared a campus dormitory with students who were half his age. He used his seniority to good effect, selling marijuana, methamphetamine, LSD and crack cocaine to his fellow students as a means of augmenting his student grant.

It is thought that Valencia had only been in Waco a week or two before being killed. "The public doesn't get as outraged when someone like Valencia turns up dead. But it's still a homicide and just as important as any other," said Richard Stroup, McLennan County Deputy Sheriff. The police described her as a "street person, but a sweet woman who loved children." She had no local address, no suitcase and no belongings. In fact, no one had a clue why she was in Waco at all. "She had no relatives there," said her father, Tommy, who lived in Bryan, and it was her mother, Roma, from Fort Worth, who finally reported her missing.

Twenty two-year-old Valencia had last been seen alive on the day she died, knocking on McDuff's dormitory door, number 118. The skinny woman was wearing a dark windbreaker, tight blue jeans, and an ornate barrette in her hair. When she received no answer, she went to the window and called out, "Are you ready yet?" She was not seen alive again.

On Sunday, March 15, 1992, walkers found a human skull, that had been exposed by animals behind the James Connally Municipal Golf Course and close to the college. An unclothed body was buried in soft, moist clay close by, and the deputies initially had just one lead to help them identify the corpse—a cloisonné hair comb lying near the body. The inlaid pattern depicted an orange butterfly among green leaves and red flowers—it was Valencia's proudest possession. Dallas medical examiners eventually identified the body by means of fingerprints.

Cause of death was recorded as strangulation.

McDuff was seen pushing a Ford Thunderbird car, a short distance from the Quik-Pak No. 8 convenience store in the 4200 block of La Salle Avenue, off Interstate 35, south of Waco, on Monday, March 1, 1992. Richard Bannister said he noticed the incident at about 3:45 p.m.

A little later that afternoon, 22-year-old Melissa Northrup went missing from her place of work, at the Quik-Pak store. Described as 4 feet 11 inches tall and weighing 110 pounds, with shoulder-length brown hair and blue eyes, Melissa was two and a half months pregnant. She lived with her accountant husband, Aaron, at 3014 Pioneer Circle, Waco. The diminutive young woman would have proved no match for a man of McDuff's height and bulk. He stood at over 6 feet and weighed in at 245 pounds.

At around 4:15 a.m., a local man, who knew Melissa, saw her car heading north on Interstate 35. She was in the front passenger seat and looked frightened.

When she did not return home, Aaron called her, and when he received no reply, he drove to the store, which was closed. The cash register drawer was open and the contents were missing. "A customer was in the store," Aaron later told police, "and when he saw me, he got real scared and threw his hands up in the air. I threw him the bathroom keys, and told him to please go look for my wife." Then he dialled 911. Police soon determined that $250 had been stolen from the cash register and, despite the fact that several people were sleeping in their cars close to the store, there were no witnesses to Melissa's abduction, although McDuff's Thunderbird was found close by.

At approximately 9:00 p.m. the same day, Shari Robinson said that McDuff arrived at her Dallas County home and he asked for some food.

Within hours of Melissa's abduction, McDuff's details were placed on the U.S. Most Wanted list, and appeals were placed in the newspapers, and on television, asking for information regarding his whereabouts. As the police intensified their manhunt, Mark Davis, a former college student friend of McDuff's, came forward to say that, on an earlier occasion, McDuff had tried to enlist him to rob the Quik-Pak store.

Another student, Lewis Bray, reported that McDuff had once boasted that the easiest way to get rid of a body was to slit the abdomen and throw it into water. It was also determined that McDuff had once worked at the Quik-Pak store and, ironically, he had been trained by Melissa's husband, Aaron.

A fisherman discovered Melissa's corpse, floating in a water-filled gravel pit in Southeast Dallas County, at 6:00 p.m. on Sunday, April 26th. The body was partially dressed, in a purple suit and a dark colored jacket. Part of her lower torso was missing. Her car, a burned-orange 1977 Buick Regal with a white vinyl top, licence plate TX LP287 XHV, was found, parked, just a mile away and close to Shari Robinson's home. After forensic tests had been completed, human hairs, identical in every respect to those taken from McDuff, were found on the car's upholstery.

* * *

McDuff was committing his murders throughout Texas, thereby creating jurisdictional problems which brought a dozen law enforcement agencies to the conference table to coordinate their inquiries. What was needed was to combine the organizational capabilities of the FBI, U.S. Marshals Service and the Texas Rangers, but rape and murder are State rather than federal offences.

Two U.S. Marshals from Waco, Mike and Parnell McNamara, had an idea which offered a way out of the bureaucratic impasse. They had been told that during the time McDuff was at the technical college, he had been supplying LSD and was known to be in possession of a firearm, both of which are federal offenses. Consequently, on Friday, March 6, 1992, the local State Attorney issued warrant No 9280-0310-

0506-Z for McDuff's arrest. Two months later, they had the break they were waiting for.

Thirty six-year-old Gary Smithee worked for a Kansas City refuse collection company. After arriving home on Friday, May 1, 1992, he tuned his TV to *America's Most Wanted* and, as was his usual practice, videotaped the program. Smithee was taken by the $5,000 reward for information leading to the arrest of Kenneth McDuff and thought he saw a striking resemblance between the face on the screen and a new co-worker named Richard Fowler. The new man had created an impression with his constant boasting about his sexual prowess, particularly with very young women.

Smithee thought very carefully about the implications of reporting his suspicions. He did not want to upset Fowler, but the chance of a fast $5,000 was too good an opportunity to miss. He discussed the tape he had made of the TV program with a work colleague before phoning the Kansas City Police. Sergeant J.D. Johnson took the call, and immediately ran a search through their computer for the name Richard Fowler. Information came on the screen reporting that a man, answering a description that fitted both Fowler and McDuff, had been arrested during a prostitution sting and been charged with soliciting. The detective then carried out a fingerprint comparison between the two names with the result that Fowler's record card matched that of McDuff.

The next morning, Johnson ascertained which truck McDuff was due to join as a crew member and determined the route that the trash-collection truck would take on Monday, May 4th. He learned that it would be going to a landfill site, south of Kansas City, between 1:00 p.m. and 2:00 p.m. The police set up a six-man surveillance team working under the guise of a commercial vehicle stop detail. "We wanted to make sure the location we picked was isolated in the event of trouble," Johnson explained. "McDuff was reported to be armed and dangerous. The site we picked was the type where some vehicles were routinely stopped, and there were no people around."

To lend further authenticity to their plans, the police borrowed a car that Kansas City Engineers used for their routine truck inspections. When the vehicle in which McDuff was riding approached, a lone officer waved it to the checkpoint. Instantly smelling danger, McDuff made an attempt to get out and make a run for it, but he was stopped in his tracks at gunpoint and made no further attempt to escape.

McDuff was indicted in the Fifty-fourth Judicial District Court of McLennan County, Texas, on June 26, 1992, for the capital murder of Melissa Northrup while in the course of committing and attempting to commit kidnapping, robbery, or the murder of another pursuant to the same scheme and course of conduct. He was found guilty as charged.

On February 18, 1993, following a separate punishment hearing, the jury affirmatively answered the first special issue submitted to Article 37. 071(b) (1) of the Texas Code of Criminal Procedure, and answered negatively to the second special issue submitted pursuant to Article 37. 071(e). In accordance with the State law, the trial court imposed the death sentence.

McDuff's conviction and sentence were automatically appealed to the Texas Court of Criminal Appeals, which affirmed the conviction on April 28, 1997.

Then, McDuff filed a petition for a writ of *certiorari* to the U.S. Supreme Court, a legal technicality requesting that proceedings be moved to a higher court. This was denied on January 12, 1998.

Next, McDuff filed a petition for a State writ of *habeas corpus* which was denied, on April 15, 1998, by the Texas Court of Criminal Appeals.

On April 29, 1998, the Fifty-fourth Judicial Court of McLennan County, Texas, set McDuff's execution date for October 21, 1998.

Counsel was appointed on April 30, 1998, to represent McDuff in the U.S. District Court for the Western District of Texas, Waco Division.

On July 8, 1998, McDuff filed a petition for a Federal Writ of *habeas corpus.* The State responded with an answer and motion for summary judgment on McDuff's claims.

The Western District Court denied *habeas corpus* relief on October 15, 1998, granting summary judgment for the State, and lifting the stay of execution. The court also rescheduled McDuff's execution for November 17, 1998.

McDuff filed a notice of appeal on October 23rd and, three days later, the Western District Court denied McDuff's request for a certificate of appealability. His appeal to the Fifth U.S. Circuit Court of Appeals was denied, and the Supreme Court denied his last appeal for a stay of execution on November 16, 1998.

* * *

Assistant Warden-in-Charge of Executions in Texas, Neil Hodges is a man familiar with the routine of carrying out executions by lethal injection. Speaking about the reality of this method of judicial death, he said, "People think this is all painless and stuff like that. It ain't! Basically, they [the condemned] suffer a lot. They are sort of paralyzed, but they can hear. They drown in their own fluid and suffocate to death really.

"Yeah, we get problems. Sometimes the guy doesn't want to get on to the table. But we have the largest guard in Texas here. He gets them on that table, no problem. They are strapped down in seconds. No problem. They go on that mean old table and get the goodnight juice, whether they like it or not."

On November 17, 1998, a large group of reporters stood outside the Walls Prison in Huntsville, Texas, in an area reserved for the press. The Walls is the oldest of all the prison units in Texas. It also houses the death chamber. Perfectly suiting the occasion, a single, heavy, dark cloud hovered over the prison. Near a concrete picnic table, a jungle of photographers' tripods looked like a flock of ostriches. Mercifully, a gentle breeze flapped at the cautionary yellow "DO NOT CROSS" police tapes. No one in the press saw a single anti-death penalty protester.

Earlier in the day, inmate number 999055, Kenneth McDuff had been taken from his cell at Ellis Unit, and driven 15 miles to the Walls. Even for a stone-cold killer like McDuff, his first sight of the death house was a sobering one. The truck that had brought him to his final destination, pulled to a stop in front of a set of wire gates topped with razor wire, glinting and sparkling in the Texas sunlight. Shackled and cuffed, he was led through two steel doors. On his left was a row of cells; he was allocated the second one, furnished simply with a bunk, a small table and a chair. The bed linen was spotless, as were the cream-painted walls. Next to McDuff's cell was a "strictly no contact" cell. The door was covered with a fine steel mesh screen, painted black. It was used by inmates, should they wish to give instructions to an attorney.

In the corridor, and to his right, was another wooden table with two chairs. On it, McDuff noticed a Bible and a telephone. There was no ashtray as smoking was forbidden.

Lethal injection was first legally introduced as a method of execution in 1977 in the States of Oklahoma and Texas. The first prisoner to die by this means was 43-year-old Charlie Brooks, who had been sentenced to death for his part in the murder of a used car dealer in Fort Worth, in 1971. Brooks finally gave up his appeals against the death sentence and died in Huntsville Prison on December 7, 1982.

The practice of giving hospital patients a pre-med injection to sedate them before going into the operating theater, prior to general anaesthesia, is a common procedure. It relaxes the patient and takes away the tension. This concept offered a number of advantages to those responsible for dispatching condemned inmates to perdition. The drugs were certainly available and cheap to use. There was also the added humane dimension inasmuch as lethal injection was a clinical procedure carried out in appropriate surroundings. Gone were the dread gallows, the ominous electric chair with all its wiring and leather helmet and death mask. Gone, too, was the evil-looking gas chamber, with its sickly green-colored walls and mass of rods, tubes and linkages. When using a lethal cocktail of drugs, the condemned inmate would be led from a holding cell to a hospital gurney to be strapped down and injected intravenously.

There were benefits as well for the state authorities. The whole idea would appeal to the media and public alike, for execution could not possibly be made more merciful. A team of paramedics would attend to the inserting of a needle into the victim's right or left arm, and a doctor would be, as with all executions, in attendance to pronounce death.

Addie McDuff had arrived too late to see her son on his last day and he was allowed no special privileges other than a choice of menu for his final meal, which consisted of two T-bone steaks, five fried eggs, vegetables, French fries, coconut pie and a single Coca-Cola. As he completed his meal, he contemplated the end, which he thought would be painless, but he didn't know that he was going to be injected with a combination of three drugs, all acidic, with a pH value higher than 6, which would burn so terribly that he would feel as if he was being injected with fire.

At 5:58 p.m., the warden received word that the Supreme Court had turned down McDuff's final request for a stay of execution, and the witnesses started to arrive through the main prison gate to be escorted to the Death House. They might have noticed the sheeting, now draped over the steel gates, hiding the hearse that was waiting to receive the body. After being given a body search to check for hidden weapons or concealed cameras, they were led to the viewing room, which was separated from the gurney by a window and closed curtains.

At 5:44 p.m. the killer was given a pre-injection of 8cc 2 percent sodium pentothal. Waiting silently, in an adjacent room, was the cell extraction team, wearing protective clothing and armed with mace to subdue McDuff if he caused trouble. Their particular skills had never been called upon at an execution in Texas.

At 6:08 p.m., McDuff was invited to leave his cell. He agreed and no guard touched him as he walked the few steps to the chamber door, which opened before him. He paused, momentarily, when he saw the gurney with its white padding and cover sheet. Two arm supports were pulled out and he saw the brown straps dangling loose with an officer by each one.

At 7:08 p.m., McDuff was strapped down, and the paramedics inserted two 16-gauge needles and catheters into both of his arms. These were connected by flexible tubes to the executioner's position which was hidden from view. The doctor also attached a cardiac monitor and stethoscope to the prostrate man's chest.

The curtains were drawn back and Warden Jim Willett asked McDuff if he had any last words to say into the microphone above his head. McDuff replied simply, "I'm ready to be released. Release me." Inside the witness area, Parnell McNamara gently placed his hand on the shoulder of 74-year-old Jack Brand.

"I've been waiting for this for 32 years," said the father of Robert Brand, who was murdered by McDuff in 1966.

"Are you all right?" Parnell asked quietly.

"I feel like 32 years have been lifted from my life," the old man said.

McDuff looked scared as, over the next ten seconds, he was given an injection of sodium thiopental, a fast acting anaesthetic which takes effect within about ten seconds. He would have felt a slight pressure, and his arm start to ache. Then he would feel light-headed.

After a one minute interval, this was followed by 15cc of normal saline, to ease the passage of 50mg/50cc Pancuronium bromide. Pavulon is a curare-derived muscle relaxant which paralyzes respiratory function and brings unconsciousness in about ten seconds.

McDuff felt pressure in his chest. It was a suffocating feeling that

caused him to gasp several times for air. He was dizzy and hyper-
ventilating; his heart beat faster and faster as his entire nervous system
came under attack. This is called the stress syndrome, a common
feature during the first stages of dying.

As the poison permeated through his body, McDuff entered the
second stage of death. He was unable to breathe or move, but he could
still see and hear. He was paralyzed and not able to swallow at this stage,
a condition which leads many witnesses to believe that death has inter-
vened. McDuff was still alive, but his central nervous system was
beginning to shut down. His eyes dilated and the hairs on his skin stood
erect as he was injected with another 15cc of saline and, finally, a
massive dose of Potassium Chloride (1.50–2.70mEq/kg). When
injected intravenously in large doses, this drug burns and hurts,
because it is a naturally occurring salt and instantly disrupts the
chemical balance of the blood. It causes the muscles to tighten up in
extreme contraction and the instant it reaches the heart muscle, it
causes the heart to stop beating. While McDuff was sedated by the
thiopental and couldn't draw breath because of the Pavulon, he was
physically unable to scream in pain when the potassium was injected,
sending his heart into a crunching, excruciating cramp.

There was a two minute wait while the doctors examined McDuff
and pronounced him dead. The curtains were opened for the witnesses
to view the body. Mrs. Brenda Soloman, mother of one of McDuff's
victims, was moved to say, "He looked like the devil. He's going where
he needs to go. I feel happy ... I feel wonderful."

The cost of the drugs administered to take McDuff's life was $86.08.

* * *

"The sad thing about this particular case is that, if Colleen had
screamed and someone had heard her, it would have been McDuff's

mother. She would have been in earshot because she lives just a few hundred yards away," commented Investigator Tim Steglich.

Inquiries into the life and crimes of Kenneth Allen McDuff included interviews with his mother, Addie, his schoolteachers and several residents of Rosebud who knew the McDuffs well. I spoke to Falls County Sheriff, Larry Pamplin; McDuff's accomplice, Roy Dale Green, who now lives in a flea-ridden shack in Marlin; U.S. Marshals, Mike and Parnell McNamara; the State prosecutor, Bill Johnston; and Tim Steglich. Background research included a visit, accompanied by Tim Steglich, to the lonely track where McDuff murdered Colleen Reed. "In the dead of night, that would be a terrible place to die," said States Attorney William "Bill" Johnston, with just a hint of tears in his eyes.

The McDuff family are a tough lot, with a reputation to match. The "Pistol Packin' Momma," Addie McDuff, had never given an interview, and even refused to speak to the police, but she made a rare exception by speaking to me. Such is her reputation for pulling a gun that the Waco police offered to keep watch, outside her isolated ranch at Belton, and waited until I emerged unscathed. Although I was expecting immediate hostility, a frail, confused old lady appeared at the door offering a traditionally cautious Texas welcome.

Addie is a protective mother, despite her son's evil deeds. Over coffee—and she apologized that she didn't have tea—she explained that one of her sons had been shot dead, while sleeping with another man's wife, and that a daughter had died in a road crash. Mr. McDuff had been buried way back, and now she had no one except a niece. Addie was about to sell up and move in with her.

Asked how she had acquired the name "Pistol Packin' Momma," she smiled. "Rosebud was a tough place to live in the early days," she said in a cracked voice. "The driver of a school bus threatened to throw Ken off as he had spent the fare. It was dark, and no boy of mine was gonna walk a long ways home. So, I just visited the bus depot the next morning, and pulled out my .22. Told him that next time he did it, it would be his last." Then she chuckled, "No one never did talk down to my family again."

She rooted through cardboard boxes of mementoes, looking for documents or any picture of Ken in his early days, but there was precious little to find. She had destroyed everything years ago.

The next port of call was Rosebud itself. A dusty, one-horse town, and, with just over 1,000 inhabitants, it has the pretension to call itself a city. Main Street is nearly always deserted, even on weekends. During a "Texas Barbeque," a mid-afternoon indoor feast, the town manager, a reporter, several residents, and the 70-year-old Chief of Police, recalled the young Ken McDuff. Clearly, they had been terrorized by the youth in those days, a feeling supported by Falls County Sheriff Larry Pamplin, whose father was the sheriff before him. Driving me around in his beat up, unmarked police cruiser, which was stocked full of shotguns and pistols, Larry explained that McDuff and his older brother, John, were among the roughest hooligans he had ever met. Larry Pamplin has since been dismissed from office, after committing aggravated assault, official misconduct and racketeering. It was proved that he had misspent funds to feed his prisoners, keeping a tidy sum back for himself.

Interviewing Regenia Moore's mother in a Waco motel proved a harrowing experience. She is now a mental wreck who, for several years, drove the dirt roads of Waco, with a spade, in search of her missing daughter's body. "I don't wish ill on McDuff," she sobbed, "I just want to give her a Christian burial, just as Addie McDuff will want for her son." Her wish has now been granted.

Finally, there was the much anticipated meeting with Kenneth McDuff, on death row, Ellis Unit, Texas. In life, he was a tall man, well built, with greasy, black hair. Wearing a constant sneer, he whinged on for an hour about the injustices committed by the judicial and prison system. He argued about the merest technicalities of his case yet, ever the hypocrite, he admitted all of the crimes attributed to him, while refusing to say where his victims were buried, unless he was paid a handsome fee.

"I don't think that the state of Texas will let me live, unless they want me to have a long drawn-out, slow life. I have sugar diabetes, so at some point I am going to have some serious problems. But the bottom line is—I want to be the one to decide when I'm to die. And I will do this by deciding when I'm going to drop my appeals. I've never been one to run, and I won't grant them the satisfaction of running me all the way to the ground. I believe there is a good possibility that both my convictions may be reversed."

Asked why he had not settled down and started some form of meaningful relationship with a woman, he replied, "I feel very old and tired. Once I wanted a wife and family just like other people do. Right now I'm like a man in the desert that is thousands of miles from the nearest water, with no possibility of reaching water, but keeps walking anyway. I don't know why I keep walking. Is it some inter-instinct [sic] to strive on?

"Now, let's talk about money. Well, on this one, I'm like the man in the desert that struck gold, and can only carry out what he can carry. I only have need for a few thousand dollars, like for burial expenses, and to maintain myself while I live. I will charge whomever, $700 per body. Use an international money order or postal orders will do. Have it sent to my inmate's trust fund in my name. When the first amount clears, I'll give you and the law a body. That way I don't get shafted, you know."

Now, that is an expression of true evil.

This chapter is based on exclusive, videotaped death row interviews between Christopher Berry-Dee and Kenneth Allen McDuff within Ellis Unit, Huntsville, Texas in 1995, and extensive correspondence.

DOUGLAS DANIEL CLARK & CAROL MARY BUNDY

"I used to be a good-looking guy, ya know.

But, see what they done to me in here.

My hair is falling out, my teeth are rotten and

still they want to kill me. Still we all gotta fuckin' die

some time. I've outlived the judge, and the prosecutor;

it's just they're killing an innocent man."

DOUGLAS CLARK TO THE AUTHOR
AT SAN QUENTIN STATE PRISON, 1995

The California Department of Corrections has an annual operating budget in excess of $3.4 billion, with around 124,000 inmates being confined at any one time. San Quentin—also known as "S.Q."—is not only the most notorious prison in the state, it is also arguably the toughest in the country. It houses the state's death row where, at any one time, up to 500 men may be awaiting execution. These days, in a gesture towards more humane methods, death is administered by lethal injection. Douglas Daniel Clark is one of these death row inmates. He costs about $50 a day to keep fit and well for his execution.

It is a 500-yard walk from the gate of S.Q. to the menacing front portico. Once through this entry, and just 30 feet down a corridor, is an interview room. Opposite, in a secure holding area, a tirade of foul language is issued by Clark, who is chained to a strong point on the wall. He is also shackled, handcuffed to a body belt, and his ankles are bound with steel chain.

Forget Hannibal Lecter, because Clark looks the epitome of evil and he is not acting. His blue eyes are wild and demonic. His hair is unkempt and prematurely grey. But it is his mouth that is so foul, in every way. The teeth in it are rotten and he spouts an incessant stream of venomous filth. Assisted by guards, he shuffles forward to meet his visitor, with intimidating hatred emanating from every inch of his powerfully built, 6-foot frame. He is wearing a grey prison sweater and loosely fitting slacks, and a baseball cap is perched, cockeyed, on his head. He is also sweating profusely.

However repulsive they may be, looks and foul language don't make a killer and, as Clark's story unfolded, it would prove to become an enthralling whodunit. Moreover, his life may even be a monument to the frustrated protestations of an innocent man.

During the summer months of 1980, a string of horrifying murders rocked Hollywood. All of the victims were hookers, trading sex for dollars along the notorious Sunset Boulevard. This prompted the press to dub the, as-yet-unknown, serial killer "The Sunset Slayer." The principal players in this dance of death were Carol Mary Bundy, Douglas Daniel Clark, and John "Jack" Robert Murray.

Carol Bundy (no relation to the serial killer, Ted Bundy) is short and unattractive. Her mother, Gladys, was part Algonquin Indian, and her father, Charles Peters, was a French-Canadian with a build that might be described as roly-poly. Carol once remarked that, "He was a male version of me with a bald head. He had blue eyes, a pleasant appearance, and a dynamite personality. He was a good father. He worshipped me because I was bright."

Born in 1943, Carol was the second of three children and the family lived in various cities across the U.S. She claims to have attended 23 different schools before the ninth grade. By the age of 11, she had already started shoplifting, and stealing money from her parents and neighbors.

Gladys Peters died of a heart attack on Sunday, June 10, 1957. The following night Carol says she was in bed with her father who "performed oral sex on me and sexually abused my 11-year-old sister." One night, just after her sixteenth birthday, she was sent out to a local store, by her father, to buy provisions. When she arrived home, she claims, she found "globs of blood everywhere and a rifle on a chair." She explained that her father, who was remarried by then, couldn't take life any more and had planned to commit murder. "That's why he sent me to the store," she said. "He was going to kill his new wife while I was gone, then kill me when I got home." Apparently, the plan literally backfired when he and his wife wrestled with the rifle, which discharged, blowing off his thumb.

After this incident, Carol's stepmother arranged for the children to be taken to a foster home. This was a temporary arrangement, for then they were packed off to Indiana to live with an uncle. Two years later, Charles Peters hanged himself. He was 52.

Carol was married in 1960, to a 33-year-old pimp whom she had known for two weeks. The marriage had lasted only six days when Carol left because her husband apparently wanted her to have sex with his friends. She was not prepared to tolerate that sort of treatment, although she later told psychiatrists that she had been involved in sex for gain before marrying, and also claimed to have been a prostitute in Portland, Oregon, in the mid 1960s.

Following her divorce from the pimp, Carol says she tried to pull her life together by attending the Santa Monica City College, where she studied to become a vocational nurse. Unfortunately, the college is unable to support her claim that she graduated class in 1968.

The following year, she married a hospital orderly named Grant Bundy. This marriage lasted 11 years and the couple had two boys. But Grant was a woman beater, and court records show that, in January 1979, Carol sought refuge in a battered women's shelter before leaving him and going on welfare. She attempted suicide on two occasions. After taking a job as a licensed vocational nurse at the Valley Medical Center in Los Angeles, Carol, now overweight, moved with her two children to Valerio Gardens, an apartment block in Van Nuys, which was managed by Jack Murray.

John "Jack" Murray—full name John Robert Murray—was a 41-year-old Australian who lived with his wife and two children. He had a reputation as a ladies' man and, in no time at all, he and Carol were in the throes of an affair. Recently divorced from her second husband, whom she called a "homosexual screaming faggot," Bundy received half the sale proceeds of her previous home. This was a substantial amount and horny Murray, to give him a more appropriate name, soon got wind of Carol's good fortune. Lavishing love, care and attention over her, Murray encouraged her to have her eyesight examined. She had appalling vision, to the extent that she was subsequently declared blind and therefore eligible for monthly disability payments from the Social Security.

Murray was not known for being a philanthropist, or even charit-

"I hate women with a passion ... they always played mind games with my head."
Harvey Louis Carignan

"The human meat, well, ah, it tastes like pork ... I don't know why I ate parts of people, but I just did."
Arthur John Shawcross, the Genesee River Killer

Courtesy of Christopher Berry-Dee

"There was nothing they could have said or done. They were dead as soon as I saw them." The author with Michael Bruce Ross on Death Row.

"It all happened so fast. Once I started, I just couldn't stop. It went so fast."
Ronald DeFeo Jr.

"Look, I can't remember their faces or their names ... but I'm telling you that he's got to be seriously dead by now."
Aileen Carol Wuornos

"Killing a woman's like killing a chicken. They both squawk."
Kenneth Allen McDuff

"I used to be a good-looking guy, ya know. But, see what they done to me in here. My hair is falling out, my teeth are rotten and they still want to kill me."

Douglas Daniel Clark and Carol Mary Bundy

"I had no intention of killing her. I don't know whether it was me or what. That was my first, my worst, and the hardest to get over."
Henry Lee Lucas

John Wayne Gacy in 1978.

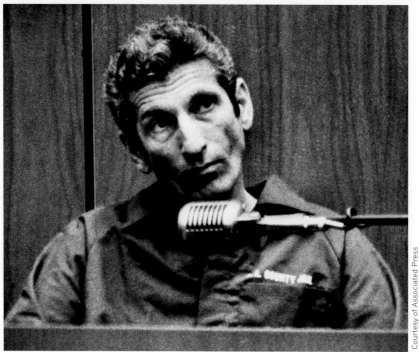

Angelo Buono, Kenneth Bianchi's accomplice, sits on the witness stand.

Kenneth Bianchi, the Hillside Strangler, in November 1978. A little under a year later, he would be sentenced to life in prison.

able, for he conned money out of his friends and frequently cheated on his wife. On one occasion, he was caught pocketing wads of notes from a telethon charity collection with which he had been involved, and there is no doubt that Bundy's disability payments found their way to Murray's pocket, too.

When he eventually learned of Carol's sizeable bank account, the relationship changed direction, becoming one of prostitute and john in reverse. Now completely infatuated with Murray, she started paying him for sex and, by the end of that year, he had wheedled $18,000 out of her on the grounds that he needed the money for his wife's nonexistent cancer operation. In reality, he used half to pay off the outstanding debt on his Chevrolet van, a vehicle that he frequently used as his mobile sex den. The balance was used to refurbish the vehicle's interior.

By Christmas 1979, Bundy was so obsessed with Murray's sado-sexual performances on her that she approached his unsuspecting wife, offering her $1500 in exchange for her husband. The woman was so furious that she insisted that Bundy vacate the apartment complex, while Jack timidly agreed to keep the peace. For him, it was a matter of selfish economics, as his wife cooked his meals and washed his clothes, services he could not afford to lose. Also, from a purely cynical view-point, Carol was simply his subservient sex partner. Now that he had acquired most of her money, she was of no further use to him. Never-theless, he did arrange for her to move into an apartment on Lemona Avenue, Van Nuys, and some three miles from his home.

On arriving at Lemona Avenue, in May 1980, Carol was immediately attracted to a neighbor's 11-year-old daughter, named Shannon. The girl was mentally and physically well developed, and the unlikely pair established a relationship by trading adult jokes. Inevitably, this arrangement took on a sexual dimension and Bundy encouraged the minor to cross the bridge from gentle petting and cuddling to full-blown lesbianism.

Despite their apparent split, Jack and Carol continued their clandestine affair, but in a less evident manner. Progressively, the sex turned increasingly deviant, and the couple tried to encourage other young girls to indulge in three-way sex with them. Fortunately, they were all put off by Bundy's unsavory looks and, now totally dejected, she took her two sons out of school and sent them to the Midwest to live with their father's parents.

* * *

"Carol Bundy, that half-blind bitch? She shit-canned her kids and sent them in a handbasket to Hell."

DOUGLAS CLARK DURING HIS INTERVIEW
AT SAN QUENTIN STATE PRISON

Douglas Clark had been born Daniel Clark, in 1948, in Pennsylvania, where his father, Franklyn, was stationed in the Navy. He was the third son of five children. In the third grade, he decided that he wanted to be called Doug instead of Daniel. The family moved regularly, from Pennsylvania to Seattle, to Berkley, England, and Japan. By 1958, Franklyn had retired from the Navy as a Lieutenant Commander. In 1959, he moved, with his wife Blanch and their children, Frank Jr., Carol Anne, Doug and Jon Ronlyn, to Kwajalein, an atoll in the Marshall Islands, where he took up a civilian position running the supply department for the Transport Company of Texas. Blanch worked as a radio controller.

They spent two years in Kwajalein, living a life of colonial privilege, in a housing complex that was built specifically for the many American families who lived on the atoll. When they returned to America, they lived in Berkley, England, for a short time before moving to India. The Clarks lived in a manner reserved for only the very wealthy back in the

States, with a number of servants who would wait dutifully on the children and parents alike.

Other Americans living in the area described the Clark family as pleasant people who kept themselves to themselves. As for Doug, none could remember any startling behavior problems, although they had found that if Doug was ever in trouble for any of the usual childhood pranks, his father would defend him aggressively, refusing to acknowledge his son's responsibility for his behavior.

Later, both Walter and Doug were sent to Ecolat, the International School in Geneva attended by the children of U.N. diplomats, international celebrities and European and Middle Eastern royalty. Unlike his brother Walt, who was popular and outgoing, Doug was considered sullen and arrogant and made few friends. He did not do well with his studies, as he couldn't be bothered to do the work or complete assignments. Doug Clark claimed that he had developed his preferences for kinky sex while living in Geneva. He was expelled from Ecolat for this reason.

After he left Geneva, 16-year-old Doug was sent to Culver Military Academy in Indiana. Frank Jr. and Carol Ann had already left home by this time and Walt was sent to a boarding school in Arizona; Jon Ronlyn joined him there later. Doug's parents continued to move around the world: first to Venezuela, then Perth, Western Australia.

Although intelligent, Doug Clark was happy to scrape through his schooling with minimal effort. He was involved in a number of sports and played saxophone in the dance band. In the three years that he attended the Academy, he did not have any close friends. Instead, he hung around with a group of kids who shared Doug's distain for authority and had a distinct "don't give a fuck" attitude. He would boast of his family's wealth and his sexual exploits, oblivious to his friends' annoyance and boredom. The fact that most of his classmates refused to mix with him, and would often avoid contact with him altogether, did not seem to bother him at all.

Doug's behavior and attitude led to many meetings with the school therapist, Colonel Gleeson. Despite the fact that Gleeson had written many letters informing the Clarks of their son's bad conduct, they showed no concern. In the time he was there, he only received one visit from his mother. The only visit his father made occurred while the boy was on vacation.

Like most teenage boys, Doug and his classmates were obsessed with teenage girls and the fantasy of sex, but for Doug it was much more than fantasy. He would often bring a girl to his room where he would record their moans and groans as he had sex with them. He would then replay the tapes to his classmates, revelling in the obvious jealousy.

At 17, Doug claimed to meet the love of his life at a Culver dance, where he took her away from another boy. Despite his claims to have been in love with Bobbi, he would take photographs of them having sex and pass them around the school, enjoying the notoriety that they brought him.

In 1967, at the age of 19, Clark graduated from Culver and went to live with his parents, who were now retired and living in Yosemite. When he was drafted, he enlisted in the Air Force in radio intelligence to ensure that he would not end up in the front line in the Vietnam War. He went first to Texas, and then Anchorage, Alaska, where he was given the job of decoding Russian messages.

The military discipline in Anchorage reminded him of Culver and he resented his senior officers' corrections, but the city life made up for it. He spent most of his time in the many strip bars where he would nurture his ego as he left each night with one of the dancers hanging on his arm. Before his term was up, Douglas Clark left the Air Force with an honorable discharge, a National Defense Service medal and his benefits intact. What the events were that led up to this are unknown as his story is different every time he tells it, and the Air Force will not reveal anything. Doug claims that he had been witness to the murder of a black man by a white man, and that he had fled when he was called in for questioning.

With over $5,000, Doug planned to drive from Alaska to the Mexican border, but stopped when he got to Van Nuys, in Los Angeles, where he moved in with his sister, Carol Ann, who was living with her abusive husband.

At 24 he met, and later married, 27-year-old Beverley in a North Hollywood bar. Blonde and heavy, the woman saw herself as fat and ugly, but felt that Doug, with his big dreams and ambitions, would always try to build her up.

They bought a car upholstery business, which Doug ran, while Beverley had a job and did the books at weekends. He insisted that he was the one with the intelligence, not she, and refused to listen to any advice she gave about the business. Whenever they began to get ahead financially, Doug would quickly blow it. During the 1970s, the business began to falter, so they sold it. To pay off their debts, Doug worked in a gas station and as a security guard before he started buying goods at auctions to resell at swap meets. Beverley had the job of loading and unloading the truck because, in his opinion, he was a better salesperson than she was.

Although Beverley could not exactly say what went wrong in the marriage, she did say that Doug was lazy. She would not consider the fact that he liked to wear her underwear as any more unusual than his desire to try wife-swapping, or three-way sex.

As Beverley gained more weight during their marriage, Doug spent less and less time at home, preferring to go to bars. According to Carol Ann, her brother drank heavily and would become over anxious and angry when drunk. Beverley would deny this, even though she had persuaded him to join Alcoholics Anonymous as a condition of them staying together. He kept off the booze for two years.

Doug was ambitious but could not commit himself to the work that was required to achieve the success he longed for. It had been Beverley's suggestion that he apply to work for the city as a steam-plant trainee. He agreed and actually completed the training course.

In 1976, four years after they were married, Doug and Beverley separated and later divorced, although they remained close friends.

Douglas Clark began work at the Jergen's soap factory in 1979. His duties as an engineer required him to tend the large boiler. While not befitting his level of education, he enjoyed the sense of power that controlling the three-story structure gave him.

In February 1980, Clark set fire to his car outside the factory, while he was working the night shift, in order to claim the insurance. He later bragged to Carol Bundy that the real reason was to destroy evidence.

By the time he met Bundy, Clark had developed quite a talent for insinuating himself into the lives of fat, unattractive women who would willingly give him free rent, food and money in return for the attention he gave them. When the women demanded more in return, he would quickly leave them and move on to the next lonely soul.

Douglas Daniel Clark had an incredibly smooth manner. He was also well read and liked to sprinkle his conversation with quotations from Shakespeare and French phrases. Thirty-one-year-old Clark was a handsome man with a soft, slightly European speaking voice, a gift which enabled him to have the pick of any woman he chose. He was a leech and a sexual hedonist who enjoyed nothing more than a varied choice of eager girlfriends who were willing to share their home with him. Indeed, at times he was so much in demand he would even forget where he was actually living himself. Just after the Christmas of 1979, Carol Bundy, then aged 37, met Doug Clark at the Little Nashville Country Club where Murray sang Tom Jones hits.

On the evening of their first meeting, Carol Bundy and Douglas Clark spent the night together. On learning of Doug's rent problems with his landlady, Carol offered him lodgings in her apartment. For a short period, the arrangement was mutually satisfactory. Put simply, Clark traded his body and sex for a roof over his head. Eventually, he came to the view that cash for sex would be more agreeable to him. During his brief stay at Lemona Avenue, Bundy introduced Clark to her sexual playmate, Shannon.

The tempting proximity of the sexually advanced youngster, and Carol's encouragement for three-way sex, proved irresistible to Clark. Bundy photographed him simulating sex with the made-up child, an exposure which would later prove to be his undoing. During an interview at San Quentin State Prison, Clark ranted on about the subject, saying, "I had sex with Bundy about three times in all our relationship, although Carol will say otherwise. Murray was her intense S&M lover. She and Jack had sex with the 11-year-old. He tried to orally and vaginally rape the kid. They repeatedly tried to engage my roommate, Nancy, in three-way sex. Carol even tried to get Nancy to join her and Shannon in three-way female sex. She told Nancy and Shannon not to let me know she was busy with Jack, trying to have sex with them, since I would not like her and her lover fuckin' around with one of my girlfriends."

* * *

The first confirmed murders committed by the Sunset Slayer were the double killing of 15-year-old Gina Marano and 16-year-old Cynthia Chandler. The naked bodies of the two attractive teenagers were found, on an incline off the Ventura Freeway, by a Caltrans street cleaner on Thursday, June 12, 1980. The medical examiner established that they had died the previous day. Cynthia was killed by a single .25 caliber gunshot wound to the back of her head, which had left the bullet lodged in her brain, and a second shot had penetrated her lung bursting open her heart. It was also determined that both shots had been fired at point blank range. Gina had also been shot twice. One round entered behind her left ear, exiting near her right eyebrow, and the second bullet blasted through the back of her head, also exiting behind the left ear.

At around 8:00 p.m., on Saturday, June 14th, a woman called the LAPD Northeast Division in Van Nuys. She told a detective that she thought her lover was a murderer. "What I'm trying to do," she said, while officers recorded the call, "is to ascertain whether or not the individual I know, who happens to be my lover, did in fact do this. He said he did. My name is Betsy."

Later in the same call, she changed her name to Claudia. The police were anxious to learn the full name of the alleged killer. The informant refused to give out this vital information, but when pressed, she did give a brief description. "He has curly brown hair and blue eyes. His Christian name is John, and he's 41 years old," she added. "I've found a duffel bag in his car, full of bloody blankets, paper towels, and his clothes."

This description matched Jack Murray perfectly, and not Clark, who was only 37 at the time. Warming now to her theme, the woman added, "He tells me he fired four shots. Two in one girl's head and virtually blew her head away. One shot in the head and one shot in the chest of the other girl. He used a .25 caliber pistol. Does that jive with what you've got?" When the caller hung up, a detective wrote on the tape cassette, "Either the killer, or one who knows the killer!"

Over the following days, investigators compiled a list of people who had purchased .25 caliber pistols in recent months. Carol Mary Bundy's name came up for she had purchased two .22 caliber Raven automatics in Van Nuys on Friday, April 25th. In fact, she was the only female on the register. The gun shop provided the police with her address, vehicle registration and social security number. Amazingly, the police chose to ignore this crucial information, despite the previous telephone call from a woman, indicating a connection with two of the murders. Why the police chose to act this way would remain a mystery for some time to come.

Meanwhile, on Saturday, June 22nd, Bundy moved from her apartment to Verdugo Avenue in Burbank. Clark, among others, helped her by taking her furniture and other possessions across town to her new home, which was a stone's throw from his place of employment at the Jergens soap factory.

At 3:05 a.m. the next day, a Burbank police officer found the fully-clothed body of prostitute Karen Jones lying in the gutter of a residential street near the NBC studios in Hollywood. She had been shot in the temple, with a .25 caliber pistol, and there were indications were that she had been thrown from a moving vehicle. Ballistic tests on a bullet retrieved from her head at autopsy proved that it matched, in every respect, the bullets that had killed both Chandler and Marano.

Later that same morning and, just a few miles away in a Sizzler parking lot, police found the headless corpse of Exxie Wilson, another hooker. The body, which had been dragged behind a trash dumpster, was naked and lying in a pool of congealing blood. Wilson and Jones shared the same pimp, and he reported that he had last seen them, both alive, shortly before midnight. They had been together.

During the late hours of Thursday, June 26th, a resident drove into the driveway of his home in Studio City and found an ornate wooden chest obstructing his access. "I'd thought I'd found some treasure," he later told police, but upon opening the chest, the man was horrified to find a severed head which had been wrapped up in a T-shirt and jeans. At autopsy, it was determined that Exxie had been shot with a .22 caliber bullet, the head had been washed and make-up roughly applied. It had also been refrigerated after decapitation, which had taken place while she was still alive. There were traces of what appeared to be semen in her throat. The recovered bullet matched, in every respect, the bullets that had been used to kill Marano, Chandler and Wilson.

* * *

Snake hunters were out looking for trophies in a ravine in the hillside country near Foothill Boulevard in Sylmar, on Sunday, June 29th, when they found the body of 17-year-old prostitute, Marnette Comer. Partially naked and covered with brush, the corpse, which had been dehydrated and mummified in the summer heat, was lying on its stomach. It was determined, at autopsy, that she had been shot three times in the chest with a .25 caliber pistol and her belly had been slit open. Marnette had last been seen alive on May 31st. The bullets recovered matched, in every respect, the rounds that had killed all of the other previous victims.

By now the police had traced the ornate chest to a Newberry's store, in Reseda, where a clerk remembered the customer being an overweight woman who wore glasses with thick lenses and short, black gloves. The sales assistant especially remembered the gloves because it had been a very hot day. "She was dumpy, and kinda ugly," the clerk told police.

By now, the clues floating around as to the identity of the mystery informant "Claudia" were adding up. Five hookers had been shot with the same .25 caliber pistol, and the description of the buyer of the chest matched that of Carol Bundy, the only woman in the whole of California who owned two Raven pistols. Yet still the police couldn't match up these leads.

On July 29th, Bundy started to deteriorate mentally. She begged Clark to shoot her. When he refused, she attempted suicide. She sat in her Datsun car and injected herself with insulin and librium. Then she swallowed a handful of sleeping pills. Despite her knowledge of drugs, gained from her nursing experience, the suicide attempt failed, and she was found and taken to hospital.

The next day, her first action was to telephone Jack Murray, from her hospital bed, and ask him to pick her up in his van. When they met, she saw that he was accompanied by a woman named Nancy Smith. Carol was so furious she refused to get in the Chevy and, seething with rage, walked home. Yet none of this prevented her and Murray from having three-in-a-bed sex with young Shannon four days later.

On Sunday, August 3rd, Bundy made arrangements to meet her lover again in the parking lot of the Little Nashville Country Club. Her timing let her down, though, for when she turned up at the rendezvous as planned, she found Murray was already in his van and having sex with a woman called Avril Roy-Smith. Carol banged on the door and Avril left.

This chance encounter with yet another woman was to be the straw that finally broke the camel's back. Bundy and Murray left from the club together and parked a few blocks away where they prepared for sex in the back of the van. Now undressed, Murray lay on his stomach while, crouching behind him, Bundy parted his buttocks and pushed her tongue into his anus. As Murray groaned with delight, she reached into her over-extended waistband and drew out one of her Raven automatics. With her tongue still in place, she touched the muzzle of the gun to the back of Murray's head. He felt the cold steel, and froze for an instant before she fired a single shot into his brain. She checked for a pulse and ascertained that he was still alive, so she fired again. Still his heart kept on beating. Throwing the gun to one side, Bundy pulled out a heavy boning knife from her bag, which she repeatedly drove into his back. After a dozen stabs he finally died. To complete her gruesome work, Bundy then slit open her victim's buttocks and mutilated his anus before hacking off his head. After rummaging through the van's cupboards, she scattered pornographic videotapes and magazines around the body. Emptying Murray's briefcase, she removed several Polaroid sex snapshots, and took his keys and his gun, before placing his head in a plastic bag. She then returned to her own car which was still parked in the club's parking lot. Now, in the early hours of Monday, August 4th, she drove to a call box and telephoned her own apartment where Clark was sleeping.

Doug Clark was in bed with Nancy Smith when the shrill ring

dragged him out of a heavy sleep. "Carol was whispering and giggling on the phone," he explained, and as the call continued, Nancy, who suffered from epilepsy, started a seizure. Doug told Bundy to shut up and get back home, and then he called for an ambulance. When Bundy arrived five minutes later, paramedics were already on the scene. After the ambulance left, Bundy took Clark to her car where, in the well of the front passenger seat, was Murray's head in the plastic bag. The ragged and bloody stump was exposed and Clark fell back and vomited. What with Nancy's fit and now this, it was all too much. But then Bundy coolly asked him if he would help her dispose of the mess. Like a complete fool he agreed, despite the fact that he was about to start his shift at the Jergens soap factory within the hour.

They drove off in the direction of the factory, with Bundy cradling the plastic-wrapped head in her lap. As they passed a pile of rubbish, she wound down the window and tossed the grisly article out. Murray's head was never seen again.

Three days later on Tuesday, August 7th, the sexually insatiable Bundy invited Tammy Spangler, one of Murray's former girlfriends, over for dinner. Clark knew that Carol was trying to initiate another three-way sex session and declined to take part. In any case, he fancied the attractive woman himself, and he also feared for Bundy's state of mind. "If she could do that to Jack," he said, "what the fuck could she do to someone else? What about my fuckin' head?"

After the meal, Tammy left to go to work, and Bundy and Clark were now alone. Her sexual expectations had been disappointed, so she convinced Doug that they should drive into Hollywood and find another girl who would treat him to a hooker's blow job. This was to be his birthday present from Bundy and, reluctantly, he agreed.

They drove to Highland Avenue where they saw a suitable whore. The prostitute was called over and a deal was agreed. The girl's name was Cathy, but before she took payment, she said, "I don't do nothing with no woman." Her concerns were allayed, and she climbed into the back seat followed by Clark, who left the driver's seat tilted forward against the steering wheel. This enabled Carol, who sat in the front passenger seat, to have a grandstand view. She gloated at the unedifying sight through her inch-thick glasses. Clark described what happened next.

"I was on the left an' Cathy was on my right, and twisted around with only her left buttock on the edge of the seat. She was working me up with her mouth, an' stuff like that. Then I noticed Carol fidgeting in her seat. She began heaving herself up and down, craning her neck to view the area around the car, like she was looking to see if there was anyone around. I saw Carol's hand reach around the seat, like she was gonna grope Cathy. Then I saw the fuckin' gun. For an instant, I thought she was going to shoot me, like she did Murray. But Carol placed the pistol to the back of the hooker's head and pulled the trigger."

The bullet passed clean through the prostitute's head and struck Clark in the lower side of his stomach. Fortunately, it was only a flesh wound, but blood flowed on to his work shirt. "I was shocked and freaking out," he explained. "Carol told me to drive the fuckin' car while she climbed in the back, tore the clothes off the dead girl and sexually assaulted her, all the while ranting that she was sure the dead girl would have liked it."

When the body had been dumped, the two drove back to Bundy's apartment where he changed his soiled clothes. He wouldn't see them again until the police arrested him.

On Saturday, August 9th, the Van Nuys police received a complaint about a Chevrolet van that had been left unattended on Barbara Ann Street. The caller also mentioned a foul smell emanating from the vehicle. Within minutes, a squad car arrived to investigate and a police officer, looking through one of the vehicle's windows, saw a body in the rear. As the scene was being cordoned off, Detective Roger Pida climbed in to conduct a preliminary investigation and, among the documents scattered about, he found a wallet, which identified the male victim as John Robert Murray. Checking through their computer, the police learned that Murray's wife had reported him missing several days earlier, and officers were able to ascertain that he spent a lot of time with a woman called Carol Mary Bundy.

The following morning, two detectives called at Bundy's apartment in Burbank. She invited them in and they were introduced to Clark and Tammy Spangler. Clark and Bundy were taken downtown for further questioning while Spangler followed in her car to bring them home after the interview.

At the police station, the couple offered different alibis for the time of Murray's murder. Clark told the truth and said that Bundy had come home later that night. In a separate interview room, Bundy lied, claiming to have been at home all evening. She was adamant that she had not ventured out. Asked if she owned any firearms, Bundy said that she had recently sold a pair of pistols to a tall guy with red hair and a scar. The only name she could conjure up at short notice was TV detective Mike Hammer. Then Tammy Spangler piped up. She told the detectives that she had seen Murray with a woman called Avril Roy-Smith on the night of the murder. "Perhaps you'd better go talk with her," she suggested.

With no solid evidence with which to hold Bundy, they allowed her and Clark to leave while they went in search of Avril, who subsequently gave a verifiable alibi to account for the time encompassing Murray's death. She said that when she left the Chevy van, Jack Murray was very much alive. As Avril departed, heading for the club where she spent the next three hours drinking with friends, she saw Carol Bundy climb into Murray's van.

The homicide cops were now very interested in Bundy. The next day, while they were completing their paperwork for the arrest warrant, Bundy walked off her job at the hospital after confessing to colleagues that she was responsible for murdering and decapitating her lover. She told them that she was going back to her apartment to "clean out the evidence before Doug gets home." As soon as she left, a senior official at the hospital reported Bundy's bizarre allegation in a frantic call to the police.

On her way home, Bundy called in to see Clark at the soap factory during his shift. She asked the gatehouse security officer to summon him. When he came out, she told him that she had told the police everything. Clark was livid. "You crazy cunt," he snapped, "get the fuck away from me."

With Bundy now off the premises, Doug stormed back into the factory where he tried repeatedly to phone Detective Pida, who was not in his office. "Bundy was trying to set me up for murder," he has said many times while protesting his innocence for the Sunset Slayings. "An' who the fuck is gonna believe a woman is doing all this murder stuff? An' she had incriminating photos of me and Shannon hidden away. Blackmail. Yeah. That's what it fuckin' is."

Just after 11:00 a.m. that morning, there was call to the Northeast Division of the LAPD, and a woman—Carol Bundy—asked to speak to homicide detectives. When Officer James Kilgore picked up the phone, the woman said, "Sometime, way back, you were having a string of murders involving prostitutes in Hollywood."

"We still are," replied Kilgore, totally unaware that the caller was recording their conversation.

"Do you still have a code name on the girl by the name of Betsy/Claudia?"

Kilgore said he wasn't sure.

"All right, never mind," said the caller. "Would you like your man today?"

She talked about the murders, and said that the weapon was a .22 caliber automatic. She said her man had told her he had "hit over 50 people." Then she said that she had killed a man named Jack Murray, and admitted her involvement with several of the other murders. "The one he cut her head off. Well, I played around with that one ... and the fat girl [Karen Jones] that he dumped off near the NBC studios, I was involved with that."

Kilgore asked how many murders there had been. "Probably 12 or 14 total," came the reply. "But I can't verify all of them. I can only verify about eight or nine."

"And you helped him on some of them?"

"Yes, I did," said Bundy. "Specifically how I got involved with it was a case of being scared to death because I knew that he had done these things. I felt I had to get involved. If I was involved he'd have no reason to kill me."

She then said she was calling to give herself up, and that her real name was Carol Bundy. Finally, referring to the killer, she blurted out, "He's my boyfriend and his name is Douglas Daniel Clark."

"Doesn't it make you feel bad that you killed somebody?" asked the detective. Bundy replied, amazingly, "The honest truth is, it's fun to kill people, and if I was allowed to run loose, I'd probably do it again. I have to say, I know it's going to sound sick ... it's like going to sound psycho, and I don't really think I'm psycho, but it's kinda fun. It's like riding a roller coaster. Not the killing, not the action that somebody died, because we didn't kill them in any way that they'd suffer. It was just killing them straight out."

* * *

After making her telephone call, Bundy started rearranging her apartment, in the belief that she had a few hours to get things in order. She was bent on doing everything she could to incriminate Clark, but she had just minutes, because detectives were about to arrive on her doorstep and arrest her. When they did, they conducted a careful search of the place.

Almost immediately, Bundy held up a cardboard box that contained a pair of panties and assorted clothing. These items later proved to belong to an, as yet, undiscovered murder victim who would later be tagged "Jane Doe 28." The box also contained a purse belonging to another unidentified victim, "Jane Doe 18."

"This box belongs to Clark," she said, "And, do you want to see what kind of guy Doug Clark is?" she asked, as she reached for her handbag on a table. An officer stopped her because he suspected that the bag might contain a gun but, inside, was Bundy's key ring. She selected a key and offered it to one of the police officers, to open the cabinet in Clark's bedroom. The cupboard contained a photo album of Clark with his numerous lovers, including photos of his poses with the 11-year-old Shannon. Also, hidden among various papers was a firearm sales receipt, made out to a Juan Gomez, which later proved to be false.

Meanwhile, Detective Pida had taken Clark in for questioning to Van Nuys Police Station where he was held for hours, without water or food and denied the use of the toilet. This treatment was illegal, especially when Clark had not even been told of the reason for his arrest. Indeed, at the time, he actually believed the arrest was all about Murray. When he was finally asked what he knew about this murder, to his credit, he admitted everything he knew. When he was asked why he hadn't gone straight to the police, Clark truthfully answered that Bundy had dozens of incriminating pictures, of himself and Shannon, which she had used as a threat.

When Pida produced the photo album, taken from his bedroom cabinet, Clark started to feel decidedly uneasy. The detective showed him a mugshot of the dead Cynthia Chandler, and Doug explained that he knew her personally. They talked about the prostitute murders, to which Clark retorted, "Someone is tryin' to lynch my ass, and I have hunch I know who it is."

With little else to book him with, the police initially detained Clark on a holding charge of child molestation. This was a stop-gap measure, for they had wider ambitions as far as Clark was concerned. There was certainly no evidence to say that he had been involved with the Sunset Slayings, other than Carol Bundy's wild accusations. Nevertheless, Clark was held, without his legal rights read to him, for another eight hours because he demanded to see an attorney.

It was now late at night and, when the police finally acceded to his request for legal representation, they informed him that all the lawyers had gone home, and it would take hours before one could be recalled. Then he was illegally moved to another police station 30 miles away. When an attorney did turn up at Van Nuys Police Station, Clark was no longer there and no one seemed to know where he had been transferred.

If the police were being "uncooperative," then Clark was quite the opposite. He gave them permission to search his apartment, his motor-cycle, and his place of work. "I gave them everything," Clark railed on. "I gave them my fuckin' boots, my fuckin' saliva, my fuckin' blood. I offered to take a polygraph, but changed my fuckin' mind 'cause I ain't never trusted the cops. I could see a set up coming from a mile off."

While he was being grilled, Bundy was unloading her story on the detectives interviewing her. She corroborated Doug's denial of guilt for Murray's murder, saying that while she had shot Murray, another man, "a psycho," had hacked the head off to remove the evidence of traceable bullets. Questioned as to why she had left the cartridge casings in the Chevy, she gave conflicting answers. At first, she stated that she didn't realize that the weapon automatically ejected the cases. Then, in a complete reversal, she said that she did realize that the cases had ejected from the weapon but, had simply forgotten to pick them up.

During the initial, and extremely thorough, search of Murray's van, there was no record of any shell casings being found. Some time later, however, a detective said that he had found a single shell casing in the van, and that it had been fired from Bundy's chrome-plated Raven pistol. This discovery took on a more sinister aspect when it transpired that a police evidence envelope, sealed and marked "2 x shell casings found at unspecified sources" had been torn open and one of the shell cases was missing.

When she was asked why she had shot Murray, Bundy gave four vague reasons in rapid succession. The first was that he had stolen money from her; second, because he had jilted her; then, she had shot him as he had planned to rape and kill Shannon; and finally, that he was going to report Doug to the police, accusing him of being the deadly Sunset Slayer. None of this made any sense whatsoever but, incredibly, the police seemed inclined to believe her. Regarding which of the four stories, they didn't seem to know.

With an attentive audience of good-looking police officers surrounding her, Bundy went on to say that she had been involved with the Cathy murder. The hooker had been shot while sitting in her Datsun. When the police told her that there was no forensic evidence of a shooting in the car, let alone a murder, she changed her account, saying that the crime had taken place in her Buick, which she had loaned to Clark. For his part, Doug says it was most certainly the Datsun because the car only had two doors, and he had to push the driver's seat forward to let the hooker in.

Bundy went on to say that she had paid the hooker to give Clark a blow job as a birthday present, but claimed that it was agreed that he would give her a signal as to when to shoot the prostitute in the head. Douglas Clark vehemently denies this, arguing, "No, man, I don't care who he is. Who would let a half-blind bitch reach over, shoot at the head of a hooker suckin' his cock and hope like hell she didn't blow a hole in his knee or chest? I mean, what if her jaw locked shut?" Perhaps Clark has a valid point!

When questioned about the Marano and Chandler murders, Bundy claimed that she had not been involved. She had merely learned of the crimes through Clark. It was Doug, she said, who had told her that he had shot both women in the head while they were giving him oral sex. During his interview at San Quentin, Clark was asked to comment on Bundy's claim.

"You are pulling my pecker," he declared. "Do you think I'm fuckin' crazy, man? Some broad is blowin' me off an' I stick a gun to her head and blast them away. What about the fuckin' blood, man? What about my dick, man? I'd have been covered with the shit and it would have been painted all over the inside of the fuckin' car."

Bundy told the police that Doug "dragged the bodies from the Buick and into his lock-up garage where he had sex with them." She added, "And it was because of this bloody mess in the car that Doug put it through a car wash." Clark has never denied washing the Buick and, indeed, he even volunteered this information to the detectives who confirmed that he had been to the carwash on June 21st, exactly a week after Bundy made her Betsy/Claudia call to the police.

Clark asserted, "Everyone who saw or rode in the Buick from June 14th to June 21st—and there will be many who testify to this—will say that the car was dry, and right after the car wash on June 21st it was soaked and damp with steamy air for a full week. The point is, what fucking vehicle was she washing out, just before the taped call to the police on June 14th? The Datsun was broken down, the Buick was dry, and only the Murray's Chevy van fits the details she made in that call."

It later proved to be the case that, indeed, Murray's van had been washed out after the first three murders, although the police chose to ignore this vital evidence that would prove beyond any doubt that Bundy was lying once again to save her own skin. Yet all of this begs the question as to why Clark washed the Buick in the first place. The answer lies in supporting evidence, given by four other people, who confirm that he is telling the truth.

During the evening of June 20th, Clark visited Joey Lamphier, one of his many girlfriends and, when he left the woman's apartment, he accidentally reversed over an alley cat, crushing its hindquarters. He lifted the badly injured animal into the Buick where it crawled under the front passenger seat. Douglas Clark is known for his love of cats and, in the past, had taken in several strays. He rescued many more from animal pounds and found new homes for them. Any cat lover will confirm, therefore, that it would have been in his nature to have been very concerned about this particular cat's welfare following the accident. Unfortunately, the cat died before he could reach a vet, so he placed the dead creature in a cardboard box and left it by garbage skip.

After work on the June 21st, Clark drove Timmy, the young son of his current landlady, and Bundy, in the Buick, to the carwash. Carol was pressing for the return of the car, in preparation for her move to Burbank. Doug hosed the cat's blood, urine and excrement from under the seat and vacuumed the excess water away. Later, Timmy told police that the small amount of blood was still wet when he got into the car, which totally contradicted Bundy's claim that the blood had been there for some ten days. And, Clark explained, "If this car wash had a sinister motive, why would I have taken a mouthy kid along?"

Police evidence technicians did find a small amount of what appeared to be blood, under and around the front seat of the Buick, yet in no way was the back seat contaminated in the manner which would have been consistent with Bundy's claim that three brutal and bloody murders had been committed in this vehicle.

Around mid-1991, Carol Bundy changed her story yet again. This time for the benefit of a journalist who was writing a book about the Sunset Slayings. She now said that the car wash on June 21st followed the murder of Cathy (Jane Doe 28), which had been committed the night before. Now, according to her latest claim, the blood was no longer that of Chandler and Marano, neither was the Cathy murder committed in the Datsun. This time it was someone else but, once again, the police seemed to ignore these contradictions.

When questioned about the murders of Karen Jones and Exxie Wilson, Bundy denied any involvement in these crimes, and merely related an account allegedly given to her by Clark. "There were three hookers working together," she said. "Clark picked up Exxie and shot her in the head before decapitating her behind the Sizzler Diner." (Witnesses heard a vehicle racing away from this precise location at about 1:15 a.m.) Bundy went on to say that Doug returned to pick up Karen Jones and he shot her while she was giving him oral sex in the car. "He killed her and dumped the body," she said. Witnesses heard a scream around 2:40 a.m., and Karen's corpse was discovered at this location less than an hour later.

Following these two murders, Bundy alleged that Clark brought Exxie's head back to her new apartment, in Burbank, where he placed it in the freezer before phoning her at her old apartment at Lemona, where she was still living. Telephone records show that this call was made at precisely 3:08 a.m.. But is Bundy's story true? She claims that it was Clark who called her to explain what he had done. Doug says that it was Bundy phoning him. The difference is that his account can be verified, for he had an alibi that night.

Tammy Spangler confirmed that Bundy had called Doug at around 3:00 a.m. at the Lemona where they were sleeping on an old mattress. "Doug was in a lot of pain because he had hurt his back while moving Carol's stuff," she said. "He was in agony and pretty wild that Carol had got him out of bed." Once again, the detectives ignored Clark's story and chose to believe Bundy, who, at best, was a pathological liar. But was there any other evidence to support Clark and Tammy Spangler's claim, that they had spent the night at Bundy's old apartment? There was.

Douglas Clark said, "I argued with Cissy Buster on that Sunday. She said, "Leave me if you don't want to live with me." I said, "Fuck it," and lugged my stuff down to the Buick. Carol had complained about the dampness and lingering smell of the cat feces from the previous day's car wash. I had offered to dry it out 'cause I needed the car. I promised to dry it out and return it in time for Carol's move to Burbank. I then drove to Lemona, at about 1:30 p.m. to 2:30 p.m. The movers came about 3:00 p.m. to 4:00 p.m. and moved her into Burbank in two trailers and pick up loads. I rode with them and Carol had a slew of kids to help her put the kitchen shit in the Buick.

"At the other end, the movers moved it all up. I helped and strained my back and ended up nearly unable to move. I left early and rode my bike to Van Nuys. I called Al Joines, my assistant at Jergens, around 6:00 p.m. I told him that I'd hurt my back, and asked him if he would start up the boiler, the following morning. I then drank several beers.

"Tammy came over and we crashed on a mattress in the now empty Lemona apartment. I was woken from my sleep by a call from Carol at a time I know to be 3:08 a.m., because the police confirmed that such a call was made."

Every detail of this statement was later shown to be true.

Most prostitutes are reluctant to trick alone, preferring to work in pairs, for safety. Contrary to this practice, Bundy claims that Exxie Wilson allowed herself to be picked up by Clark, who killed her and then returned to the red light district on his own with the intention of enticing the now dead girl's colleague into the Buick. Furthermore, as was later shown at autopsy, Exxie Wilson was still very much alive during her decapitation, and that it would have been impossible to accomplish this act of mutilation without Clark being sprayed with arterial blood, which was not the case. Even more startling was the coroner's statement, which claimed that both Murray's head, which Bundy had admitted cutting off, and Exxie Wilson's headless body, had been decapitated by the same hand, using knives which had been found in Bundy's apartment.

The time interval which elapsed, between the murders of Exxie

Wilson and Karen Jones, is also of interest, for it has the Bundy/Murray modus operandi written all over it. Bundy revealed her M.O. when she offered Clark his birthday present and shot the hooker into the bargain. That Exxie had been decapitated by the same skilled hand that had cut off Murray's head, and that it had been Murray's van that had been washed out several times, just after the murders, all points to Murray and Bundy as being the real murderers of Exxie Wilson and Karen Jones.

Then there is Bundy's telephone call to the police on Saturday, June 14th when she described the killer as a man called "John" and gave a description that matched that of John "Jack" Murray down to his correct age.

During her tape recorded interrogation, on Monday, August 11th, Carol Bundy made reference to Clark murdering another hooker (Jane Doe 18) "two weekends ago," and she was adamant about the date. Somewhat curiously, she was allowed to change this all-important date when the police ascertained that Clark was 380 miles away, attending his brother's wedding, on the weekend pinpointed by Bundy. Eventually, Bundy could only say "some time in July." But if this female killer was allowed to change a specific date to any one of her choosing in a given month, it paled into significance when she added that the crime committed on that date had been "Doug's last murder."

"He told me nothing about it," she explained to the detectives. "Absolutely nothing at all, and if he won't tell me, then he won't tell you, so you might as well forget it."

But, within minutes, she changed her tune yet again, by giving a full description of the crime, including the nickname Clark had supposedly assigned to the victim—Water Tower—and then offered up the location of the body. She even described Doug placing the girl's body on the hood of her Datsun, and having intercourse while the motor ticked over and he simulated "coital movements."

With Bundy lying, and changing her story at every twist and turn, it may come as no surprise to learn that she told police that the handbag they found in her apartment belonged to the Water Tower victim, too. But the bag actually belonged to someone else, and it contained a woman's business cards, telephone numbers and a driving licence; yet, no effort was made by the police to check out these vital details, or to try to find the rightful owner.

Quite rightly, Clark believes that if Jane Doe 18 had been identified, that information could have established a date when she was last seen alive and probably murdered, thereby giving him the opportunity to confirm an alibi. More recently, he has also commented on the nick-name he allegedly gave to this victim.

"I have never named anyone by that name, dead or alive," Clark says. "The police say the body was found by an oil tank. I am a four-year educated engineer, and tanks are not towers, and oil is not water. This location was probably in the oil pumping area of those hills, and I would never nickname a girl Water Tower. Only a layman who didn't know the difference might do that."

Even when confronted with her lies, which the police anxiously accepted as "truths" to suit their case against Clark, Bundy continued to lie and lie again. She further confused the already vexed situation by claiming that the cosmetics she had used to transform Exxie's head into a "Barbie Doll" had been taken from the purse belonging to Jane Doe 18. She insisted on this, despite the obvious fact that Wilson had been killed a month earlier than Jane Doe 18, ruling out Bundy's possession of her purse.

During her trading of accusatory testimony to escape execution, Carol Bundy insisted that Clark was a necrophile. She said that he shot the prostitutes through the head as they performed oral sex on him. In such a bizarre case, anything is possible, but common sense suggests that even the most deviant sexual psychopath would be deterred from such perverse activity. Not only was there the real danger of exiting and ricocheting bullets, as in the case with Cathy, but also the very real peril of reflexive, death-spasm bites on the penis, and Doug was very proud of his manhood.

While there was no evidence to support Bundy's claim that Clark was a necrophile, there was strong evidence to say that she was. She had admitted to having her tongue in the anus of Jack Murray when she fired the bullets into his head. Furthermore, when her Datsun car was stored after it had been released from the police pound, a letter was discovered which seemed to have been missed during the first police search of the vehicle. In Carol's handwriting, and signed "Betsy"—the pseudonym she had used in her first call to the police—the letter contained sexually explicit details of "vaginal death spasms." She continued by describing, in sexually graphic detail, how Doug had taken the severed head of Exxie Wilson from the freezer and into the shower, where he performed oral sex with the icy remnant.

Yet again, her account is a pack of lies and testimony to her powers of grisly imagination. Now, this is not about a "chilled head." The alleged object of Clark's sexual outrage was not simply "chilled," it was frozen solid. The severed head had become a solid block of ice, as both Bundy and the police confirmed, when it was discovered, and it took several days to thaw out. When interviewed, Clark said, "The cops said it was froze solid, and Bundy says the same fuckin' thing. The jaw was locked shut. So how do you get a penis into that mouth? Give me a fuckin' break, will ya?"

This argument, nevertheless, could be missing the obvious. There was nothing to say that the head had not been used as a sexual receptacle before it had been frozen.

Despite Bundy's claim that Clark ejaculated into the mouths of both Marano and Chandler, internal swabs taken from the bodies showed no traces of semen. Traces of blood and sperm were found, though, on Exxie Wilson's body and Chandler's external vulva area. When tested, this was shown to be blood type A, the same type as Murray's, and distinct from Clark, who is type O. Traces of acid phosphates were found in Exxie's throat, but this probably came from her spinal fluid, although the prosecution later insisted it was Clark's sperm, even though it did not match his blood type.

Shortly after her arrest for murder, detectives took Bundy for a meal. During this break in proceedings, she was given the freedom to empty her bank safety deposit box, while the police stood by, making no record of the contents. She also took officers to Clark's private post box, where, without a search warrant, they unlawfully ordered the clerk to hand over the mail it contained. Then, Bundy was allowed to return to her apartment so that she could arrange the sale of furniture, despite the fact that much of it belonged to Doug Clark. He stated quite correctly that "they [the police] then let her have her car back before it was tested by the defense team," emphasizing, "They never let murder cars back, never."

Someone who was storing the Datsun for Bundy after her arrest, found the death spasm letter and a bloodstained jacket, which has never forensically tested or bloodtyped. The garment did not belong to either Clark or Bundy, or to any of the known victims. Subsequent research identified the true owner as Jack Murray. When his wife was shown a photograph of the jacket, she unequivocally identified it as belonging to her late husband.

Incredibly, the generosity shown by the police to their star witness knew no bounds, even though Bundy was shown to be a pathological liar. On August 29th, and only 18 days after her arrest, they allowed her access to Jack Murray's bank deposit box and allowed her to remove $3,000. This was cash to which Mrs. Murray had lawful title. The money simply vanished into thin air. For many years, the police adamantly denied that this incident took place. It was only when Clark finally proved the lie in court that the police admitted that the deposit box was opened in their presence.

"Oh, yeah. That day. Sure, but what money are we talkin' about?" asked a detective. "Money, we ain't seen no money."

At the time of writing, the police deny that any back-handed deal was done with Bundy. If they did admit that favors-for-cash deals had been conducted, three attorneys and a dozen police officers would be facing court proceedings. For her part, Carol Bundy insists she gave the $3,000 to the police for safekeeping and says that the money hasn't been seen since.

* * *

If mystery after mystery surrounds the lies and accusations of Carol Bundy, then the firearms involved in this case create a veritable minefield of problems and enigmas. It was established that she had purchased two .25 caliber Raven automatic pistols on May 16, 1980. These guns were similar, but not identical, in their appearance. They were distinguishable insofar as one was chrome-plated, while the other was nickel-plated. Ballistic tests identified the nickel-plated firearm as the weapon used in all of the murders, with the exception of those of Cathy (Jane Doe 18), and Jack Murray. In the latter case, no ballistic evidence was possible, for the very good reason that his head was never found. By now, both of the two cartridge cases, allegedly found in his truck, had mysteriously gone missing, in much the same manner as Mrs. Murray's cash. Not to be beaten, Bundy now came up with the explanation that the nickel-plated gun actually belonged to Clark. He denied it, and other people, whom the police chose not to believe, corroborated his denial.

During the Memorial Day weekend, which began on May 24th, Clark and a girlfriend, Toni, had made arrangements to travel north, to Yosemite, with the intention of visiting his parents. He planned to make the journey on his motorcycle and, just in case Toni was too nervous to travel by this means of transport, he telephoned Bundy to see if he could use her Buick, should the need arise. It was during this phone call that Bundy told him that she had recently bought the Raven pistols, and she asked him if he could check them over because one kept jamming. When Clark took possession of these guns, they were unloaded but they came with a two-thirds-full box of shells.

On his return from Yosemite, Clark told Bundy that the chrome-plated gun was still jamming. She retained the nickel-plated pistol, which was later proved to be the murder weapon, and gave the malfunctioning chrome-plated pistol to Clark as a gift. She confirmed as much to the police.

On June 16th, Clark gave the gun to Joey Lamphier, showing her how to clear it if it jammed again. Early in July, Bundy demanded the return of this gun. There was an argument, following which, Clark returned the Raven to Bundy. The next time he saw it was on the night of August 7th, when Carol used it to shoot Cathy through the head.

The two pistols surfaced again, on August 9th, after the police discovered Murray's headless corpse. Bundy handed the firearms to Clark, saying, "Get rid of these where they'll never be found." He took them to the soap factory, where they were eventually discovered by police, still in Bundy's make-up bag, which was hidden on the top of a boiler.

Police investigators had had a field day, combing through Bundy's apartment and, in her bedside cabinet, they found 29 rounds of .25 caliber ammunition. An officer flicked through the pages of *Hustler* and *Playboy* magazines, while another detective amused himself by studying a particular bondage and domination magazine. Also in the living room, investigators found several film reels of "Super" pornography, and a book that contained an illustration of a severed head. All of this material was owned by Bundy, but at Clark's trial it was all attributed to him.

During her lengthy interviews with the police, Bundy told them that Clark had had sex with the dead bodies of Marano and Chandler in his garage where he stored wood, along with his motorcycle and several boxes of his personal belongings. The detectives' ears pricked up and they obtained a search warrant for the place. No sooner had this accusation poured from Bundy's mouth than she frantically insisted that they wouldn't find any evidence there. "We scrubbed the place out," she confided. Nevertheless, police found Clark's boot print on the floor and they were keen to ascertain if the stain was blood.

Forensic experts carried out a "presumptive" blood test, which gave a positive indication that the stain was organic in origin. Further tests were required to authenticate the true nature of the stain. This was never done, and the reason, according to the police, was to "preserve the boot print for identification and comparison." This was a relatively lame excuse, as the print was recorded photographically, and there was no reason why a positive blood test could not have been completed after photographs had been taken. Another possible explanation lies in the concerns that the stain might fail the test, thus proving, for the umpteenth time, that Carol Bundy was a liar.

Police also claimed to have found another bloodstain, measuring 2 feet by 8 feet in size, on the floor of Clark's garage. They concluded from this that heavily bleeding bodies had been dragged across the floor. This, they reasoned, corroborated Bundy's testimony about the necrophile orgy that had supposedly occurred in the garage with the bodies of Marano and Chandler. As with the boot print, only a presumptive test was carried out and, again, the test proved inconclusive. Furthermore, when examined, the girls' bodies showed no signs of blood smears or streaks, as would have been the case if they had been dragged in such a manner. Post mortem abrasions on Chandler's back were attributed, by investigators, to the act of dragging the body across a rough surface. On the other hand, the medical examiner argued, these marks could have been the result of the body being dumped down the ravine.

Clark was astonished that the police should be so surprised to find his boot print in his garage, and with his usual droll sense of humor, he commented, "What the fuck am I supposed to do? Levitate around my garage?" He also provided an explanation for the long drag marks which had been discovered on the floor.

"There was a track where the bike went in and out over a period of six months right down the middle of the garage. I stored raw wood, ply and particleboards there. There were four woodworking shops within a 50-foot radius that directly dusted the area. The door allowed leaves and dust to blow in, round and under it." This would certainly explain why the drag marks were organic in origin.

After careful investigation of Clark's garage, the police could only say that there "might have been blood on the floor." There was certainly not a shred of evidence to support Bundy's allegation that Clark had had sex with two dead and heavily-bloodstained bodies there. Moreover, Bundy's other statement, that they had scrubbed the place clean, proved to be another of her lies, for it was patently obvious, even to the police, that the place had not been cleaned out for years.

If anything could save Clark from the death sentence, it lay in establishing solid alibis for at least a few of the murders. But alibis seemed to be lacking, especially for June 11th, the date of the Marano and Chandler killings. Doug argues that he could not even remember where he was living on that day, let alone what he did after work, when, Bundy says, the crimes were committed. It soon became apparent that he was lodging with Cissy Buster, one of his many on-and-off again girlfriends. She told detectives that he arrived home around 8:00 p.m. that evening, but time-keeping records from the soap factory suggest that he finished much earlier, at 1:00 p.m. Cissy Buster added that Clark had called her to say he would be home late, and she remembers this because it was her son's graduation party. It was subsequently shown that these events actually took place on Friday, June 13th, and not on the day of the murders.

One thing that could seal the case against Doug Clark would be a survivor who could identify him. While he and Bundy were under lock and key, a regular jailbird named Charlene Anderman, a mentally-unhinged woman who had been frequently arrested on drug and prostitution charges, was also behind bars. Around the same time as the Sunset Slayings occurred, a series of savage knife attacks and robberies were committed against hookers. In April, Charlene had fallen victim to one such assault. She had joined a john in his car when the man pulled out a knife and stabbed her several times in the back before kicking her out of his vehicle on to the street.

Police arrested Jerome Van Houten, whom Charlene Anderman identified in a line-up, but her recollection of the attack was hazy because she was high on cocaine at the time. She told the police that the attack had taken place in a motel room, then she changed her story to say that she had been stabbed in a car, the color and make of which constantly changed. Understandably, the police deemed her identification to be unreliable, but they had enough on Van Houten to secure his conviction based on positive identification provided from other victims.

Now locked up in jail, Anderman started bragging about Clark being her assailant, so the police decided to interview her again. They showed her a photograph of Doug and, suddenly, she decided that he was the knifeman, adding that she was willing to testify to this in court providing that the police would free her from custody after the case was over with. Fortunately for Doug Clark, the court thought that she was totally unreliable and her evidence was thrown out. The police had to honor their part of the deal, and Charlene, whom her sister said was "a liar who would say or do anything to get out of trouble," was released almost immediately.

Doug Clark has always maintained that Bundy and Murray killed most of the victims while driving around in Murray's Chevy van. During the forensic investigation of this vehicle, a vital piece of evidence was found, hanging from the roof vent hatch. It was a sliver of human scalp with strands of blonde hair attached to it. This gruesome artifact was approximately two inches in length, dehydrated, and probably detached from a head as the result of a gunshot blast. As most of the victims had been blonde, and Murray was dark haired, it would seem evident that at least one of the prostitutes had been killed in the van, which would support Clark's claim. The state, however, desperately needed to convict Clark. After all, Murray was dead, and if he had been the Sunset Slayer, then the crimes had been allowed to run their bloody course. None of this would have gone down well with the police departments involved, especially as they had now gone out of their way to implicate Clark. The skin tissue, with hair attached, was taken away and no investigation was carried out to determine its origin. Clark was also refused the right to have it submitted as evidence at his trial.

With all the cards stacked against him, what luck Clark had remaining totally evaporated when an attorney was appointed to defend him who was inexperienced and ill-equipped to handle such a serious case of serial homicide. Clark's attorney had recently been declared bankrupt, and had appeared in court to answer matters against him of legal malpractice and theft of a client's funds. As a result of this, the lawyer had turned to drink and, when he appeared for Clark, he was an out of control drunk. He addressed the court claiming that he was an alcoholic and, throughout the trial, he was so distracted by his own bankruptcy that he paid little attention to Clark's case. Family, friends, witnesses for the District Attorney and court officials all saw him drinking, usually doubles, before the court convened. The bailiff even complained to the judge about the lawyer's alcoholic smell, which pervaded the air during his appearance at morning sessions.

On the first day of the trial, the attorney simply opened the proceedings by saying that Clark was guilty as charged, but that he was insane and should, therefore, be given a lenient sentence. Quite rightly, the judge was shocked by such an admission and, as the attorney staggered back to his seat, the judge was forced to remind him what the proceedings were all about. This was just the first phase of the trial in which an attempt was made to discover who had committed the crimes, and any suggestion of sentence would be dealt with at the later penalty phase.

Muttering under his breath, the lawyer sat down, only to rise, momentarily, an hour later, to say that he was ill prepared because he had not seen Clark for weeks. This was not so, for jail records of visitors, and the attorney's own financial records, proved he had been taking instructions from his client almost every day, right up to the first day of the case.

As the trial progressed, Clark became increasingly aware that his lawyer was a major liability. In a desperate effort to do something to save his own skin, he requested that he be allowed to represent himself. Several times, while he was being cross examined by the prosecutor, he noted that his attorney was asleep, and had to wake him up. On other occasions, he had to interject the legal objections to lines of questions the court had ruled inadmissible. The prosecutor saw the defense attorney nodding off and, taking advantage of the situation, tried to slide contentious problems past him, an underhand tactic that worked on several occasions. The court ruled that Clark could not object on his own behalf; only his lawyer could do this, whether he was in dreamland or not.

From the outset, it became obvious that the state was determined to get a conviction at any cost. Faced with a defense in the hands of a totally incompetent attorney, who was either asleep or drunk, the prosecution was likely to have its wish granted.

Occasionally, Clark burst out with angry rants and accusations. One afternoon, he was manacled and tied to a chair in which he was gagged with a leather strap and a towel. At other times, he was escorted from the courtroom and locked up in a small holding-room, equipped with speakers, so that he could listen to his right to live being eroded away.

Eventually, with the trial having reached its midpoint, Judge Torres acceded to Clark's insistence that he should be allowed to represent himself. Despite this being exactly what Doug had wanted from day one, nothing improved. Indeed, if it were possible, things became far worse. He was denied co-counsel, advisory counsel and the services of a law clerk, and the judge, illegally, told him to "go it alone." At one point, Clark gave the court a list of items he required as evidence, including the items found in Murray's van. Some of these were sex toys and home-made pornographic videos. (Bundy had bought Murray a video camera, and it has always been suspected that they may have been recording their murders as snuff movies.) Needless to say, the judge blocked Clark's request. The accused man was astounded, screaming, "If I had a color movie, with the sound of Carol and Jack committing these murders, you would not let me bring it in?"

The judge smirked and said, "You are right, Mr. Clark. I would not."

At another stage of the trial, it became evident that Clark did indeed have an alibi for the night that Exxie Wilson's head was deposited in the ornate chest. Several people recalled that he had been partying with a go-go dancer who was about to return home to New Zealand. Clark had also written her a check that night, and he was able to provide banking documents to support the fact that it had been cashed the following day. Not even the most adept serial killer can be in two places at the same time, and Bundy had told police that it had been Clark who had dumped Exxie's severed head, so this provided a problem for the prosecutor. The dancer even offered to return to the USA to give her evidence if her airfare was paid.

In vain, Clark asked for this dispensation, rightly arguing that the District Attorney had flown in scores of witnesses, one of whom had been an FBI agent from Virginia, to confirm that the boot print found in Clark's garage was indeed Clark's, something that he had admitted from the outset. Indeed, the prosecution spent over $10,000 on travel for their witnesses, and Clark was allowed just $20—which amounted to his entire defense funding—in dimes, for a single telephone call.

In a last-ditch effort to get the dancer to testify, he begged that she be allowed to give her evidence over the telephone. This is a legally accepted procedure, if the witness is positively identified and sworn in at a local court. But, once again, his request was denied.

Meanwhile, another problem surfaced, when the court began hearing about the discovery of Exxie's head, and the clothing it was wrapped up in. The police had made efforts to identify the jeans and T-shirt, and detectives Stallcup and Jaques of the LAPD, who were working the Marnette Comer murder, telephoned the Sacramento PD. Stallcup required contact with known associates of Comer, such as co-hookers and pimps, and also wanted to interview Marnette's sister, Sabra, who was also a prostitute.

Sabra categorically told the two investigators that the T-shirt and jeans had belonged to a hooker called Toni Wilson, a Caucasian, aged 19, with natural blonde hair and, blue eyes; she was slim, 5 feet 7 inches tall, and had freckles. This was a positive identification and one which was supported by numerous other characters, including a pimp named Mark. These witnesses even told Stallcup that the last time they saw Toni Wilson, she had been wearing the very same clothing described.

In his handwritten report, timed and dated 1600 hrs, August 9, 1980, Stallcup made a careful note of this information. Then, later in the evening, he inexplicably reproduced an "official" version in typewritten form, the substance of which somewhat changed the testimony of Sabra Comer, to read that she had identified the T-shirt and jeans as belonging to her deceased sister, which was not the case. During the trial, the prosecution called Sabra Comer as a witness, to identify the clothing, and she did identify the items as belonging to her sister, Marnette. Somewhere, there was a major discrepancy and Clark picked it up. He called Detective Stallcup to give evidence.

He asked the detective about the handwritten notes he made from replies given by Sabra, and inquired whether it was his usual practice, when typing them up, to turn the details around 180 degrees. Stallcup answered, "No. I would put myself in a very bad spot of jeopardy there. The crime for doing such ... something like that, if it ended up to be a capital case, I would be under the same problem that you have got sitting there."

Stallcup knew that for a police officer to falsify evidence and to commit perjury in a capital case left that officer open to a capital charge himself. After being pressed on this issue by Clark, the detective agreed that he made the handwritten notes. Stallcup "thought" the typed version was his, too, but only after his signature was pointed out to him on the page. This incident was allowed to pass, without a stain on Stallcup's character.

A similar situation to the one Clark found himself in occurred in the more recent case of Roger Coleman, who continually protested his innocence of murder. When Coleman's defense submitted solid proof of innocence for a retrial, it was deemed too late, but he was given the benefit of doubt and offered a polygraph test, which took place just a few hours before his execution. This test, which simply detects any slight heartbeat increase, or sweat secretion, when the vital questions are asked, was unsurprisingly failed by Coleman, who was about to die an agonizing death, and he was escorted to the electric chair on May 21, 1992.

Like Clark, Coleman had solid alibis, witnesses and forensic evidence, suggesting he had not committed murder. Furthermore, a woman claimed that another man, who was a known killer, had confessed to her that he had carried out the murder attributed to Coleman. This witness was found dead on the day following her statement. Also, in the Coleman case, the State offered a fellow inmate freedom if he would say that Coleman had told him that he had committed the crime. He talked and walked, while Coleman died. On his subsequent release, the jailhouse snitch retracted his admission.

Douglas Daniel Clark was found guilty on six counts of first-degree murder and sentenced to death. For her part, Carol Bundy was found guilty on two counts of first-degree murder, those of Jack Murray and Cathy (Jane Doe 28), and she was sentenced to two life terms of imprisonment. But is Clark really a serial murderer?

He had alibis and witnesses for all the murders except one. The police obtained statements from many of these witnesses and allowed them to be altered in order to circumvent the alibis and thereby incriminate Clark.

The weapons and vehicles, associated with all the murders, belonged either to Carol Bundy or Jack Murray.

Bundy lied at every twist and turn. Money went missing and she says she gave it to police officers who, in turn, granted her extraordinary indulgences.

Most of the prosecution witnesses had criminal records representing leverage, by means of which, the police could coerce the "required" testimony from them. Indeed, Sabra Comer has recently said that she was forced to change her evidence because the police officers had threatened to put her "out of business" if she didn't cooperate with them.

The judge refused to allow the jury to hear tape recorded evidence of Bundy confessing her involvement and pleasure in the murders.

Murray's van was returned to his wife before the trial began, thus denying Clark any opportunity to have the interior independently examined.

Vital trace and ballistic evidence was either mislaid or "lost" by the police.

The state's Attorney General admitted that Bundy had been given a deal to testify against Clark in return for her life.

* * *

Today, Clark awaits his appointment with San Quentin's executioner. As his time is just about to run out, it is perhaps unfair to criticize him for being a very angry man who is full of contempt for the police and the justice system.

Without any doubt, Doug Clark was a fool. He most certainly was an accessory after the fact, in the case of Jack Murray, for he has admitted he was with Bundy when she threw her former lover's head out of the car. And Clark was certainly present when Bundy shot a hooker through the head as she gave him oral sex in a car. He did not report this murder either, which would have bought at least a life sentence when he was arrested.

Clark's early years still remain something of a mystery, and he is loath to discuss this part of his life when he has far more pressing matters on his mind. Unlike Bundy, it is known that Doug came from good stock, enjoyed a healthy childhood, and a first-class education.

Doug Clark used to be a handsome man, well read, and he spoke, as most would agree, beautifully. He was a philanderer who wooed different women on an almost weekly basis and he was a Don Juan of almost epic proportions, too, but all of his lady friends say he treated them well and he has never been accused of using violence against them, even though his sexual interests were hardly conservative. Clark also used women to provide him with lodgings, often in return for sexual favors, a practice, which ultimately proved to be his undoing when he fell in with Bundy. Therefore, in every respect, and even by the FBI's own reckoning, he does not fit the psychological profile of a serial killer.

Like so many serial killers, Carol Bundy had had a troubled upbringing. She is an ugly, duck-shaped woman who could hardly see 2 feet in front of her. She paid men to have sex with her and Murray was a willing partner who satisfied all of her perverse sexual needs. By her own admission, she was a necrophile, and a hedonist killer.

Hedonist killers may be divided into sub-types. Lust murderers kill for sexual enjoyment. Thrill killers kill for the excitement of a novel experience. Both of these sub-types may show evidence of sadistic methods, mutilation, dismemberment and pre- and post-mortem sexual activity. Bundy fits both categories extremely well.

There is little evidence to contest the view that it was Bundy and Murray who killed at least five of the Sunset prostitutes, following which, Bundy, spurned and inducted by her lover and accomplice in serial sexual homicide, killed and decapitated him in a fit of jealous rage. Indeed, the Betsy/Claudia telephone call to the police, when she pointed an accusatory finger in Murray's direction, proved beyond any doubt that the seeds of anger and resentment had already been planted well before she shot him.

Doug Clark distanced himself from Bundy at this time and, in an act of spite, she turned him in. Casting herself in the role of the State's only—and totally untruthful—witness, she engineered a life sentence for herself and a death sentence for Clark. Good luck, Doug Clark.

* * *

Carol Mary Bundy died, while still in prison, on December 9, 2003. The cause of death was heart failure.

This chapter is based on exclusive videotaped death row interviews between Christopher Berry-Dee and Douglas Daniel Clark within the San Quentin State Prison, California, 1995, and extensive correspondence.

Doug Clark welcomes correspondence, and his address is: Inmate C-63000, San Quentin State Prison, San Quentin, CA, 94974.

HENRY LEE LUCAS

"I had no intention of killing her. I don't know
whether it was me or what. That was my first, my
worst, and the hardest to get over. I just couldn't see
what happened. I would go out sometimes for days,
and I'd be looking behind me and watching for police
and be afraid that they were going to stop me and
pick me up. But they never did bother me."

HENRY LUCAS TO THE AUTHOR AT ELLIS PRISON, 1996

"Texas has the second-largest prison inmate population in the U.S., and some time during their lives, 560 out of every 100,000 Texans will spend time in jail. At any one time, there are about 100,000 inmates within the Texas penal system, 46 percent of whom have killed somebody. At the time of writing, there are 453 inmates on death row at Ellis Unit in Huntsville. Henry Lee Lucas used to be one of them until his sentence was commuted, in 1998, to life without parole. On Monday, March 12, 2001, he died of a heart attack at the age of 64.

* * *

FBI statistics say that the majority of serial killers have come from broken homes, or they have suffered from some form of extreme abuse as children. Henry Lucas was no exception. His father, Anderson "No Legs" Lucas, had been a habitual drunken hobo who had fallen from a freight train and lost both of his legs as the result. "My pa," Henry once said, "well, he hopped around on his ass all his life. Done sold pencils, an' skinned mink for a living."

Henry's mother, Viola Dison Wall Lucas, was a prostitute who had been previously married. She dumped her first four children in foster homes prior to marrying Anderson. At the age of 35, she bore a son, Andrew, and five years later, during the early hours of August 23, 1938, Henry Lee entered this world.

Viola was of mixed race; somewhere in her genes was part Chippewa Indian, and those who knew her claimed that she could be as mean as an overheated rattlesnake. "She was a dirty old woman you would not want to be around," was how her granddaughter described her.

Henry described his mother as having just two teeth. She was prone to outbursts of extreme violence and she chewed tobacco. "Some people say they gonna give a whipping with a switch or something,"

Lucas said to me. "When she went and got a switch, she done went and got a broomstick, an' she'd wear it out."

Henry was born in a four-roomed, run-down cabin, nine miles from the hick town of Blacksburg, Montgomery County, Virginia. The place, with no plumbing or electricity, was tucked into a steep cleft between the rolling slopes of the Get and Brushy Mountains, which form part of the Appalachian Mountain system of East North America, extending from the Quebec province in Canada to central Alabama. The cabin is still in existence today. Several miles from the nearest neighbor, the Lucas smallholding was fit only for raising a scrubby cereal crop and equally lean livestock, which included a few scrawny chickens and a cow. The outbuildings, of which there were two, were in the same state of disrepair as the cabin, and everything, including the family, looked like something that had been sucked out of an earlier century by a twister and dumped unceremoniously into nowhere land. The house has been left to the ravages of time and weather. Most of the windows were broken, or simply non-existent, their sun-bleached, peeling frames, hanging limply from rusty hinges, and primed for firewood and nothing else. The roof was rotten, as was the stoop, where Anderson Lucas washed away his days.

The Lucases inhabited the property with Viola's pimp, Bernie, who was a scrawny lowlife and always on the make. Henry, Andrew, Anderson, Viola and Bernie all shared the same filthy bedroom, and Lucas says that he was forced to watch his mother and Bernie, or her many clients, have sex.

In the tradition of the local people, the Lucases distilled a particularly volatile moonshine. With the kick of a southern mule, the making of this spirit was a profitable venture for Anderson who was, in every sense of the word, continually legless and literally out of his mind on drink. Any surplus hooch was sold to supplement the family income. Therefore, it is not surprising to learn that, by the age of ten,

Henry, who tended his father's still, was hooked on the illegal corn liquor. For this work, Henry and his brother were paid the occasional nickel, a quarter on a good day, as wages. With a few cents in their pockets, they would scoot into Blacksburg and watch a movie. The Lucases usually ate food that was stolen or scavenged from trash dumpsters. It was eaten off the dirty floor because Viola wouldn't wash the plates. She cooked only for herself and Bernie, while the rest of the family were left to their own devices.

Forced to wear a girl's dress by his mother on his first day at school, Henry turned up as a scrawny, undernourished child with long, blonde hair. His teacher took pity on him. Annie Hall found him a pair of trousers and, before the day was out, she had even cut his hair. In return for this act of Christian goodwill, Ms. Hall was severely reprimanded by Viola Lucas. Henry had fond memories of his teacher, who bought him his first pair of new shoes. She also made him sandwiches, and occasionally took him home with her for a decent, hot meal.

Brutal physical abuse was a common enough event in the Lucas home; more so was the psychological battering Henry received on an almost daily basis. On one occasion, Viola took him into town where she pointed out a strange man. "That's your real pa," she sneered. "He's your natural pa." The seven-year-old was devastated and, when he arrived home in floods of tears, he asked Anderson if this were true. It was.

The same year, Viola smashed Henry over the back of the head with a wooden board. He lay where he fell for three days before Bernie, fearing that he would never get up again, took the boy to hospital. In the admission room, Bernie claimed that Henry had fallen from a pick up truck. After his discharge, Henry suffered from dizzy spells and blackouts—and they continued until the day he died. He described the sensations as "like floating on air."

Those who have met Henry Lucas, or have seen his photograph, will also notice that his left eye is artificial and made of glass. This came about as he and his brother, Andrew, were attempting to make a swing in a maple tree. While Henry was holding a vine, Andrew slashed to cut it with a knife, but the blade slipped and slashed across the bridge of Henry's nose and into his eye. During the following six months of hospitalization, his mother only visited him once. On the day he arrived home, she shot his pet mule in a fit of rage, then whipped him for costing her the few bucks to have the carcass hauled away.

Although the injury caused Henry great discomfort, gradually the wound began to heal. Nevertheless, for a long time afterward, he tended to see only shadows and because his peripheral vision was damaged, he walked sideways like a crab.

It seems that the only love and attention Henry received during his formative years came not from a rare, helping hand at home, but from his teachers at school. Due to his long periods of absence from class, he fell a grade behind his contemporaries. Annie Hall, in the true American schoolmarm tradition, not only kept him well fed, but she went to other lengths to help him overcome his new problems with reading. With a weak eye, he had trouble with small print, so she bought him books with large type so that he continued to learn. Then, ironically, it was at school that his problems surfaced again, when he walked into the hand of a teacher called Mrs. Glover, who was about to strike another pupil. His eye injury opened up, and this time it was beyond repair. The glass eye was fitted a year later.

Out of the 13 "family background characteristics" the FBI have found to adversely affect a child's later behavior, among their study group of serial killers, Lucas experienced ten of them, a staggering 77 percent, which, by FBI calculations, would have placed him at the top of their "At High Risk" register. Lucas would have checked off alcohol abuse, psychiatric history, criminal history, sexual problems, physical abuse, psychological abuse, dominant mother, negative relationship with male caretaker figures, negative relationship with mother and he had been treated unfairly in the FBI's questionnaire.

There is no way of knowing when Lucas's criminal career started, but he says it was when he stole a battery-powered television, because he liked to watch *The Lone Ranger*, and *Sky King*. He is quoted as saying, "I just started stealing, I guess, as soon as I was old enough to run fast, 'cause I didn't want to stay at home, I figured if I could steal, I could get away from home."

Henry's sexual history also goes way back. He claims that he was encouraged into bestiality by his half-brother, cutting the throats of the animals and then having sex with them. He told a psychiatrist that he had sex with his half-brother's wife when he was 13 years old. "I just went along with it … I didn't feel it was right," he said. Then Henry graduated to attempted rape and murder, or so he claims in his unverified account of a crime he says he committed at the age of 15.

In March 1951, Henry spotted a 17-year-old girl at a bus stop. He cornered her on an embankment, where he attempted to rape her before strangling her. Years later, when Lucas was finally brought to justice for the last time, law enforcement officers from all over the United States descended upon him in their efforts to clear up unsolved murders. During these lengthy interviews, Henry never mentioned this first murder and, despite more recent, careful research into this case, police officers now believe that it never took place.

In March 1952, Henry's brother joined the U.S. Navy, and then his father left home, in a simple wooden coffin. "He went out and lay in the snow to get away from his wife having sex with another man," Henry said. "That's what made him die. He laid down in the snow and caught pneumonia and he was drunk and he just died."

That very same month, the law caught up with Henry Lucas, who was now an accomplished thief. He was charged with petty larceny and sent to the Beaumont Training School for Boys. He claims to have liked the place because this was the first time he ate regularly, and he was able to enjoy hot water and electricity. But, this statement contradicts his behavior, as school records show that he was continually trying to abscond. Henry was released from Beaumont in September 1953, and he periodically worked as a general hand on a farm. In October, he raped his 12-year-old niece.

Nine months later, he was back in custody for the second time and the 18-year-old Lucas was sentenced to four years in the tough Virginia State Penitentiary, for burglary. He became an accomplished carpenter in the prison chair factory, learning skills that would serve him well when he was released. The tailor shop taught him a little about sewing, the chain gang showed him how to break sweat.

On May 28, 1956, with the very real chance of being brought down by dogs, or a bullet in the back, Lucas and a fellow convict escaped from an outside road repair detail. They stole a car and sped off for Ohio. When they ran out of gas, they stole another vehicle and crossed the state line into Michigan. Interstate flight and auto theft across a State line are federal offences, and State Troopers arrested them in Toledo in July, after which, Henry started a 13-month term at the Ohio Federal State Reformatory at Chillicothe. After his federal term had expired, he was returned in shackles to the Virginia State Penitentiary to complete his original sentence. He was back on the streets in September 1959.

After his release, he moved to Tecumseh, Michigan, to live with his half-sister Opal. While there, he met a woman called Stella, and after dating her for a short time, he asked her to marry him. She agreed and they announced their engagement. During the evening of January 12, 1960, he was boozing the evening away with Stella. "She was my first true love," he said. "She just understood me, an' we had plans to marry, an' stuff." However, there was another visitor in town that night; his irate mother had gotten wind of where he was staying. Viola tracked Henry down to the bar where he was drinking, and she demanded that he get rid of Stella, and that he return to Virginia forthwith. This outburst reduced Stella to tears.

It was an inappropriate moment for the "mother from Hell" to force her way back into Henry's life, for that night he and Stella were making plans for the wedding, and he was as drunk as a skunk. In a telephone conversation with me, Stella remembered, "When Henry was drunk, he got as mean as mean can be. He drank Jack Daniel's like it was water in the desert. That night, the old girl really upset me. I threatened to break off the marriage and I walked out and went home. He truly hated his mom, and what she got, she deserved."

Lucas was now at risk of losing the only woman he loved, and 20 minutes later he was hammering on Opal's apartment door where his mother was staying. Viola, who was also drunk, started cursing him, and wrongly accused him of being intimate with Opal. She berated him for leaving her all alone in Virginia, for by now Bernie had found pastures new. What happened next is best told by Lucas himself.

"I'd gone back to where she was staying to calm her down, and she done picked up a broom handle and smacked me with it. I guess it was about 12 o'clock that night when she finally made me so mad that I hit her. All I remember was slapping her alongside the neck, but after I did that, I saw her start to fall, and went to grab her. But she fell to the floor, and when I went to pick her up I done realized she was dead. Then I noticed I had my knife in my hand, and she had been cut.

"I got scared and turned out the lights and went outside and drove back to Virginia. I only stayed there one day, and I started to worry about my mother and wondering if she had been found. I left Virginia and started back to Tecumseh to give myself up. I was picked up by the police in Toledo, Ohio, and later returned to Tecumseh. It was a terrible thing to do, and I know that I have lost the respect of my family and people who know me, but it was one of those things. I think it had to happen."

As it turned out, Viola hadn't died immediately after the attack. She was still alive 48 hours later, when Opal returned to the apartment and found her lying in a pool of blood. An ambulance was called but, because of the length of time she had been bleeding and the resulting shock, they were unable to save her and she died a short time later. The official police report stated that she had died of a heart attack, precipitated by the assault.

Henry was picked up in Toledo, Ohio, and returned to Michigan where he was charged with second-degree murder. Despite assuring police that he had acted in self defense, he later pleaded guilty and was sentenced to 20–40 years in the State Prison of Southern Michigan. Far from losing the respect of members of his family—along with the multitudes of relations, distant or otherwise—Henry was lauded by the Lucas clan, and the citizens of Blacksburg. Viola had been a nuisance for as long as they cared to remember, and everyone was delighted to see her disappear under 6 feet of dirt.

When interviewed in Ellis Unit, Texas, Henry, a slightly-built man, with his weeping false eye, which he constantly wipes on the sleeve of his shirt, had changed his mind about the murder of his mother. After having first admitted to murdering his mother, he contradicted himself. "My half-sister, Opal, done the killing, an' now she's dead," he argued pathetically.

Understandably, Henry says that his incarceration in the State Prison of Southern Michigan was not a happy time in his already distorted life. He claims he was plagued by the voice of his dead mother, who haunted him in his cell. "She kept tellin' me to do bad things," he recalled. "She told me I had a destiny with death behind them walls." He slashed his wrist with a razor and slashed open his stomach with a knife in two suicide attempts, and none of this behavior went unnoticed by the prison guards.

In his own interest, the doctors decided that Lucas would be better off in the Ionia State Mental Hospital where he underwent electroconvulsive shock treatment and was placed under close observation. He stayed there for almost five years before being returned to prison, in 1966, after a psychiatrist concluded, "Lucas is making good progress. I am impressed with his growth." However, another psychiatrist disagreed. "Lucas is totally lacking in self-confidence, self-reliance, willpower and general stamina," he reported. "He does not have the courage to take responsibility for his behavior, but blames others for his mistakes and misfortunes, and he is inclined to engage in aggressive social behavior, aimed at alleviating some of his discomfort."

Lucas had been prescribed Prozac, an antipsychotic with sedative side effects, and this more or less kept a lid on his boiling emotions, but it is known that he had warned the authorities not to release him from prison because he knew that his murderous tendencies would flare up again. He even told the doctors, "Let me out, an' I'll leave a body on your doorstep. I guarantee you that."

During that period of imprisonment, the Michigan Department of Corrections housed around 37,000 inmates and ran at 125.5 percent of capacity. Each facility was bursting at the seams with prisoners. For his part in the scheme of things, Lucas had simply been reduced to a prison number and, despite his protestations and murderous threats, anxious to make more cell space for the 9,000 new inmates that are admitted every year, on June 3, 1970, correctional staff literally dragged him to the gates and threw him out.

That afternoon, a young woman was murdered in Jackson, just a few miles from the grim prison walls. Another girl's body turned up, a few blocks away from where the first corpse was found, on the following day. Officially, neither of these murders has been attributed to Lucas, although the cases are still classed as "open."

For his part, Lucas claims responsibility, adding, "They [the prison authorities] know I meant what I said. I hated everything. I was as bitter as bitter can be. I was madder than hell."

Unofficially, the story is somewhat different. A senior law officer who cannot be named told the author, "Sure, everyone knew it was Henry who killed those girls. The decision not to arrest him went right to the top, and I mean the top. But those assholes didn't want the shit that would come their way if the press knew that he had threatened to kill somebody on the day he was released. If they had, the rinky-dinks and the governor would have been thrown out of the gates with him."

* * *

Many of the incidents in Henry's checkered history, sandwiched between his release from prison in Michigan to his final arrest in Montague County, Texas, 13 years later, are shrouded in mystery. Initially, he was paroled to live with Almeda Kiser, another half-sister, in Maryland and, for almost a year, he kept out of trouble with the police. In August 1971, his supply of Prozac ran out, and he failed to renew the prescription. Lucas said that this lack of medication made him restless and very angry.

In October 1971, he approached a 15-year-old girl, walking to school. He ordered her to get into his car or he would shoot her. An approaching school bus came into view, and he raced off in a cloud of dust, leaving the terrified girl by the roadside. A few days later, he tried to abduct another schoolgirl and she escaped without harm. However, both potential victims had made a note of his licence plate number and they reported it to the police.

In March 1972, Lucas was back before the courts and sentenced to another five years in prison, for attempted abduction and kidnapping. Following his release, on August 22, 1975, Lucas traveled to Port Deposit, Maryland, to visit his half-sister, Almeda, and her daughter, Aomia Pierce. Records show that he stayed there for three days, after which he moved to Chatham, Pennsylvania, with Aomia Pierce and her husband. He found menial work as a farm hand before being introduced to Betty Crawford, the widow of one of his nephews. Initially, they were just friends but the relationship developed steadily until they were finally married, on December 5, 1975.

After living with the Pierces for a short time, Lucas, Crawford and her three children moved back to Port Deposit to live in a trailer park. Henry drifted from job to job earning only small amounts of money. The bulk of the family's income was provided by Betty's social security payments. The family lived in this manner until June 1976, when, in company with another family from the trailer park, they moved to Hurst, Texas. The plan was for Betty to visit her mother while Henry looked for work. When this plan failed, they moved to Illinois, before returning to Maryland.

Shortly after returning, Betty Crawford accused Lucas of molesting her daughters. Lucas denied the charges but told her that he had decided to leave anyway. On July 7th, Lucas packed his few belongings and headed off towards Florida. On the way south, he stopped off to stay with Opal. Less than a month later, Henry and his brother-in-law, Wade Kiser, traveled to West Virginia for a family reunion. On the way, while caught in heavy traffic, Henry struck up a conversation with another man and, shortly after, he left Kiser to team up with the stranger for a trip to Shreveport, Louisiana. After a brief stop over in Virginia, to visit his half-brother, Harry Waugh, Lucas arrived at his destination.

While in Shreveport, Henry was offered the job of driving a car to Los Angeles but declined after he became convinced that he would be working for the mafia. He left Louisiana and went back to Port Deposit. He didn't stay long and moved on to Wilmington, Delaware, where a relative, Leland Crawford, gave him work in a carpet store. This employment lasted for several months, then he returned again to Port Deposit to spend Christmas with another relative, Nora Crawford. The following January, he left Nora and moved to Hinton, West Virginia, and went to work for Joe Crawford, who was not only a relative, but also owned a carpet store. While in Hinton, he met a woman called

Rhonda Knuckles and lived with her, until March 1978 when he tired of the relationship and returned yet again to Port Deposit. Lucas stayed for a short time until his sister Almeda offered him lodgings and a job in her husband's wrecking yard. Henry seemed settled until Almeda accused him of sexually molesting her granddaughter. Again, he denied the accusation.

On or about September 4, 1977, Lucas says he was in California, where he claims to have murdered Elizabeth Wolf in Davis, a medium-size city, some 25 miles west of Sacramento. What he was doing so far south remains a mystery, although his late mother had had a relationship with a man named Dixon, who hailed from a city of the same name, 15 miles from where he killed Elizabeth Wolf. Perhaps he was searching for his natural father?

After stabbing Mrs. Wolf, Lucas hightailed it to Houston, Texas, where, on September 7th, he shot to death Glenda Beth Goff. On September 17, 1977, he was arrested for a misdemeanor in Jacksonville, Florida, and was jailed for 45 days. The morning after his release, he told the Kisers that he needed their truck and tools to collect a couple of wrecked cars for the yard. When Lucas didn't return that night, or the following day, the Kisers reported the car as stolen. The vehicle was later recovered outside Jacksonville, Florida, in an undrivable condition. It was here that Lucas met his future sidekick, Ottis Toole.

* * *

Ottis Elwood Toole was born on March 5, 1947, in Florida. His background was similar to Henry's. At age four, Ottis was run over by a car. By the age of six, his alcoholic father had been sexually abusing him for several years and, when his genetic father left home, Robert, an equally perverted stepfather, moved in and took over where his predecessor had left off.

At eight, Ottis fell through a broken board on his front porch, impaling his forehead on a nail that went three inches into the frontal lobe of his brain. That injury, it is said, resulted in his suffering from *grand mal* epileptic seizures for the rest of his life.

The youngest of four children, Ottis had been born into a family that was totally inbred, schizophrenic and psychopathic. His mother, Sarah, a Bible-thumping Baptist who chanted verse at the drop of a hat, had grown accustomed to her second husband passing young Ottis around to his drinking cronies for sex. And if that form of abuse was not bad enough, the boy was bullied 24 hours a day, by his elder brothers and sexually abused by his sisters, Drusilla and Vonetta, who made him dress up as a girl and made him wait on them like a little Cinderella. Notwithstanding this torment, Ottis grew into a strapping, 6 foot 2 inch hulk, with large hands and a powerful 200 pound physique.

The Tooles's run-down, clapboard house was set deep in alligator country, in Springfield, Florida, and it put a leaking roof over the heads of Ottis's family as they came and went in this explosive powder keg of overcrowding, poverty and sexual deviation. Perhaps no one can sum up Ottis Toole better than the author Sondra London. Sondra interviewed Toole at the Appalachee Correctional Institute, in July 1991, and she made this observation about this serial killer in her book, *Knockin' on Joe*:

> To him, life itself is so unmeaning, and the distinction between living and dead people so blurred, that killing is no more than swatting a fly. Retarded and illiterate, he has been out of control since his early childhood. Born in the shadow of the "'Gator Bowl," Ottis is a real live "'gator"—a bottom feeder, more reptilian than human, scuttling through the swamps of society, ceaselessly scanning for helpless prey.

Lucas and Toole met in a soup kitchen, not far from Jacksonville. At this time, Ottis was sharing a house with his mother, Sarah, and her husband, Robert, Ottis's wife, Novella, a nephew, Frank Powell Jr. and Frieda "Becky" Powell, Ottis's 11-year-old niece. It seems that the Toole family was quite used to Ottis bringing home strange men from the mission. Sarah Pierce, a one time house guest, later told police that Ottis, a known bisexual, often picked up men to bring home for sexual purposes. As well as his homosexual tendencies, Ottis also enjoyed watching his male guests have sex with his wife and the under-age Becky. Henry soon adapted to his new home, and he shared the main bedroom with Ottis after Novella was sent to stay with neighbors.

Ottis got a job for Henry in the paint factory where he worked, but it was only a few days before Lucas quit and headed south to his former hunting grounds in Texas, where, on October 22, 1977, he shot dead Lily Pearl Darty with two bullets to the back of her head. On November 1st, in Bellmead, near Waco, Texas, he shot Glen D. Parks, twice, with a .38 caliber revolver, after first hog-tying his victim.

Lucas's next murder spree started in and around Jacksonville in late 1978, but not until he and Toole had, by Lucas's own claim, joined a satanic cult called The Hand of Death. In fact, Lucas attributed his most heinous crimes—The Crucifixion Killings—to the devil and "his doings." Later, he claimed that he underwent cult training in the Florida everglades some time after he was released from prison. According to a 1985 book, *The Hand of Death*, which was written by Lucas and coauthored by Max Call, there were some 200 inductees in his class, representing six different nations, and all ethnic groups and social classes. Henry further claims that during his first week of training, he began by teaching a class in the techniques of killing with a knife. They practiced hand-to-hand combat, studied law enforcement manuals, and memorized radio communication codes. All of this must have been an uphill struggle for Henry because of his extremely low IQ. After careful research by this author, it was realized that this large class of students, and the training they enjoyed, only existed in the fantasy-driven imaginings of Lucas's mind, and nowhere else. He also says that they read a satanic bible, and since the participants believed that acts of perversion would provoke the reincarnation of the devil, and glorify Satan, the group leaders encouraged the practice of sodomy, sado-masochism, bestiality and necrophilia that followed each black mass, all of which were subjects that Lucas was already at home with.

During these alleged devil-worshipping ceremonies, Henry told the author that they sacrificed kidnapped children, or traitorous members, on an altar within a sacred circle. Dancing worshippers carried the luckless victims on their shoulders while the remainder of the group chanted "*Ambe iske ho a secco*," the meaning of which remains a mystery! Nevertheless, Lucas has it that a high priest, called "The Hand," wearing the obligatory cloak, walked, through rings of fire, to the altar where he slaughtered the victims, and everyone was required to drink the blood and eat the flesh. Henry says that he left the camp after seven weeks to carry out the murderous orders of a superior named Don Meteric.

On his first mission, presumably with the devil sitting on his shoulder, Lucas claims he kidnapped small children and dropped them off at a large sheep ranch, just across the Mexican border. When he returned to the cult, his superiors tattooed a scorpion on his hand. Meteric then asked Lucas and Toole to kill a man. This victim was lured to a beach where Lucas cut his throat as the victim took a drink from a bottle of whisky. Lucas's reward, for committing this crime, was a second tattoo. Later, he was tattooed with a snake, then the Devil hold-ing a cross, for abducting young prostitutes, who were forced to take part in pornographic snuff movies.

When I asked Lucas to reveal his tattoos, he blandly explained that they had vanished after he turned to Christianity. He apparently turned to God immediately after murdering 72-year-old Librada Apodaca in El Paso, Texas, on May 27, 1983.

If one were to believe a single word about the cult—and there isn't one iota of evidence to support even a hint that it ever existed—one is left wondering how Lucas and Toole found the time to drive to Kennewick, Nevada, where it is known that the duo raped and killed Lisa Martini, in her apartment, on October 31, 1978. By his own reckoning, Lucas was either in the everglades learning radio procedures—obviously vital for devil-worshipping—or in Mexico, trading in kidnapped children, of which law enforcement has no knowledge whatsoever. The killer then returned to Jacksonville and resumed his old job. Later, Ottis's mother bought a house and moved her extended family into it. Henry quit his job again and went into the scrap metal business, soon filling the backyard of the new house with wrecked vehicles and parts.

On November 5, 1978, police established that the two serial killers were driving along Interstate 35 in Texas, when they spotted a teenage couple walking along the side of the road after their car had run out of gas. Toole shot Kevin Kay in the back and head with a .22 caliber pistol, while Lucas raped Rita Salazar, before firing six bullets into her. Kevin Kay, who had a minor criminal record, was identified through fingerprints, and the attractive Rita was his steady girlfriend.

Now, ever mobile, the two men drove to Michigan where, on October 3, 1979, they robbed, raped and murdered Sandra Mae Stubbs. Then, they turned around and headed south, to Austin, Texas, where Harry and Molly Schlesinger were shot to death in their liquor store ten days later. Throughout this short period, the killers financed their criminal activities through robbery, culminating in murder.

* * *

Arguably, the most infamous Lucas/Toole murder was the raping and shooting of a still unidentified young woman in the case that has become dubbed "The Orange Socks Murder." Found in a culvert on

Halloween, October 31, 1979, the victim wore no clothes except for a pair of orange socks. A motorist, who had been driving north on Interstate 35, stopped to relieve himself and, to his horror, he found himself peering down at a corpse, lying face down and hugging the dirty concrete. "I had just taken ma pecker out," he told a police officer, who arrived quickly on the scene, "an' shit! Ya know, Jesus, fuckin' shit! It was there, ya know. Took a pee anyways, though."

This murder fell under the jurisdiction of Williamson County Sheriff Jim Boutwell and, back at his jail in Denton, some ten miles north of Fort Worth, the veteran cop pored over the few clues available. He was hoping that they would reveal something positive. He was looking for anything that could lead to identifying "Orange Socks" and her killer.

The attractive female was in her mid-twenties. She had reddish-brown hair, weighed between 125 to 130 pounds, and was 5 feet 9 inches tall. Apart from the orange socks, she wore a silver, inlaid abalone ring. There was no purse, handbag or driver's licence. There was nothing else whatsoever.

At autopsy, the body gave up a few clues, one of which indicated that she had venereal disease. There were tiny insect bites on her ankles, probably flea bites. Her stomach contents contained traces of a partially digested meal—burger, fries and Coke. Her teeth were almost perfect, so dental records might not even exist, and an X-ray showed no broken bones. On more intimate examination, a makeshift tampon made from toilet tissue was removed from the vagina, and that was all Boutwell had to go on. There was nothing that could help identify her to family or friends, and circulating her photograph around the entire North American continent was out of the question.

After his arrest in Montague County, Texas, Lucas admitted that he had killed "Orange Socks," but he refused to name Toole as an accomplice. Lucas says he picked her up while she was hitchhiking out of Oklahoma City. He thought her name was either Joannie or Judy.

They drove south down Interstate 35, and he said they had consensual sex before they ate a meal at a truck stop. He described the meal, which was consistent with the medical examiner's evidence.

After eating, they drove further south, and Henry said he asked her for more sex, but she refused. A struggle ensued with him nearly losing control of the car, which screeched to a standstill in a cloud of dust after almost leaving the road. "After I pulled over," he said, "I done choked her until she died. I had sex with her again, then I pulled her out of the car and dropped her down the culvert." He also mentioned that she wore some kind of sanitary towel, which he called a "Kotex."

Sheriff Boutwell would not leave this particular case alone; he was determined to solve it for he reasoned that this was just one of a string of sexually-related homicides committed along the Interstate 35 corridor. Bodies just kept turning up on the much-traveled highway between Laredo on the Mexican border, and Gainesville, Cooke County, in the north.

On November 27, 1979, Lucas and Toole were back in Jacksonville. In Cherokee County that night, during the course of robbing a motel, Lucas raped, then shot to death, 31-year-old Elizabeth Dianne Knotts. Two weeks later, an 18-year-old was raped and stabbed to death in her home. Debra Lynn O'Quinn's remains were later discovered in woods close by.

On January 5, 1980, the two men wheedled their way into the home of 76-year-old Jamie L Collins, whom the two men sexually assaulted and stabbed.

March 27th brought the beating and hacking to death of 45-year-old Jo Scheffer. Her body was found, in a day care center, 12 hours later.

On July 12th, 24-year-old Regina Azell Campbell was found dead underneath a car. She had been raped by both men, then strangled.

July 20th witnessed the brutal rape and murder of Tammy Keel Conners. Aged 19, this beautiful young woman, with aspirations of becoming a model and actress, had been dragged screaming from the roadside, and subjected to unspeakable acts of savagery before being tossed, half alive, into a ravine, near Jacksonville.

There is no way of ascertaining the total victim count of Lucas and Toole. These eight murders may only be the tip of the iceberg. However, it is known that the two men struck again, on December 22nd, when the 28-year-old mother of two children, Brenda Elaine Harden, was found raped and stabbed to death in her bedroom.

1981 brought no respite for the residents of the area as the festive season ended. Lucas says they killed again and again. Certainly they ended the life of down-and-out, 58-year-old Shirley Ogden, for her mortal remains were found near trash cans, on an alley, on April 14th.

Toole was also enjoying his criminal hobby of arson. He has claimed to have started a "100 of 'em." On January 4, 1982, the two men killed 65-year-old George Sonenberg, who died an agonizing death a week after Toole poured gas over him, while he lay in a drunken stupor, and set him alight. By all accounts, this offense started as a robbery which went wrong, and as was their usual practice when committing arson, the men watched from the brush as the flames shot into the night sky, laying low as the firefighters fought the inferno, rescuing a fatally burned Sonenberg during the process. With any evidence of the robbery and attempted murder reduced to cinders, the police believed that the victim had tragically set fire to himself after dropping a lit cigarette as he dozed off. That Sonenberg reeked of gasoline appears to have been overlooked by the police. Toole later confessed to this murder when law officers visited him, after his arrest, and while he was a resident at the Raiford Penitentiary. For this crime, Toole received the death sentence.

On January 9, 1982, and just five days after torching George Sonenberg, Lucas and Toole broke into the Jacksonville Home for Children and "rescued" Becky and Frank. The foursome hit the road on a crime spree that would encompass many more states, including Nevada, New Mexico and Texas.

* * *

Back at the ranch, so to speak, the indefatigable Sheriff Boutwell had a list of 20 unsolved homicides cluttering his desk. It had not been an easy four months for him and, back in October 1981, he had been forced to take a bold initiative. With the assistance of Texas Rangers company "F," based in Waco, and the Crime Analysis section of the Department of Public Services, in Austin, Boutwell had organized a meeting to pool any information on the Interstate murders. From border to border, 29 officers and agents, from the 500-mile stretch of I-35, came together for the first time. Methodically, they sifted through photographs, witness reports and evidence, comparing modus operandi in an effort to disentangle the mystery surrounding the killings.

After Christmas, Sheriff Boutwell summed up the results: most of the victims had been dumped along I-35. They had been shot, beaten to death, strangled, set on fire, crucified, raped or sodomized and stabbed. There had also been a hit-and-run, which smacked of murder. The sheriff was up to his eyes in murder most foul, and up the creek without a paddle.

In Florida, the Jacksonville City Police and Sheriff's Department were experiencing similar difficulties, as were their colleagues in Michigan and elsewhere. But Lucas and Toole were ever-mobile interstate killers and, unless they made a mistake, they might carry on with their murderous spree for years to come. The two men also enjoyed another advantage: they were not committing federal crimes, so the FBI and U.S. Marshals Service had no interest or jurisdiction. In every respect, it was left to the relatively inexperienced local police agencies to solve their own crimes. State by state, city by city and town by town, these agencies had neither the budget and the time, nor the interest to liaise with each other.

* * *

Henry Lucas was 40 years old, and he had fallen in love with the 13-year-old Becky, who looked every bit of 19 when it was required of her. The two men often used her as jailbait to lure unsuspecting truckers into their murderous net. Hauling long distances, the bored and lonely drivers were unable to resist the temptation of a scantily-dressed girl, thumbing a ride. It became an all-too-familiar scenario; the hiss of air brakes, a cloud of dirt and dust, the throbbing engines of those big trucks. "Hop up here, gal," they'd shout. Then, as soon as the cab door was thrown open, the driver would find himself examining the dangerous end of a loaded pistol.

A similar technique would be used with Becky "dressing down" for the killing to be done. On one occasion, their car overheated under the blistering Texas sun, so they stopped in Tyler County. Becky knocked on an elderly woman's door, asking for water to top up the radiator. The trusting lady cooked them all breakfast, and while Becky and Frank finished off their over-easy eggs, grits and ham, the two men finished off their host with a brutal rape and two well-placed shots to her head.

Eventually, though, Lucas claims that Toole began acting weird and doing things that he didn't approve of, such as mistreating Becky, mutilating bodies, even barbecuing and eating their victim's flesh. And, there was another problem. Ottis had fallen in love with Henry who, in turn, was in love with Becky. It seems that Ottis didn't want to share Lucas with Becky—or anyone else, dead or alive. That Lucas raped his victims didn't help the problem with the possessive Toole, and the rift was the starting point for the men parting company. They broke up in late January 1982, when Lucas raped and sodomized a young girl, while Becky and Frank watched and Ottis seethed with anger.

Now at the point of almost complete mental disintegration, Toole took out his hatred on this victim, beating her mercilessly and slashing her until she died. When he had finished, Toole headed home to Jacksonville, while Lucas, Becky and Frank made for California.

Fifty miles east of Los Angeles, they stopped at the unremarkable city of Hemet and, while searching for work as a carpenter, Lucas met Jack and Becky Smart, who owned an antique refurbishing business. Using his skills learned in prison, Lucas exchanged his labor in return for room and board. As time passed, Mrs. Smart grew to like Henry and, at some sacrifice to her own business, she decided that he would make a much-needed handyman for her 80-year-old mother, Kate Rich, who lived in Ringgold, Clay County, Texas. The Smarts bought bus tickets for the trio and, pressing some cash into their hands, stood and waved their goodbyes.

* * *

Kate Rich was an energetic widow who had difficulty walking. She was well liked by her neighbors, sewed patchwork quilts, enjoyed fresh crayfish, and delighted in the frequent visits made by her many children, grandchildren and great-grandchildren, several of whom lived in the vicinity. When Henry knocked on her door with a message from her California daughter, Granny Rich ushered him in with open arms. Inadvertently, Mrs. Smart had sent her mother the Angel of Death.

Before long, however, Henry's dingy clothes, backwoods talk, foul language and strange behavior began to make Kate's family and friends feel uneasy; besides, he didn't seem to be so handy after all. It was either that, or he was just bone-idle. For the better part of each day, he chain-smoked cigarettes and drank coffee or beer. Then, making one mouth less to feed, Frank departed, to hit the road on his own. Shortly after this, Kate told Henry and Becky that they had to go. He was a waster, she wanted nothing more to do with him, and the following morning, they went in search of another place to live.

The sun had climbed high in the Texas sky, and the temperature was well over 100 degrees when preacher Rubin Moore spotted Henry and Becky trying to thumb a lift near Ringgold's bus station. He picked them up and drove them to his House of Prayer, ten miles south, in Stoneburg, Montague County. In 1994, when the author visited the place with Paul Smith, an investigator for the District Attorney, the place had changed little. It was, and still is, a converted chicken farm inhabited by a small group of religious fundamentalists, who keep the gates padlocked and do not entertain visitors.

Rubin Moore owned a roofing company, and the preacher and Lucas agreed that the couple could live in a shack and use the communal kitchen. In return, Henry would work for Rubin Moore, while Becky would stay behind to help out with the chores around the House of Prayer.

For a while, all seemed rosy in the garden. Becky was very happy, and she attended Sunday services, visiting Granny Rich who had a soft spot for the young girl, whenever she could. And, considering her close contact with the religious comings and goings, it was not long before she got caught up in the spirit of things.

In August 1982, she renounced her life of sin, and decided to leave Henry and return to Florida. Henry could join her, if he wished to mend his unrighteous ways, she told him. On August 24th, they argued well into the late hours, with Henry finally caving in to her demands: he would go with her when she left. Around midnight, they silently gathered together their belongings, slipped out of the property without telling a soul, and started to hitch a ride for Florida.

A typically hot and sticky Texas night found them under a flyover intersection in Denton. There, in an open field, they spread out a blanket and undressed. Henry set aside his heavy Bowie knife for protection and asked Becky for sex. She refused, and they started to argue again. Lucas had changed his mind; he didn't want to return to

Florida after all, he wanted to remain at the House of Prayer. Becky was determined to go her own way, then she slapped him across the face. Without thinking, he heaved the knife into her chest. The blade sliced her heart, and she died minutes later. When he realized what he had done, Lucas cradled her in his arms and wept.

Before sunrise, Lucas decided that he should bury the body. He removed a ring from her finger, cut her into pieces, put all but the legs into pillowcases, and placed her in a shallow grave. Then he tied a belt around the legs, and dragged them into the brush where they would be eaten by wild animals. Henry returned to the House of Prayer with the story that Becky had hitched a ride from a truck driver. He appeared calm as he reiterated the phony account to Rubin Moore, who apparently found it all quite plausible.

On September 16th, a Sunday evening, Lucas announced that he was taking Granny Rich to church. He went to her house, and, as it was too early for the service, they decided to drive across the State line, into Oklahoma, for several six-packs of beer. They drove and talked for almost two hours while the church service started and finished. Then murder took place.

Kate was a regular attender and she was furious at having missed church. As they turned in the direction of her home, Lucas suddenly veered off Route 81, drove along a track, crossed a railway line towards a disused oil well, and slammed on his brakes. Why Lucas killed Kate Rich is unknown and he won't discuss the matter, but it is known that the old boy was very fond of Becky, therefore it seems feasible that she had been asking Lucas a few, very awkward questions. He stabbed Kate and, as her last breath was leaving her lungs, he slashed an upside-down cross between her breasts and had sex with the dead body. Afterward, he dragged the corpse over a nest of fire ants, and down into a reedy ditch, where he stuffed Kate Rich into a dried out culvert. He lodged the corpse in place with a length of two-by-four timber, which he found by the railroad. He buried her clothes nearby and returned to the House of Prayer.

Known as "Hound Dog," Sheriff Conway of Montague County, told me that Kate's relatives had grown anxious about her disappearance and had reported the matter to him. The sheriff soon learned that she had last been seen alive in the company of Lucas, so he hauled him in for questioning. But the ugly man just clammed up. "There was not enough evidence for me to arrest that little sonofabitch," Conway said. "I checked his name through the National Crime Information Center's computer and, yes, Lucas had a criminal record. But, that wasn't enough and I had to set him free. We did keep an eye on him, believe me."

The end for Lucas was not far off, for he had two serious problems. Kate Rich and Becky Powell were now reported as missing, both having last been seen alive with Lucas and, in that neck of the woods, news travels fast. Dozens of accusatory fingers were now pointing in his direction, so he left town, spinning the yarn that he was off to find Becky.

From Ringgold, he made his way to California, where he intended to lay a smokescreen by talking to the Smarts. But, while he was there, Mr. Smart noticed blood on Henry's car seat and he contacted the local police, who, in turn, contacted Sheriff Conway.

Lucas spent the remainder of October bumming around the country before he foolishly returned to Montague County. There, Hound Dog had found an old 1981 Maryland arrest warrant for Lucas, who had previously violated his parole conditions. Sheriff Conway arrested his man and hooked him up to a polygraph machine, and the print out indicated that Lucas was not telling the truth about Kate Rich. This was not sufficient evidence with which to charge him with capital murder, so, in an attempt to detain him longer, Conway faxed his colleagues in Maryland. The Maryland police curtly informed Sheriff Conway that they were no longer interested in Lucas, and they certainly would not pay the extradition costs to have him brought back to their jurisdiction. Lucas was set free again.

* * *

For several months, Lucas drove the interstate highways of America. He visited Mexico, California and Illinois, where he met Gloria Ann Stephens, whom he brought back to Texas with him. He killed her and dumped the body outside the town of Magnolia, near Huntsville. Then, shamelessly, he returned like a bad penny to the House of Prayer. Fearing that someone might stumble across the corpse of Kate Rich, he drove out to the culvert and retrieved the remains, which he later cremated in a wood burning stove at the House of Prayer. He dumped the ashes into the garbage for their regular collection.

On October 9, 1982, Wise County Sheriff Phil Ryan from Decatur, and Denton County Sheriff Weldon Lucas interviewed Henry at the House of Prayer, but still no charges were pressed. Within an hour of the law leaving, he went to Kate Rich's home and set it ablaze, before traveling back to California. His car broke down in Tucumari, New Mexico, so he called Rubin Moore, asking him to collect him and take him back to Montague County.

Hound Dog Conway didn't earn his name from being anything less than a tenacious law enforcement officer, and it transpired that Rubin Moore had taken possession of a .22 caliber pistol, which Lucas had given to him for safekeeping. With the Maryland parole violation a dead duck, Conway now had a rock solid reason to arrest Lucas. "It is a felony for any ex-prisoner, convicted of a violent crime, to possess a firearm," Conway explained, "I was rubbing my hands with glee."

Hound Dog arrested Lucas at the House of Prayer. He threw him into a cell where the prisoner complained about the cold—the sheriff had deliberately turned up the airconditioning to freeze his suspect into talking. He also stopped Lucas's ration of cigarettes and coffee. For his part, Lucas bitterly complained, "You sure know how to put a man down, sheriff."

It was perhaps inevitable that a deal would be struck, as Lucas habitually smoked up to 80 cigarettes a day, drank coffee by the gallon, and hated the cold. He was soon confessing to a large number of murders, drawing pictures of his victims, and writing pages of notes, such as these,

one killed in new
york
light Brown hair
Blue eyes
New York
Buffalo
would Have Been Strangled
with white cord
gold ear
pins
had dress
inside apartment
Joanie
white pretty teeth
with gap in front
Top Teeth
Blue eyes small pin
Ear
Hair below shoulders
through over
Bridge
with head and fingers
missing

In Wichita Falls, on October 1, 1983, Lucas pleaded guilty to the murder of Kate Rich, and he was given a 75-year sentence. But he still had Becky's murder to account for, and he stood trial for this at Denton County Court. His defense was that it was an involuntary act, committed in the heat of the moment, during an argument. In addressing the jury, Henry's attorney, Tom Whitlock, threw in the only defense he had. "I think it happened in such a way it was strictly an accident," he said. However, what Tom Whitlock said, and what the jury of seven men and five women believed, were poles apart. On November 10, 1983, they deliberated for two hours before reaching a verdict of guilty. The judge gave Lucas a life sentence.

A Texas life sentence does not necessarily mean life, and there was every possibility that Lucas might be paroled in the future. However, Williamson County Sheriff, Jim Boutwell, had other ideas. If he had had his way, he would have seen to it that Lucas went to the electric chair, for the murder of Orange Socks.

Boutwell had questioned Lucas while he was being arraigned for the murder of Kate Rich. He had shown him a photograph of the body of Orange Socks, being careful to cover the neck area so that Lucas wouldn't see the cause of death. The suspect could have come up with a number of causes; instead, he claimed, "Yeah, that one was a hitch-hiker, and she would have been strangled." He went on to give other details about this murder, along with another 156 homicides across the country. But his confession to the Orange Socks murder was all Sheriff Boutwell needed, and so that there would be no retraction, he filmed the confession on a video camera.

In the United States, the death penalty is usually sought when murder is accompanied by another serious offence, making the crime "aggravated." With his attorney strongly advising his client to shut up, Lucas rambled on and on, saying that he had raped Orange Socks before and after her death. Death by execution is merely a legal formality after that type of admission. Lucas had bought a ticket to his own perdition.

* * *

Captain Bob Prince, of Texas rangers Company F, is a law officer who is larger than life. Weighing in at well over 200 pounds, he stands 6 foot 4 inches, and he is a formidable cop in every sense of the word. As a sergeant who was placed in charge of coordinating the 875 police agencies, with more than 1,000 investigators who wanted to interview Lucas about unsolved murders committed in their respective jurisdictions, Bob Prince was kept so busy that he had to book the interviews six months in advance. So popular was Lucas that Bob Prince kept extensive records of most telephone calls and written requests.

Lucas now held center stage during the greatest crime show on Earth and he was revelling in every moment of it. Dressed in an expensive new suit, shirt and shoes, he visited the dentist for the first time in his life and had a set of dentures fitted. Police officers competed to be photographed with Henry Lucas, who was becoming known as the most prolific serial killer in American history. It seems that no expense was spared as the police were as anxious to clear up as many crimes as possible.

By April, police had cleared up 190 cases, although Bob Prince explained that if Henry had had it his way, the number would have totalled 3,000 and more. In their rush to clear up unsolved homicides, and wipe the red chalk from their incident boards, officers did not concern themselves that he often confessed to murders committed on the same day, some 600 miles apart, when his only form of transportation was his feet.

As the files built up, police assumed that common patterns between the murders might emerge, although very few did. Apart from the I-35 and Jacksonville murders, when there was a common M.O., the murders had been committed using pistols, rifles, shotguns, table legs, telephone cords, vases, knives, hammers, tire irons, two-by-four lengths of wood, axes, vacuum cleaner cable, nylon rope, burned, and even a car. Although Lucas has said, "They was killed by every way known to man, except poison," it is now commonly agreed that he may have only actually killed a fraction of the total he admitted to.

Sheriff Boutwell was adamant that Lucas had killed hundreds of people during his reign of terror, but when confronted with solid evidence that suggested otherwise, he refused to comment further. Bob Prince now agrees that Lucas may have murdered 30 people, if that, in his time.

* * *

The structure and quality of family interaction is an important factor in a child's development, especially in the way the child perceives family members, and their interaction with the child, and with each other.

The FBI states, "For children growing up, the quality of their attachments to parents and to other members of the family is most important as to how these children, as adults, relate to, and value other members of society. Essentially, these early life attachments (sometimes called bonding) translate into a map of how a child will perceive situations outside the family."

Reflecting on Henry's childhood, there is no doubt that he was psychologically damaged during his formative years. However, as most authorities will agree, millions of people, from all walks of life and cultures, suffer similar abuse, and they don't turn into serial killers.

In his book called, *Serial Killers—the Growing Menace*, the late Joel Norris mentions Henry's diet as a child:

These years of malnutrition, especially during childhood, resulted in stunted development in the cerebral tissue as well as an impaired judgement and cognitive performance. It was only during his incarceration that his diet was stabilized to the point where he no longer suffered from elevated levels of blood sugar and severe vitamin deficiencies.

Yet, although this may have the ring of truth about Lucas's problems, I doubt, given the available case history, that this is the entire story.

We know that Lucas's behavior, while in prison, was extremely psychotic and antisocial to say the least, and that is why he was prescribed Prozac, a drug that effectively controlled his emotions. It was this treatment, perhaps in concert with the balanced diet, that combined to settle Lucas down during his lengthy periods behind bars. However, inmates often calm down and act more responsibly within the structured penal system, so in this respect, Lucas was not unique.

Before his death, I interviewed Lucas a number of times. He comes across as something of a zombie, but an affable zombie. Without a doubt, the cocktail of psychological and physical child abuse, use of drugs, accidents, four packs of cigarettes a day, large consumption of alcohol and a poor diet, caused a progressive degeneration of his neurological system. As Joel Norris points out, "The physical connections between the different areas of the brain, the hundreds of millions of electromechanical switches that balance primeval feelings of violence with logical, socially disordered behavior, simply didn't work properly."

So, here is a man, therefore, who, like so many of his killer breed, died emotionally and socially before he was into his teens, and for whom life itself had just become a search to satisfy his dysfunctional urges from one day to the next. Of course, none of what has been suggested is intended to imply that Lucas was, by legal definition, insane. He knew the difference between right and wrong, good and evil. He knew he was taking long strides outside the social order, and he didn't care about the consequences, the carnage and heartbreak that he caused during the years of his homicidal spree.

During my last interview with Lucas, he argued that he had never killed anyone. Becky Powell was still alive and well, he said, even though police have since recovered a set of bleached bones from a site in Denton County identified by Lucas. But there was no forensic evidence categorically stating that these were the remains of Becky Powell. Furthermore, it would be in Lucas's interest to report that, recently, a woman has come forward to claim that she is Becky Powell. She has even offered to take a polygraph test and give blood samples, which could be used for DNA analysis. The police will not entertain the idea, even if it was for a little fun, or an interesting exercise. But what if Becky was still alive? The devil's work, with his Black Hand of Death cult of followers? Real life zombies returning from a Texas grave?

"I did not kill Kate Rich, either," Henry protested. And it could be argued that only the widow's ashes were left blowing in the wind. No one could identify her from those grey traces. Nevertheless, parts of her glasses *were* found near the wood burning stove, the very same stove in which he originally claimed he had cremated the body.

As our last interview drew to a close, I asked Henry how it was that he had led so many law officers to shallow graves, how he had described details that could only have been known to the murderer. His convoluted answer was that he had been shown pictures of the bodies *in situ*, so he was able to repeat that information. This, of course, begged the question, "How did you know where the bodies had been dumped?"

Once again, Lucas gave what he thought was a credible answer. "They [the police] done took me there beforehand, and then they came back to me afterward and asked me where the bodies were."

The problem with this answer is that the police had no idea where these corpses were until Henry told them.

In a last ditch effort to get Henry to tell the whole truth, he was asked about the murder of his mother. Wiping the dripping green slime from his false eye with his shirt cuff, he replied, "Nope. I just never killed no one. I just always thought I'd killed her dead. But my sister said on her deathbed that she'd killed my mom ... I never knew that. There was a witness to that, but she's dead, too."

Just two weeks previously, Lucas had been visited by police officers. During that interview, he confessed to another two murders, and gave them details of the burial sites. The bodies were subsequently recovered.

Henry Lee Lucas was like a rare, prehistoric specimen preserved in amber. He was insidious in a fascinating sort of way. Ugly, mentally flawed, he wore perfectly the persona of a serial killer in that human warehouse known as the Texas Department of Corrections.

* * *

Ottis Elwood Toole died in prison, of cirrhosis of the liver, in September 1996. Convicted killer Henry Lee Lucas was rescued from death row and almost certain execution by the then Governor of Texas, now President of the United States, George W. Bush, on June 25, 1998.

Bush said, "While Henry Lee Lucas is guilty of committing a number of horrible crimes, serious concerns have been raised about his guilt in this case [Orange Socks]."

Work records and a cashed paycheck indicated that Lucas had been in Florida, where he worked as a roofer, and these records coincided exactly with the date of this murder. Clearly, Lucas could not have been in two places at once, and now there is good reason to believe that the late Sheriff Boutwell knew this, too.

In Texas, a governor has the legal authority to commute a death sentence only on the recommendation of a majority of the 18-member Board of Pardons and Paroles. The same panel rejected a clemency plea from Karla Faye Tucker, a 38-year-old woman, who confessed to the pickaxe slayings of two people, but said she had become Christian in prison and asked for mercy. She was executed on February 3, 1998.

Since Governor Bush had been in office, a majority of the Board voted to recommend commutation of a death sentence on only one occasion. The only independent authority that a Texas governor has, in a death penalty case, is to grant a one-time, 30-day delay of execution. There had been 134 executions between the time Bush took office and the date of Lucas's commutation.

"There's an 80 percent chance I will walk out of prison some day," Lucas told the Associated Press. "He [Bush] stood up for what he believes in the law and law says no innocent person should be executed," added Henry, who had been set for lethal injection on June 30th for the 1979 slaying, in Williamson County, of Orange Socks.

On June 30th, he was taken from death row to the Texas Department of Criminal Justice Diagnostic Center in Huntsville, where he underwent medical and psychiatric tests to see if he was sane enough to be executed. His conversation with psychiatrists lasted about a minute. "They changed my record," he said afterward. "They said I was a nut. They sent it back over here; I went back down to these people. They said, 'They changed you to a nut.' These people changed my record back to the way it's supposed to be. I'm just a person trying to do their time, trying to clear these false cases and get back to my own life. That's all I am trying to do."

Escaping execution by the skin of his teeth, Henry was returned a week later to Ellis Unit, about 15 miles northeast of the town. But instead of returning to death row at Ellis, he was placed among the general prison population.

His life in the general population was not without adjustments. He still walked the corridors with his hands behind his back, a routine procedure on death row, where inmates are handcuffed. He also had a new prison number, trading his three-digit death row ID for a six-digit regular number.

"Down there, it's something different completely," he said of death row. "It's a tight feeling. Once you get to population, it's not that way."

He explained that when he arrived at his new cell, his cellmate requested an immediate transfer when he learned Lucas would be his partner. Henry was given a cell of his own.

Bush, who had said that Lucas would never be released from prison, said questions raised by Lucas, and others, about the murder for which he was subsequently given the death sentence, convinced him to allow the commutation. "It shocked me, to be honest," Lucas said. "I didn't think he was going to do it. Everybody was against it. He stood up for what he believed in. I gave up, yeah. Anybody would, with the kind of record I've got. But I only killed my mom, an' I served my time for that."

At age 64, Henry Lee Lucas died of a heart attack during the late hours of Monday, March 12, 2001. He was removed from his cell and transported to the medical area at Ellis Unit after complaining of chest pains, and he was pronounced dead at 10:17 p.m. After an autopsy at the University of Texas Medical Branch, in Galveston, he was buried at Peckerwood Hill Cemetery, the final resting place of thousands of Texas Department of Criminal Justice inmates whose bodies have been unclaimed by friends and family.

Over 500 people attended the service, more than three times the number to attend any killer's funeral in history.

This chapter is based on exclusive death row interviews between Christopher Berry-Dee and Henry Lee Lucas within Ellis Unit, Huntsville, Texas in 1996, and additional correspondence and research.

JOHN WAYNE
MICHAEL GACY

"It was all their [his victims'] fault.

They stalked and came on to me."

JOHN WAYNE GACY, DEATH ROW

Most of the things all of us value,

John had no value for at all. John didn't value

other life. John didn't value other emotions.

John didn't value any institutions.

John didn't value the feelings of other people.

GREG ADAMSKI, JOHN GACY'S ATTORNEY 1990–94

Smaller than I imagined, he bustles into the interview room, shackled and scrubbed as clean as a new pin. He smells of cheap disinfectant, a prison odor not unlike that exuded by a mortuary attendant. He has a slight, almost effeminate lisp. Potato-faced, round-shouldered, porcine blue eyes, he is two inverted cones joined together, bulging at his gut, a repugnant sight.

I have some patience for killers like Kenneth Bianchi because they are at least able to communicate at length. However, for this doughy monster, a creature that tortured and slaughtered at least 33 young boys, I have little time at all.

Gacy, among all other serial killers I have met, repulses me the most with his presence; his self-important attitude, declaring, "I grant you an audience at my behest," was all too apparent.

His handshake was like a damp cloth, his fingers feminine, the nails oh-so-carefully manicured like the words in his day-to-day diary, well clipped and cleaned for the observer's consumption.

It was not so much his catalogue of mind-sickening crimes that troubled me, it was more this gutless bisexual who degraded the word "humanity" that turned my stomach; how weak and pathetic can a "real" man be?

* * *

Born on a Tuesday, and executed on Tuesday, blue-eyed John Wayne Michael Gacy came into this world at Edgewater Hospital on St. Patrick's Day, March 17, 1942. He was to be the second of Marion and John Stanley Gacy's three children and their only son. Joanne was born two years earlier and, two years later, along came Karen.

Marion Elaine Gacy, née Robinson, was an outspoken and gregarious woman from Racine, Wisconsin. She loved to dance, sing and enjoyed a few drinks with her friends. She was also hard working, having supported herself as a pharmacist prior to her marriage at the age of 30. Her upbringing had been solid to the core, so here we find no abusive, hard-drinking butterfly; indeed, she was a thoroughly decent woman.

The family patriarch, John Stanley Gacy Sr., was born in Chicago, the son of Polish immigrants. Quite the opposite of his wife, he was serious, known to be self-contained, somber and largely incapable of displaying the gentler emotions such as happiness or sorrow. Nevertheless, he was applauded by colleagues as an industrious machinist, a perfectionist in a perfectionist's trade, and he earned a good living.

At home, John Sr. could do anything with his hands—carrying out household repairs, decorating, even creating his own tools and beating his wife, which he did frequently. Quick tempered, he could explode without any warning. At dinner, he would lash out at anyone who said so much as a word that displeased him. He also drank heavily and believed that to spare the rod was to spoil the child.

* * *

"I've always looked after my children—even now. A lot of things my dad did, I refuse to do 'cause... I... I... don't believe in hitting children... I always felt that service to the community... and community service to others, you know, in my religious background. If you serve other people, it will come back to serve you.

JOHN WAYNE GACY, DEATH ROW 1993

The Gacys' home on Opal Street, Norridge, Chicago, a location that gave a nod to suburbia, was one of six houses on the street but retained its rural charm. Visitors noticed that prairie grass grew like electric hair in every direction.

Norridge was a small community of proud, like-minded people who cared for their homes and their children. They kept livestock, including chickens and goats, and carefully tended their vegetable gardens. Doors were never locked, curtains never twitched with gossip, for they attended to their own business and expected their neighbors to attend to theirs.

John Jr.'s start in life was not without problems. One day, as John Stanley worked on his car, his four-year-old son wanted to help. However, he messed up a pile of parts that his father had neatly laid out in a specific order. For this slight infraction, Gacy yelled at his son and gave him a whipping with a belt. It was a thrashing John Wayne would remember for the rest of his life.

Around the same time as the thrashing, a neighbor's 15-year-old daughter, who had minor learning difficulties, took John out into the long prairie grass and pulled his pants down. The boy ran off home, shrieking at the top of his little voice to blurt out an account of what had happened to his mother. Much acrimony existed between both sets of parents for years afterward.

John Jr. loved animals and, aged six, he was given a mutt named Pal. In a drunken rage one day, John Stanley Gacy shot and killed the dog to punish his son, leaving the dead animal on a riverbank, where young John found it. The boy stole some flowers from a funeral parlor and gave Pal a proper burial.

The Gacy children enjoyed a Catholic education in the north of the city. Regarded by his teachers as a good student, John wasn't much liked by his schoolmates. He was overweight, clumsy and inclined to be dreamy and unimaginative. He was useless at sports and he wasn't good with his hands, either. Added to this was the fact that he was a sickly child. His mother had told him that he had a heart problem from birth, an "enlarged bottleneck heart," which kept him away from the rough-and-tumble play of childhood. The doctors could find nothing of this bad heart, but they were soon to have cause to wonder.

John was subjected to a pitiless campaign of mental and physical abuse from his bullying father in the years to come. It seemed that never a day passed without the boy getting into trouble. The elder Gacy never missed an opportunity to let his son know he was a disappointment, and was always berating the boy for the slightest mistake, calling him "dumb" and "stupid." This label must have fixed itself in Johnny's psyche like an unwelcome mantra.

At around age five, Johnny started to have seizures, causing him to pass out for no apparent reason. The doctors who examined him did not immediately settle on a precise diagnosis; nevertheless, advising caution, they prescribed large quantities of strong barbiturates along with anticonvulsant drugs such as Phenytoin (Dilantin) and Phenobarbital, which are used to treat seizure disorders and status epileptics.

Taken in small doses, these drugs have few harmful side effects. However, John Jr. was packed full of these pills and, if he wasn't well before he started taking them, he was most certainly a lot worse off under their influence, because Dilantin produces a veritable harvest of side effects.

First was gingival hyperplasia of the gums; apart from being uncomfortable and socially embarrassing, he noticed an uncontrollable growth of rapidly reddening gums which spread throughout his mouth, and this was followed by ataxia, nystagmus (involuntary movement of the eyeballs), slurred speech, decreased coordination with an inability to execute fine motor skills or manipulate objects, and unpredictable muscle movements. Not surprisingly, John suffered insomnia, dizziness, transient nervousness and was plagued with headaches, nausea, vomiting, constipation and, quite understandably, chronic depression. To cap it all, he also ran a very high risk of suffering toxic hepatitis and liver damage.

John's father had his own ideas about what was causing the seizures, putting it down to malingering, in an effort to miss out on school and gain attention. Marion Gacy thought differently. She knew her boy was ill and she did the best she could to protect him. As an experienced pharmacist, she should have known that her pre-adolescent son was growing steadily more dependent on the painless highs of these mood altering drugs, and she would have noted the adverse side effects. However, her main concern was directed at the ceaseless friction between the boy and his father. She acted as a buffer to such an extent that John Stanley taunted the boy about being a "mamma's boy" and told him he was going to be a "queer." Calling the child a "he-she" was another of his favorite labels of derision.

It was not until John was ten that the doctors eventually diagnosed his malady as a form of motor epilepsy. By then, the damage had been done, for he had been taking the powerful anti-seizure drugs for five years.

When he was nine, John Wayne claims he fell prey to sexual molestation from a friend of the family, a contractor who began giving the boy rides in his truck. These trips always included episodes of tickling and wrestling. Invariably, these sessions would end up with the boy's face caught between the man's legs, John claimed while on death row. He knew in some way that he was being victimized, but he felt powerless to do anything about it. Telling his father was out of the question.

Although the precise date is unavailable to us, around 1952 the family moved to a more spacious house at 4505 Mamora Street, in northwest Chicago. John later recalled that his father had a "secret place"—the large basement. Here, the man would soak up music by Richard Wagner and a lot of drink. The basement was off limits to the rest of the family. However, when drunk, Gacy Sr. would talk to himself in two different voices.

Before long, young John had found a secret place of his own underneath the front porch where he could see others but not be seen himself. Like his father, who enjoyed his own private den, the boy now had his own lair and what he did there was his secret, too. That was until he took an item of his mother's underwear to his playhouse and hid it in a paper bag. In later years, Gacy would explain to interviewers that he had not used the underwear for sexual purposes; as he had previously told his parents, he just liked the feel and smell of it.

When this infraction was discovered, John was subjected to yet another beating. He was to get another hiding when his younger sister, Karen, found her panties in his bed. After being thrashed by his father, his mother compounded the punishment and, in an effort to end this troubling habit, she forced him to wear women's panties to school under his clothes.

So John Wayne Michael Gacy staggered with faltering steps into his teens, only managing to get by with the support and the partial protection that his mother offered him from even more fatherly abuse. Nevertheless, even with the storm fence in the form of the matriarch around him, the psychological battering from John's father continued relentlessly. There would be no let up until Gacy Sr. died.

At age 11, young John Gacy was doing as well at school. He had few friends among his peers, although, again, his teachers considered him a good pupil. With that being said, he was a withdrawn boy who kept himself to himself. He wanted, indeed desperately needed, to meet his dad's high expectations, paralleling Mr. Gacy's desire for a son who shared his own interests and did things the way he did. John met some of the criteria—he was always neat and well turned out, he kept his room orderly and clean—but his father demanded so much more.

John Stanley Gacy took his 11-year-old son on a week's fishing trip to Wisconsin. This was the boy's first real chance to prove himself. Unfortunately, it rained the entire time. The fishing was ruined with the result that Gacy Sr. retired to the tent and drank to excess, all the while brooding and blaming his son for the failed adventure. He never took his son fishing again.

In the same year, John was playing by a swing when he was hit in the head by one of the seats. The accident caused a blood clot in the brain; the trauma wasn't discovered until he was 16 when the blackouts ceased after he was prescribed medication to dissolve the blockage.

The tough, brutal, hard-working, hard-drinking perfectionist and disciplinarian that was Mr. Gacy admired his own attributes in others, so young John set out to prove he could work hard. And it would be fair to say that, throughout his life, the "good" John Wayne Gacy was a workhorse who never let up.

At school, he ran errands for the teachers; he helped the school truant officer by telephoning parents to check up on absentees; at 14 he took on odd jobs after school; he had a paper route, and he worked as a stock clerk and delivered groceries for a local store. This work gave him his first salary.

John was a diligent young man, anxious to please. He helped his mother paint the house and do chores, and he made sure his school homework was still excellent. But this was still not enough in his father's eyes. Nothing John did was right.

* * *

"This is Christ as I see him in myself. And it is monolithic because Christ to me is monolithic; he's all things to all people."
JOHN WAYNE GACY, DEATH ROW 1992, DESCRIBING ONE OF HIS
PAINTINGS OF CHRIST

Although not commonly known, least of all agreed upon, it seems probable that Gacy started killing in his fourteenth or fifteenth year, for years later he admitted stabbing a youngster to death when he was about 15. This startling claim made by Gacy can also be supported by an unimpeachable source—none other than the former Des Plaines Chief of Police, Joe Kozenczak, who was the prime investigator in the 33 murders.

In the summer of 1989, Joe Kozenczak says he was sitting at his desk when Sergeant John Sarnowski of the Chicago PD came in. The officer had just read Russ Ewing's book on Gacy called *Buried Dreams*.

In 1955, Sarnowski had been a detective with the Chicago PD. In October of that year, John and Anton Schuessler and their friend Robert Peterson were found brutally murdered.

In his book *A Passing Acquaintance*, Joe records that "the boys' battered bodies were found in a forest preserve area on the northwest side of Cook County. About a year after the murders, Sarnowski was assigned to the case, and now thirty years later, he was still haunted by it."

While the sergeant had been reading about the young John Gacy in Ewing's book, he suddenly realized that Gacy, Peterson, and the Schuessler boys, aged 11 and 14, had lived within close proximity of each other on the northwest side of Chicago.

Gacy lived at 4505 North Mamora. The Schuesslers at 6711 North Mango Avenue; Robert Peterson at 5519 Farragut Street. Therefore, Gacy lived about a mile from the Peterson household, and a very short distance from the Schuesslers. Of some added significance, the school John Gacy attended at the time was at Prussing, which was close to the Farnsworth School attended by Peterson.

What had also piqued Sergeant Sarnowski's interest was that, as a youth, Gacy had frequently visited the Monte Cristo Bowling Alley. Coincidentally, this was the same bowling alley attended by the three other boys.

John Sarnowski had seen a photo of Gacy taken shortly after his arrest for serial murder, and he couldn't help but notice the strong resemblance between it and an artist's conception of a boy who used to meet with Robert Peterson when he took his sister to an eye doctor's surgery. According to the sergeant, the drawing was developed with the help from the eye doctor who described the boy [Gacy] as looking like Mr. Potato Head and having a limp.

At first, Joe Kozenczak couldn't believe his ears. The very notion that Gacy might have become a serial killer at such a young age was completely alien to him. It would have probably been alien to the entire U.S. law enforcement system as it is extremely rare to find a person committing serial murder at such a young age.

* * *

Sergeant Sarnowski persisted, continuing to add weight to his theory by suggesting that the modus operandi used to murder the three boys seemed to reflect a young serial murderer who had not yet perfected his method.

But that was not the end of it. Sarnowski added that Peterson had been strangled, that there was an indentation on the front of the throat from a sailor's knot, or from something else. (Gacy would often kill his victims with a ligature twisted tight with a length of dowel rod, which would have caused similar trauma to the throat area.)

The evidence found on the boys' bodies in 1955 indicated that they might have been killed in a machine shop type of environment. Sarnowski reminded Kozenczak that the Gacys had had a machine shop in the basement of their house on Mamora Street.

There were a few other correlations, some which interested Kozenczak and others that didn't. The idea that one boy could overpower three boys at the same time seemed most unlikely, yet it was not impossible. Sarnowski had brought this matter to his superiors, who found no reason to pursue the theory.

Shortly after their meeting, Kozenczak and Sarnowski visited the crime archives at Maybrook. The officer in the records section pulled down a box—a cardboard box that should have contained the complete files on the three murders. When they blew the dust off, they found to their utter dismay that the container was empty. The vitally important files were lost forever.

* * *

At the age of 17, Gacy was diagnosed with a non-specific heart ailment. He was hospitalized on several occasions for this problem throughout his life, but the doctors were not able to find an exact cause for the pain he was suffering. Although John complained frequently about his heart, even more so after his arrest for serial murder, he never suffered any serious heart attack, and many thought it was an attempt to gain sympathy votes, of which he received none.

The year 1960 started on a sound note for 18-year-old John Wayne Gacy, for by now he had learned that people admire volunteer workers. He knew that trusted and respected public servants such as law officers and firemen were at the top of the popularity list. Deprived of respect by his father at home, he had gained respect at school for his volunteer work. The grocery store boss admired him for being a hard working and industrious young man, and this was sufficient reward for the moment.

John formed a civil defense squad at his high school. As the organizer, he awarded himself the rank of captain. He even attached a flashing blue light to the dashboard of his car and, wearing his cop-type uniform, he delighted in racing off to a fire or traffic incident. It made him feel important, needed, respected. It gave him a sense of belonging, a kind of acceptance that came with his new responsibilities, something he'd sought so frequently from his father at home, to no avail.

In his late teens, it would seem that, at last, the friendly and earnest John Wayne Gacy was starting to succeed and move up the social ladder. However, in one area, he considered himself an abject failure— he was useless and pathetic with the opposite sex.

John was an unappealing sight: his doughy shape and potato head simply didn't appeal to the girls. On the rare occasions when he did find himself starting a sexual encounter, his nerves got the better of him and he failed. On one occasion in his car he passed out, just as he had done so many times before when under stress. The girl had partially stripped and they were groping each other when he fainted. The girl was shocked, Gacy was mortified, and, when he told his father, Gacy Sr. was furious with his weak son. Mr. Gacy hated homosexuals, and told young John he was becoming a queer, that he was a sissy and a weakling. But 18-year-old John refused to give up trying to please, so he threw himself into politics.

John ventured into political life by placing one toe in the water, starting volunteer work for an alderman candidate in the 45th Ward. For such a young man, he had taken on a great responsibility, yet, despite his success, his father ridiculed him. "Politics is all bullshit," his father ranted, "politicians are phonies; you are a patsy for working for free."

Nevertheless, John loved the work and long hours. He had found new friends who trusted and admired him. He had found another home in politics, a place where he was wanted and respected. Here, he could succeed and make his mark, so he dropped out of high school in 1961. Now 19, the rift between himself and his father widened more than ever before.

We could never accuse John Wayne Gacy of being work-shy. Despite all of his faults, here we find a young man who was driven to hard toil by his brutal and domineering father—not so much because Mr. Gacy demanded it of his son, but because John wanted to please in any way he could.

Not merely content with his political work, John labored away on behalf of the Catholic church, turning his hand to anything asked of him with zeal. Carrying out repairs, picking up the elderly and dropping them home after services, collecting and delivering their groceries—nothing was too much trouble. In fact, he spent so much time at church, he considered the priesthood. He even became a member of the St. John Berchmann's parish bowling team and showed some promise.

John recognized that the church was not meeting the needs of some parishioners, particularly the young ones. And, while it is easy for us to denigrate John's well intentioned ambitions, knowing as we do now that he was to become one of the most heinous serial murderers of all time, it's true that he formed a young adults group called the Chi Ro Club. Ever the organizer and eager to please, he put together social events, ran yard sales to raise cash and scheduled a formal winter dance. Gacy later told Lt. Kozenczak, "I really wanted to become a priest. Even went to confession and hinted this. But all they wanted was someone to do plumbing and carpentry. Stuff like that. One time, during confession, all the priest wanted to discuss was a building quote from my father."

During one of his more generous days, it is claimed that Mr. Gacy Sr. purchased a new 1960 Chevrolet Impala for his son. It was to become John's pride and joy and he kept it spotless. However, there was a catch. The truth was that Mr. Gacy loaned John the money for the car and John suddenly found himself in debt to his dad. Now John's father had more control over him than ever before.

After one argument, Gacy Sr. removed the distributor cap, saying he would replace it when the arrears were up to date. John was not only humiliated but also inwardly fuming. Unable to get to and from work to carry out his tasks for the church or fulfill his other social obligations, he brooded. After three days, he paid his father back and the distributor part was replaced. This time, though, John had had enough. Telling his mother that he was off out to put air in the tires, he vanished for three months.

Having by now dropped out of no less than four high schools and with no diploma, John Jr. drove to Las Vegas where he found work as an ambulance driver for the Palm Mortuary and Memorial Park. This employment was soon terminated when the staff discovered that he was too young to drive ambulances; John was 20 and the minimum legal age was 21. However, rather than lose the enterprising young man, his boss assigned him to the mortuary; work that necessitated contact with dead bodies.

Not knowing where her son was, Mrs. Gacy was beside herself with worry and couldn't sleep. Knowing that John was physically and emotionally sick, she fretted for his wellbeing. For his part, John Gacy, Sr. could not have cared less, that is until a letter about medical bills from his insurance company dropped through the mailbox.

Mr. Gacy flipped.

Marion called the hospital where her son had been receiving treatment and was informed that young John was paying off the bill, and that he was working at the Palm Mortuary in Las Vegas.

* * *

There was something about the detached, professional way the morticians went about their work that appealed to John Gacy. He found himself fascinated with cadavers and death. The stillness of the corpses, white, bereft of life, skin bat-like tight over fragile bone, touched something primitive in him. He learned how the bodies were cleaned, treated and embalmed. And, because he had no proper lodgings, he slept on the premises, which gave him access to the deceased at night.

Alone in a strange city, without friends and social life, John Gacy became a ghoul. When all was secured in the funeral home and the staff had left, he would shuffle over to the cabinets and pull out a drawer. In the weak, yellowy light, he would converse in hushed tones with the corpses, explain his troubles and touch the bodies ever so gently, curiously examining them. Sometimes he would undress them, neatly fold the clothes and leave them next to the caskets. He did this night after night until the director became suspicious and telephoned the Las Vegas Police to get some advice on what to do, but nothing was ever proven, and Gacy soon moved on to another job.

Later, the Des Plaines Police learned that the John Gacy was a necrophiliac. He enjoyed having sexual relations with his victims both before and after he killed them, sometimes keeping their bodies around and sleeping with them for a day or so after their deaths.

Tiring of Las Vegas, John called his mother and asked if he could come home. It would take him three months to save enough money for the trip back to Chicago.

* * *

In 1963, with the newfound confidence he had found by living and working in Las Vegas, John Wayne Gacy enrolled in a year-long course at a local business college, and moved in with a maternal uncle and aunt. When he completed his studies, he found a position as a management trainee for Nunn Bush, a large shoe company based in Illinois. He proved to be a born salesman, a hit with the staff and customers alike. Easy-going and hard-working, he soon was promoted to departmental manager for the company at the Robinson department store, 821 East Cook Street, near Springfield.

Then John discovered the Junior Chamber of Commerce—the Jaycees—established in 1920 to provide opportunities for young men to develop personal and leadership skills through services to others. In 1963, the Jaycees enrolled 21-year-old John Wayne Gacy. John took to the Jaycees like a duck to water and was in his element. Out of the reach of his domineering father, he blossomed, for he was now in the company of like-minded young people whose watchwords were "honor" and "achievement." And, as he had done previously while working as a volunteer for the Catholic Church, he threw himself into the organization with such determination that he won the "Key Man" award for April 1964; no small achievement for he had only been in Springfield for three months.

Indeed, John was now on a roll. He met a young woman, Marlynn Myers, who worked at the Robinson store, and they dated. "It was kinda like love at first sight," Gacy later claimed.

But he then discovered other highly charged feelings. John had been out drinking with a male colleague—a man several years older than himself—and, at the end of the evening, they returned to the man's house for coffee. A homosexual encounter soon followed with the two men ending up naked with Gacy receiving oral sex.

After his arrest for murder, Gacy said somewhat hypocritically to the author, "Although I enjoyed it at first, I felt ashamed and violated. He outsmarted me and I felt used."

In September 1964, Gacy, now 22, married Marlynn, whose father, Fred Myers, was a successful franchiser of Kentucky Fried Chicken with outlets in Waterloo, Iowa.

The year 1966 found Gacy being named as the first vice president of the Jaycees, the outstanding first-year Jaycee in his area, and the organization's third outstanding member state wide. His wife became pregnant with their first child, Christie. Although his father remained tight-lipped, perhaps secretly he was somewhat impressed by his son's exceptional achievements.

Gacy's new father-in-law was not overly impressed with his daughter's choice of husband. He didn't regard Gacy as good breeding stock; nevertheless, he was crazy about his daughter, so he offered the couple a house and his son-in-law a job managing three chicken franchises in Waterloo.

The position paid $15,000 a year, plus a percentage of the profits. John went on to take a course at the Kentucky Fried Chicken University, joined the Waterloo Jaycees and revelled in the best years of his life.

1966 brought even more success for John Gacy. His son, Michael, was born. He worked 10 to 14 hours a day, and maintained his tireless devotion to the Jaycees, organizing events, recruiting new members, coordinating fundraising efforts, and devoting his skills to community projects. At meetings and events, he always arrived with buckets of chicken to hand out in a well meant public relations exercise. John also joined the Waterloo Merchant Patrol, a kind of auxiliary made up of citizens who helped augment the police protection of businesses. He carried a sidearm and even had a red flashing light put on the dashboard of his car. And John also liked being around young boys. If they had blond hair, all the better.

John Gacy was voted the Jaycees' outstanding member for 1967, and he was chaplain of the local organization. In line for presidency of the Waterloo club in 1968, Gacy was almost there. He had political connections, boasting friends in just about every type of business, and many of his pals were in the police and fire department. He was married with two adorable children, a nice house and a secure income. What could possibly go wrong now?

Everything seemed to be looking good for John Wayne Gacy Jr. Yet his lucky streak would not last too much longer. Rumors were spreading around town, more importantly among Jaycee members, regarding Gacy's sexual preferences. It seemed that young boys were always in Gacy's presence. Everyone in town had heard the stories that Gacy was a homosexual—or, more correctly, bisexual—and that he made passes at the young boys who worked for him at the fast food franchises. However, people close to him refused to believe in the gossip.

That was until May 1968 when rumors became truths and John Wayne Gacy's world imploded.

* * *

20 MAY 1968—WATERLOO, IOWA—SODOMY—10 YEARS

09 SEPTEMBER 1968—CONSPIRACY—ASSAULT WITH ATTEMPT TO COMMIT FELONY DD 3036939

12 SEPTEMBER 1968—BURGLARY AND ENTRY

11 DECEMBER 1968—(REF # 26526 BLACK HAWK COUNTY)

EXTRACT FROM GACY'S FBI RAP SHEET # 585181 G

In the spring of 1968, Gacy was indicted by a grand jury in Black Hawk County for allegedly committing the act of sodomy with a teenage boy named Donald Voorhees.

The story which developed was that Gacy was driving along when he heard a young boy call out, "Hey, Mr. Gacy…" He pulled his car over and, when he realized that the boy was the son of another Jaycee, he offered him a ride. Donald had been at his girlfriend's home and was walking home. Gacy seized the moment to bring up the subject of sex. He mentioned some stag films which several of the Jaycees had allegedly been watching. Donald said that he had never seen such a film, and by now Gacy's heart was racing. With Marlynn out of town, he had his house to himself so he invited Donald to join him at home.

They had a few drinks, and Gacy manipulated the boy into exchanging acts of oral sex. Indeed, after that night they met several times for sex. Gacy claimed that these liaisons were at Donald's request and he paid him some money in return. But Gacy had crossed the line. In March 1968, Donald learned that Gacy was planning to run for Jaycee president and that his own father had been approached by Gacy to act as his campaign manager. Ron spilled the beans about his relationship with Gacy, and soon police were hammering on Gacy's front door.

While executing their search warrant, officers found pornographic videos portraying oral sex among men, so they charged Gacy with sodomy. Donald told the court that Gacy had tricked him into being tied up while visiting Gacy's home a year earlier, and had violently raped him. Gacy denied all the charges, claiming that Donald had willingly had sexual relations with him in order to earn extra money. Gacy further insisted that Jaycee members opposed to him becoming president of the local chapter organization were setting him up.

Rapidly, the case moved on to a grand jury, where, for the first time, Gacy learned that he was in even more trouble. In late August 1967, another boy, Edward Lynch, a 16-year-old employee of one of the chicken franchises, had been invited to his boss's home while Marlynn was away.

First, they went to the basement, had a few drinks and played pool, the lecherous Gacy watching Edward's every move. The winner would give oral sex, and Gacy lost each frame. Gacy argued that the suggestion of the prize was the boy's idea, however, after the game, Edward baulked, so they repaired to the front room where Gacy played a few videos. Now extremely sexually aroused, Gacy suggested that they go to the master bedroom and he pulled out a kitchen knife with which to force Edward into submission. The boy was terrified and tried to run. A short scuffle ensued, during which Gacy lost possession of the knife, and Edward suffered a few cuts. Then the steam went out of the older man and Gacy apologized.

Having calmed Edward and himself down, Gacy insisted on showing another film. The boy reluctantly agreed. After all, he wanted to keep his job, and Gacy had apologized. The next thing he knew, the boy's boss had produced a padlock and length of chain; Gacy also wanted to bind the boy's hands.

Reluctantly, Edward agreed. He was lucky to escape with his life.

Once again, Gacy would later argue that the idea of the chain and padlock came from Edward; however, Edward claimed that, when Gacy tried to sit on his lap, face-to-face, he head butted Gacy, who then tried to force the boy's face down on to a cot and began to choke him. He released his grip only when the boy fell unconscious for a few seconds. Then Gacy reverted back to normal. He apologized again, then drove Edward home. Despite Gacy's promises that there were no hard feelings, Edward was fired from his job a few days later. Gacy was now facing charges relating to Edward as well as those arising from the case brought by Donald.

Despite it all, Gacy persisted in his bid to become president of the Jaycees. He even volunteered to take a lie detector test to prove his innocence to his friends. He undertook two polygraph examinations and failed both.

Notwithstanding this, many of his fellow Jaycees rallied around Gacy, refusing to believe that such a "fine, upstanding brother" could be a sexual deviant. He stayed in the running for president until he was nominated and then, quite suddenly, he did the decent thing: he fell on his sword, emotionally announcing his withdrawal "in the interests of the organization and my family."

Moral support for John Gacy had all but evaporated by now. His wife could hardly hold her head up in her beloved community. John's father was incandescent with rage and Fred Myers was on the verge of firing his son-in-law. For his part, Gacy thought he could wheedle his way out of his problems by simply threatening Donald with his life if he testified against him.

In September, with the court case looming, Gacy hired an 18-year-old thug named Russell Schroeder to persuade Donald not to testify. Without this witness, Gacy reasoned that he could beat the rap against him for assaulting Edward. The police had the chain and padlock as evidence, and they had also recovered the stag movies, but John Gacy maintained that there had been no sex, only a fight, which had merely been a high-spirited tiff between young men after a drink.

Gacy, with his high social standing in the community and support from his powerful friends, thought he could win the case hands down. He convinced himself that he would resume his social life and business life as if nothing had ever happened.

For his part, Schroeder jumped at the chance to earn the $300 offered by Gacy for his services. It was money he could use to pay off the loan on his car. He approached Donald, who dismissed the threat out of hand, so Schroeder fired mace at the boy, burning his face. In agony, Donald rushed home sobbing. His parents took him to the hospital and reported the incident to the police. Under questioning,

Schroeder soon cracked and implicated Gacy, who was manifestly now in more trouble than before.

As the investigation into the sodomy allegation was being prepared, other witnesses lost their fear of Gacy and came forward. At the front of the line was 17-year-old Richard Westphal. He had worked for Gacy, and he told investigators that Gacy often played pool with him, the prize being oral sex, which the boy declined. Gacy had also coerced his wife, Marlynn, into sleeping with Richard, who was a virgin. After they had finished in bed, Gacy ambled into the room saying the boy "owed him one."

Another 18-year-old who worked at the same restaurant as Richard reported that Gacy had threatened him with a pistol. Gacy played a bluff game of Russian roulette with him because the boy had talked to Richard and knew too much about Gacy's perverted sex life.

A 15-year-old boy came forward claiming that Gacy paid him and other boys $5 each for helping out in "sex experiments" which he claimed he was conducting for the Governor of Iowa.

John Wayne Michael Gacy, age 26, was ruined.

As with the majority of sex offenders, the courts can order that a person attend a psychiatric hospital for evaluation prior to a court case. Gacy could not make the $10,000 bail bond so he was packed off to the psychopathic hospital at the State University of Iowa to await his trial. There, he was examined over a period of 17 days. Apart from being overweight, the doctors could not find anything physically wrong with him.

Dr. L.D. Amick was one of the psychiatrists assigned to Gacy at that time. He found that Gacy had an IQ of 118, which was "bright and normal." But the shrink also concluded that Gacy enjoyed a total denial of responsibility for anything that went wrong in his life. He had an excuse for every accusation; he would twist the truth about every wayward move to deflect blame from himself, and make himself look good, however damning the circumstances.

As for molesting boys? Gacy had "no remorse over his admitted deeds," Dr. Amick penned in his trial report. "We regard Mr. Gacy as an antisocial personality—a diagnostic term for individuals who are basically unsocialized and whose behavior pattern brings them repeatedly into conflict with society." Dr. Amick concluded, "No known medical treatment can help such people because they do not learn from experience."

So, it could be argued that John Stanley Gacy Sr. had much to answer for. He had created a sexual psychopath, a young man who would later turn into a creature of monstrous proportions.

Days before his trial, Gacy changed his mind and decided to throw himself at the mercy of the court by pleading guilty to the sodomy charge. This was a calculated move by Gacy to wheedle his way out of a prison sentence, and he almost succeeded.

Investigating probation officer Jack Harker had been so impressed by Gacy's convincing manner that he supported John, arguing that a period of supervised probation would serve just as well as any prison term. Also in Gacy's favor was the fact this was his first offence and he had agreed to move back to Illinois, well away from Iowa.

Judge Peter Van Merte had been a sitting judge for years. Here was a hardliner who had heard this type of claptrap before. Sitting patiently while the defense made its argument in favor of a lighter sentence, the judge thought long and hard about John's abuse of his position at work, and how the respected Jaycees had been brought into disrepute in his own city. The judge took a very dim view of the accused, more so because there seemed to be a pattern of molestation, which, if not stopped now, would only escalate.

To exacerbate the issue, Gacy was not an Iowa homeboy. Facing the judge was a city slicker from out of town, a man who had abused his position in the judge's own community to abuse young boys.

The judge sentenced Gacy to ten years in the grimly ornate Iowa State Reformatory for Men at Anamosa—25 miles east of Cedar

Rapids, in the heart of "nowhere land."

That very same day, Marlynn Gacy filed for divorce. She later remarried and John Wayne Gacy would never see his wife and children again. Somewhat shamefully, however, this pervert was released back into the community after serving just 18 months of his sentence, paroled back to Chicago on Thursday, June 18, 1970. His rap sheet informs us that his parole was discharged on Tuesday, October 19, 1971.

Prisoner #26526, John Wayne Gacy, threw himself into prison life with the same degree of enthusiasm as he had done when at liberty. In fact, not a day passed when Gacy was not organizing or doing something. He passed the examinations for a high school equivalency, something he had failed to achieve before, and took college credits in psychology.

Setting out to impress inmates and staff alike, John toiled in the prison kitchen and was thrilled to find that the facility had a Jaycee chapter. Working all the hours allocated to him, he spearheaded the design and building of a miniature golf course for the inmates' use, and prepared Jaycee banquets. He won a number of Jaycee honors, including the club's Sound Citizens award, and the roles of chaplain and legal counsel became his. In a controlled environment, John was as good as gold.

However, prison life had not all been a complete bed of roses. Of course, on "the outside" he had lost everything he had worked for, and then he lost something else. On Christmas Day, 1969, John Stanley Gacy died of cirrhosis of the liver. The man had been completely broken by his son's crimes and the disgrace John had heaped on his family. Several times, John Sr. had been reduced to tears—the only times he had cried in his life.

Upon his release from Anamosa, the prison warden shook Gacy's hand, explaining that, because John had been a model prisoner, he was sad to see him walk out of the gates.

Gacy traveled to Chicago, moving back with in his mother who now lived in a new condominium. He found work as a cook at a popular restaurant called Bruno's, and his employment brought him into contact with members of the Chicago Black Hawks hockey team and a number of Cook County Police officers, many of whom he befriended.

In February 1971, having only been out of prison for eight months, 29-year-old Gacy was in trouble once again. He picked up a teenager near the Greyhound bus station and tried to force him to have sex. Gacy would later claim, once again, that it was the teen's fault. The boy, he alleged, had offered sex. Despite this, Gacy was arrested and charged with assault but, for reasons unknown, the complainant didn't show up at court so the case was dismissed. Had he been found guilty, perhaps 33 young men would not have lost their lives.

By the time his period of parole expired, Gacy was found hanging around with a young man named Mickel Reid. They had met on a street corner as early as November 1970 while Gacy was trawling for sex. The two men had talked about setting up a home maintenance business and they chose to name it PDM Contractors (Property Development Maintenance Contractors), a name that John's mother had suggested.

Trade boomed and the backyard at the condo soon became too small for all of the building materials, so mother and son bought a three bedroom, ranch-style place at 8231 West Summerdale Avenue, Des Plaines. The financial arrangement meant that John owned half of the property, while his mother and two sisters owned the other half. Two boys then moved into the spacious house. They were Mickel Reid and one of John's coworkers at Bruno's named Roger.

Like most of Gacy's homosexual relationships, the one between Reid and John was destined to fail. For some bizarre reason, one evening when the two were working in the garage that adjoined the property, Gacy struck Reid over the head with a hammer. This assault, as we may imagine, drew some blood and, when the older man raised the weapon a second time, Reid fought him off. Gacy stopped and apologized, but the incident terrified Reid and he left immediately. Roger followed.

If we are to believe Gacy, his first murder—other than any killings committed when he was in his middle teens—took place on New Year's Day in 1972.

John, now 30, had joined his mother at a family party and he got drunk on Scotch. That night, Marion Gacy stayed with friends, while her inebriated son sat around brooding. Then he suddenly got into his car and disappeared into the night. "I just went looking around," Gacy later told police.

By Gacy's own admission, he drove to the Greyhound bus station in Chicago where he spotted a light haired youth whom he remembered as "the Greyhound Bus Boy." Tim McCoy was from Omaha, Nebraska, and had just arrived in Illinois. Gacy invited him back to his house where they had drinks and sandwiches, followed by sex. According to Gacy's later statement—which can be safely taken with a grain of salt—he retired to his own room while Tim slept in the guest room.

Gacy said that he awoke to find the youth walking towards him brandishing a butcher's knife. He claimed that, in the ensuing struggle, the boy fell on the knife and stabbed himself to death.

In a second version of the story, Gacy claimed that the boy didn't fight back; rather, Tim seemed surprised and frightened. As Gacy grappled for the knife, he was accidentally cut on the left forearm and felt "a surge of power from my toes to my brain." Then he said he plunged the knife into Tim's chest. "When it was all over," Gacy claimed, "I looked down at the pants he'd worn to bed. They were covered with blood—but with something else, too. During the struggle, I had experienced a powerful sexual release."

After the stabbing, Gacy had a problem, how to dispose of the body. No one would believe it was self defense, so he cleaned up the blood, dragged the corpse to the foyer closet, opened the crawlspace trapdoor and pushed it through. He would bury it later. However, the truth of why the boy was walking towards Gacy with a knife soon became patently clear. When Gacy went into the kitchen, on the worktop were a carton of eggs and a joint of unsliced bacon. The young guest had not been planning murder, but was preparing breakfast for his host.

On Thursday, June 22, 1972, posing as a police officer, Gacy lured a young man into his car and handcuffed him. After a short conversation, Gacy said, "What's it worth to you to get out of this?" When the boy explained that he didn't have much money, Gacy asked, "Would you suck my dick?"

Fearing for his life, the passenger consented. Gacy drove to the restaurant where he worked and forced the boy into the bathroom. It was between 3:30 and 4:30 a.m. Once inside the building, the boy resisted Gacy's attempts to make him perform oral sex and he was hit on the head several times and kicked. Somehow, handcuffed though he was, the boy managed to open the door to the bathroom and ran off down the road. Gacy followed in his car and knocked him down. The victim survived to testify, but the overworked court system got into plea bargaining and finally granted Gacy the disposition "Stricken on Leave to Reinstate." This meant that Gacy had been issued with a warning that if he were brought in front of the courts again the charge would be reinstated. Once again, the criminal-justice system had failed the community, for, if the case had gone ahead, a number of young boys would not have been slaughtered and ended up, their remains rotting, in the crawlspace beneath Gacy's home.

There are many who claim that John Wayne Gacy was a homosexual. To be accurate, he was bisexual and, to prove this point, he married a woman named Carole (Huff) Lofgren on Saturday, July 1, 1972—just nine days after the Northbrook Police had arrested and bailed him.

Gacy and Carole had known each other from their school days. Carole, herself recently divorced, found John "a very warm, understanding person, easy to talk to." She claimed that he was comforting to her and her two daughters, four-year-old Tammy and April, age two, from her first marriage, and she accepted the fact, when he told her, that he was bisexual.

What we do know is that Gacy's mind had split in two. On the one hand, there was Gacy the successful contractor, community builder, event organizer and friendly neighbor, while, on the other hand, he was a sexual pervert, a sadist, whose murderous compulsions were growing out of control. The stronger personality, the killer, would soon dominate, to turn John Wayne Gacy into one of the most heinous serial murderers of all time.

Carole, her two daughters and her mother, Jean Cienciwa, moved into Gacy's home on West Summerdale. Carole would later tell police that she was aware that he had been married previously with two children, and had been in trouble in Iowa. She had believed John when he had told her that the charges were primarily concerned with pornography. She knew nothing of the sodomy charges. Had she known the truth, she would have never married him.

Initially, the two little girls were pleased to be around John Gacy. They tried hard to please him and readily climbed on to his lap to share what they had done with him during the day or just in an effort to communicate with their new father. However, Carole recalled that her daughters quickly discovered that the man they called their "Daddy" had no time for their affection and they, in turn, eventually stopped trying. John was mirroring the lack of affection and the rejection his own father had meted out to him. Carole and her mother now sensed something was very wrong.

After John Gacy's arrest for murder, Detective Lt. Joseph Kozenczak and Detective Greg Bedoe spoke to Carole at length. She recalled that her husband's unusual behavior didn't stop with his rejection of Carole's daughters, and that it was not uncommon for John to lounge around the bedroom, naked, and to masturbate while flicking through homosexual magazines. When she taunted him, he would push her across the room. There were stag magazines everywhere, even under the sink in the kitchen. She found semen-stained silk bikini underwear behind the bedroom dresser and under their bed. Initially, she thought that he was trying to turn her on, however, around the same time, she began to notice some other unusual activities involving her husband. He was staying out late and, occasionally, he would pull his car into the driveway up to the garage with its lights out, park the vehicle and go into the garage. Often, he had a young, blond haired boy with him.

Carole was scared; although she loved John, her suspicions were now truly aroused. She told the detectives that on one occasion she took the key to the garage and had a look inside. What she found shocked her. The interior had been decorated. There were mattresses over the floor, red lights plugged into the walls and mirrors on the ceiling.

And there was something else. The new bride started to smell a strange, sickly sweet odor emanating from the crawlspace under the house. Carole called upon neighborly Mrs. Grexas, who thought that a rat had died under the floor. John blamed the stench on the damp crawlspace.

On one occasion, Carole claimed she awoke at around 4:00 a.m. when she heard his car entering the driveway. When John turned on the light, Carole's presence startled him. He became angry and ordered her back to bed. She asked him what he was doing, but he became madder, so she retired without another word. Sometimes, he would arrive home during the early hours and sleep on the couch in the recreation room, which he had decorated with a bar and a pool table.

Later, she learned that John was having sex with young men who worked at PDM. Not all were compliant, however, and one strong youth beat up Gacy in the driveway. Gacy told Carole it was merely a dispute over money. Years later, she would learn the truth. Gacy had tried to rape the youth and had come off much the worse for wear.

Despite his bizarre and depraved domestic behavior, by 1974 the nice guy in Gacy had truly ingratiated himself into the community. While some considered that he was a loudmouthed braggart, he was generally popular, and always willing to help his neighbors out, even if this meant shovelling snow from their driveways when he had more pressing matters at hand. To the locals, he was a great guy, even more so when he started to host theme parties.

One event had a Hawaiian luau theme, another had a cowboy Western flavor; with around 300 guests attending each one, they were usually held on Independence Day, and his barbecues became the talk of the town.

By now, John's reputation had outgrown Des Plaines. At one function, the groundbreaking of a new retirement center for the elderly he had helped raise money for, Gacy had his photograph taken with the then mayor, Michael Bilandic. As he had a criminal record, Gacy could never aspire to such high office, but he was able to nourish his long-standing taste for politics in less influential ways.

It was not long before Gacy caught the attention of Robert F. Matwick, the Democratic township committee member for Norwood Park. As a free service to the community, Gacy and his employees volunteered to clean up the Democratic Party headquarters.

In 1975, Gacy achieved an appointed post, his first political position: Secretary-Treasurer of the Norwood Park Township Street Lighting District. He headed up Chicago's Polish Constitution Day Parade, and it went like clockwork. He ran the River Grove Moose Lodge, at age 33 he was now too old to be a Jaycee, and, as part of the organization's Jolly Jokers Club, Gacy further impressed Matwick when he arrived dressed up as Pogo the Clown to entertain children at parties and hospitals.

Indeed, Gacy invented two clown characters. One was the tattered Patches and the other was Pogo. "Pogo was the happy clown," he said, "while Patches was more serious." Gacy's interest in clowns remained with him right up to his execution.

Trouble started to brew again when gossip began to circulate about Gacy having a homosexual interest in teenage boys. One of the rumors stemmed from an incident that took place during the time Gacy was involved with cleaning the Democratic Party headquarters. A teenager who worked with Gacy on that particular project was 16 years old and, according to the boy, Gacy made sexual advances towards him, yet backed off when the youngster threatened to hit him with a chair. Gacy joked about the situation and left him alone for a while.

The following month, while the boy was visiting Gacy's home, Gacy again approached him. Gacy tried to trick the young man into hand-cuffs and, believing he was securely cuffed, he began to undress the boy. However, the boy made sure that one of his hands was loosely cuffed and he was able to free himself and wrestle Gacy to the ground. Once he had Gacy on the floor, he handcuffed him, but eventually let him go after Gacy promised he would never try touching him again. Gacy honored his promise, and the boy continued working for Gacy for another year following the incident.

At his office in Chicago, Joe Kozenczak recalled that one of the most significant things Carole had told him related to an event that took place on Mother's Day, 1975. John had risen early and told her that he was going to give her a Mother's Day gift, and that, when he had done so, he would tell her something interesting. He started to have inter-course with her and, when they had finished, he announced that she should never expect sex again. "I am through with women," he said. Carole thought that this was a morbid joke but, as time marched on, it turned out to be the truth.

After this Mother's Day incident—her gift being intercourse—John had no qualms about commenting on young men and their bodies. He'd sit at a bar and lewdly comment on a "guy's tight ass" or describe the hair and build of the type of young man who turned him on. Of course, at this stage, no one knew just how far John's obsession had actually taken him… or would take him.

Seventeen-year-old John Butkovich was like most young men who enjoy cars and he took great pride in his 1968 Dodge upon which he was continually working. He particularly loved to race his car. It was an expensive hobby and, in order to pay for new parts, he knew he had to get a job.

Butkovich, who had lived at 4835 North Kenmore, Chicago, began doing remodelling work for Gacy at PDM Contractors. It was a position that he enjoyed and one that paid well. He and Gacy had a good working relationship, which made the long hours pass by more quickly. However, their working relationship ended abruptly when Gacy refused to pay Butkovich for two weeks' work. Gacy often refused to pay his employees in order to save money for his own purposes.

On Tuesday, July 29, 1975, angered that Gacy had withheld his pay, Butkovich went over to his boss's house with two friends to collect what he believed was rightfully his. When Butkovich confronted him about his paycheck, Gacy refused to pay him and a heated argument erupted. Butkovich threatened that he was going to tell the authorities that he was not deducting taxes from earnings. Gacy was enraged and screamed at him. Finally, John and his friends realized that there was little they could do, so they eventually left Gacy's house. John dropped off his friends at their home and drove away, never to be seen alive again.

Gacy later told police that he had called Butkovich back to his house on the promise of payment. He apologized about the disagreement and they had a drink. Then the argument started again, and Gacy, now alone with the teen, handcuffed him and said nothing more.

John told Detective Larry Finder, "That Butkovich kid owed me money for the damn apartment carpeting… carpeting… oh, the … that happened when I stored one of the guys upside down… it usually ran out of his nose or mouth or something… but Butkovich, usually takes three knots and the stick to kill these guys with the rope… it only took two with him. I covered his body with tarp before the concrete."

When Gacy awoke in the morning, he said the boy's body was just where he had left him, alive, but now he was dead. There was a rope around the boy's neck. Gacy rolled the body up in a tarpaulin and dragged it into the garage. He planned to dump it later. When his wife returned home, he told her Butkovich had left his employment and that was the end of the matter.

However, disposing of the body was not as easy as John would have liked it to be. With his wife now on the premises, there was no way he could get it down into the crawlspace unseen, and the corpse was beginning to stink. So Gacy dug a hole in the only part of the garage that was not concreted, a section three feet by one-and-a-half feet, where he had planned to install a drain.

The corpse was stiff and, as much as John jumped up and down on it, it would not bend in half and compress enough to get it into the small grave. Eventually, after an hour of strenuous exertion, Gacy managed the task and covered the grave with concrete.

Butkovich's car was later located by police approximately one block from his home. Inside was his wallet, the cash intact, his jacket and many other personal items.

The marriage between Gacy and Carole had now completely broken down so Carole asked for a divorce. Gacy was thrilled and even sent her to his own lawyer and helped her move out. After their divorce in 1976, Carole occasionally met John for dinner. The divorce was finalized on Tuesday, March 2, 1976, and she finally stopped seeing him after she remarried.

The 17-year-old Michael Bonnin was not too different from John Butkovich in that he enjoyed working with his hands. He especially liked doing woodwork and carpentry and he was often busy with several projects at a time. On Thursday, June 3, 1976, he had almost completed work on restoring an old jukebox, yet he never had a chance to finish the job he'd started. While en route to catch a train to meet his stepfather's brother, he disappeared.

Ever since his parents could remember, Billy Carroll, Jr. was the kind of boy who seemed to be always getting into trouble. At the age of nine he was put in a juvenile home for stealing a purse and, at 11, he was caught with a gun. Billy was mischievous and spent most of his time on the streets in uptown Chicago. At the age of 16, he was making money by arranging meetings between teenage homosexual boys and adult clientele for a commission.

Although Billy came from a very different background from that of Michael Bonnin and Johnny Butkovich, they all had one thing in common—John Wayne Gacy Jr. Just like Johnny and Michael, Billy also disappeared suddenly. On Sunday, June 13, 1976, he left his home saying that he was going out to paint a friend's garage. He was never seen alive again.

When talking later about another of his victims, Gacy recalled that 17-year-old Gregory Godzik loved his job with PDM Contractors and, although he had been working at PDM for two weeks, he didn't mind doing the extra odd jobs that his boss required of him. His wages allowed for him to buy parts for his 1966 Pontiac car, a time consuming hobby. He was proud of his car and, although it was a bit of an eyesore, it served its purpose.

On Sunday, December 12, 1976, Gregory dropped off his date, a girl he had had a crush on for some time, at her house, then drove back towards his own home. In fact, he intended to visit Gacy and take him some marijuana, but he hadn't been able to buy any, and needed to apologize.

Gacy stated that he retired to bed and, in the morning, he had found the boy dead, sitting in a chair wearing only his underwear. There was a rope around his neck.

The body of Gregory Godzik ended up in the crawlspace with the others. The following day, police found the boy's Pontiac. The windows were open and the doors unlocked, but Gregory was missing. John Gacy later remarked to Detective Larry Finder, "One guy, Godzik, dug his own grave." Godzik's parents had last seen their son on December 12, 1976, and had reported him missing the following day.

Towards the end of December 1977, 19-year-old department-store employee Robert Donnelly was walking along a northwest Chicago sidewalk on his way to a bus stop when a black Oldsmobile pulled over to the curb. It was late at night and the boy suddenly found himself fixed in a spotlight shining from the driver's side of the car. Gacy played a tough cop and asked for identification, then he pointed a gun at his victim and shouted, "Get in or I'll blow you away."

Placing handcuffs on the young man, Gacy drove him back to West Summerdale, forced whisky down his throat when he refused a drink, and anally raped him. Gacy then dragged Robert into the bathroom and repeatedly dunked his head into a bath full of water until the boy lost consciousness. After Robert came to, Gacy urinated on him, dragged him back into the recreation room to watch homosexual movies and continued the torture.

Robert would later testify in court that Gacy made him play Russian roulette with a revolver, spinning the cylinder and pulling the trigger 10 to 15 times until the gun finally went off. It was loaded with a blank round.

Gacy then bound and gagged his terrified victim and raped him again. His rage nearly spent, Gacy ordered the weakened youth to take a shower and get dressed, then he put him in the car for what he promised would be Robert's last ride.

"How's it feel, knowin' you're going to die?" he taunted as he drove Robert back downtown. But then, inexplicably, Gacy released his captive with one last threat. "If you go to the cops," he said, "I'll hunt you down."

Robert, who was afflicted with a stutter, and had been receiving treatment from a psychiatrist following the death of his father, did report the attack to the police, describing the black car and the distinctive personalized number plate, "PDM."

As had happened three times before, the police interviewed Gacy, who corroborated the incident, but claimed that it was a "slave routine," and the sex was consensual. The prosecutor who reviewed the case dropped it because it was one person's word against that of another. Gacy had slipped through the net again with further terrifying consequences.

On Thursday, January 20, 1977, a 19-year-old street hustler called John Szyc—Gacy called him a "he/she"—also disappeared, much like the other young men before him. Cruising in his 1971 Plymouth Satellite, he was never seen alive again. Gacy had spotted him while he was driving through North Chicago, and the boy told the contractor that his Plymouth was up for sale. Gacy said that he might be interested so they drove to West Summerdale Avenue, supposedly to settle the deal. Szyc died that night and he, too, was buried in the subsoil of the crawlspace.

Interestingly, a short while after the young man vanished, another teenager, Tom Costa, was picked up by police in a 1971 Plymouth Satellite while trying to leave a gas station, allegedly without paying. A police chase ensued, which started in Cicero and ended in Chicago. He was charged with running a stop sign, eluding the police and reckless driving. The theft charge was dropped through "lack of evidence." The charges for running the stop sign had been SOL. He had pleaded guilty to eluding the police and reckless driving and, as a result, had his driving licence suspended for two years and was fined $50.

Tom Costa had originally worked for a plumber called Max Gussis but found the pay inadequate, so, when Gacy offered him $10 an hour, he jumped at the offer. Prior to his marriage in 1977, he had moved into Gacy's house, with the agreement that he would pay his boss $25 a month rent. He would later describe Gacy as "a workhorse whose first concern was business." Tom had apparently slept at Gacy's home on the night of the Szyc murder but says he saw nothing untoward.

Tom and Gacy soon struck a deal of their own. Tom would buy the dead boy's car from Gacy for $300, and pay him back at $50 a week until the bill was settled. After he had paid $200, he could take possession of the vehicle. Costa and Gacy went and picked up Szyc's car near Clark and Ohio Street in Chicago. It had been parked close to a gay movie house, and they took it for a "test drive." According to Gacy, Tom forged the title, signing the vehicle over to the two of them. Tom Costa would later deny the forgery and he was never charged with the offence. A television and a clock radio, taken from the trunk of the Plymouth, went home with Gacy, but Szyc's wardrobe of clothes and wigs was left behind a dumpster.

Jeff Rignall, a 26-year-old homosexual, was walking to a Chicago gay bar when Gacy picked him up in his black Oldsmobile. Though Rignall climbed into Gacy's car willingly, Gacy chloroformed him for the drive back to West Summerdale Avenue. There he stripped the man and strapped him to what the victim would later describe to the police as a "pillory device" that held his head and arms immobile. His attacker then forced him to perform oral sex and repeatedly raped him with a number of blunt objects.

Rignall was later dumped in the snow at the base of the Alexander Hamilton statue in a downtown Chicago Park. He was bleeding from the rectum and his face felt as if it was on fire; he had suffered facial burns and liver damage from the chloroform, and spent several days in the hospital.

In a later television interview, Rignall changed his story, albeit slightly, saying, "I got in the car with him [Gacy] and a short way after I got into the car with him he placed a rag over my face which turned out to be chloroform, and proceeded to have a lengthy drive and every time I came to the rag would go back over my face, and I remember him carrying me into his house. And then he put the rag over me and that's the last thing I remember until I found myself at about 5:30 a.m. at the steps of Lincoln Park, half-dressed, my face completely burned."

This attack transformed Jeff Rignall into an avenger bent on tracking down Gacy. However, once the police realized that the complainant was a homosexual, they lost interest in the case. Undeterred, Rignall hired a civil lawyer and sued in civil court. Gacy countercharged that Rignall had abused him verbally and had pushed him. In September, Gacy settled the suit for $3,000.

In May 1978, Gacy was in charge of the Polish Constitution Day Parade, which was attended by Rosalynn Carter, wife of the then president, Jimmy Carter. Thirty-six-year-old Gacy was in his element. At a reception, he was even photographed shaking hands with the smiling first lady. This was an extraordinary lapse of security, for the Secret Service had even given him a lapel pin as a sign that he had been cleared as having no criminal record.

Up to this point, an astonishing number of young men had either been listed missing, or had been discovered as murder victims, pending inquiries. The official records from various morgues stated,

CLOTH-LIKE MATERIAL IN THE THROAT. MALE, WHITE, FIVE FOOT THREE, 119 POUNDS. IDENTIFIED NOVEMBER 14, 1978, AS FRANK LANDINGAN, AGE 20.

MALE, WHITE, FIVE FOOT TWO, 140 POUNDS. IDENTIFIED DECEMBER 20, 1978, AS JAMES MAZZARA, AGE 20.

MALE, WHITE, FIVE FOOT SIX, 130 POUNDS. IDENTIFIED DECEMBER 29, 1978, AS RICK JOHNSON, 17, STUDENT.

MALE, WHITE, SIX FEET, 165 POUNDS. IDENTIFIED JANUARY 6, 1979, AS JOHN PRESTIDGE, AGE 20, A STUDENT.

MALE, WHITE, FIVE FOOT TEN, 130 POUNDS. IDENTIFIED JANUARY 6, 1979 AS JOHN SZYC AGE 19.

LIGATURE AROUND THE NECK. MALE, WHITE, FIVE FOOT SEVEN, 150 POUNDS. IDENTIFIED JANUARY 6, 1979 AS MICHAEL BONNIN, AGE 17.

CLOTH-LIKE MATERIAL IN HIS THROAT. MALE, WHITE, SIX FOOT, 175 POUNDS. IDENTIFIED JANUARY 6, 1979, AS ROBERT GILROY, AGE 18, A STUDENT.

MALE, WHITE, FIVE FOOT SEVEN, 135 POUNDS. IDENTIFIED JANUARY 9, 1979, AS TIMOTHY O'ROURKE, AGE 21.

LIGATURE, A ROPE AROUND HIS NECK. MALE, WHITE, FIVE FOOT EIGHT, 145 POUNDS. IDENTIFIED JANUARY 27, 1979, AS JOHN MOWERY. LIGATURE AROUND NECK. MALE, WHITE, FIVE FOOT EIGHT, 140 POUNDS. IDENTIFIED JANUARY 29, 1979, AS MATTHEW BOWMAN, AGE 19.

CLOTH-LIKE MATERIAL ON THROAT. MALE, WHITE, FIVE FOOT NINE, 145 POUNDS. IDENTIFIED IN THE SPRING OF 1979 AS RANDALL REFFERT, AGE 15, STUDENT.

PAPER-LIKE MATERIAL IN THE THROAT. MALE, WHITE, FIVE FOOT EIGHT, 140 POUNDS. IDENTIFIED APRIL 9, 1979, AS ROBERT PRIEST, AGE 15.

CLOTH-LIKE MATERIAL ON HIS THROAT. MALE, WHITE, FIVE FOOT EIGHT, 155 POUNDS. IDENTIFIED MAY 16, 1979, AS WILLIAM KINDRED.

ROPE AROUND HIS NECK. MALE, WHITE, FIVE FOOT SEVEN, 145 POUNDS. IDENTIFIED SEPTEMBER 11, 1979, AS ROBERT WINCH, AGE 16, A STUDENT.

MALE, WHITE, FIVE FOOT SIX, 145 POUNDS. IDENTIFIED NOVEMBER 14, 1979 AS SAM STAPLETON, AGE 14.

LIGATURE AROUND NECK. MALE, WHITE, SIX FEET. IDENTIFIED NOVEMBER 16, 1979, AS DAVID TALMA.

CLOTH-LIKE MATERIAL ON THROAT. MALE, WHITE, FIVE FOOT FIVE, 140 POUNDS. IDENTIFIED NOVEMBER 18, 1979, AS DARRELL SAMPSON, AGE 18.

CLOTH-LIKE MATERIAL IN HIS THROAT. MALE, WHITE, FIVE FOOT SEVEN. IDENTIFIED AS RUSSELL NELSON, AGE 21, A STUDENT FROM MINNEAPOLIS.

Of Robert Priest, a victim discovered in April 1979, Gacy said later, "Well, the Priest kid never fit in... he probably would have told someone, though... even if he wanted fast money... that's the truth... the kid was scared I was going to kill him. He couldn't do anything—no erection—sometimes we used Amyl nitrate... Godzik and I would smoke marijuana and then take it... more kicks... no females, no Blacks, no Puerto Ricans."

* * *

With 16 years on the Force, and promoted to Chief of Detectives on July 1, 1978, Lt. Joe Kozenczak had never been a cop to treat a missing person's report lightly, and there was something that immediately troubled him early on the Tuesday morning of December 12th that year.

Midway through a stack of paperwork, he came across a missing-person's report numbered 78-35203. It concerned a 15-year-old boy named Robert Jerome Priest. The complainant was Elizabeth Priest, the boy's mother, and she had reported him missing at 11:00 p.m. on Monday, December 11th.

Scanning the report, Kozenczak noted that Robert, born March 16, 1963, was described as having brown hair, brown eyes, five feet eight inches, 140 pounds, with a shag haircut. Rob, as his friends and relatives called him, was a student at Maine West High School and a stockroom boy at the Nisson Pharmacy in Des Plaines.

On the night he disappeared he was wearing tan pants and a blue down jacket. By a remarkable coincidence, Mrs. Priest had taken a photo of her son outside the pharmacy a year earlier. Even more remarkably, the very day that Rob went missing, his father, Harold, had bought him his own camera and, anxious to see what kind of photographs it would produce, he purchased a roll of color film and took a snapshot of his son, who was wearing exactly the same clothes as when he disappeared. It was roll of film that would catch a serial killer.

Lt. Kozenczak soon established that Rob worked from 6:00 to 9:00 p.m., when usually his mother would pick him up. This Monday was special to the family because it was Elizabeth's birthday. Earlier in the day, Harold had bought a birthday cake, and they would cut it when Rob arrived home.

Mrs. Priest arrived at the pharmacy exactly at 9:00 p.m. Rob asked her to wait a few minutes while he went outside to talk to a man about a summer construction job. She waited for 20 minutes then went outside to find him gone. After hanging around for another five minutes, she drove home and started to phone her son's friends as well as the co-owner of the pharmacy, Phil Torf.

Torf seemed to recall that Robert might have been talking to a local building contractor, John Gacy of PDM Construction. He had heard part of a conversation about "summer employment." To help Elizabeth, Torf telephoned Gacy, who had been in the store about a refurbishment contract, but he could only leave a message on the answering machine.

Tragically, and unknown to Torf, at that precise moment Robert was restrained in handcuffs. At 11:00 p.m., Elizabeth Priest contacted the Des Plaines PD.

After Lt. Kozenczak had tidied up his morning paperwork, he summoned Sergeant Ken Fredericks, the supervisor of the Youth Bureau, to his office. When the sergeant arrived, he told Kozenczak that Mrs. Priest and her children—Ken, 21, and Carrie, 22—were downstairs talking to Detective Ron "Ronnie" Adams. The time was around 9:10 a.m.

At around 9:30 a.m., Adams called Gacy at home, and asked him what he had been doing at the Nisson Pharmacy. Gacy confirmed that he had been there to discuss renovation work, and had enquired if there were any materials left over from previous work he had carried out on the premises. He was adamant that he had not had any personal contact with the missing boy.

On face value, Gacy's account was honest enough. However, Adams double checked with Kim Byers, a young girl who worked with Rob at Nisson. She recalled Rob saying when he left the store at 9:00 p.m. that the contractor wanted to speak to him outside. Now Adams knew that Gacy was lying... but why?

At lunchtime, Kozenczak, Fredericks and Adams met up for lunch at The Pot and Pan restaurant, where they discussed the Priest case. Adams hadn't wasted a moment; he had already called the pharmacy and had spoken to the co-owners. The Torfs had told the detective that Gacy had been in their store twice on the Monday. Possibly, Rob had overheard a conversation with Gacy regarding hiring high school students for summer work. But the Torf brothers also revealed something else. They believed that Gacy ran a Christmas tree lot on the northwest side of the city.

When he returned to his office after lunch, Lt. Kozenczak assigned Detectives Mike Olsen and Jim Pickell to the case, and by 1:30 p.m. they had traced Gacy's address to 8213 West Summerdale, Norridge, Illinois.

Pickell drove out to a Christmas tree lot and the detective soon learned that the Torfs' information was incorrect, so he went to Gacy's house. Although a black 1978 Oldsmobile, four door sedan, licence PDM 42, was parked in the driveway, no one appeared to be at home. A neighbor thought that Mr. Gacy might be out in one of his two black company vans.

It is possible that after Detective Adams's phone call to Gacy in the morning, the contractor, now forewarned that the police were being proactive, put the corpse into his black van or his car and disposed of the body that day. It later became clear, though, that he actually did the deed at night.

On his return to the police station, the detective checked out Gacy's name and was mortified to learn that he had a significant criminal record, which included a lengthy prison term for committing buggery on a boy. Throughout the rest of the afternoon, detectives called Rob's school friends. Everyone said that Rob was a stable, intelligent boy who did not appear to be having problems at school or personally. He had, however, recently broken up with a girlfriend, but the relationship was getting back on track.

At around 4:30 p.m., Joe Kozenczak went home for dinner and then, at 5:30 p.m., he received a call from Ronnie Adams who wanted to know what he should do next. Joe asked him to call back. Joe was sufficiently worried to feel that he needed to interview Gacy as a matter of urgency, so he called the duty state's attorney in downtown Chicago for advice.

Joe explained about the missing boy. He recognized that, for the moment, he had no grounds for arresting the man, but it was important to interview him at home without telling Gacy that anything he said could be used against him without issuing the Miranda warning.

The advice that came back from the DA was simple. Kozenczak would merely treat Gacy as a witness and he would avoid accusing him of anything. Gacy was not required to say a word and, as the attorney put it, "If he says go, you go."

At 9:00 p.m., Kozenczak met up with Detectives Olsen, Pickell and Dave Sommerschield. They drove to Gacy's residence in two unmarked squad cars, and Olsen and Sommerschield went to the side of the premises where they waited. After knocking several times on the door, Kozenczak and Pickell saw the shape of a head move behind the glass of the front door. It was an eerie sight and sent a chill through them. Then, at that very moment, a black van pulled up and out climbed Tom Costa. The officers identified themselves and Costa explained that Gacy never answered the front door, and that they would have to try the side entrance. They did, and saw through a window Gacy reclining in a chair watching television.

Gacy invited the detectives into his home. He confirmed that he had been at the pharmacy the previous day, initially claiming that he had returned home at around 8:45 p.m., 15 minutes before Rob had vanished.

Upon his arrival home, Gacy said he had listened to his answering machine, upon which was a recorded message from his aunt stating that his uncle was dying at the Northwest Community Hospital in Chicago. Gacy drove to the hospital to meet her but he was informed that his aunt had gone home. He followed her there to discover that she had gone on to a neighbor, a relative, to discuss the funeral arrangements. He had stayed with them for a while, and then drove home, arriving between 12:30 and 1:00 a.m.

What Gacy didn't say was that he had, in fact, left the store at around 7:15 p.m. and returned at 8:00 p.m. to pick up his appointments book, and that he had then left the store at 9:00 p.m. when, outside, he spoke to Priest.

Kozenczak had noticed that Gacy's clothing was "rather strange." Joe Kozenczak remembers, "Gacy was forty or fifty pounds overweight, around six foot tall, and every inch of him matched the description of a slob."

Over a flannel shirt he wore a thin navy top, similar to those worn by joggers. Nevertheless, Joe was sympathetic and suggested that Gacy might like to accompany him back to the police station where they could take a statement. Gacy refused the offer, saying that he was expecting a call from his mother in Arkansas about his uncle's death. Kozenczak was persistent, though. He explained that Rob's parents were very upset and that anything that John could do to help would be appreciated. "Why don't you call your mother, rather than wait for her call?" Joe asked. Gacy looked sullen and was annoyed.

After more persuasion, Gacy agreed to call his mother and spoke to her for ten minutes. Kozenczak furtively looked around the room, then his eyes settled on a piece of office paper. Moving closer, he made out the words "Nisson Pharmacy" written on the bottom of it. He slipped it into his jacket pocket.

As Gacy was preparing himself for the drive to the police station, Tom Costa walked into the room. Until then, the other two detectives had been talking to him outside, but the weather was cold, and Costa had had enough. Gacy's confidence was obviously boosted by the arrival of his coworker and, standing up, he suddenly said, "I have more important things to do. I am not going with you. Haven't you got any respect for the dead?" The police had to leave.

Rob Priest's body was just yards away and John Wayne Gacy was minutes away from taking the biggest gamble of his life.

There was little point in the four detectives watching the Gacy residence all night, so while Sommerschield and Olsen set up an observation point half a block east on Summerdale, Kozenczak and Pickell made their way back to the police station. They had gone only a few miles when their radio crackled. It was Olsen saying that Gacy was on the move, and in a hurry.

The killer had rightly assumed that the cops would be watching him. He arranged for the van to pull up to the front of the house so that he could walk along the length of the property without being seen, then he ran to his car and sped off with the van in close pursuit.

Sommerschield and Olsen followed, requesting assistance from their two colleagues. Kozenczak spun his car around and drove back across the Robert Kennedy Expressway to try to intercept Gacy, who was obviously up to no good. Unfortunately, moments later, they heard Sommerschield's garbled words over the radio, "Bureau 6 to Bureau 1… we lost him!"

At 11:00 p.m. that night, Gacy called the Des Plaines Police Station demanding to know if Kozenczak still wanted to see him. The Chief of Detectives said that he did and that he would wait for the contractor to turn up. After two hours, Gacy had still not arrived so the detectives asked the desk officer to inform the man that they would see him the next day.

Gacy eventually turned up at the police station at 3:20 a.m. The contractor looked dishevelled. He had mud on his pants and shoes. His eyes were "glassy," and the desk officer, Jerry Loconsole, reported that the man had claimed he had been in an auto accident near his house. He had skidded in the snow, and had had problems getting his car moving.

On reading all of the available material on this case, confusion seems to exist as to when Gacy actually killed and disposed of Rob Priest's body. The murder had to have taken place between December 9th and 11th, when Rob was abducted, and before Gacy left his home at about 10:00 p.m., and drove to the Northwest Community Hospital in Chicago after he was notified that his uncle was dying. Or, if the boy had been restrained and gagged, Gacy might have killed him after he arrived home at around 1:00 a.m. the following morning, and most certainly before the police arrived to talk to him at around 9:30 p.m. that night.

When questioned by police after his arrest for murder, Gacy claimed that at around 8:30 p.m. on the evening of December 12th, the day after Rob Priest vanished, he called Tom Costa and asked him to come over. They were going to look for a Christmas tree, he told him. This is of some significance because the Torf brothers had told the police that Gacy owned a Christmas tree lot, which he didn't.

While he waited for Costa to arrive in the van, Gacy says that he brought the body down from the attic and laid it in the hallway, an extremely bizarre action considering that his coworker would arrive at any moment and see the body. However, when Costa rang the doorbell, Gacy says he told his visitor that he couldn't go and sent Costa away. The killer then claimed that he wrapped the body up in an orange blanket and placed it in the trunk of his car, before driving south to throw the corpse into the Des Plaines River. According to Gacy's later statement, Costa had come and gone, and the body had been disposed of in the Des Plaines River before the police arrived.

Costa has always maintained that he knew nothing of any murders, or the disposal of any bodies. He says he turned up at Gacy's place and they drove off in the van. He was at the wheel while Gacy gave directions. They were driving north on a street east of Cumberland Avenue when they passed a wooded area used for dumping trash. The area, Costa told police, "looked something like a prairie, and almost the size of a city block."

Costa told Joe Kozenczak that Gacy, who had been staring out of the windshield with intense eyes, told him to drive along the perimeter of this area. As they drove slowly north, Gacy suddenly ordered Costa to stop the vehicle and turn the lights off. Not understanding why, Costa did so and eyed the contractor who sat motionless, gazing into the open prairie. This incident seemed rather peculiar, claimed Costa. They stayed there for a few minutes, and Gacy seemed to be in a trance. Then he came out of this trance and they drove off. The two men did not find a Christmas tree, so Costa drove his boss back home and left.

* * *

332

At 11:00 a.m. on the morning of Wednesday, December 13, 1978, sounding businesslike and cooperative, John Gacy telephoned Lt. Kozenczak. "Did you still want to see me?" he asked.

Forty minutes later, Gacy arrived at the Des Plaines Police Department, while Joe was still making arrangements with District Attorney Terry Sullivan to obtain a search warrant for the suspect's home. Detective Pickell took the man through his movements on the evening Rob Priest had vanished, and Gacy was adamant that he had not spoken to the missing boy.

With the search warrant now in his possession, Kozenczak asked Gacy for his house keys. The man looked shocked and was angry. He refused. "Either give me the keys, John, or you'll have to buy a new door," said Kozenczak, and Gacy threw them to him.

A short while later, seven officers—Lt. Kozenczak supervising, along with Detectives Pickell, Adams, Olsen, Kautz, Tovar and Evidence Technician Karl Humbert—assembled at Gacy's red brick ranch house. The place was in darkness.

Kozenczak remembered that the house "had an aura of coldness and neglect. It lacked a woman's touch… it felt barren and uncomfortable. The interior decoration, if you could call it that, was uncoordinated and chaotic." As Kozenczak scanned the rooms, he noticed a small grey terrier that moved about apprehensively. "What seemed really ironic," says Joe, "was the dog's physical appearance, particularly its enlarged anus."

The house had three bedrooms (one of which Gacy used as an office), a very large dining room, a combination family/living room, and a kitchen and bathroom. The seven detectives went everywhere, opening closets, pulling out drawers and photographing everything as they went along. One of the officers also went into the garage while another checked out the attic.

Kozenczak walked into the kitchen. He saw a red photo receipt lying in the bottom of the trash basket. Picking it up, he made out "No.

36119, Nisson Pharmacy Inc., 1920 Touhy Ave., Des Plaines, Illinois." This was later to become an invaluable clue in the Priest murder.

Detective Kautz had been checking out the closet in the hallway. As he pulled things in and out, he noticed a crack in the floor running alongside the edge of the closet door. He called Kozenczak over and, after removing a golf bag, they put a screwdriver into the crack and found that they were lifting up the closet floor. Indeed, the entire floor was a trapdoor that led down into the crawlspace under the property.

While Kautz held a flashlight, Kozenczak and Humbert climbed down looking for signs of a freshly dug grave. There was nothing unusual except the smell of damp soil.

John Wayne Gacy was released and placed under surveillance.

The highly trained surveillance team—Delta Unit—was made up of the force's most experienced drivers. Formed into two teams and supervised by Sergeant Walter Lang, it was mobilized at noon on Thursday, December 14th. Officers Shultz and Robinson were assigned to watch Gacy's house until 1:00 a.m., when they would be replaced by Hachmeister, who would work alone.

Although a specialized squad, it was widely agreed that the equipment they used was not the best. "The Delta cars," recalls Joe Kozenczak, "were items which we referred to as 'Article 36,' from the Illinois Revised State Statutes, having belonged to an individual who has been convicted of a serious crime." One of the cars, a Plymouth, had been used in the abduction of a girl; the vehicles were ill-equipped for such work and not suitable for high-speed pursuits.

While every move Gacy made was being watched and recorded, back at the police station, Lt. Kozenczak was leaving no stone unturned in his hunt for Rob Priest. He interviewed a number of people, while his colleagues conducted more inquiries into Gacy's shady background. They had heard a rumor that Charles Hattula, a former coworker of Gacy's, had been found drowned in a river some 60 miles southwest of

Chicago. They also discovered that Gregory Godzik was missing—Godzik's car was found in the possession of Tom Costa, and the vehicle identification number (VIN) had been slightly altered.

Another workmate of Gacy's, David Cram, was also brought in for questioning. He explained that his boss had been down in the crawl-space and said that there was a drainage problem. Gacy kept wallets and driver's licences from dead people, he told the investigators. There were also a number of watches that had mysteriously come into the contractor's possession.

On Saturday, December16th, John Gacy's former wife, Carole, came into the Des Plaines Police Station where she was asked about her life with her former husband. She told officers all about his perverse ways and that he liked to have sex with young men. John Butkovich's name came into the conversation. He had been missing since July 21, 1975. Other young men had worked for Gacy and had vanished—Bruce Dorc, Donny Bingham, Chris Cottles, Don Bacon, Chris LaCore, Jerry Caldwell, as well as Gregory Godzik. The names were piling up thick and fast. Other officers followed up a lead that their prime suspect had buried bodies at the Maryland Cemetery. Extensive searches found nothing.

Following up the information on Charles Hattula, on Monday, December 18, 1978, Detective Tovar managed to get a lead. Hattula had driven a van with Texas plates, so Tovar contacted the driver's licence division of the Public Safety Department in Texas. Tovar was informed that Charles Antonio Hattula resided at 50567B Val Verde Lane in Houston, Texas. He was described as a white male, blond with blue eyes, six feet tall and 170 pounds. His date of birth was April 24, 1953. After failing to obtain a telephone number, Tovar contacted Sergeant Cooper of the Harris County Sheriff's PD, of which Houston is a part. Cooper sent an officer to the residence. In the meantime, it appeared that there was neither a missing report nor any criminal history on Hattula in Texas.

Having apparently reached a dead end, Tovar tried something else. He conducted a driver's licence check on Hattula in the State of Illinois. Charles Hattula resided at 3120 North Western Avenue, Chicago. He had had a driver's licence but it had been revoked on April 14, 1978. He also had a criminal history.

Hattula had been arrested for possession of a controlled substance and marijuana at his home on April 20, 1976. At the time, he was employed by PDM Contractors as a carpenter. He had also been arrested in Freeport, Illinois, on March 12, 1971, for a curfew violation and possession of marijuana. Charles Hattula's aunt explained that her nephew had drowned in Freeport on Mother's Day, 1977. His body was recovered from the Pecatonica River on May 13, 1978. Cause of death was listed as asphyxia by drowning. But had he been a Gacy victim?

Officer Tovar and Detective Ron Adams also interviewed Mrs. Szyc. They showed her the Maine West ring found at Gacy's property. She positively identified it as the property of her missing son; however, she went one step further. Missing from her son's apartment—and later from the trunk of his car—was a 12-inch screen black and white Motorola television set. She had found the warranty card and had brought it with her.

A large number of photographs had been taken when the police searched Gacy's home, and among them was a snap of Gacy's bedroom. It clearly showed a light-colored Motorola TV sitting on an ornate jewelery box between two dressing mirrors.

Not wasting a moment, the officers called at the Motorola corporate headquarters at Schaumburg, not far from Des Plaines. They were told that the television in the photograph was a Model BP-3050KN, which matched the number on the warranty card in Mrs. Szyc's possession. There was also an identification number for the actual television set on the card. Would it match the TV in Gacy's bedroom?

Lt. Joe Kozenczak recalls, "On the morning of December 19, 1978, I was confronted, once again, with the hardcore reality and horror of a case which, from all indications, would make history in the world of criminal justice." The Priests had come to see him.

Ever since their beloved son had gone missing and from right under the nose of his mother on her birthday, the distraught parents had been conducting inquiries of their own. They had staked out Gacy themselves, followed him, watch him, fretted and cursed. Now they were at their wits' end. Their patience had run out and they were at the police station to demand answers, for there was little doubt in their minds that Gacy had killed their Rob.

Over coffee with Kozenczak, Elizabeth Priest mentioned Kim Byers, the girl who had worked with Rob at the pharmacy. It was an off-the-cuff remark, but one which, as is so often the case, oiled the creaky wheels of justice.

"Does she have any new information?" asked Kozenczak.

"No, not really. She was just telling me that Rob had something of hers that day, he…"

"Yes, what was that?"

"Well, it's a little complicated, lieutenant. She says she got cold and so she decided to put on Rob's jacket while she was working. And then she decided to leave some film for developing and, well, she thinks she forgot and put the receipt for it in Rob's jacket pocket, because she's never seen it since. So, I just thought maybe that would help."

"You mean the jacket he was wearing when he disappeared?"

"Yes, of course. Kim gave him back the jacket later, but she left her film receipt in his pocket."

Kozenczak says his heart missed several beats. He rushed down to the property room and retrieved, "like a piece of gold," the bright red receipt which he had found in Gacy's trash bin. It was possibly the only item of evidence to show that Rob had been in Gacy's home.

Within minutes, Kozenczak summoned a marked patrol car and, with lights flashing, the envelope containing the film receipt was on its way to the Cook County Crime Laboratory in Maybrook. Another officer rushed over to the Nisson Pharmacy. Here he would look for Kim Byers's entry in the log sheets. They were able to match the receipt number to the order number. Meanwhile, lab technicians determined, through analysis of the fibers, that the receipt and the envelope had been joined.

Kozenczak would later say, "When this was going on, I was giving the Priests hope, but I knew that I was killing all hope. It was a bad time." Rob Priest's jacket was later found hidden in a wall when police demolished the house.

While the noose was tightening around Gacy's neck, he was giving the police plenty to think about. At times, he was convivial to the extent that he invited the surveillance team into his home for drinks, while at other times he was obnoxious, full of hollow threats and boastful. "Fuck you, halfwits. I am gonna sue ya fuckin' ass," was one of his favorite outbursts. "Tell that fuckin' shithead Pollack, Kozenczak, that I'm gonna have his shield."

On one occasion, when he left his home, he shouted, "What am I doing this afternoon? Oh, I've just got to drop off a few bodies behind the railway bridge in Chicago. Care to lend me a hand?"

With the temperature well below zero, Wednesday, December 20th became a hectic day as all of the threads linking John Wayne Gacy to the murder of Rob Priest were slowly coming together. While Kozenczak interviewed Tom Costa using the polygraph machine—the results were inconclusive—Jim Kautz was developing a complete roster of names, addresses, phone numbers and record checks of young men whom the police knew had been in contact with Gacy. "It was a massive project," Kozenczak remembered. However, the final interview of the day produced an amazing result when they again talked to David Cram,

Gacy's coworker, who said that he had dug trenches in the crawlspace under Gacy's house.

"Can you draw a sketch for us?"

"Yeah, sure."

Cram took a pencil and drew a rough plan showing trenches around the perimeter of the foundation on three sides. Looking from the north wall, where there were none, they formed a sort of "upside-down 'U'."

"You notice anything down there?" asked Greg Bedoe.

"Yeah, sure, it stunk."

"What d'ya mean?"

"It smelled real bad, man, like nobody would want to stay down there long. I came up every chance I could."

Upon hearing this conversation, Kozenczak recalled a remark made by Sergeant Walter Lang, the Delta boss who had said that, when Bob Shultz had used the bathroom, on the invitation of Gacy, he had noticed a "peculiar odor that seemed to be coming from the heat vent directly in front of the toilet." While he was standing there, the furnace kicked on, and the smell came up so rich and strong it almost choked him. It reminded Shultz of some unsavory odors he had encountered when his duties had sent him over to the Cook County morgue.

The surveillance quickly took its toll on Gacy. For years, he had been sinking into the habits of a confirmed pill abuser, knocking back handfuls of Valium tablets to calm down, then amphetamines to pep himself up. He swilled beer and whisky. During this last week of freedom, he was on a rollercoaster ride of liquor and drugs. He openly defied traffic laws, smoked a joint in his car and drank heavily as he led officers on a merry chase. He introduced the surveillance team to his pals from the Moose Lodge, calling them his bodyguards. He also delighted in eluding his pursuers and succeeded on a number of occasions. Once, after openly joking with his attorney about taking a long vacation, Gacy vanished and a squad car rushed to O'Hare Airport to block his departure.

It was only a trick; Gacy had spent the time driving around, making a brief stop to see a friend who sold Christmas trees.

* * *

That Thursday morning started bright and early with Joe Kozenczak and DA Terry Sullivan putting together a fresh application for a second search warrant. Despite all of the evidence, which appeared to implicate Gacy, they still had to convince Judge Marvin Peters, who was soon on their side.

At 10:00 a.m., the surveillance team reported in. Gacy, it appeared, was "cracking up." He had spent the night at the office of his attorneys, Stevens & Amirante. Soon after he had arrived, Sam Amirante came out of his office visibly shaken. He walked down the hall to the two surveillance officers, and said, "Whatever you do, don't let this guy get away." The astonished officers then watched while the attorney took out a cigarette and tried to light it, only to discover that he had been trying to ignite the filter end. Then he turned his back, still visibly shaking, walked slowly back to his office and quietly shut the door.

Early that morning, Gacy left the office and, driving like a maniac on the slick icy streets, led the members of the surveillance team to the gas station in Park Ridge. Hachmeister and Albrecht watched him give four marijuana cigarettes—"Thai sticks"—to the station attendant. As soon as Gacy left, they recovered the cigarettes and reported it to Sergeant Lang.

Things out on the street were happening quickly, too. Gacy, feeling the effects of stress, fatigue and pills, seemed to be making the rounds of his friends' homes, bidding them goodbye. By 11:30 a.m., Gacy, carrying a rosary, had called on David Cram at his apartment. At 11:45 a.m., the two men drove through the snow to De Leo's Restaurant to meet Attorney Leroy Stevens. While Gacy went inside, Officer Shultz spoke to Cram. The contractor had been popping pills and drinking all morning, Cram said, and was going next to the Maryland Cemetery where his father was buried. The man had a knife with him and was talking about suicide.

"Anything else?" asked Shultz.

"Sure… he says he's killed more than 30 people," came the blunt reply.

Gacy's confession was quickly transmitted to Sergeant Lang, who, having heard about the drug deal at the gas station, knew he could arrest Gacy at any time. He also knew that his suspect was falling apart at the seams and might kill himself.

"Walter Lang, westbound on Elston Avenue, called me," remembers Joe Kozenczak. "He called me on the red phone and related all the facts."

"Do you want him arrested?" asked Lang.

"Yes, pull him… now," Kozenczak replied.

The actual arrest took place at Oakton Street and Milwaukee Avenue in Niles at 12:15 p.m. In this highly congested and commercial area, Shultz managed to block Gacy's car with his own and, drawing his revolver, searched Gacy and found a bottle of Valium tablets in his pocket. By 12:45 p.m., Gacy was in the custody of the Des Plaines Police Department. He was 36, and he would never be a free man again.

Lt. Joe Kozenczak obtained a second search warrant and arrived at Gacy's home at 6:30 p.m. Alone, he went inside. "When the door opened," Joe recalls, "I saw nothing but darkness—total darkness. I felt a chill, the kind that makes your entire body jolt. I quickly walked down the hallway to the front foyer area where the closet was. By now, Lang was in the house. We didn't waste time. I opened the closet door, threw all the contents on the floor outside it and lifted the cover to the crawlspace."

The search team entered the crawlspace expecting horrors, but the reality, if anything, exceeded their worst forebodings. What they found was a hellish graveyard that assaulted both their noses and their sanity.

After an hour of preparation, during which they had to remove the ground water using submersible pumps, the evidence technicians finally got down to digging. Ice cold water kept seeping into the crawl-space, turning the search area into a sea of viscous mud. The pumps spluttered and clogged on bits of floating, greasy, soap-like flesh, called "adipocere." When the pumps finally stopped, the officers used buckets to bail out the water. Suddenly there was a muffled yell.

"What in the hell have you found?" shouted Kozenczak.

David Genty answered, "I've got a body down here."

Having informed the press that bones that had been found in the house were indeed human, the Cook County medical examiner Dr. Robert Stein, Chief Investigator Francis J. Flanigan and the Cook County medical examiner's photographer, dressed in overalls, set to work on the house. The evidence technicians were Genty, Humbert, Zakas, Cox and Jones.

Floodlights illuminated the work and made it more ghastly. The men laboring in the lurid glow wore heavy protective clothing, including surgical gloves; contact with the noxious matter that they were unearthing could mean blood poisoning and gangrene. But the flimsy gloves were soon torn by the bones and gravel, exposing the workers' hands to the sting of the many bags of lime that Gacy had poured into the water.

The digging continued. The officers down there spoke of hair protruding from the ground which was still covered with remnants of lime. Small red worms scattered from the shock of the light. There was the unforgettable stench of death and decaying flesh. Genty unearthed three bodies in less than ten minutes.

Right from the outset, the police tried to impose some order on the chaos. They sawed through the floorboards and joists to allow easier access to the burial space. They divided the area into a grid, and, when a bucket was lifted from a particular grid, it was taken behind the house and placed in a corresponding grid to dry. No one imagined that it would freeze instead of drying.

The police soon realized that it was impossible to remove bodies methodically one at a time; in most cases, decay had left little intact. Technicians merely searched through the mush for bones, which were crudely rinsed—using a bucket of water and Gacy's own deep-frying basket—before they were passed along for inspection by Dr. Robert Stein. It soon became clear that small bones from wrists, fingers and toes would be lost. Only when shoes or socks survived could evidence technicians recover the tiny remains.

As the law prescribes, Dr. Stein wrote a death certificate as each body was exhumed. Then he and his assistants piled the bags near the front door to be picked up for delivery to the morgue. Each body was reduced to a number, each number was placed on a wooden stake, and the stake driven into the mud of the crawlspace as near as possible to where the skull had been found. As the graves emptied, the number of stakes increased, the chilly ground water seeping relentlessly in, pooling around the posts.

In a bizarre deal, Gacy agreed to help the searchers if the police allowed him to visit his father's grave. This done, the contractor was taken to his house where he railed at the officers for wrecking his property. There was mud on the carpets, the houseplants had been knocked over, and his neatly ordered tools had been messed up. He began cleaning up, petulantly announcing that he would not cooperate with the police any longer if they were going to be so careless. State Attorney Terry Sullivan, in charge of building the prosecution's case, screamed, "Cuff him." He was furious and ordered Gacy out of his home. "Drag the bastard out, if you have to," he shouted.

Police coaxed Gacy to spray-paint an "X" on the spot in the garage where he'd poured concrete over Butkovich's grave. The body, preceded by a cloud of noxious gas, was chipped out of the floor by members of the North Investigation Unit of Cook County, Lundquist and Swartz.

By Saturday, December 23rd, Joe Kozenczak received a mittimus, a legal order remanding Gacy to the custody of the Cook County Sheriff, from Judge Marvin Peters, which authorized the Des Plaines PD to take John Gacy to Cook County's Cermak Hospital where he would be segregated from other prisoners and subjected to psychiatric examination.

Identifying the bodies was a nightmare. Only after developing a technique of defining each grave site by depth and length could searchers be reasonably sure they were lifting parts of one corpse and not another as they explored. In some graves, Gacy had buried one body on top of another. In one grave, the skeletons were so jumbled together that the two skulls were almost touching. The problem was resolved by simply placing bags between the corpses and removing the soil by the handful.

The search team fought the horror of their work with black humor. Officers warned against throwing chicken bones into the pit, saying that Dr. Stein might flip out. Then there were the inevitable John Gacy jokes—Gacy wouldn't be going out this New Year's Eve because he couldn't dig up a date. Officers held a "Ghoul Pool" on the number of bodies. The guesses ranged from 5 to 14—all too low.

On Sunday, two more bodies were recovered and, keeping with a directive issued by Chief Dobbs of Cook County Police, the next day would be a holiday.

On Tuesday, December 26th, six more bodies were recovered from the crawlspace. One was found under a concrete slab. Several had only socks on their bodies. Ligatures were around the throats of a few, and some had what resembled underwear or cloth in their throats. In many instances, a plastic bag, like those used in dry-cleaning establishments, was wrapped around the victim's upper body and head. Gacy had learned as he went along. Cloth in the throat and plastic bags made things neater for him.

Police were taking souvenirs such as bricks, ballpoint pens with the PDM logo and Gacy's business cards. Photos of the diggers and technicians were taken for posterity. They posed in front of a huge blow-up of Gacy adorned with Polish flags and a collection of dildos. Officers postured before this grotesque background, their riot helmets under their arms, while a colleague displayed the day's body count on a film-style chalk clapper-board.

Scuba divers were brought in to supplement the helicopter search of the Des Plaines River around the bridge in Grundy County where Gacy had said he had disposed of a body. Nothing was found.

Five more graves were added to the police diagram the next day. Officer Ralph Tovar found a blue parka jacket between the floor joists adjacent to the laundry room. The jacket wasn't the only item hidden by the contractor. Like so many serial killers, Gacy kept and hid souvenirs of his murders. Several pieces of jewelry, various items of clothing, adult books, smoking materials—including pipes and bongs—25 badges and stars, a folding knife, pieces of rope and items used for torture were collected.

Later, highway diggers excavated the entire crawlspace down to undisturbed clay. In April 1979, the house, now unsafe from all the digging, was razed to the ground. But still the digging continued. The total number of bodies unearthed from the house, the garage and driveway eventually totalled 29. Six of the bodies have never been identified.

James Mazzara's body was recovered from the Des Plaines River on December 28, 1978.

On April 9, 1979, a man strolling along the river's towpath, five and a half miles downstream from the I-55 bridge, found Robert Priest's corpse. Joe Kozenczak remembers the day as if it were yesterday, "It was late afternoon when Ron Adams and I started the trip down I-129 in back of Bedoe and Sullivan's car. They had detailed directions from the Sheriff's Department as to where we were to meet our escort in Grundy

County. Bedoe decided to use his red light and siren, and we zoomed down the interstate like that until we reached the Morris exit and found the Sheriff's police car waiting for us.

"The body was being held in a nearby hospital where a dentist was comparing its teeth with Rob Priest's dental charts. It was a positive match."

* * *

"When they paint this image that I was this monster that picked up those altar boys on the street and swatted them like flies, this is ludicrous. Whether it's Berkowitz, whether it's Bundy, whether it's Wayne Williams down in Atlanta, or any of the others, or Charlie Manson, I don't comment about any other cases because of the simple fact I wasn't there. I hate it when they [the public] put me in the same club with them.

"If the people want to know the truth, or the honesty of it ... that they want to be brainwashed into what they want to believe, then, OK, fine, go ahead and kill me. But 'Vengeance is mine' sayeth the Lord, because you will have executed someone who didn't commit the crime."

JOHN WAYNE GACY, DEATH ROW, MENARD CF, 1992

The trial of John Wayne Gacy started at the Central Criminal Court in Chicago on February 6, 1980, Judge Louis B. Garippo presiding. Terry Sullivan and William Kunkle, Chief Prosecutor for the county, were to face Sam Amirante for the defense.

Judge Garippo has since retired from the bench, but recalled the trial clearly. "It was a straightforward murder trial," he said. "There was, from a judge's point of view, nothing unusual in the proceedings. Jury selection was very fast, only taking four days." And what of Gacy's defense? "Well, there is no doubt that he had suffered a bad childhood.

That undoubtedly created some sympathy in my courtroom. But, unfortunately for Mr. John Gacy, it no doubt occurred to the jury that millions of people have similar abusive childhoods, and very few of them have some thirty bodies buried on their property."

As for the death sentence Judge Garippo handed down, he said that he had no qualms, "none at all. I have my own private thoughts, of course I do. I was merely an instrument of the criminal justice system. My job was to see that John had a fair trial, which he did. Based on the evidence, it was overwhelming, the jury found him guilty, and I passed the only sentence for his crimes prescribed by the law in Illinois."

William Kunkle's team brought in one expert witness, in the form of James Cavanaugh, who evaluated Gacy at Cermak Hospital. He recalls, "My impressions of him during these approximate 18 hours were that he was a well organized, very intelligent man who was very particular about the way he organized his environment. He made the best possible use of all the space he had in Cermak Hospital. He had decorated it. He had worked out an exercise program that was quite interesting, showing a great deal of imagination. Walking a number of miles each day, which he kept track of by flipping and checking cards out of a deck and each card represented a certain amount of feet. My impression was that this was a person who was a little compulsive, meaning he had to do things over and over and over again in a ritualized manner.

"Other general observations were that, after we got over the hurdle of the ground rules for us during the examination, meaning that we, in a sense, capitulated to his desires to sign this form that we wouldn't release our work product, he was generally quite cooperative and answered questions quite fully and was able in about 18 hours of interview to retrace many of the pertinent details of his life up to the time when these evaluations began."

Cavanaugh's general conclusions about Gacy were that he showed a sexual sadistic behavioral pattern, was narcissistic—meaning he had "a grandiose sense of self-importance or uniqueness"—and was anti-social. In layman's terms, all of this added up to a mixed personality disorder. But Cavanaugh didn't feel Gacy's mental problems in any sense met the state's legal definition of insanity.

Dr. Helen Morrison, forensic psychiatrist for the defense, claimed that Gacy was insane, while other psychiatrists labelled him as "very dangerous, borderline personality, amnesiac and schizophrenic." Then the final nail was put in Gacy's coffin when a defense psychiatrist said that, if Gacy was found insane, he would be put back out on the streets because "he cannot be hospitalized against his will."

In 1995, William Kunkle offered this insight into the case, "Basically, the defense claimed that John was a deeply sick individual who was crazy all of the time. That one doesn't wash. He certainly wasn't crazy when he was working at his job and socializing. He wasn't crazy at all … According to Illinois law, John was sane. He was just evil."

And what of Gacy's claim that someone else had killed and buried the victims without his knowledge? "Within hours of his arrest, John was confessing to the murders. He drew a very accurate diagram of where the bodies were in his crawlspace before the digging started. It was very accurate. He told police where he had disposed of Mazzara and Rob Priest. This was correct, too. Yes, John Gacy was guilty. I lose no sleep over this."

Kunkle also had an opinion on Gacy's state of mind. "A real medical, model psychiatrist who treats patients and understands mental illness will never believe that you can turn this type of serious mental illness off like a faucet. Did he have personality disorders? Absolutely. Was he a sexual deviant? Of course. But psychotic? Not even close."

And, of course, William Kunkle is correct. If his crimes were not premeditated, why would Gacy have burial trenches dug in advance? Why did he keep handcuffs and a rope ready? If he didn't understand the criminality of his behavior, why did he choose victims who might not be missed? If he had amnesia, how did he draw a precise sketch locating each body on his property?

William Kunkle added, "Clearly, when you have this kind of behavior, the preplanning for all those things, the covering up, the post-planning, the postconduct for all these things, and all this going on against the backdrop on the surface of what appears to be a perfectly normal existence … just doesn't fit."

* * *

"Do you realize that, by 1993, 50 percent of American families will be single parented? And that shows a breakdown in the Church in not being able to hold families together. And, for this reason, children run away from home and seek love in other places."

JOHN WAYNE GACY, DEATH ROW, 1992

The prosecution had called 79 witnesses, the defense 22. Now, on March 12, 1980, at 4:40 p.m., the jury presented 35 signed verdicts of murder. They also found Gacy guilty of taking "indecent liberties with a child upon Robert Priest" and guilty of "sexual assault upon Robert Priest."

Because the Illinois death penalty statute became effective on June 21, 1977, it applied to the 12 murders that occurred after this date, and affected the sentencing. In fact, the final verdict stated that Gacy, who had "attained the age of 18 years at the time," murdered 12 individuals after June 21, 1977 and was sentenced to death.

Judge Garippo, with his black robe and grey hair, sat looking distinguished and stately behind the bench, announcing that the execution date would be June 2, 1980.

On March 13, 1980, Gacy was sent to Menard Correctional Center in Illinois. He would remain there for just over 14 years until he was transported by helicopter to the Stateville Penitentiary near Joliet for execution. Gacy would become the hundredth person executed in Illinois since 1928, when the state took control of executions.

Barring any last-minute delay, Gacy was to be the second person to die by injection, and the first killer whose appeals had run out since the reinstatement of the death penalty.

John Szabo was the first person sentenced to death under the state's new death penalty. Szabo, 36, has avoided execution since 1979 through various legal challenges. He was convicted of four murders in Will County. Court challenges also kept alive George Delvecchio, James P. Free, Jr., Kenneth Allen and Hernando Williams, the other killers sentenced to death before Gacy.

During the evening of May 9, 1994, Gacy sat down for his last meal—fried chicken, French fries, Coke and strawberry shortcake. Prison officials later described his demeanor as "chatty... talking up a storm." In a phone interview shortly before his execution, he told a Knight-Tribune reporter, "There's been 11 hardback books on me, 31 paperbacks, two screenplays, one movie, one off-Broadway play, five songs, and over 5,000 articles. What can I say about it?" But, of course, he quickly protested, "I have no ego for any of this garbage."

Hours after having exhausted legal appeals that had filled and perpetuated his life, Gacy, aged 52, was strapped to a gurney in the execution room shortly after midnight. For his last words, Gacy snarled, "Kiss my ass." His execution was a minor media sensation and large crowds of people gathered on the grounds of the penitentiary where it occurred. In a display of what has been called "shocking bad taste," vendors sold T-shirts and Gacy merchandise, and the people cheered at the moment when Gacy was pronounced dead. But all had not gone as planned. There was a problem with the machine.

Executioners had started the chemicals flowing at 12:40 a.m.. The process was scheduled for ten minutes, not eighteen. The first injection causes sleep, the second stops the breathing and the third stops the heart. Gacy was not unconscious when the problem occurred and suffered a great deal of distress when there was a blow back and his blood and chemicals sprayed around the death chamber.

Howard A. Peters III, head of the Department of Corrections, said that the second of the three chemicals that were to flow into Gacy's arm apparently gelled, or were blocked by a clot of Gacy's blood. Officials attached a new tube to the needle and resumed the execution.

* * *

I do not consider myself unique in that I managed to interview John Wayne Gacy prior to his execution. Many other criminologists, psychiatrists and friends of John managed this, too.

I cannot say that his correspondence with me was of much assistance either. As with everyone who visited this man on "The Row," most had to complete a two-page questionnaire which was subject to his approval before he would even consider agreeing to the visit. Nevertheless, by taking a lateral approach in examining what we do know about John Gacy, we can learn much about the workings of his mind.

On a number of occasions, individuals who wanted to meet with him—those whom he thought worthy of the effort—would be sent his "bio review." I was considered important enough to receive one, and it makes for an interesting read. I have included it here verbatim, without his permission, for the obvious reasons.

BIOGRAPHICAL REVIEW

Full name:	John Wayne Michael Gacy
Date of Birth:	March 17, 1942
Age, Height, Weight:	50; 5' 9"; 220 pounds
Home:	Menard, Death Row, Chester, Ill.
Marital Status:	Twice divorced

Family:	2 sisters, 5 children
Wheels:	Last car '79 Oldsmobile 4 dr.
Brothers:	None
Sisters:	Two
Most Treasured Honor:	3 times Man of the Year, Jaycees, 3 different cities.
Perfect Woman or Man:	Woman: independent thinker, self-starter, mind of her own. Man: Bright, bold, honest, dependable, says what he is thinking.
Childhood Hero:	J.F. Kennedy, R.W. Daley
Current Hero:	M. Cuomo, Donald Trump
Favorite TV Shows:	*Unsolved Mysteries*, National Geographic specials
Favorite Movies:	*Once Upon a Time in America, GoodFellas, Ten Commandments*
Favorite Song:	"Send in the Clowns," "Amazing Grace"
Favorite Singers:	Judy Collins, Bob Dylan, Neil Diamond, Roy Orbison, Sha Na Na
Favorite Musicians:	REO Speedwagon, Elton John, Zamfir
Hobbies:	Correspondence, oil painting, study of human interests
Favorite Meals:	Fried chicken, deboned lake perch drawn in butter, salad, tea
Why you wrote J.W. Gacy:	I don't, I just answer for him. [sic]
Recommended Reading:	*Texas Connection, Question of Doubt*
Last Book Read:	*Naked Lunch* and *Wild Boys*, William S. Burroughs
Ideal Evening:	Dinner and concert or live show, drinks and a quiet walk by lake.

Every Jan. 1st I Resolve:	Correct things that I let go the year before.
Nobody Knows I'm:	A character who loves to tease and joke around (sic).
My Biggest Regret:	Being so trusting and gullible, taken advantage of.
If I Were President I'd:	Make sure the people of this country had jobs and a place to live before worrying about other countries.
My Advice to Children:	Be yourself, think positive, respect parents.
What I Don't Like about People:	Phonies, people who don't keep their word.
My Biggest Fear:	Dying before I have a chance to clear my name with truth.
Pet Peeves:	People who say things they have no intentions in doing.
Superstitions:	None, it's for negative people.
Friends Like Me Because:	I am outspoken and honest, fun-loving and dependable.

John Gacy married two independent-thinking, self-starting women with minds of their own, and they were clearly not right for him. Where he describes his ideal man, of course, he is suggesting his own self-perceived attributes.

Gacy was a man with political aspirations who considered himself as a hard working entrepreneur, so his childhood heroes will come as no surprise to us: J.F. Kennedy had been president of the United States; R.W. Daley was a well-liked mayor of Chicago; Mario M. Cuomo, a State of New York governor, was the youngest child of poor and illiterate immigrants whose father worked cleaning sewers until he had enough money to start a small grocery store; and Donald Trump needs no introduction.

With his various preferences, the reader will note that he has conveniently omitted to include the masses of stag magazines, pornographic literature and homosexual videos that must have taken up a great deal of his free time. The real John Gacy is also apparent when he refers to the last books he has read; these publications would not have been supplied to him in prison.

Naked Lunch by William S. Burroughs was published in 1962 and sparked a landmark obscenity trial that served to end literary censorship in America. *Wild Boys*, also written by Burroughs, contains shocking, pornographic imagery of a violent world of renegade homosexual boys; it was a book well thumbed by John Gacy.

John's ideal evening seems somewhat out of sorts with his true self, for it is known that he rarely attended a concert or live show. This preference suggests decent sensibilities with the "drinks and a quiet walk by a lake." Nowhere here do we find any reference to swilling back bottles of whisky and six-packs of beer, smoking reefer after reefer and constant pill-popping to either knock him out or wake him up.

The reader does not have to be a psychiatrist or psychologist to realize that John's bio review has to be taken with a grain of salt. It is what John *doesn't* say which is of more importance to us when trying to understand him and this can no better be illustrated than in his New Year resolution, "to correct things that I let go year before," a well-intended resolution maybe, yet one which, for some decades, he singularly failed to realize.

Of course, as Pogo the Clown, John loved to tease and joke around, while once again neglecting to mention that he loved to "tease and joke" around with his many young victims, the ploy in getting them to try on his handcuffs to see if they could escape was one of them. Towards the end of John's review, we see a little more of the psychopathic personality coming through. Ever the hypocrite, he claims that his biggest regret was "being so trusting and gullible, taken advantage of." We can say without any doubt that his many victims were trusting, gullible and taken advantage of… but John Gacy? He was the ultimate user and abuser. And he has the gall to suggest that he hated phonies and people who didn't keep their word!

His greatest fear was of dying before he had a chance to clear his name with the truth. But, with his having confessed to all of the murders—and, at one point, John Gacy claimed to have killed up to 50 young men all over the United States—and, having described in great detail the locations of the corpses under his home on Summerdale, which turned out to accurate, going on to say where he had thrown at least five bodies into the Des Plaines River, that, surely, must be where the real truth lies.

One might ask, what more truths had to come out which would "clear his name"?

"At the time of my arrest, there were four other suspects, all employees of PDM contractors, all with keys to the house … if you've lived your life the right way then you have nothing to fear in my case. I am fairly comfortable with Him. I've been at Catholic services for the past ten years. I've had confession. I've had communion. I've no qualms about that. I am at peace with myself."
JOHN WAYNE GACY, AT INTERVIEW

Indeed, he nails his hypocrisy to the cell door when he says that his pet peeves are "people who say things they have no intention of doing." It's clear that Gacy had more than sufficient time to come up with the truth—to be precise, between 12:15 p.m. on Thursday, December 21, 1978, when he was arrested, and 12:40 a.m. on Tuesday, May 11, 1994, when he was executed.

* * *

John Wayne Gacy was emotionally stunted as a child and, as he grew older, where there should have been a conscience there developed a void. During this period, his formative years through to his very early teens, I would suggest that John's mind split in two, for as he developed he held two differing sets of thinking processes, values, attitudes, emotions and aspirations. There was the hardworking, honest, upright pillar of the community with his social and political dreams. But, on the other hand, he harbored dark and perverted secrets.

Of course, John loved his mother. As he grew older, he probably regarded her as a strong, gregarious woman who had turned weak. He had witnessed how his domineering father had heaped verbal and physical abuse upon her. And, with almost overwhelming ambitions to be like his methodical father, to be able to prove himself as a "real man," he would subsequently have subconsciously had little respect for women in general.

His father was a precise patriarch whom the impressionable young John secretly looked up to, despite the beatings and abuse meted out to him. He would do anything to please his father, and it is interesting to note that John was devastated when, while in prison, his father passed away and he wasn't allowed to attend the funeral. We will also recall that, on the day he was arrested, John Gacy was on his way to his father's grave where he intended to place a rosary and possibly commit suicide.

Mr. Gacy Sr. was a control freak and a perfectionist. It is no mere coincidence that John would become a perfectionist in his work and a control freak, too. He aimed for perfection in organizing social events, his dedication to fine detail and long hours gained him high recognition with the Jaycees. This was no small feat and we must give John Gacy credit for that.

There may be those who smirk at Gacy's achievements, but the Jaycees do not give out honors lightly. We may also recall that he organized the Polish Constitution Day Parade in 1978—one of the few years that this event has gone off without a hitch. And John did not gain the position in 1975 of Secretary-Treasurer of the Norwood Park Township Street Lighting District because he was a fool. It may also be argued, though, that, because he could not succumb to the temptation of young boys while in prison, he was destined to become a model prisoner anyway.

It could be suggested that the torture, sexual abuse and seething anger Gacy directed at his helpless victims was an echo of the way his father treated him as a youth. The victims were John himself. He became his father, heaping ridicule on them and exercising power and control over them, punishing them for his own weaknesses in mind, body and soul. It is also of some interest to note that John never assaulted a woman, nor did he attack older males—he was too much of a coward to strike out at mature men. His targets were young male prostitutes, runaways, the innocent and often gullible. They were his desired prey.

But why, if John thought so little of women, did he marry? I suggest that he married because this was the socially acceptable thing for him to do. The good Mr. Gacy wanted to be a successful businessman, a politician. To fit in with the social set and political circles in which he needed to mix, a wife was an asset to him, a tool he could use to promote himself as an upstanding member of the community. And it is of interest to note that both of his marriages failed when the "bad" John Gacy came out of the closet.

His first wife understandably left him when he went to prison for sodomizing a young boy; his second wife left him when she ran out of patience and refused to condone his homosexual leanings and perversions a day longer. John had no choice when Marion left him because he had effectively dug his own grave and was on his way to prison. Things were different, however, when he lost his second wife. Our aspiring politician was now aware that, because of his previous prison sentence, he was barred from high office. PDM Contractors was doing very well. Effectively, his second wife, Carole, and her two children were unwanted baggage. He was managing in his social and business circles quite well without her. In fact, the "bad" John Gacy would have viewed her as a hindrance, one which prevented him from fully exploiting his carnal desires. Once she had left, the leash was taken from around his neck and the monster inside his head could now run amok, which it did.

John would later claim that his alter ego, "Mad Jack," committed the murders and, in a strange way, with the great gift of hindsight, it appears that John Gacy did have an alter ego of sorts, though this was never medically proven. At one time, Gacy had befriended, although it was never reciprocated, a police officer by the name of Jack Hanley, a detective with the hit and run unit of Cook County law enforcement. Gacy developed a fixation for this cop. Jack was all the things Gacy was not: muscular, commanding and a devoted hater of homosexuals. Jack Hanley was the punishing type of lawman that Gacy both admired and feared. He became a kind of obsession figure for Gacy and, later, a scapegoat.

It has been claimed that, when John started drinking or taking drugs, it seemed that his alter ego Mad Jack would take over and do things that Gacy would never do sober. Gacy would eventually confess to police that when he couldn't really remember the crimes or exactly what he had done with some of the bodies before he buried them under his house because Jack had been in charge. However, this explanation does not fit with the John Gacy whom we have met so far, because we find a man who was trawling for sex with young men when he married for the first time, a man who was committing serious sexual offences long before he met Jack Hanley.

We have come to know an individual who used his role as the manager of several fried chicken outlets to procure young boys, and he used the same technique and opportunity when working in politics and around the community. It is more than probable, though, that drugs and drink fuelled his sexual cravings.

Like so many serial murderers, Gacy never accepted the blame for his actions. It was always, without exception, the fault of Mad Jack, or the boys themselves.

There are many observers who argue that John did not have a conscience. However, I contend that the good John Gacy did have an honorable conscience, and the work and honors he gained working for the community are good testimony to this. Conversely, the bad John Gacy had no conscience whatsoever; tragically, the bad John Gacy prevailed during the last few years of his freedom. There would be no cure, and it stayed with him until the end of his days.

There is one final scenario which is terrifying in the extreme, one almost too awful for contemplation. Had John Gacy not served a ten-year prison term, and he had managed to emulate the achievements of his heroes, there is little doubt that he would have achieved high political office. He may have enjoyed a glittering political career and Illinois might have enjoyed a mayor in John Gacy, or even a Governor.

Perhaps, however, the last word should go to William Kunkle, who said after Gacy's execution, "He got a much easier death than any of his victims. In my opinion, he got an easier death than he deserved. But the important thing is he paid for his crimes with his life."

This chapter is based on several visits by the author to Chicago and Des Plaines, Illinois; unique archive material; interviews with many of the principal police players; an interview with John Wayne Gacy at Menard, and a 63-minute police video of the exhumation of Gacy's victims from his crawlspace.

KENNETH ALESSIO BIANCHI

"If this person is more real than just my dream, and if this is the same person haunting me, which is more likely, this person could have been responsible for the uncontrollable violence in my life, the instigator of the lies I've done. The blank spots, amnesia, I can't account for, and the deaths of the girls, all the ones in California, and the two here. But if he is in me, then he killed them using me— why can't I remember for sure?

I want to know if this is so—what if?"

KENNETH BIANCHI IN HIS PRISON DIARY

y nerves are on edge. I am about to be locked into a small cell with a sadosexual psychopath. Kenneth Bianchi is an exploitative homicidal maniac who ripped away the lives of some 15 young women, including two little girls, and dumped their bodies like so much trash.

I am about to get up close and very personal with this monster who has vowed to tear my face off. With a heavily pockmarked face, he is a powerful, dark haired human predator with ink-black eyes which never blink, the cold, wet eyes of a great white shark, soon to stare deep into my head with his evil tentacles of enquiring thought.

An arm's length away, a touch away now, Kenneth Bianchi does not smile as he walks into the room. He sits down. His breathing is shallow. I can almost hear his mind working like the ticking of a clock, even a bomb about to explode, for his hatred towards me radiates like red hot coals.

Two long minutes pass. Not a word is said. Tick, tick, tick, tick. I lean back in my chair; I smile. "You don't like me one bit, do you, Ken?"

There is no response and no movement from the man simmering a heartbeat away. To break the ice, I rise to my feet and slowly walk around the table to him. I place my left hand on his shoulder. "Hey, Ken," I whisper. "You are some miserable son of a bitch. Come on, where is that fucking smile?"

Within a millisecond, a switch flicked inside his head. The tension seemed to wash out of him in an instant and a cruel smile slowly came to his thin mouth. It was this human contact, the physical touch and a dangerous up close encounter—which could have played out either way—that now enabled me to have a 60-minute interview with "The Hillside Strangler."

When we parted, Ken stopped in his tracks, reeled around and snarled, "Don't ever, *ever*, come near me again."

I did—not once, but twice!

On the second occasion, as instructed by the guards who waited at the entrance of the tier, I slowly walked the yellow line down the Special Housing Unit (SHU). Cross the line and the spittle, excrement and urine from angry inmates will cover you. I stopped at cell number 8. Ken was lying on his bunk, headphones on, watching TV. I walked to his cell door and called his name. He stirred. He ignored me. Then he flew at the bars in a frenzy.

"Nice house you have here, Ken," I said, smiling. Then I stepped away.

Third time, it was yard time. Bitterly cold, wet and windy at the pen. Bianchi saw me watching him as he walked during exercise. This time mute, he turned up his collar, pulled his cap down over his eyes, and I would never see him again.

* * *

"One girl was killed and, when she was dead, she was put inside the bedroom blindfolded. I took her girlfriend [Sonja] into the bedroom and raped and buggered her before killing her. She screamed for her mom, and the last thing she saw was the face of her dead friend lying under the sheets next to her."

KENNETH BIANCHI TO THE AUTHOR AT INTERVIEW, ON THE
MURDER OF 14 YEAR OLD SONJA JOHNSON

After four years of continual correspondence with Bianchi, I was finally granted a rare interview with him. The meeting took place in September 1996, at the notoriously tough Washington State Penitentiary (WSP) at Walla Walla, a medium sized city that squats in dry flatlands just a stone's throw from the Washington–Oregon border in the southeast corner of the state.

Bianchi stands around five feet eleven inches tall, and he is extremely well built. A tough exercise regime has toned his muscles to perfection; with a washboard stomach and powerful shoulders. Today, well into his fifties, he is a fine specimen of a man. Ken's once rich, black mane of hair is thinning and turning grey, however, he still has the drop dead handsome looks that the women always found so attractive. But it is his eyes that one finds fascinating, if not disturbing. They are small and jet black. They are unblinking, devoid of any emotion whatsoever, they glitter with distilled evil. When one looks into Bianchi's eyes, I kid you not, you are looking into the abyss and that abyss is looking straight back at you.

* * *

Kenneth Alessio Bianchi was born on Friday, May 22, 1951, in Rochester, New York. He was the last of four children to Florence King, an attractive, precocious 17-year-old go-go dancer. She dumped him like an unwanted puppy shortly after giving birth. Kenneth never knew his genetic father, so, throughout his life, he suffered the social stigma of knowing he was a bastard.

Within weeks of his birth, Ken was fostered out to an elderly woman who had little time for him, so she farmed him out to a number of her friends and neighbors. It would be fair to say that, during this crucial period, Kenneth did not enjoy the benefits of having a mother. In fact, he did not have anyone to give him this vital attention. Indeed, it was quite the opposite, for he was shuffled from home to home, with each minder exhibiting different opinions of him, ranging from short term curiosity to unwelcome nuisance. So, in this respect alone, and in much the same way as so many other serial murderers, from day one, Ken was being emotionally deprived and damaged.

Italian immigrants Frances Bianchi and her husband, Nicholas, a manual laborer at the American Brake-Shoe foundry in Rochester, adopted Ken when he was three months old. He was to be their only child.

Born in 1918, Frances had wanted a child since her late teens, but she could not conceive. Time dragged by and, now 32, the only option open to her was adoption, to which her husband somewhat reluctantly agreed. Unfortunately, Frances was a hypochondriac and emotionally insecure; furthermore, she suffered frequent bouts of depression. Nonetheless, she was successfully able to conceal much of this under a veil of overt assertiveness, which manifested itself in an oversolicitous and totalitarian style.

In order to survive emotionally, Frances was capable of splitting off from her weaker self. She used denial and repression, which broadly speaking means, when one is not happy with a situation, one puts the conscious thought out of one's mind. This was her mental defense mechanism, a vital requirement as her husband further aggravated the family's weak infrastructure with his inveterate gambling through which he lost the better part of his wages to the bookies.

Although a hard worker and a loyal spouse, Nicholas was weak-willed. As a direct result of him not being able to pay off his gambling debts, the family was always on the move because loan sharks threatened to shoot him if he didn't pay up. This confused package of mental and financial instability spilled into the Bianchi home on a daily basis, and it was Frances who felt it the worst with her paranoia soon rubbing off on her adopted son.

If Frances Bianchi needed anything from this unsettled and worrying existence, it was security. She wrongly reasoned that she would be better off if there was someone who really needed her and, in turn, she would satisfy her maternal instincts by having a child. Ken would have to pay a very high price, and he was forced to give Frances his undivided admiration and full attention during the years to follow if he were to survive psychologically himself. A hint of these troubles surfaced just a year later.

Ken's adoption agency records reveal that, although he was a "sturdily built baby with bluish eyes and wavy brown hair, appearing happy, contented and alert," Mrs. Bianchi was described as being "over-solicitous." A footnote added that Nicholas Bianchi was "quiet, unassuming, but very friendly, able to control his incessant stuttering, which has troubled him since childhood, only when Kenneth is around him."

In 1953, with loan sharks forever chasing Mr. Bianchi for his gambling debts, the family were forced to leave their home on Saratoga Avenue in Rochester, New York, and move to Glide Street where they kept a low profile. The loan sharks soon caught up with them, so a year later they moved to Los Angeles where they stayed with Frances's sister, Jennifer Buono. By now, Ken had developed asthma.

While in California, Ken attended the Century Park School, where, at age five, he suffered the first of two bad falls. He tripped while running up a flight of concrete steps, cracking open his head, then, a month later, he fell headlong from playground equipment, hitting a number of steel rungs and breaking his nose when he hit the floor. After this accident, he started wetting his pants during the daytime. He developed a facial tic which was apparent when he was stressed, and he was significantly accident prone; choosing to run rather than walk, he was always falling over.

During the family's time in California, Nicholas Bianchi managed to save some money, which he used to pay off his gambling debts, so the family decided it was now safe to return to Rochester. Ken's asthma had all but disappeared, although his mother noticed that her boy had become withdrawn. He would retire to the attic where he spent hours gazing vacantly at the trains as they passed the house. Then, as might be expected, Nicholas started running up large gambling debts again.

The family's stay at 529 Lyell Avenue, in the red light district where serial killer Arthur Shawcross trawled for victims, was short-lived. According to Ken, "In 1958 we moved to a pink-painted house on Wildwood Drive, then in 1959 to 60, Villa Street, then on to Campbell

Street," and, all the while, Kenneth was changing not only any friends he had made, but schools as well.

In 1960, the nine-year-old was seen briefly at the Strong Memorial Hospital Clinic in Rochester. His appointment was prompted by a complaint from the Society of Prevention of Cruelty to Children. In a nutshell, this issue was based on school and adoption agency evidence suggesting that the boy was not being properly cared for and, of course, there was every reason to believe this was the case. The report which followed Ken's visit, claimed, "Kenneth is a very anxious boy who has many phobias and counter-phobias. He uses repression and reaction formation. He is very dependent upon his mother. She has dominated him, and indulged him in terms of her own needs. He is anxious, protective, and this clinging control has made him ambivalent. But he represses his hostile aggression, and is increasingly dependent upon her."

Therefore, as far back as nine years old, there appear to be significant indications that Kenneth Bianchi was made up of two opposing sets of attitudes and emotions. Echoing the psychopathology of his neurotic mother, he, like John Gacy, was mentally splitting in two. Undeniably, he had for years been the victim of a subtle form of child abuse and, unless something changed, he would be emotionally scarred for life.

But nothing did change. Indeed, matters became worse when, in 1961, two doctors at the DePaul Psychiatric Clinic in Rochester saw Ken again. On this occasion, the complaint came from the Monsignor at Ken's school because of his continual absenteeism. The facial tics and the enuresis (wetting himself) were also cause for concern, as was the asthma, which had returned with a vengeance. Doctors Dowling and Sullivan strongly recommended treatment for the boy, although, after two visits to the clinic, Mrs. Bianchi bluntly told the doctors that she didn't see the need for any more treatment. She refused to let the doctors see Ken again and, in doing so, Frances placed her adopted son in great peril.

In June 1965, tragedy struck when Nicholas Bianchi died at work following a massive heart attack. He was on the telephone to Frances when it happened, and he collapsed with the handset clutched tightly in his hand. Later that year, Frances and Ken moved house yet again, and once more he was uprooted from his school, moving to the McQuaid Jesuit High School in the same city.

In his unpublished manuscript, Kenneth Bianchi devoted just half a page to the subject of his father, whom he says he "adored." However, over five pages contain explicit details of his early sexual experiences, and this is all rather sinister for a convicted serial killer who is intent on proving his innocence for a string of sexually related homicides, which include the rape, buggery, torture and murder of two little girls.

Nevertheless, the following is Ken's account and, although some may find this shocking, it is significant that this beast refers to young girls, aged around ten, as "women." He also claims to have been sexually active since the age of 11.

While my hormones increased, it was not until my sophomore year when I had my first sexual experience with a partner. It was when I was about eleven years old when I had my first solo experience. My first love was blonde, thin build, and easy to speak with. She had a cute way of flirting, head tipped a bit. A beautiful smile across her face. She smelled divine, as women do.

Our first sexual encounter was at her home, with her parents and sister away. It was brief and I was so nervous my hands shook. I tried my best to be patient and gentle as I assumed a man would be. I'm certain I was hurried and, with a touch of experience, I wore no protection, which she had insisted on. When we finished, I just held her. It was the most beautiful and memorable experience I'd had up to that point in my life.

KENNETH BIANCHI ON HIS EARLY SEXUAL EXPERIENCES

In fact, the girlfriend in question was just nine years old, but this did not prevent Ken adding that she was not his steady girlfriend. "We coupled for a week or so," he claimed, "but her heart belonged to several other guys in the neighborhood. She and I had sexual relations twice more before ending our relationship." Warming to his theme, Bianchi admitted that he had "scholastic problems" because his real interest was always the female sex. "I was crazy about girls … I dated different women on a regular basis. Romance is wonderful, life was my opiate, women were my fix. I could easily be distracted from my studies by the right woman."

With equal clarity, Kenneth Bianchi also remembered Sue Davis, a young girl from his school who was younger than him, it seems, who invited him to her home where there was a swimming pool. And, at this point in his writing, Bianchi launches into a more complete quasi-erotic explanation of a problem that occurred during that very same swimming session, and it bothers him some 40 years later.

She was a little chubby. She had a spinal problem, and was bubbly and full-figured. We were in the pool, and I reached out to hug her. She turned and my hand brushed against her breast. I wasn't disappointed, but it was unintentional. We broke up after that. She thought I had touched her breast without her permission. That allegation upset me.

KENNETH BIANCHI ON SUE DAVIS

Sue Davis was eleven years old, and Bianchi did more than touch her breast, he touched just about everything else. So, it is clear from the pen of the killer himself that, by the age of 18, the oldest girl he had had sex with was 14, and the youngest, at least three of them, were aged nine.

In 1970, Ken resumed his studies and set his sights on joining a police academy. He enrolled at college, and now 19 he was living with his adoptive mother at 105 Glenda Park.

With only a decent showing in geography, in all other subjects Ken struggled abysmally, so it is not surprising to learn that Ken not only failed to obtain his degree, but he was also deemed to be totally unsuitable to become a police officer. He was, however, offered the more menial job of jail deputy, a position he promptly turned down while all of his fellow students were joining the police academy. Ken was now a laughing stock and he didn't like it one bit. But his narcissistic obsessions were to have further, far wider-reaching and more dangerous implications than anyone could have predicted around this low point in his life.

With his dream shattered, he took to petty thieving and was soon being dismissed from every part time job he took. Ken did, however, have something in common with one small group of people, that subculture of society called emerging serial killers, for he was a pathological liar. Telling lies was his way of making himself seem cleverer than he actually was. Kenneth could not allow himself to be seen as inferior in the eyes of his peers, and looking back at him as he was then it is clear that this young man suffered from a manifest grandiosity—and he still does to this day.

Upon leaving school in 1971, Bianchi married an extremely attractive girl called Brenda Beck. He took a part time job at the Two Guys store, and he furthered his education at the Rochester Monroe Community College where he reviewed plays and films for the college newspaper, The Monroe Discipline. Ken's enthusiasm then faltered; he failed to complete many of the classes, which included psychology, in which he drew an "incomplete." However, psychology was a subject he would return to under somewhat less than honest circumstances eight years later.

At the same time as Ken's academic efforts were tottering on the edge of a cliff, his personal life suddenly collapsed around him when his

wife caught him in bed with another woman, Janice Tuschong. Brenda
threw him out on to the street where he became the subject of much
ridicule among the few friends that he had.

Brenda has never given interviews, although, in 1994, Frances
Bianchi (now Piccione) broke her silence, telling me, "Ken was a blatant
liar. You'd catch him doing something, ask him why he did it, he'd tell
you, 'I didn't do it.' I'd catch him in lies, and he would deny everything.
And, in the end, you felt like you were the crazy one, and not him. He
is such a smooth liar. He tells such lies that you believe him. You really
believe what he says until you prove it for yourself."

So, Bianchi needed to be admired for something he was not. This
was his way of compensating for his shortcomings. He *had* to excel in
everything he undertook; after all, this was what his mother had drum-
med into him, expected of him and, like all grandiose people, woe
betide if something fails them. When that happens, a bout of severe
depression is imminent and, in Ken's case, the catastrophe was immediate and lethal.

The collapse of Bianchi's self esteem during this period of his life
proved just how precariously his self esteem had been hanging by a
thread, for nothing genuine that could ever have given him strength, or
support, had been allowed to develop inside his mind. As Dr. Alice
Miller says, "The grandiose person is never really free. First, because he
is so excessively dependent on admiration from others; and second,
because his self respect is dependent on qualities, functions and
achievements that can suddenly fail."

At the very time Bianchi's desperate attempts at becoming a police
officer were foundering like a ship in a hurricane, his marriage lay in
tatters, too. Then, out of the blue, a number of horrific child murders
shook his hometown of Rochester. These killings took place within a
mile radius of Ken's front door, and he soon found himself being interviewed as a suspect in the killings. The media dubbed the cases "The

Alphabet Murders" or "Double Initial Murders," because each victim's Christian name began with the same letter as the surname.

The first murder, that of ten-year-old Carmen Colon, was on Tuesday, November 16, 1971. Her body was found at Churchville, and this event took place within days of Bianchi learning of his third set of failed exam results, and of him being kicked out of the marital home. There was a gap of 17 months before the murderer struck again. The murder of 11-year-old Wanda Walkowitz coincided almost to the day of Bianchi being thrown out of Janice Tuschong's apartment in April, because she had caught him sleeping with one Donna Duranso.

Bianchi's affair with Donna collapsed in November 1973 and, a day later, the Monday after Thanksgiving break, 11-year-old Michelle Maenza went missing. Two days later, her body was found fully clothed along a lonely road in Macedon, Wayne County.

All three girls had been raped, then strangled to death. There were other links between the murders as well: all lived in rundown neighborhoods; all were walking alone when they were snatched from the streets; all were from broken homes, their fathers gone, the mothers on welfare; all had eaten a small meal just before they met their deaths; all had white cat hair attached to their clothing; and each girl was last seen alive in the company of a young, white male who was driving a white car. The description of the car and the man matched Bianchi perfectly.

All three children were streetwise. They had been warned by their mothers not to speak to strangers, therefore, investigators reasoned that whoever had abducted them might have been disguised as a police officer, or even a clergyman. Of course, there were other suspects, and one man committed suicide before the police arrived to interview him. Post-mortem blood tests, though, proved that this man—Miguel Colon, the uncle of Carmen whom FBI profiler Robert Hazelwood thought fitted the bill—could not have been the killer because the culprit was a nonsecretor, an individual of blood group A, B or AB who does not secrete the antigens characteristic of these blood groups in bodily fluids (such as saliva, semen, etc). Bianchi is a nonsecretor, a group making up just 20 percent of the U.S. population.

During his interview with Rochester homicide cops, Bianchi was as sympathetic as ever. A natural-born liar, well able to sell ice cream to Eskimos, he convinced the officers that he had watertight alibis for the three murders in question. However, he refused, as was his legal right in those days, to give body fluid samples, which would have confirmed that he was a nonsecretor. Then, amazingly, even more so as Mrs. Bianchi owned a white cat, and he drove a white car, suspicion fell away, and no one checked to confirm the veracity of Ken's alibis. The author has since carried out research on these three murders, and quickly learned after speaking to the providers of the alibis in question, including Janice Tuschong, that Ken's claims were not worth the paper they were written on. And this poses some intriguing questions. Why did Ken lie about his alibis, and why would he refuse to give body fluid samples?

When he was questioned by the author at the Washington State Penitentiary, Ken confirmed that his mother had owned a white cat during the time of the murders, that he did, indeed, own a white car, and he argued that it was not in his interests to give bodily fluids, but that he had been telling the truth about his alibis. Ken also says that he has been ruled out as a suspect in the Double Initial murders, when this is not the case. When I visited the Rochester Police, Captain Lynde Johnston claimed that Bianchi has always been in the picture.

Frances (Bianchi) Piccione told me in 1992, "It seemed that, whenever Ken had a fight with a girlfriend, or had a problem, he went out and killed someone. I even told the police the same thing."

Bianchi's early life shows that he is atypical of the serial murderer type in psychological make up. He was superficially attractive to women, although, when his partners looked deeper, they found that he was transparent, immature, unfaithful and a pathological liar. Such men might seem to have many female friends, but they are unable to form or sustain any meaningful, lasting relationships. Deep down, they have formed a growing dislike, even a rage towards women in general.

There is no doubt that Ken felt that the world was stacked against him. He sat for hours, asking himself why, if he were so clever, which in a bigoted way he thought he was, he had failed, when all around him were enjoying success. And, like so many of his breed, it is not what Kenneth says or does that is so important, but what he will *not* say, or patently avoids saying, which is vital when trying to find the reason why he turned into such an abhorrent killer. For instance, Bianchi has always claimed that he is a secretor, therefore he could never have been involved in other well-documented murders. Indeed, he went further by stating in countless letters that he can produce his medical notes to support this claim. However, when pressed to supply these documents, Bianchi avoided the subject by saying, "Actually, I am not sure if I am a secretor, or nonsecretor. I just don't know."

In a search for the facts about his claim, the author contacted the FBI, who released a document dated Wednesday, June 2, 1982. In it, Agent Robert Beams, a specialist in blood grouping and body fluids, confirmed that, after taking samples from Bianchi, he was able to say that Bianchi was a nonsecretor. More to the point, a recent discovery was made in Bianchi's cell. He has had a copy of that very same document, and it has been in his possession for decades.

No account of Kenneth Bianchi's life and crimes would be complete without mention of his adoptive cousin and accomplice, Angelo Buono, who lived in Los Angeles.

Ten miles north of L.A. is the sprawling suburb of Glendale where, in 1975, Kenneth Bianchi alighted from a bus at the Eagle Rock Plaza terminal minus his worldly possessions. His two suitcases had been lost during the gruelling trip from Rochester and he wouldn't retrieve them for several days. Meeting Ken at the terminal was his adoptive cousin,

Angelo Buono, known variously by his cronies as the "Italian Stallion" and the "Buzzard."

Buono's background offers some clues to his subsequent dysfunctional, violent and sadistic adult life: his mother and father had violent rows and split when he was very young; his mother found it almost impossible to make ends meet, and young Angelo was sucked into petty crime while still at school. His childhood idol was a rapist called Caryl Chessman, who lulled victims into trusting him by impersonating a cop.

Angelo spent some time in prison, had six kids by several mothers, all of whom ended up on the receiving end of his violent temper, and he bragged of abusing a 14-year-old girl "to break her in." Interestingly, his business, an auto upholstery workshop, lent him an air of respectability, as he was a skilled technician, numbering Frank Sinatra and other stars among his clients.

One of Ken's first priorities upon arriving in Los Angeles was to find a job to help him pay his way with Angelo, and he managed to land himself employment as a real estate customer services clerk with California Land Title (Cal Land). Ken had learned of the vacancy through Buono's female bank manager who put in a good word for him when he applied for the position. Then, at the firm's 1977 New Year's Eve party, he met Kelli Kae Boyd, who worked at the company's head office in Universal City.

A stunning brunette with large brown eyes, she fell for Bianchi's smooth approach, and they dated for a month before she decided to end the relationship because of Ken's immaturity and insecurity. "He was very possessive, and he always wanted to know where I was going, who I was doing it with, and I didn't really like that very well," she later told Detective McNeill of the Bellingham Police Department.

With enough cash now to find a place of his own, Ken left Buono's place and rented rooms at Tamarind Apartments, and no sooner had he slammed the door shut than he picked up the phone and started wooing Kelli again. As was his practice with previous girlfriends, he sent her bunches of flowers and, before long, he was treating her at the most expensive restaurants he could afford. They moved in under the same roof and, at the beginning of May 1977, she announced that she was pregnant with his child.

Life with Kenneth was always going to be a rough ride. The couple argued frequently, and more than once Kelli kicked him out. Each time, he returned to Angelo's place where he slept on the floor, or he would call his mother who mediated reconciliation. Throughout all this, Kelli still worked at Cal Land, although she was heavily pregnant.

Bianchi earned considerably less than Kelli and, although he had now been promoted to Assistant Title Officer, he decided to earn a little more cash on the side. He would become Dr. Bianchi with a doctorate in Psychology, and here, published for the first time, is his account of why he formed this bogus service.

People in California are big on widow dressing. Joining the Psychology Today book club, I took in books to decorate my shelves. I was introduced to Dr. Weingarten, and I asked him if I could rent part of his offices at night. I sounded literate, and he accepted me on the reference of a mutual friend. There was no extraordinary effort to fool the doctor, and if he'd asked me just some basic questions about psychology, he would have seen right through me. Placing ads in The Los Angeles Times, *I received credentials from other psychologists and students applying for a job with me. A diploma replacement service supplied more decorations for my walls and shelves. Also, I had several basic psychology books from back east. I knew I was doing wrong, but I took every precaution to not harm anyone.*

KENNETH BIANCHI ON HIS QUALIFICATIONS

So, now we find our "Dr. Bianchi" obtaining genuine diplomas by sleight of hand from students who applied for a position with him and, as soon as they dropped into his mailbox, he substituted his own name. To add further authenticity to the phony venture, he forged letters from various well-known institutions, who thanked Dr. Bianchi for his "generosity," and for the "small cash donations, and his valuable time in giving such enlightening lectures." Of course, all of this was a figment of his overactive and crooked imagination. He then told Kelli that he had earned his Psychology degree way back in Rochester, and that he was helping two colleagues, one of whom was the unwitting Dr. Weingarten, with their overload of patients. But then, like all of Bianchi's schemes, it fell apart.

During a visit to California to see her son, Frances could not fail to notice the many fraudulent diplomas which he had displayed in his apartment as well as his office. She was not impressed, and she berated Ken, threatening to expose him as a cheat. However, the warning went unheeded. Ken continued to pour money into advertising until his funds dried up. Patients failed to materialize, and he dumped the fabricated sideshow when Kelli heard the truth from his mother. And, yet again, Kelli Boyd threw Kenneth on to the streets. This time she had had enough.

But Ken had another ace up his sleeve. He told the gullible Kelli that he had lung cancer, and begged her to take him back. In a statement to the police, she later said, "Those days were very fretful for me. I took time off work to be with him. He had appointments at the hospital, and I drove him there to make sure he was OK. But he made me wait in the car. He had many bad ways, and very good ways. He was bad at paying the bills, and he was always skipping off work. On balance, I loved him, and I didn't want him to die without seeing our child. Yet, all the time, he was lying to me about the cancer. Then he got dismissed from work for having drugs in his desk drawer. That's when I kicked him out for good."

Poor old Ken was now falling apart like a cheap suit. The guy who was so bent he couldn't lie straight in bed had lost his job with Cal

Land, his bogus counselling service had flopped, Kelli was heavily pregnant, he had no home and the bills were mounting daily. So, apart from wrecking his own life, he was destroying Kelli's, and perhaps she made the wisest move of her life by moving in with her brother at 200 East Palmer, the day after Thanksgiving, 1977. Within a week, she moved again, this time to Adelaide Avenue. Shortly thereafter, she traveled north to Bellingham, Washington, where her parents put a secure roof over her head. Sadly, however, a dormant serial killer would follow in her tracks.

A week after Kelli left him, Ken, who was never one to allow grass to grow under his feet, bounced back when he was introduced to a drop dead gorgeous blonde at a party. Just turned 16, Sabra Hannan was an aspiring model with all the physical attributes to match her ambitions. For his part, Bianchi was loveless and penniless, and Angelo was sick and tired of handing out cash to his immature cousin, so, within minutes of meeting Sabra, the quick-thinking Ken came up with another scam which would raise money, and also please Angelo into the bargain.

After placing a drink in her hand, Ken slipped his arm around Sabra's waist and he gently eased her to another room where he explained that she was the most beautiful woman he had ever seen. He told her that he had friends in the movie business, and that she could easily earn $500 a week from the outset, and this figure would rise when she became better known.

That night, Sabra, now a little the worse for drink, was lured to the Buzzard's nest, and Buono's eyes lit up when he saw the slim-figured, busty teenager. As the hours drifted by, Sabra fell asleep, totally unaware of the scheming cousins who were whispering quietly in another room. This time, Ken had come up with a great idea. The two men would force Sabra into prostitution and, before the week was out, she was left under no illusion that they would kill her if she attempted to leave. By then, she was already their sex slave and soon-to-be hooker.

Fearful for her life, Sabra was now coerced into introducing her friend, 15-year-old Becky Spears, to the cousins. She, too, was forced into prostitution, and every night both men sodomized the girls to the degree that the young women had to wear tampons in their rectums to stop the bleeding. Then life for the girls took an unexpected turn for the better.

After a fortnight of this living hell, Becky was summoned to a wealthy lawyer's apartment for sex. On her arrival, she looked so down-hearted her client asked her how she had become involved in prostitution. With tears flooding down her face, she explained that Buono and Bianchi subjected her and Sabra to degrading sex acts and sadistic cruelty. She said that the two men had threatened to track them down and kill them if they ran away.

To his credit, the lawyer acted immediately. He drove Becky to the airport where he bought her a ticket to her home in Arizona and, just before she boarded the aircraft, he stuffed a large wad of notes into her pocket. Then, he kissed her on the cheek and said goodbye.

As might be expected, Angelo went ballistic when his youngest hooker failed to return home, so he made several threatening phone calls to the lawyer, stammering, "Give me her fuckin' address, or I'll fuckin' shoot you." Through his real estate contacts, Bianchi obtained the lawyer's address then placed an ad in a local paper, advertising the luxurious property and its entire contents for sale. However, these were the types of threats which the attorney could easily deal with, for among his clientele was the local chapter of the Hell's Angels, and he asked them to pay Mr. Buono a visit.

Fitting new mats into a customer's car, Angelo was still fuming with rage when he was tapped smartly on the shoulder. At first, he ignored the leather-clad bikers, which was not exactly the diplomatic thing to do. Then, as one biker produced a sawn off, pump action shotgun, the largest of the group, six-foot-four-inch, 350-pound "Tiny," reached through the car window and extracted the struggling Buono by his shirtfront. "Do we have your attention, Mr. Buono?" he asked.

Unfortunately, there is no record of the discussion that followed; unsurprisingly, the cousins didn't bother the lawyer again, and the remaining girl was allowed to go free.

This incident was certainly the crucial turning point which led the perverted Buono to become a serial murderer. Word of his humiliation flashed around the neighborhood like a bush fire. He lost face with his cronies, and the intensely macho crook was outraged that he had been shown to be a weakling in front of Bianchi. At Henry's, Buono's favorite eatery, regular customers and staff alike sniggered behind his back. It was rumored out loud that the Italian Stallion could no longer control his women.

When the author questioned Bianchi about his role in the stable of hookers, he denied that he ever touched the girls. He added that a man called J.J. was a partner with Buono and himself, and that he was only the driver and responsible for collecting the cash, of which he might receive a small percentage.

After his arrest many years later, Bianchi was interviewed by Sergeant Frank Salerno of the LAPD about the call girl service. The following transcript has never been published before.

Salerno: What was the financial arrangement for the call girl service? You guys obviously were going to get something out of what the girls made.

Bianchi: The girls would be working for J.J. completely, and the girls would have to pay Angelo... I can't remember the exact percentage because it varied.

Salerno: So, it was coming out of the girls' take?

Bianchi: Right, and it would go to Angelo.

Salerno: Strictly to Angelo.

Bianchi: Yeah, and then Angelo would, you know, give me

	what I...
Salerno:	What? What would he give you?
Bianchi:	It varied. It just depended on what the girls got. Sometimes if the girls got only, came home with only $20, there would be no take or very little take and I wouldn't get anything, you know, it would just be a pass situation. Sometimes the girls would come home with like $100 or $200.
Salerno:	What would you get out of that?
Bianchi:	I would probably end up with about $20 or $30 out of that.
Salerno:	Out of $100 or out of $200?
Bianchi:	Out of about $200.
Salerno:	What would the girls end up with?
Bianchi:	The remainder. Probably about $140.
Salerno:	And Angelo would get $20 or $30?
Bianchi:	Right, about the same.
Salerno:	So, in essence, you and Angelo were still partners in ... a call girl service or something along that line?
Bianchi:	Right.

* * *

With the slave girls gone, Buono's pimping income dried up, so the two men had to find more teenage girls. They tried to abduct one girl, then suddenly realized she was the daughter of a famous actor. Snatching her from the streets was far too risky. Eventually, they found a young woman and installed her in Susan's former bedroom. They also bought a "trick list" from a prostitute named Deborah Noble with names of men who frequented prostitutes. However, the truth was quite the opposite, because it was a list of men who wanted to visit one particular good time girl in her own apartment. To make matters worse, this prostitute already had a pimp, and she had no intention of going into business with the likes of Buono and Bianchi. The list was useless; the dirty duo had slipped up yet again and, to explain the effect this rip off had upon the two men, Bianchi wrote in a letter, "We went off in search of the vendor, madder then hell."

The police have always maintained that Bianchi and Buono never found the seller of this list, and that an acquaintance of the seller, Yolanda Washington, was the first victim in the Hillside Strangler series. However, Bianchi told me that this was not the case. Ken argues that Laura Collins had sold them the phony list, and that is why she was the first to die.

Also of some interest is the fact that when the Hillside Strangler task force was assembled in December 1977, Laura Collins's name was erased from the victims' list, and it was not until January 1978 that the then Assistant Chief of Police, Darryl Gates, publicly indicated that Laura was indeed a victim of the strangler.

Laura Collins, 26 years old, was last seen alive just after noon at Ventura Freeway and Lankershim Boulevard, on Sunday, September 4, 1977. Her partially clothed body was found near the Forest Lawn exit ramp off the Ventura Freeway, Burbank, at 10:30 a.m. on Friday, September 9th. She had been strangled, and this homicide became the blueprint for all of the subsequent killings.

At 1:34 p.m. on Monday, October 18, 1977, a naked body was found perversely sprawled on its stomach alongside Forest Lawn Drive, close to the famous cemetery of the same name, and just south of the Ventura Freeway. Lying in a crucifixion position, with the right hand crooked over, the legs apart, it appeared that she had been dragged from a vehicle by two men and dropped near a pile of broken concrete just a yard from her head. Behind the body was a yellow "No Trespassing or Loitering" sign.

Tall and leggy, the black woman was immediately identified by Vice officers as Yolanda Washington, a particularly attractive 19-year-old, who had almond-shaped eyes and medium length black hair. She was a part time bar waitress and hooker who was known to have prowled for business with Laura Collins.

Inquiries soon established that Yolanda had last been seen alive just before midnight the previous day as she solicited for business at Vista and Sunset Boulevards. The autopsy showed that she'd had sex with two men shortly before death—one of whom was a nonsecretor. With her killer kneeling over her, she had been strangled with a piece of cloth while she was lying down. There were marks around her wrists, and Yolanda had been anally raped, too. Bianchi confirmed this to me, saying that he had killed her in the back seat of his car and had removed a turquoise ring from her finger which he later gave to Kelli Boyd.

Just after midnight on Monday, October 31, 1977, a white female was abducted from the Hollywood area of Howard and Wilcox. Unattractive, with medium length reddish brown hair, 15-year-old Judith "Judy" Ann Miller lived in a ramshackle hotel, which was her base as a part time hooker. From trailer park stock, her mother was wanted in connection with a welfare fraud, and her father had jumped bail for a similar offence.

It was a pretty grim sight that Halloween morning at Alta Terrace and La Crescenta. The naked body lay close to the curb in a middle-class residential area, covered by a tarpaulin by a property owner to shield the corpse from the children in the neighborhood. The bruises on her neck showed that she had been strangled. She had ligature marks on both wrists and ankles as well. Insects feasted on her pale skin. On her eyelid was a small piece of light colored fluff that Sergeant Frank Salerno of the Los Angeles County Sheriff's Department saved for the forensic experts, and it did not appear that she had been murdered at this location. The coroner determined that she had been strangled to death around midnight, some six hours before she was found. It was also clear that she had been raped and sodomized.

Bianchi says that Judy had been taken back to Buono's house where she had been raped. Bianchi sodomized her, then strangled her. He finished her off by suffocating his victim with a plastic supermarket bag. "She involuntarily urinated after death, just as Washington had done," Bianchi claimed, with an evil grin playing across his mouth. "We made her go into the washroom before we killed her to stop it happening, but it didn't work. She was tied by the arms, legs and neck to our special chair in Angelo's bedroom. She didn't like dying one bit."

A white waitress at the Healthfair Restaurant near Hollywood and Vine, and part time prostitute, 21-year-old Teresa "Terri" (a.k.a. "Lissa") Kastin became the stranglers' fourth victim. Moderately attractive, with a Roman nose and bushy dark hair, Terri was stopped by Bianchi and Buono, who were posing as police officers, at 9:15 p.m. on Saturday, November 5, 1977. They ordered her into their black over white sedan and, like Miller, she was taken back to Buono's home for what Bianchi called "questioning." There, she was tied down into the special chair, and her striped sweater and short skirt were cut off with scissors. The two men were repelled because she had hairy legs, and Bianchi was reduced to raping her with a root beer bottle as he throttled her. When she kicked out in her death throes, Buono sat on her legs, shouting, "Die, you cunt, die." Terri was allowed to suck in lungfuls of air many times before she lost consciousness for the last time.

At 1:15 a.m. the next day, Terri's body was found at Chevy Chase and Linda Vista. Identification was made swiftly after a news broadcast reported the murder and Terri's father telephoned the police reporting his daughter as missing. At autopsy, no semen was present in the vagina or anus, which supported Bianchi's confession that neither of the two men had physically raped this victim.

Jill Barcombe was an 18-year-old white hooker who had moved to

Hollywood following a string of prostitution convictions in New York. She was last seen alive at Pico and Ocean Boulevards at around 7:00 p.m. on Wednesday, November 9, 1977. She was found naked and strangled at 5:50 a.m. the following morning at Franklin Canyon Drive and Mulholland. Jill had put up a fierce fight for her life; as severe head trauma was present.

A 28-year-old aspiring actress and part time model with a real "wow" factor, Jane King was rated by the "Hollywood set" as a stunning blonde bombshell who had literally exploded on the scene when she was just 16. Over the years, Jane had raised the eyebrows of every hot blooded male and film producer who saw her. She was also a Scientology student and a follower of L. Ron Hubbard's work on dianetics, the eradication of negative thought and energy to lead a more fulfilled life. Police claimed that she was a part time hooker, although this was incorrect.

Jane was last seen alive outside 9500 Lemona, at 10:10 p.m. on Wednesday, November 9, 1977. Posing as police officers, Buono and Bianchi cruised up, "arrested" her on suspicion of prostitution and took her back to Angelo's home where she was dragged screaming through the living/dining area into the east bedroom where she was stripped naked. Bianchi confessed that they "were delighted to find her pubis was shaven." However, because she struggled while she was being raped, the two men decided to teach her a lesson. A plastic bag was placed over her head while Bianchi sodomized her. Jane pleaded desperately for her life during a four hour period of terror before she was allowed to suffocate to death as Bianchi climaxed.

Jane's naked body was found on a bed of dead leaves in undergrowth at the Los Feliz exit ramp of the Golden State Freeway on Wednesday, November 23rd. She lay on her back, legs open, with the right knee drawn up.

The murders of Sonja Johnson and Dolores "Dolly" Cepeda, and the violence and brutality they suffered, shocked everyone involved in the case. Aged 14 and 12, they were two innocent little girls who happened to be in the wrong place at the wrong time. Judge Roger Boren, former prosecutor at Bianchi and Buono's trial in L.A., told me, "Angelo Buono and Kenneth Bianchi followed the girls on a bus as they traveled from a shopping mall, and apparently used some police ruse that they were being arrested. They took these two young girls to Angelo Buono's house and did with them what they did with the other victims— tortured them and strangled them to death.

"They took the girls to a hillside overlooking one of the largest freeways in Los Angeles and discarded their bodies. That particular hillside was used by many people to discard trash. There were couches, mattresses… things of that sort had been thrown down that hillside. And these two bodies had been discarded in a like manner. In fact, they were not discovered for two weeks."

The 14-year-old Sonja and 12-year-old Dolly were both pupils at the Saint Ignatius school. They were last seen alive on Sunday, November 13, 1977, boarding a bus at the Eagle Plaza stop, which was just a quarter of a mile from Angelo's home. They followed the vehicle and, when the girls disembarked near their home, again, posing as a police officer, Bianchi approached the girls and accused them of shoplifting. They were taken "downtown" and interviewed in Angelo's house. Sonja was raped and murdered in a bedroom by Buono, while Dolly sat outside with Bianchi.

"Where's my friend?" asked the girl when Buono came out alone.

"Oh, don't worry," said Bianchi, "you'll be seeing her in a minute."

The last thing Dolly saw was the dead face of Sonja on the bed beside her as Bianchi raped and sodomized her. Children playing on a dumpster at Landa and Stadium Way found the girls' naked bodies at 4:00 p.m. on Sunday, November 20th.

The crime scene photographs showed Dolly and Sonja sprawled out among the discarded beer bottles and tin cans. Sonja rested almost on her right side, her left hand tucked up under her breasts, the hand nudging her chin. The right arm, hand gripped tight in a death spasm, was outstretched and underneath her right side. The legs were almost straight, the left foot draped over the neck of Dolly who was on her stomach; her torso slightly crooked and leaning to the right of her legs, which were parted. Dolly's left arm was also tucked underneath her body, her hand covering her mouth as if to stifle a scream. The right arm, bent at the elbow, was outstretched. There were a set of human bite marks on her left buttock.

When one sees such terrible things, only then can one understand the true, evil nature of Kenneth Bianchi and Angelo Buono.

* * *

"The public were just outraged that we, as law enforcement officers, could not do anything to stop these brutal murders. Especially the single women in this city who went to work at nights, going to the markets, going to see their families. They were petrified."

DETECTIVE RICHARD CROTSLEY, LAPD, TO THE

AUTHOR AT INTERVIEW

Like Jane King, 17-year-old Kathleen "Kathy" Robinson was another attractive blonde who was well known around the hotspots of Hollywood. Her flowing blonde hair caught the attention of the Hillside Stranglers at 9:30 p.m. on Wednesday, November 16, 1977. She was walking towards her car which was parked near Pico and Ocean Boulevard, when Buono and Bianchi drew up alongside her. Flashing a phony police badge, they ordered her into their car. She was found fully clothed, strangled, with her throat cut, at Burnside and Curson, at 8:30 a.m. the next day.

A quiet young woman, 20-year-old Kristina Weckler was an honors student at the Pasadena Art Center of Design. She lived at Tamarind Apartments, 800 Garfield, Glendale. This was the same apartment block where Bianchi had once resided, and he knew the young woman and had pestered her for a date. Kristina, who knew that Ken was living with the pregnant Kelli Boyd, rejected his advances.

Kristina's naked body was found at Ranon's Way and Nawona on Sunday, November 20th. Detective Sergeant Bob Grogan immediately noticed the ligature marks on her wrists, ankles and neck. When he turned her over, blood oozed from her rectum. The bruises on her breasts were obvious. Oddly enough, there were two puncture marks on her arm, but no signs of the needle tracks that indicate a drug addict.

Bianchi told me that, at around 6:00 p.m. on Saturday, November 19th, he knocked on Kristina's door, telling her that he was now a police officer, and that someone had crashed into her car parked outside. Once in the lot, she was bundled into his car and driven to Buono's home where they tried to kill her using a new method. They had intended to inject Kristina with caustic cleaning fluid; however, when this barbaric method of murder failed, they covered her head with a plastic bag and piped coal gas into her lungs. Bianchi raped Kristina, ejaculating into her during the moment she convulsed in death. She died as the result of strangulation by ligature.

The truth, however, was slightly different. Bianchi told police that he had knocked on Kristina's door and had asked her if she wanted to go to a party. At first, Kristina said that she was tired. But Bianchi was insistent and she soon took up the offer, slipping on a pair of brown loafers, a beige, long sleeved blouse and a skirt, and followed Bianchi to his car, in which Buono was sitting.

They arrived at the murder house at about 12:30 a.m. It was obviously deserted and the men said that the other guests would soon arrive. Within minutes, they were killing her. Using the method described above, the terrified and totally compliant Kristina took over an hour to die. Describing how Buono injected the poor girl, Bianchi told police:

> He [Buono] suggested that… he said, 'How about just injecting air into her? The air bubble would probably kill her.' I said, 'Oh, you want to try something different. Whatever.'
>
> We both walked back into the dining room, put the chair back at the dining room table. He grabbed her underwear and her socks and he went back into the room and set the needle down on the bed… at one end of the bed and he said, 'Come on, now, we're going to stand up,' and we both helped her up. He said, 'Sit down here,' and he sat on the edge of the bed and he helped her get her clothes on, her underwear and socks, he said, 'OK, now, come on. Stand up.' And he helped her stand up and we walked her to the open part of the room at the bottom of the bed and set her down on the floor, face up. He took the needle, took the cap off of it, he pulled back the plunger and he told me, he said, 'Hold her legs.' I held her legs, he crouched down. He's on her left side. He stuck the needle in her neck [left side] and pushed the plunger in and pulled it out.
>
> He did it a couple of times. She flinched and made a murmuring sound and he stood up and he said, 'Let go of her legs,' and he walked towards me and pushed me lightly back towards the doorway and he says, 'Just stand here and see what happens.' So I stood there for about five to ten minutes. Nothing happened. He says, 'What I should do is put something in the needle. Stay here. I'll be right back.' He went into the kitchen area. When he came back there was a blue solution, some kind of blue solution, in the needle.
>
> He injected her and said, 'Help me to get her up.' We helped her to her feet and she was still shaking. Walked her into the kitchen and walked her into the front where his stove was being put in, or the connection was, and lied her down on the floor. He stood up and

started to walk away from her and he indicated to me to walk away with him, he had to talk to me. We walked into the dining room, and in the dining room he said, 'What I'll do is put a bag over her head,' he says, 'I'll use the twine; I'll cut off a piece of twine, so we can make a seal on the bag,' he says, 'and the pipe, the bendable pipe is long enough,' he says, 'stick that under the bag and when I tell you, turn the gas on and when I tell you, turn the gas off.'

After we'd had a little discussion in the dining room, we walked back into the kitchen. Kristina Weckler's lying on the floor in this direction, in front the fixture. Angelo is standing here to her left side. She's still shaking really bad, probably from that blue stuff that was injected into her. He put the bag over her head and there was no unusual movement when he did that. He told me to get the pipe and stick the pipe under the bag, which I did. He then wrapped the twine a couple of times around her neck and pulled it tight and said, 'OK, go ahead. Turn it on.' I turned on the gas, the bag inflated. He said, 'Turn off the gas.' I turned off the gas, and he waited until it deflated. Turned it on again. We repeated this probably about four or five times.

Finally, it was obvious that she had stopped breathing, so he said to take the tubing out, which I did… put the tubing back and made sure the valve was turned off all the way. He took the rope off of her and the bag off her head. He took out his keys and rolled her over and I held her shoulders while he rolled her over and unlocked the handcuffs. I took off the tape and gag from her mouth and took the blindfold off and he removed her pants and underwear. We both walked into the dining room and put everything into a paper bag. He then got the roll of tape and taped up the bag. I walked to the back door. He walked to the dumpster. Moved a few things around and tossed the bag in there. Put things on top of the bag. He came back in, asked me for the keys to my car. He said, 'I'll open up the trunk.' When he *got through opening up the trunk, he walked to the street, looked around and came back again… then we dumped her off.*

KENNETH BIANCHI AT POLICE INTERVIEW

* * *

A promising lead in the hunt for the killers came on Monday, November 28, 1977, the day after a student and trainee secretary disappeared from 9500 Lemona, Sepulveda, in the San Fernando Valley. The father of 18-year-old Lauren Rae Wagner found her car parked, with the driver's door open and the interior light on, near his house and directly in front of the home of an elderly woman called Beulah Stofer. Mrs. Stofer told police how she had seen the young redhead abducted by two men. They were driving a black over white sedan, and first she thought that it had been a police car.

At 7:30 a.m. the following day, a driver on his way to work found a naked body at 1200 Cliff Drive in the Mount Washington area. Lauren was lying on her back, her left arm outstretched, her left lower leg just touching the road. Her mass of rich, red hair framed her pretty face, and her eyes were peacefully closed. Strangely, it looked as though she had burns on her palms. Like the unusual puncture marks on Kristina Weckler's arms, it looked as though the killers were experimenting, possibly with methods of torture. There was also something else that was different, a shiny track of some sticky liquid, which had attracted a convoy of ants. If this substance was semen or saliva, there was the possibility that the killer's blood type could be determined. Tests on semen found on the earlier victims had revealed nothing.

Bianchi told the author that, back at Buono's house, Lauren pretended to enjoy being raped in the desperate hope that her attackers would allow her to live. However, they tried to electrocute the woman by attaching live electrical wires to the palms of her hands, but this only caused extreme pain and superficial burns. Bianchi then raped her, and Buono strangled Lauren to death with a ligature.

The two killers now realized that they had been seen by Mrs. Stofer, so they obtained her telephone number, and called her from a pay phone in the Hollywood Library in North Ivar Street, where they subjected her to death threats. Undeterred, though, she was able to furnish police with an excellent description which matched Bianchi and Buono in every respect.

On Monday, December 14, 1977, police were called to a vacant lot on a steep slope at 2006 North Alvarado Street, where they arrived at 7:03 a.m. The sun had just come up, and it was a clear day with very few clouds in the sky. Rampart Divisional Patrol Unit 2-A-47, consisting of officers Lewis and Akeson, had responded to a radio call alerting them to a dead body lying by the road, which ran through the floor of the canyon splitting Lakeshore Drive and Alvarado.

When homicide detectives Oakes and Richard Crotsley arrived, they noticed that the tall, blonde victim was lying on her back in the now usual spread eagle position, and that post mortem lividity had started to form in her toes. The young woman was Caucasian, and in her twenties. There were ligature marks around both wrists, ankles and her neck. On her left forearm she had a tattoo, a square "cross" with four dots within its border. On the right ankle was a second tattoo of faint design bearing the name "Kim." With no other identification to be found, she was labelled as "Jane Doe #112," and the stranglers' penultimate victim was on her way to the morgue.

Using documents furnished by the LAPD, and confirming this with Bianchi himself, it is now possible to plot the victim's last hours in some detail. She turned out to be Kimberley "Kim" (a.k.a. "Donna') Diane Martin and, for the first time, using this previously unpublished material, we can see the cunning of the Hillside Stranglers as they entrapped their victim.

At precisely 8:30 p.m., on Tuesday, December 13, 1977, the phone of Climax Nude Modelling, 1815 Serrano Avenue, rang, and Michelle Elaine Rodriguez answered it. The call came from a man who gave the name "Mike Ryan" (Kenneth Bianchi), and below is the transcript of that recorded conversation.

Rodriguez: Hello, modelling service.

Bianchi: Hello, yes. Can you get me a girl?

Rodriguez: That depends where you are located, sir.

Bianchi: I'm in Hollywood.

Rodriguez: That will be no problem. I can have a girl with you in about 15 minutes.

Bianchi: How much does it cost?

Rodriguez: $40 for a modelling service.

Bianchi: OK. My wife has left town for the first time in two years, so I would like you to send me a pretty blonde model if you could. Possibly wearing black stockings and a dress.

Rodriguez: That will be no problem, sir. May I have your name?

Bianchi: Michael Ryan.

Rodriguez: And could you spell your last name, please?

Bianchi: R-Y-A-N.

Rodriguez: May I have your phone number?

Bianchi: 462-9794.

Rodriguez: Sir, that is a payphone. (Once again, Bianchi was using the phone in the Hollywood Library in North Ivar Street.)

Bianchi: Ha, ha, ha. You know it's funny. A lot of people seem to think that this is a payphone. It must be a digit in the number or something.

Rodriguez:	That must be what it is. The reason I thought it was a payphone is that the fourth digit of the number is a "9," it's a payphone.
Bianchi:	That must be it, or the fact that you hear my TV in the background. Would you like me to turn it off? (The "television noise" was the customers' conversations who were using the library.)
Rodriguez:	Oh, no. I'll verify it.
Bianchi:	All right.
Rodriguez:	And what is your address, sir?
Bianchi:	1950 Tamarind.
Rodriguez:	Sir, could you spell that for me?
Bianchi:	T-A-M-A-R-I-N-D.
Rodriguez:	Is this a house, or an apartment?
Bianchi:	This is an apartment. Number 114.
Rodriguez:	Sir. How are you going to pay?
Bianchi:	Cash.
Rodriguez:	May I ask where you found our advertisement?
Bianchi:	The Freep. (A local free paper.)
Rodriguez:	OK, sir. I'll have a girl out to you shortly.

This was end of the first conversation, and Michelle then called the operator to verify the number. She always followed this practice to ensure she didn't send a girl out to a prank call. First, she asked the operator if the number was a payphone. If it was, under normal circumstances, the operator would confirm it; however, if it was a private number, the operator would advise the caller that she could not give out that information. But, on this rare occasion, Bianchi had luck on his side. On this occasion, the operator spoke to her supervisor, and she came back to Michelle, saying, "No. My supervisor won't allow me to give out that information." Of course, Michelle understood this to mean that her client had booked one of the girls from a private address—which it wasn't—and therefore the call was good. She called "Mr. Ryan" back, and he picked up the handset immediately "as if he was waiting for the call," Michelle later told the police. Unwittingly, Michelle had now sealed the fate of Kimberley Martin.

Bianchi:	Hello.
Rodriguez:	Hello. Michael?
Bianchi:	Yes.
Rodriguez:	This is just the modelling agency calling to verify your call.
Bianchi:	OK. Thank you. How much longer will it take before the girl will call me?
Rodriguez:	Very shortly.
Bianchi:	OK. Thank you. Goodbye.

Michelle then called Kimberley Martin who worked under the name of "Donna."

Rodriguez:	I have a call. It's a cash call out in Hollywood in an apartment. Do you want it?
Kimberley:	Yeah. Give me the information.
Rodriguez:	Michael Ryan. Phone number 462-9794. 1950 Tamarind, Hollywood. Cash. Apartment 114. Sounds like a good call to me. It's an apartment. It's near your location, but always be careful and make sure he's not a cop.
Kimberley:	Sounds good to me. I'll give him a call.
Rodriguez:	Call me and let me know whether you'll go on it?
Kimberley:	OK. Goodbye.

Kimberley Martin called her prospective client, then she rang the agency back.

> Kimberley: Sounds good to me. I'm going right on it.
> Rodriguez: Call me when you get there. Goodbye.

The distance from the library on Ivar Street to 1950 North Tamarind Avenue is nearly a mile, taking an average of five minutes to drive. Bianchi was seen sitting on the library steps by a witness at around 9:00 p.m., then he suddenly stood up and walked off. Buono was picking him up.

At around 9:05 p.m., Kimberley left her apartment, and it took Kim 15 minutes to drive the 3.8 miles to Tamarind, where she parked up and walked into the lobby, where several people saw her at 9:25 p.m.. Shortly thereafter, residents heard a woman screaming, "Please don't kill me," but all of them thought that this was a domestic dispute. Minutes later, though, they found the contents of a woman's handbag strewn along a hallway.

Bianchi claims that he and Buono dragged the woman out through a rear entrance and into the underground garage where they had left their car. They drove her to Buono's home, where she was tortured, raped and killed. "We killed her because she was fuckin' useless in bed," he explained to me.

* * *

Even though 84 officers were assigned to the Hillside Strangler investigation, the general public now thought that the police were helpless, and they were about right. With some 10,000 leads to follow up, thousands of fingerprints to be processed and a reward of $140,000 posted for information that would lead to the Hillside Strangler's arrest, the task force were no nearer catching the killers than they were on day one.

After press headlines suggested that the killers were posing as police officers, the public trusted no one, and it was even suggested that two renegade policemen might be running amok on some kind of sick vendetta. It had got to the point where nobody could be certain of the true identity of a man wearing a uniform, or waving a silver badge, and citizens were simply not stopping when requested by any cop, uniformed or not. So the police implemented a new policy which allowed motorists to drive to a police station with a flashing patrol car following them, and this prompt action partially put people's minds at rest.

Nothing happened on the murders during the month of January, possibly because Angelo Buono's mother was in the hospital with a terminal illness. But in February of 1978, the last of the Hillside Stranglings murders in Los Angeles occurred when Cindy Hudspeth's body was found up in the mountains above Glendale on the Angeles Crest Highway.

JUDGE ROGER BOREN, FORMER PROSECUTOR AT BIANCHI AND
BUONO'S TRIAL IN LA, TO THE AUTHOR AT INTERVIEW

On Friday, February 17, 1978, the crew of an Angeles National Forest helicopter spotted an orange Datsun, which was parked precariously close to a ravine by the Angeles Crest Highway. Upon opening the trunk, police found the body of 20-year-old Cindy Lee Hudspeth, a brunette who worked as a receptionist. She was also employed as a part time waitress at the Robin Hood Inn, a restaurant frequented by Angelo Buono.

In his statement to police, Bianchi claimed that he had arrived at Buono's auto upholstery shop where he found Cindy's car parked outside. "She had called to inquire if Angelo could make new mats for her," he said. The two men spread eagled Cindy on a bed, hog-tied her, then raped and strangled her for almost two hours. Then, with the dead body in the trunk, Bianchi drove her car, closely followed by Buono in another vehicle, to the ravine where they tried to push the Datsun over the edge. It rolled 50 feet then stopped, but by then the killers had fled. Cindy's naked body was found about 30 feet down the incline. Her arms were by her side, her legs apart.

The murder of Cindy proved to be the last of the Hillside Stranglings, for after a heated argument with Bianchi, during which Buono pointed a loaded revolver at Ken's head and told him to "F-f-f-ff-fuck off," Bianchi packed his bags and left Los Angeles. Buono went back to refurbishing cars and did not kill again, while Ken scooted north to Bellingham, leaving 13 dead bodies, countless broken lives and a mountain of debt behind in his wake. His new hunting ground awaited him.

* * *

"Well... Mr. Bianchi? He was ... a wannabe cop. He wanted to be a police officer. He tried in his hometown of Rochester to be a reserve. He moved to California, got involved down there, wanted to be a deputy police officer in Los Angeles. He actually got into their ride along program. Because of his ability to con, he talked a security agency into thinking he was really hot stuff, so they made him a captain in their organization. He became friends with several Bellingham police officers, and he took the test, the examination for the Bellingham Police Department."

CRIME SCENE OFFICER ROBERT KNUDSEN, BELLINGHAM PD,
TO THE AUTHOR AT INTERVIEW

The small, seaport city of Bellingham had a population of about 60,000, and it lies 20 miles due south of the Canadian border, on the northwest seaboard of Washington State. Bellingham is the gateway to the Mount Baker recreational area, which looks over one of the most magnificent vistas in the area—the pine-clad slopes of San Juan, the Vancouver Islands and the Strait of Juan de Fuca.

When I visited Bellingham in 1996, the place was wrapped in an icy coat, a typical winter in those parts, and my thoughts traveled back in time to January 1979, when the weather was similar, but laced with the cold chill of murder. Violent crime in this neck of the woods was such a rarity in those days that, when Chief of Police Terry Mangan was informed one Friday morning that two young women had been reported as "missing under suspicious circumstances," his first thought was that they had left town for an early vacation without telling anyone.

Co-eds 22-year-old Karen Mandic and her roommate 27-year-old Diane Wilder both studied at the Western Washington University, and several friends were concerned about their welfare.

Chief Mangan was a former Roman Catholic priest whose close friend, Sister Carmel Marie, once ran the Saint Ignatius School in Los Angeles. She had introduced Terry Mangan to the bookkeeper of her diocese, one Tony Johnson. In November 1977, when the Hillside Stranglings were at their peak, Mangan had read in a paper that Johnson's 14-year-old daughter, Sonja, had become one of the victims. Now, however, in January 1979, and following an amazing string of tragic circumstances and coincidences, Mangan would secure the arrest of one of the Los Angeles killers, 1,050 miles north of Tinseltown, and in his own backyard.

Karen Mandic was a beautiful student with long, blonde hair. She had last been seen alive at 7:00 p.m. on Thursday, January 11th, when leaving the Fred Myer department store on Interstate 5, where she worked as a part time cashier. Earlier in the week, she had told two friends, Steve Hardwick and Bill Bryant, that a man who had recently asked her for a date had offered her a house sitting job for that Thursday evening, and it paid $100 an hour. In fact, he had asked her out several times, and his name was Kenneth Bianchi.

Ken, who by now was back living with Kelli and his son Ryan, had previously worked at Fred Myer as a security guard, and he was now employed as a security officer with the Whatcom Security Agency (WSA), a local company that provided mobile and static security patrols throughout a 50-mile radius of Bellingham. Ken had pledged Karen to secrecy; nevertheless, she was thrilled with the opportunity to earn some extra cash.

Upon learning of the offer to Karen, Steve Hardwick was suspicious from the outset. Karen, however, would have none of it, insisting that everything was OK. She explained that the house, owned by a Dr. Catlow, was in an upper class area, that the doctor was going on vacation with his family, that the alarm was not working, and that she had asked a friend called Diane Wilder along for company. It was easy money, she told Hardwick. All they had to do was wait until the burglar alarm repair people turned up later in the evening, and then she could return to Fred Myer and cash up. Besides, Bianchi worked for WSA; it was a highly regarded firm, and even Hardwick knew that.

Hardwick, who could smell a latrine rat from miles away, was still highly suspicious, so he pressed Karen further. "Don't worry," she snapped back, "it's only for two hours, and I'll be back to finish up at the store by 9:00 p.m. Everything will be OK. I'm taking Diane with me. Besides, Ken has given my name to the insurance company who are paying the bill. I can't change anything now."

When Karen failed to return to Fred Myer later in the evening, the manager telephoned Hardwick, who immediately drove to Dr. Catlow's house at 334 Bayside, where the split-level property appeared deserted. Although he could not recall Bianchi's name, Hardwick did remember WSA, so he telephoned the night dispatcher, Wendy Whitton, and requested any information on the Bayside account. Wendy, who was not authorized to reveal details of her employer's business, promised the anxious Hardwick that she would call the firm's co-owner, Randy Moa, and, as soon as she did, alarm bells started to ring.

Moa and his partner, Joe Parker, had just completed a somewhat belated security check on Bianchi's résumé and, in doing so, they had spoken to one Susan Bird, an attractive woman who lived locally. Susan had been shocked to hear that Bianchi had obtained work in the security business because he had recently suggested to her that, because of her stunning figure, she would make a good prostitute, and he could become her pimp. Susan was even more concerned because she knew that Ken had applied to the Bellingham Police Department for a job as a cop.

At first, Moa and Parker didn't believe Susan Bird, so she put them in touch with a girlfriend called Annie Kinneberg. Annie and her pal, Margie Lager, confirmed what Susan Bird had said, relating that Bianchi had also wanted to photograph lesbian models for clients that he said he had back in L.A. "He's a kinky bastard," Annie explained. "He's living with a woman called Kelli, and they have a little boy. That guy is real weird, you know."

Upon receiving the call from Wendy Whitton, Moa sprang into action. First, he radioed Steve Adams, and ordered the night patrol officer to check out the Bayside address himself. Unfortunately, Steve went to the wrong address, 302 Bayside, where he woke up the bleary-eyed owners who knew nothing at all. Then, having realized his mistake, he called the office, and waited in his truck until the police turned up.

In another effort to solve the problem, Moa telephoned Bianchi at home. Ken denied all knowledge of the house sitting job. He also denied knowing anyone called Diane Wilder or Karen Mandic, adding to his protestations of innocence by claiming that he had been to a Sheriff's Reserve first aid meeting that evening.

Moa was now not only confused but also becoming increasingly alarmed, so, in an effort to clear up matters, he summoned Bianchi to the firm's office. Then Moa contacted the instructor of the Sheriff's Reserve to confirm what Bianchi had told him, and learned that Ken had been lying. Ken had failed to turn up for the class, so Moa then called the Bellingham Police Department.

Upon their arrival at WSA, the cops asked Ken if he knew the two young women. Initially, Ken flatly denied the suggestion, then realizing that he was painting himself into a corner, he backtracked, saying, "Maybe Karen." A gut feeling told the officers that Bianchi was lying because he wouldn't look them straight in the eye. He appeared shifty and nervous, too. However, with little evidence to take him into custody, Bianchi was allowed to return home.

At 6:00 a.m., Bill Bryant, who was a university campus cop, obtained a key to Karen's apartment. By the telephone, written in red ink, was a message in Diane's handwriting. It read, "Karen. Ken B. called. Phone 733-2884." Picking up the scrap of paper, Bill decided to call the number. It turned out to be WSA, and, lo and behold, it was Bianchi who answered the phone. "I know your voice," said Bryant. "You called Karen's apartment on Tuesday, and I told you that she wasn't in." Once again, Ken denied knowing Karen Mandic, adding that anyone could be using his name.

Bryant then called his father, who was also a police officer, and he, in turn, called the Bellingham Police Department who re-interviewed Bianchi later in the morning. Officers Geddes and Page confronted him with the note, and Ken reacted angrily. "I'd sure like to know who has been using my name," he snapped. "I'm well known. I was in the newspaper when I left Fred Myer to come here in charge of operations."

Nevertheless, even though Bianchi was now the chief suspect for the girls' abduction, the officers could do little more than allow him to carry on with his work, despite the evidence mounting against him.

* * *

"They were told to lay face down and then they were separated, tied up and, individually, one by one, untied, undressed and I had sex with them. Then they were both dressed again. Then I killed them separately. I believe, ah, Diana Wilder was first and Karen Mandic second. Then they were carried out and put in the back of the car and driven to the cul-de-sac."

KENNETH BIANCHI CONFESSING TO THE AUTHOR

AT INTERVIEW

At 4:40 p.m. the same day, Karen's green Mercury Bobcat was found. Just a mile from the Bayside address, in a cul-de-sac in Willow Drive, the vehicle contained the fully clothed bodies of Karen Mandic and Diane Wilder. At autopsy, it was determined that both young women had been raped and strangled with a ligature. Officer Knudsen recalled that, "The car was locked; however, the passenger door was only on the first catch and so I had no trouble getting into the vehicle that way. I opened both doors, and took a closer look, and the bodies of two young ladies had been tossed in like two sacks of potatoes, one thrown on top of the other."

With this grim discovery, an order went out for Bianchi's immediate arrest, but first they needed the help of Randy Moa. Knowing that he might be armed, and considered dangerous, Moa radioed Ken in his truck, instructing his unwitting employee to check out a disused guard shack at the south terminal, a remote area of the docks, and, moments after he arrived, Detective Terry Wight, who was brandishing a pistol, arrested him.

With Bianchi now in custody, the investigation moved up a gear and, while police broke the tragic news to Karen's father, Detectives Nolte and McNeill, and Field Investigator Moore, conducted a thorough search of Bianchi's home, where in the bedroom they picked up a pair of blue uniform trousers. The crotch had been ripped and Kelli confirmed that these were the trousers that her common-law husband had been wearing the previous evening. She also pointed to a red, plaid shirt, and there was an identical one lying underneath it. Kelli said that Ken had been wearing one of those shirts the night before, and fibers, identical in every respect to those of these shirts, were later found in Dr. Catlow's home. The officers also took possession of a pair of cowboy boots, and they soon matched the sole tread pattern with imprints found both at Willow Drive and Bayside.

Hanging in the bedroom closet was a .357 caliber, a highway patrolman's revolver, complete with a standard Sam Browne belt and holster. Again, in the same closet, Nolte discovered a shoulder holster and several cameras. The firearm was licensed and in extremely good condition. The cameras and photographic equipment were of professional quality, and this added veracity to the claims of Susan Bird, Annie Kinneberg and Margie Lager that Bianchi wanted to photograph them.

The officers now turned their attention to Kelli's dressing table, where they found a quantity of jewelry and seven watches. Kelli explained that Ken had given her most of these items as presents—in fact, these had been taken from former Hillside Strangler victims. They were his trophies from the crimes.

Bianchi's home was now searched from top to bottom. In the basement, officers found several thousand dollars' worth of brand new tools, all in their original boxes without price tags or sales receipts. It was soon discovered that this treasure trove had been stolen from Fred Myer when Ken had worked there as a security guard.

However, the stash of stolen goods didn't end with the tools, for on one shelf there was a large quantity of medical supplies, enough to supply a doctor's office. Ken had stolen it all from the Verdugo Hills Hospital in Los Angeles. And, when Detective Moore made the mistake of prying open a cupboard, he was literally buried under scores of tins of crabmeat that tumbled out. Ken had taken the horde from a cold storage company where Whatcom Security had assigned him as a guard. Finally, a box full of brand new jackets and touch-tone telephones was opened. These had been stolen from the Uniflite Corporation, whose offices were at the dock's south terminal.

But this merely proved that Bianchi was a thief, not a murderer, and at this stage there wasn't the merest hint that he had been involved in the Hillside Stranglings.

Both of Bianchi's vehicles had now been impounded at Bellingham Police Station, where Detective Knudsen waited for Kelli Boyd to arrive before he could search them. At 2:00 a.m. on Saturday, January 13th, though, he started looking for clues on Karen's Bobcat. Crawling underneath the car, Knudsen noted that the gasoline tank had a fresh dent on the driver's side. It appeared from the angle of the damage that this was a back-up dent and, later that day, the investigator found paint on a dislodged rock in the driveway of 334 Bayside. This evidence was solid proof that, at some time, the Bobcat had been on Dr. Catlow's property.

When Kelli eventually arrived at the car impound, Knudsen went through Ken's beat up VW with a fine toothed comb and, in the front passenger foot rest, a brown leather attaché case was discovered. Tipping the contents of the case on to a table, officers found that every document tied a "Dr. Bianchi" to a psychiatric counselling service in Los Angeles. Taken together, these were unusual items to say the least, so Nolte and Knudsen took stock. It seemed that they might have captured a double murderer, sex pervert, thief, security guard-come-pseudo cop and psychiatrist all in one hit.

Nolte was cautious and he decided to make further inquiries. He called the LAPD. "We've got a real fruit under arrest here in Bellingham," he explained. "We got him in on suspicion of two homicides, an' rape. Do you know the name 'Kenneth Alessio Bianchi'?" Within the hour, the LAPD called back. "Sure," said the breathless voice, "we got a Bianchi, K.A., on our list. He applied to join the force; he even had a ride-along in a squad car. Yeah, his name has come up several times during the Hillside Strangler investigation, but, ya see, no one has gotten around to speaking with him yet. We can wire you an ID F.I.T. of our suspects if you need it."

One face from the printout was Bianchi to a tee.

At the time of his arrest, Ken had been in possession of a large bunch of keys, which were now in a police property box. Detective Nolte had overhead Randy Moa saying that a ring of keys, along with several client account cards for the southside district of Bellingham, were missing from the office, so Nolte went to the property box and retrieved them, and Moa identified them as belonging to those accounts for which Bianchi was solely responsible. One key in particular fitted Dr. Catlow's front door. Indeed, the account card was tied to this key, and this proved that Bianchi had had access to the Bayside address.

With the very real prospect of them having arrested a cold blooded serial killer dawning upon them, the police then searched Ken's Whatcom Security Agency pick up, call sign 5. However, the only item of note recovered from Bianchi's truck was a striped towel. Tests later proved that it was stained with the semen of a nonsecretor and, as we now know, this fitted Bianchi exactly.

On Monday, January 15, 1979, Nolte and his colleagues searched Karen Mandic's apartment for the second time. In a drawer, Nolte found a business card in Ken's name indicating that he was the self-styled "Captain Kenneth A. Bianchi" of Whatcom Security. Nolte spoke to Randy Moa who reported that no such "Captain" title had been authorized by his company.

A few days later, police carried out a thorough search of the south terminal area where Bianchi had been arrested. Here, they found a coat belonging to Diane Wilder and, in one of the pockets, were the keys to Karen's car. Obviously, the two young women couldn't have dropped the coat off at the south terminal; their killer must have done so. The noose was tightening around Bianchi's neck.

It was now crucial for the police to establish Bianchi's movements for the relevant times in question because, if he produced a solid alibi to say he couldn't have committed the murders, the police would have been back at square one.

Kelli Boyd was positive that Ken had arrived home on Thursday evening at about 10:30 p.m. She told the cops that she noticed that he had ripped the seat of his jeans, which she thought was "kinda comical," but she was surprised when he threw the garment into the trash. She had retrieved the pants because she thought that the cloth might come in useful as her mother was making a rug, and she needed all the denim she could lay her hands on. Kelli also recalled that Ken had been sweating profusely when he walked through the door, and this was unusual. "He smelled kinda strange," she said.

When Kelli was asked about a little gold Italian "Good Luck" horn on a chain, which had been found on her dressing table, she explained that it had been a gift from Kenneth way back in Los Angeles. Later, this item of jewelry proved to be identical to one belonging to the murdered Yolanda Washington.

With Kelli placing Bianchi at home around 10:30 p.m. on the night of the murders, the police looked elsewhere for witnesses who might have seen him out and about, and first they spoke to a Mrs. McNeill who lived at 327 Bayside, almost opposite Dr. Catlow's home. She reported that, at around 9:30 a.m. on Thursday, January 11th, she had seen a yellow WSA pick up truck enter Dr. Catlow's driveway. At noon, she saw an identical vehicle enter and leave the property and, at around 7:00 p.m., or shortly thereafter, she heard a vehicle enter the drive but did not see it. When questioned about the sound of the engine, Mrs.

McNeill said that it had sounded like the vehicle that had made the earlier visits.

On Saturday, January 13th, a vital witness came forward in the form of Raymond Spees, who claimed that, during the late evening of the murders, he had been to church. Between 10:00 and 10:30 p.m., he said that he was returning to his home past the cul-de-sac where the bodies were found in Karen's car. As he passed the cul-de-sac entrance, a vehicle came out rapidly, and he had to swerve to avoid it. Spees described the vehicle as a yellow WSA pick up truck with a flashing light bar on the driver's side. Spees was positive about this identification because he knew the firm, and noted its emblem on the cab door. Spees also noticed that the driver was shielding his face with his hand.

With overwhelming evidence mounting against him, Bianchi consistently refused to admit guilt, and then he asked for legal representation. Attorney Dean Brett advised his new client not to talk to the officers again without him present and, initially, Ken found Brett "a shining example of an energetic champion of justice." This flowery accolade was withdrawn a week later after he started to sum up his predicament. Ken was furious that Kelli had held a yard sale to dispose of his property, and then he accused her of having an affair with Dean Brett. Ken was also worried about the lies he had told police about his movements during the time of the murders. He had told officers that he had attended a Sheriff's Reserve meeting, and this was blatantly false. In the years to follow, he wrote to me with a pathetic excuse for telling the lie:

I hate confrontations. People only have their whereabouts checked when they are suspected of doing something wrong. So, knowing I hadn't done anything wrong, and nothing to hide, I had given the original, short answer, about going to the Sheriff's Reserve class. That was simpler than the longer, true explanation. Besides, if I had

*killed the girls, I would have remembered it. I didn't, and that's
what I kept telling the police.*

KENNETH BIANCHI

Poor old Ken! This is yet another example of deep-seated, psychopathic denial, and it is illustrative of Bianchi's thinking process around the time of the murders and, indeed, his warped thought processes today. Of course the "true explanation" to which he refers is that he had just raped and strangled two innocent young women. Now, that would have taken some explaining away.

* * *

When Bianchi was charged with the two counts of murder, he pleaded "not guilty." An affidavit of probable cause set out the allegations in detail, and this was the first opportunity for Bianchi and his legal team to study the case presented by the state. It was also the chance for Ken to embark on the first of his many "fly specking" exercises, where he examines everything in minute detail, for which he has become notorious ever since.

The main thrust of the prosecution was to file for the death penalty, but there was a plea bargain offer on the table: if Bianchi pleaded guilty, the State wouldn't press for the death penalty, and Bianchi would live. This somewhat rocked Bianchi's boat, for he had no intention of simply throwing his hands in the air and admitting guilt. Dean Brett, however, was quick to point out that protestations of innocence would no longer wash; the lie-detector test to which he had submitted had failed him. Nevertheless, Bianchi tore up the plea bargain offer, and he returned to his cell to sulk.

In the United States, the moratorium on capital punishment was lifted in 1976, and Brett was anxious that his client would not be the first killer to be hanged in Washington, so he attempted to mitigate Ken's culpability for the Bellingham murders by suggesting that he should plead "not guilty by reason of insanity." To this end, Dean Brett felt obliged to inform Ken of the horrors of death by hanging, going on to paint a morbid and terrifying picture of this form of execution. "Most go to the gallows screaming," he told the white faced Ken. "Some collapse and have to be strapped to a board. An' hanging is goddamn painful if it don't work out right."

"That meeting scared me straight," Bianchi wrote in a letter. "I was in a corner not of my own making, an' I had nowhere to run or hide." So now confronted with the stark choice between death or a life behind bars, Bianchi reluctantly agreed to plead insanity.

With their client's permission, Ken's legal team employed the services of John Johnson, an investigative social worker, who started to probe Bianchi's history right back to day one. Johnson was an excellent researcher, and before much time had passed he reported back to Bianchi and Brett. It was good news, for it was suggested to Ken that he might have been abused as a child and this would have unhinged his mind. In fact, the defense team went even further. Ken's failure in having remembered killing the co-eds could be due to some form of amnesia. Therefore, with this information now at hand, there was the possibility of Ken receiving a reduced custodial sentence with a specific period before parole or, better still, his time could be served in a psychiatric institution where the silver tongued killer could work his ticket to freedom, as so many killers do.

Talking to this author, Dean Brett denied any such attorney/client manipulation, although it is certain that he advised his client to undergo a series of hypnosis sessions, which Bianchi called "the modern version of the rubber blackjack." And then Ken seized on what he thought was a great idea. He would invent a multiple person-ality disorder.

Although the medical profession had been aware of the enigmas of the multiple personality disorder (MPD) since the early 19th century, the general public learned of the illness largely through the 1957 film *The Three Faces of Eve*, which was based on the book of the same name written by two psychiatrists. MPD seems to be caused by severe psychological traumas in childhood, such as sexual abuse or extreme cruelty, and these experiences can be so painful that the victim blocks them out. In later life, a violent shock can reactivate the trauma, causing the "everyday" personality to blank out. The most remarkable case of MPD in recent years was that of Billy Milligan. In 1977, he was arrested in Columbus, Ohio, for rape. Billy later declared to a social worker that he was not Billy but "David," and subsequent examinations by psychiatrists made it clear that Milligan was a genuine MPD case.

Sexually abused in childhood by his stepfather, Billy had become another personality to escape the misery. Eventually, he split into 23 separate personalities, including a lesbian, a suave Englishman who also spoke Arabic, an electronics expert and a Serbo-Croat. (It has never been explained how Milligan came to speak Serbo-Croat.) Nevertheless, all these personalities were so distinctive that only a remarkable actor could have simulated them. It was later discovered that the lesbian personality committed the rape, and another of the personalities had turned Billy in to the police. And it is now thought that the Milligan case—much publicised in the late 1970s—may have given Bianchi the idea of pretending to be a "multiple."

Ken had watched *The Three Faces of Eve* while he was in custody. He had even read the book, and it is known from his custody records that he also saw the movie *Sybil*, which concerned another multiple personality disorder. So the whole idea of MPD was a gift from the gods, and Bianchi rubbed his hands with glee.

Kenneth Bianchi was sitting in his cell beaming with delight as his attorney arranged the first of many hypnosis sessions. Once again, the killer was playing center stage, and the immediate follow up came about when forensic psychiatrist Dr. Donald T. Lunde recommended that Ken accept a course of hypnosis under the expert supervision of a Dr. John Watkins. Dr. Lunde reasoned that, if anyone could find a genuine MPD, then it had to be Watkins.

On Wednesday, March 23, 1979, Dr. Watkins, a specialist in multiple personalities and hypnosis from the University of Montana, was brought in to perform the first of many sessions with Ken. By now, Bianchi was more than eager to cooperate and, within minutes, it appeared that he was in a trance. He started speaking in a strange, low voice, introducing himself as "Steve Walker." This Steve came across as a highly unpleasant character with a sneering laugh. He told those present that he hated Ken. "Ken doesn't know how to handle women," he said. "You gotta treat 'em rough. Boy, did I fix that turkey. I got him in so much trouble, he'll never get out."

Dr. Watkins believed that what he was witnessing was indeed a genuine multiple personality, and he bought Ken's performance hook, line and sinker. With little prompting, Steve turned to the Los Angeles murders, describing how Ken had walked in on Angelo Buono while he was murdering a girl. At this point, Steve admitted he had taken over Ken's personality, and had turned Ken into Angelo's willing accomplice for all the Hillside Stranglings.

"Are you Ken?" asked Dr. Watkins.

"Do I look like Ken? Killing a broad doesn't make any difference to me. Killing any-fuckin'-body doesn't make any difference to me. Angelo is my kind of man. There should be more people like Angelo in the world. I hate Ken," snarled Bianchi in response.

To Watkins, at least, it seemed perfectly clear that Kenneth Bianchi had two opposing personalities—the loving father, kind friend and hard worker who made up Ken, and the vicious rapist, sadist-come-serial murderer who made up Steve Walker.

Watkins firmly believed that Ken had subconsciously invented Steve as a repository for all his hateful feelings towards his adoptive mother, Frances. And, in this way, Ken could remain a loving, devoted son, the affectionate guy that almost everyone knew and liked, while Steve, who was apparently unknown to Ken, would periodically emerge to wreak terrible vengeance on young women. Yes, Kenneth Bianchi had done his homework very well.

Word soon leaked out that Bianchi was "coughing" to the L.A. murders, and that he had implicated his accomplice, Angelo Buono, so L.A. task force detectives rushed to Bellingham and sat outside Ken's cell door in anticipation of what might happen next. However, dissatisfied with this not quite Oscar winning performance, Bianchi expanded on his scheme and, knowing that the inquisitive police would read his prison diary, on Wednesday, April 18, 1979, he penned a note for them to read.

To be absolutely sure of his diagnosis of multiple personalities, Watkins also administered the Rorschach inkblot test to check out both Ken and Steve, the results of which appeared to support his overall hypothesis—both tests differed and were consistent with two personalities—so he reported back to Dean Brett, saying, "It is one of the clearest cases of Dissociative Reaction and Multiple personality I have diagnosed in over 40 years."

Somewhat condescendingly, Bianchi would later write, while shooting himself in the foot, "Dr. Watkins is a kind, soft spoken, honest behavioral expert who was caught up in the excitement of the moment. When all the hypnosis sessions stopped, the MPD never appeared again."

But the damage had been done and a leak prompted *Time* magazine to pronounce: "BIANCHI—A MULTIPLE PERSONALITY." These headlines so outraged Judge Kurtze that he decided to appoint a panel of experts to evaluate Bianchi, and the judge summoned Dr. Watkins and Professor Donald T. Lunde to act for the defense. Doctors Ralph Allison and Charles Moffett represented the court, and Doctors Martin Orne and

Saul Faerstein acted for the State, in an effort to sort, as the police suggested, "the bullshit from the bullshit."

Fortunately for Dr. Watkins, he had an ally in the judge's camp in Ralph Allison, who was also the author of a famous book called *Minds in Many Pieces*. Dr. Allison's credentials were impeccable and, under apparent hypnosis, Ken, through Steve, claimed, "I fuckin' killed those broads... those fuckin' cunts. That blonde haired cunt, and the brunette cunt."

"Here in Bellingham?" asked Allison incredulously, while gripping the arms of his chair.

"That's right."

"Why?"

"Cause I hate fuckin' cunts."

After that short exchange, Dr. Allison pressed his subject about the murder of Yolanda Washington in Los Angeles, and Steve piped up again. "She was a hooker. Angelo went out and picked her up. I was waiting on the street. He drove round to where I was. I got in the car. We got on the freeway. I fucked her and killed her. We dumped the body off and that was it. Nothin' to it."

In apparently regressing Ken back to his childhood at around the age of nine, Dr. Allison found an environment filled with pain and suffering, which, he thought, had spawned Ken's Steve alter ego. Under the so-called hypnosis, Ken claimed to have met Steve while he was hiding under his bed. "Mommie was hitting me so bad, I met Stevie," he whined in a childlike voice.

Dr. Allison was now in his professional element, and probed a little deeper. "How did you first meet him?" he asked quietly.

"I closed my eyes. I was crying so hard," Bianchi whimpered. "All of a sudden he was there. He said 'Hi' to me. He told me I was his friend. I felt really good that I had a friend I could talk to."

Outside in the corridor, police officers rolled their eyes towards the heavens, while others stuck their fingers down their throats. Detective Terry Wight popped a mint into his mouth and remarked, "That fucker is blowin' smoke in our yard. He's either fuckin' innocent or he's a damn good actor." And he was right on the money. This was going to be a tough case, weeks of unpaid overtime and little sleep, just to get Bianchi into court. With a bit of luck, they might get a judge who suffered from insomnia, and a jury with at least one brain between them, but the cops also reasoned that, even if the judicial train did manage to haul itself into the right station, the shrinks would say that he was nuts, and he would end up doing the rounds of psychiatric interviews long after even they were dead.

Of all the experts who were summoned to evaluate Bianchi, Professor Donald T. Lunde, MA, MD, was perhaps the most qualified. A clinical associate professor of psychiatry and behavioral science, and emeritus lecturer at Stanford University, he is the author of *The Die Song, Murder and Madness* and *Fundamentals of Human Sexuality.* He is also a member of the American Academy of Psychiatry and the Law. Therefore, it might not seem unreasonable to infer that Professor Lunde would provide a correct assessment of Kenneth Bianchi's state of mind. However, in all fairness, he did not, and he later agreed with me on this point, all of which goes to show that even the finest psychiatrists in the world, of which Professor Lunde is one, can be manipulated and conned by a cunning and murderous psychopath.

Lunde began his report, dated Monday, July 23, 1979, by explaining how he had formed his evaluation of Bianchi, and on what sources he had based his diagnosis. His four month study included three short sessions with the subject which took place on July 11th, 12th and 13th. He had read some 3,000 pages of police documents, witness statements, medical and psychiatric reports and school records. He also gained access to the information compiled by Dean Brett, John Johnson and the DA's Office, he reviewed the audiotape and videotape interviews, and read transcripts of examinations performed by his colleagues. Donald Lunde even interviewed Kelli Boyd, along with dozens of other people who knew Bianchi, although Mrs. Bianchi refused to speak to him.

Lunde started by making a glaring error when he reported that Ken had been fostered for the initial 11 months of his life, when it had only been three months. Mistake number two came when he misread the DePaul Clinic evaluations by stating that Mrs. Bianchi had blamed her husband for being unable to have children, when she had said no such thing. And he compounded this error by saying that Nicholas Bianchi was "overshadowed and overpowered" by his wife, when this was not so.

Professor Lunde also gave the wrong dates for Kenneth's schooling, and he was fundamentally inaccurate when he claimed that Ken's enuresis problems were psychosomatic in origin when they were physiological. Professor Lunde suggested that Bianchi's mental condition was of a "dissociative reaction, with extreme stress bordering on psychosis." In his report, the professor wrote,

> *This condition (dissociative reaction) has been present since at least the age of nine years, and is manifested by periods during which the defendant acts without awareness of his actions, and for which he subsequently has amnesia. During some of these periods, the incredible amount of unconscious (repressed) hostility towards women present in this man surfaces. The best demonstration of what I have just described is seen in some of the videotapes, which were made while Bianchi was under hypnosis, and emerged as a quite different personality calling himself "Steve Walker."*
>
> PROFESSOR DONALD T. LUNDE

It was debatable, said Professor Lunde, whether Bianchi represented a true case of multiple personality, as he felt Bianchi could have been capable of faking his symptoms given the wealth of literature in his possession and the fact that he had tried unsuccessfully to pass himself off as a medical expert. But Professor Lunde went on to conclude that "Bianchi is not psychologically sophisticated enough, nor is he intelligent enough to have constructed such an elaborate history which gives him the mental defense if he were subsequently charged with a crime.

"Furthermore, one would have to assume that Bianchi began plotting his strategy for these crimes and his defense at about age nine, since this is when the first documented symptoms of his mental disturbance occurred."

Professor Lunde could not contemplate for a moment that Ken had coached himself on multiple personality disorder simply by watching a few movies and reading a book in his cell, or that the crooked idea had only entered his head as he considered his fate at the end of a hangman's rope. The professor had completely underestimated the cunning of Bianchi, who is the greatest cock-and-bull storyteller since the beginning of time.

But this was not quite the end of the matter as far as Professor Lunde was concerned, because, while stating that Bianchi was mentally competent to stand his trial, he reported that, in his opinion, Ken was indeed suffering from Dissociative Reaction.

"It [dissociative reaction] has affected him in such a manner that he would have been unable to perceive the nature and quality of the acts with which he has been charged. It is my opinion that the defendant did not have a moral sense of right and wrong, but was aware that what he was doing was against the law, and for this reason, precautions were taken to avoid incriminating evidence."

So, Professor Lunde believed that Bianchi was only taken over by Steve when he needed to rape and murder, and at no other time, which turns out to be highly convenient for a defendant facing the death penalty. But, although Ken had no moral sense of right and wrong, conversely, Bianchi knew that, when he was committing his heinous crimes, and undertaking the careful preplanning, the murders themselves and the elaborate cover ups, that he was in fact breaking the law.

Having studied the case file, and having interviewed Bianchi for some eight hours, Dr. Moffett felt it wiser to sit on the fence, believing Bianchi to be "psychotic and probably schizophrenic," which did nothing to endear him to Dr. Allison, who was effectively on the same team. However, Moffett still plunged into the same trap as Watkins, Allison and Lunde in believing that Bianchi had genuinely been hypnotized.

Having now sown the seed of a multiple personality in the minds of three eminent psychiatrists, with a fourth leaning towards a different diagnosis altogether, Ken had only to sit back and watch with amusement as the experts argued about his state of mind, for each psychiatrist who examined him was predisposed to stake a claim on being correct. By cooperating with the psychiatrists, Ken pleased them, and they are the first to agree on this point. When Ken tried to ram normality down their throats, it was a successful and calculated attempt to prop up their beliefs that he really had been hypnotized; therefore, any words that fell from his lips had to be the truth. Dr. Moffett, like Lunde and Watkins, firmly believed that Ken had been hypnotized, which led him to conclude that Steve was the result of an "ego, or an identity split" rather than the "different personality" which his colleagues had now agreed upon. Moffett added, "Is this so different from a patient hearing the voice of Satan and struggle against alien control?"

In believing that Steve existed as a "split" rather than an entirely "separate" personality, Dr. Moffett missed another vital observation which would have proved Bianchi to be a bare-faced liar, for Ken was delighting in reliving his wicked crimes in all their gory detail, safe in the knowledge that this was coming from Steve. Safe, too, in the knowledge that he could confess without blame being apportioned to him personally. He was suckering the doctors; he was playing the starring role to a well established and well intentioned audience who could make him internationally famous. Ken had struggled all his life to be someone and, at last, he had almost achieved his goal.

Dr. Moffett's diagnosis, actually, wasn't wildly off the mark. He claimed that Ken was suffering from "delusional grandiosity," but added, "Ken lives on the brink of regressed and infantile terror. He literally wakens in his cell at night, hiding under his bed in nameless terror."

Ken did wake from his sleep, and he did hide under his cell bed. However, not unlike the phony notes he penned in his jail diary, that were sure to find their way to the attention of the authorities, these nocturnal activities were feigned sideshows to arouse the attention of his guards, to further bolster his act, and to substantiate the façade of his vulnerability.

Dr. Moffett eventually concluded in his summary to Judge Kurtze, "He [Bianchi] intellectually knows right from wrong. The combination of his grandiose alter ego, and his dissociation, and his lack of awareness of the violent aspects of his own being, would not permit him to effectively control and govern his actions."

When Doctor Orne from the Department of Psychiatry at the Pennsylvania Medical School arrived in Bellingham blew not only his colleagues, but also Bianchi, out of the water in a flash of brilliance. Aware of the benefits to Bianchi if he succeeded in faking a multiple personality disorder, Dr. Orne decided to analyze, not so much Ken's personality, but the assumption of multiple personality itself. This was a unique move, a lateral test to see whether Bianchi had been really hypnotized at all, for Dr. Orne figured that, if this man could fake a multiple personality disorder, then he could easily fake hypnosis. In Dr. Orne, Bianchi was about to meet his nemesis.

Before attempting to hypnotize Bianchi, Dr. Orne mentioned in passing, and deliberately almost out of Ken's hearing, that it was rare in the case of multiple personalities for there to be just two personalities. Bianchi overheard the doctor, and, shortly after he entered a phoney trance, out came "Billy," who amounted to personality number three. Minutes later, Dr. Orne asked Billy to sit back and talk to his lawyer who wasn't present in the room, but, on this occasion, Ken overplayed his part. Of course, Billy had no lawyer at all, but this did not stop Ken from leaning across the table and shaking the invisible attorney's hand. Then Dr. Orne had Dean Brett walk into the room. Bianchi, or Billy, immediately shifted his attention to the visible lawyer, asking, "How can I see him in two places?" This behavior proved beyond a shadow of a doubt that Bianchi was faking hypnosis and, following a few other tests, it was shown that Bianchi was faking MPD, too.

So, at long last, Ken had come unstuck and he was now exposed as the faker he really was. And the entire fabrication completely collapsed when a detective recalled seeing the name Steve Walker among the documents found in Ken's attaché case. Steve Walker, it transpired, was the real psychology student who had unwittingly furnished Bianchi with his diploma, the very same item that Ken had altered to suit his own ends, back in Los Angeles. Checkmate.

After pleading guilty to seven murders, which included the Bellingham slayings, Kenneth Alessio Bianchi was sentenced on Friday, October 19, 1979. Three days later, Angelo Buono was arrested in Los Angeles, and he was charged with ten murders. On April Fool's Day, 1984, Buono was sentenced. A plea bargain meant that neither would face the death penalty if they gave evidence. Of course, Steve and Billy never again surfaced, but someone else did, and she was a beautiful, part time actress and writer. Her name is Veronica Wallace Lynn Compton.

* * *

"Let's deal with our mutual friend, Bianchi. Ken's not stupid. Ken is the slickest criminal I've ever met in all of my years, and I've met a few criminals. But, without doubt, Ken is the master of them all.

He is very circumspect … that's where his brilliance lies, in his ability to premeditate things, and to protect himself. He is very good at that."

VERONICA COMPTON, IN CONVERSATION WITH THE AUTHOR

While held in custody at the Los Angeles County Jail during Buono's trial, Ken almost engineered his freedom when a young actress and budding screenplay writer fell in love with him. "VerLyn" was a statuesque beauty with sultry, raven hair. She had a figure that made most men, and many women, drool and, as one woman observed, "VerLyn has a figure that most women would die for." Indeed, even after serving 15 years in prison—she has since been released—Veronica is still an extremely beautiful woman.

Veronica was, and still is, highly intelligent, too, but it would be fair to add that she has never fully applied her many abilities to any studies or goals and, around the time of the Hillside Stranglings, she was deeply hooked into a downward spiral of cocaine and sexual perversion, the latter of which would become her downfall. In the waning days of 1979, Veronica was into sadomasochism, practicing as a dominatrix. She was partying every night, heavily dependent on the cocaine high that fuelled her fantasies and fed her enormous bisexual appetite for whipping the flesh of LA's movers and shakers.

When I met Veronica at the Western Washington Correctional Center for Women (WWCCW) in Gig Harbor, she explained, "In those days, I was inexorably slipping deeper and deeper into the nether world of the leather and the lash scene. The more lurid, the more wickedly cruel the fantasy, the better." She also explained that she had had aspirations of becoming an actress and a screenplay writer. In fact, she had penned a number of frantic, blood dripping fiction pieces, which were far too extreme for any mainstream publisher to commission. One of those stories was called *The Mutilated Cutter*, concerning a female serial killer who injected semen into her victim's vaginas to make police think that a man was the murderer.

The Los Angeles trial of Bianchi and Buono was in full swing at this time, so Veronica wrote to the handsome Ken, asking him to help her research *The Mutilated Cutter*. Within a short space of time, they were meeting frequently in the county jail, and Veronica fell in love with Bianchi, who had now convinced her that he was an innocent man.

Week after week, they shared fantasies and intimate love letters and, quick to take any advantage that came his way, with the plot of *The Mutilated Cutter* appealing to him, Ken persuaded VerLyn to carry out her literary plot in real life—in Bellingham, of all places. This, he said, would prove that the Hillside Strangler was still at large. "If you can do this, I will be let out of prison and be free to marry you," he told her.

The first and most important part of the scheme was to obtain Bianchi's semen and smuggle it out of jail. Bianchi soon solved that problem when he cut the finger from a stolen kitchen rubber glove. He masturbated into it and then tied the open end with the cord from a string of rosary beads, which he had acquired from a visiting Roman Catholic priest. He then stuffed the small package into the spine of a law book, which had been loaned to him by Veronica, and, when she called to visit him a week later, she walked out of the jail with the book tucked under her arm.

With the first part of the plot completed, they now had to establish alibis for the times of the Los Angeles murders, for even Bianchi could not be in two places at once and, if he could prove that he was elsewhere when the murders took place, he reasoned that he would be home and dry.

To achieve this difficult feat of establishing alibis, Veronica traveled out of state, staying at hotels, where she granted sexual favors to the staff in return for blank bar tabs and backdated receipts for rooms Ken had never used; it proved easy. She forged Ken's signature on these documents, but, to add even further credence to the plan, she stole gas station receipt books and filled them in. The idea was that, in the weeks to follow, she would miraculously uncover this "new evidence," present it to the police and hope that this would ensure her lover's release from prison.

In 1980, and now completely under Ken's spell, VerLyn flew to Seattle, and from there she drove up to Bellingham, where she befriended a young woman called Kim Breed in a bar. In an audiotape she sent to me, Veronica's exact words were:

The task would be settled in mere hours. The victim would fit the needed requisites. I would arrive in Bellingham, Washington, on a fall afternoon. Another woman's body would be discovered shortly afterward. The method of killing would be familiar to the Whatcom County Homicide team. Their worst nightmare would be relived: a serial killer had apparently returned to town to continue the reign of terror he had enjoyed only 20 months previously. What they were not to know was that this individual was not a serial killer, neither was it a man.

The peculiar murder tools remained undisturbed in the luggage I retrieved from the airport conveyor. There were no suspicious glances and, with a small pillow under my clothes, I was just another pregnant woman, dressed perhaps a bit too "California," with my long, blonde hair held back with a silk scarf, a muslin dress and designer sunglasses, more suited to a beach side patio than gloomy Washington. Still, even with the clothes, I could hardly qualify as anyone noteworthy.

My purse contained plenty of cash and a cache of narcotics; both would be essential in my work ahead. A taxi took me to my destination, a small motel off the town's main boulevard. I signed the register with a fabricated name, the same one as I had used for my plane tickets, to keep my real identity a secret. Without taking off my gloves, I picked up the room key, and said, 'Thank you,' in my best affected Southern drawl. It, like everything about me, was a performance. A creation. A fiction.

The motel room was standard, but it held everything necessary for my purpose. There was a queen size bed, a mirrored vanity area and a small bathroom. Still keeping my gloves on, I unpacked the one suitcase, and arranged the items in a vanity drawer. I carefully laid out two pieces of rope, one with a pre-tied noose, the other loose, to be used to tie the victim's wrists.

Satisfied with my organization of the items, I started the ritual of medications—tranquillizers, cocaine and alcohol, to be taken as he [Bianchi] had directed. Finishing with them, and with my addictions sated for the moment, I felt hopeful that the hallucinations would be kept at bay, so I settled into tending the blonde wig and adjusting the padding that made my flat stomach give the appearance of pregnancy under my dress. All part of the fictitious creature partly of my making and partly of Ken's.

VERONICA COMPTON

During her first evening in Bellingham, VerLyn met Kim Breed in a local bar. After a few drinks, VerLyn invited Kim back to her motel room. Once there, she slipped the noose over the unsuspecting woman's head, then tried to tie her wrists. However, Kim Breed was a martial arts expert, so she athletically threw her assailant over her head, and rushed into the street, leaving Veronica dazed and scared on the bedroom floor. When she recovered, Veronica fled back to Los Angeles with the police in hot pursuit, having traced her airline ticket.

When she was arrested and returned to Bellingham, she knew that she was in a serious predicament. In this conservative town, where wearing a garter belt was considered kinky, and drug addicts thought to be the curse of the nation, VerLyn was about to stand her trial with the odds a million-to-one in favor of a guilty verdict. Subsequently,

Veronica was sentenced to 15 years for trying to duplicate a Kenneth Bianchi murder in an effort to free one of the most hated men in American criminal history. Only recently, and after one escape bid in which she climbed under the wire and almost got clean away, is Veronica a free woman, married and living near Seattle.

* * *

Kenneth Alessio Bianchi arrived at the Shelton Reception Center in January 1985, and was furious that his file had "Sexual Psychopath" over the cover, with the words "Child Killer" underneath. This file was supposed to remain out of the sight of other inmates, but, by the time Ken arrived at his cell, the prison grapevine had ensured that his true identity was known throughout the pen. Now he had a price on his head, as everyone wanted the kudos of having murdered one of the infamous Hillside Stranglers.

In February 1985, Bianchi was taken to the Washington State Penitentiary at Walla Walla, where he was immediately placed in punitive segregation. Known as "The Hole" in prison parlance, Ken was confined here for almost two years, living in terror of his life. During this period, he had the gall to apply for parole, while reasoning that, if this failed, he would turn to God to see if the Almighty could help him out.

William B. Matthews, a 63-year-old former communications technician who doubled as a Christian visitor, recalls meeting Bianchi shortly after his arrival at Walla Walla, saying, "I remember it was a time of duress for Ken. He told me that urine had been thrown over him several times, and feces thrown at him once by other inmates. I might explain that Ken gave his life to Christ during the first week of his stay at WSP. I wish that it was possible to convey what it was like when I walked through that filthy tier called 'The Hole', and to see this man, Ken, with so much joy and peace within himself."

So, wily Kenneth Bianchi was up to his old tricks yet again, this time by flicking a switch and becoming a devoted servant of God almost overnight. And delighted he would have been, for with the threat of murder around every corner, it goes without saying that he would have been very pleased to see the friendly, if not naïve, face of William B. Matthews staring at him through the cell bars.

In support of Bianchi's somewhat premature parole application, which was scheduled for December 17, 1985, residents of Walla Walla, Gordon and Dorothy Otter, wrote to the Board of Prison Terms and Paroles on August 16th, stating, "From our observations of Mr. Bianchi, we feel that he is sincere and a dedicated Christian man, who has a very positive attitude. He is always pleasant, takes an active part in the religious services, and he is concerned about the welfare of others." The Otters' intentions may have been good, but it seems that they failed to grasp the fact that the main reason inmates attend religious services is to get out of their cells for a few minutes, grab a decent cookie, enjoy a cup of coffee—with sugar—and suck up to any do-gooders who might be inclined to influence parole hearings in their favor. Kenneth was no exception, and the Otters fell for it. Unfortunately, the Otters had also failed to appreciate the true extent of Ken's concern for the "welfare of others," which did not extend to the many women and children that he had raped and murdered over the years. The more obvious fact that Ken hadn't been within a mile of a church in his life didn't concern the Otters at all.

On the very same day that the Otters' letter arrived at the parole office, a reference from Pastor Dick Jewett, of the Stateline Seventh Day Adventist Church in Milton-Freewater, Oregon, dropped through the parole board's mailbox. It read,

I am filing this reference on behalf of Ken. He is a member in good standing of my church. I have baptised Ken myself and, after exten-

sive interviews, I have satisfied my mind as to his sincerity. He is an active member and regular attendee at our services on the prison campus. His attitude and conduct at the present time is exemplary.

PASTOR DICK JEWETT

It was obvious that Ken had been very busy indeed, especially when parole officials opened yet another letter which had been sent by a Mr. and Mrs. Black:

We had the privilege of witnessing Ken Bianchi make a commitment to the Lord in Baptism. Ken appears to be very sincere, devoted and earnest. His views are conservative, but he never fails to look at both sides. He has always been polite and sensitive concerning this. He wants to attend college, which shows he has goals. My husband and I have been involved in the prison ministry just over two years. We have written and talked to many prisoners. From these experiences we have learned to be fair judges of character. It is obvious to us that Kenneth Bianchi truly loves the Lord and his behavior and attitude strongly proves it.

MR. AND MRS. BLACK

Another letter of recommendation was received from Father Frederick Ellsworth, a well meaning priest from the Christ the Healer Orthodox Mission, saying, "Ken is open, willing to share and quite responsive. I have two young daughters, and I would even welcome him into my home. He would fit in well with my family and his writing has been a highlight."

And the icing on the cake came from one Bruce Zicari a tax consultant from Penfield, New York. Bruce declared, "I would certainly like to reiterate my confidence and high regard for Kenneth Bianchi, and I am certain that he has the capabilities to be successful at whatever field of endeavor he might choose."

Of course, Bianchi's endeavors in the field of sadosexual serial homicide had been highly successful. Fortunately, however, none of this impressed the parole panel who rejected Bianchi's application out of hand. So Ken settled down to his studies, and he started by attending a Saturday morning computer class, and in doing so he was paving his way to participate in regular college programs. For the time being, Bianchi would put God on the back burner, but not before offering some enlightenment in a letter to me.

I have academically completed a ministerial training program given by the Evangelical Theological Seminary, and I am blessed to have been ordained by a Full Gospel Church back in 1986. My faith had taken an exploratory course with independent studies in Eastern religions, earth religions, Judaism and Biblical archaeology. I even mailed out, free of charge, a written homily entitled "Word on the Word." I ceased doing it because it became too expensive. I would not, and cannot, accept donation.

KENNETH BIANCHI IN A LETTER TO THE AUTHOR

Well, Ken *is* being a little economical with the truth here, for, after speaking to prison officials, I learned that he raked in as much cash as he could before the Department of Corrections stopped him from running his own "Save Ken Bianchi" campaign. And, it also transpires that, for years, Bianchi's church had sent him quarterly newsletters detailing forthcoming religious events. They addressed correspondence to none other than "Reverend K. Bianchi." This, however, did not last long, for, when James Blodgett, a new, tough, no-nonsense prison administrator took over, Bianchi's ordination certificate and letters were confiscated.

But Ken keeps on trying—or trying, at least, to pull the wool over everyone's eyes. In June 1988, he received his Associate in Arts Degree. In truth, he cannot draw a straight line; he paid more able inmates to draw fine pencil pictures which he then signed as his own, making a few bucks into the bargain.

Then, on Thursday, September 21, 1989, Ken Bianchi married Shirlee Joyce in the prison chapel. Shirlee, who was a pen pal, met him for the first time and spent just two hours with the killer the day before the ceremony. He wore an immaculate tuxedo. She wore a white wedding dress and veil, and the guests included representatives of both families.

The following day, prison records show that Ken refused to work, claiming, "You must be joking. It's the day after my fuckin' wedding." This caused Officer Estes to give Bianchi an infraction. Shortly afterward, Officer Grudzinski overhead Bianchi threatening to "fuckin' get Estes" at the first opportunity. This loose remark, although probably made in the heat of the moment, resulted in Bianchi being disciplined and thrown again into The Hole. He lost his job in the law library—a rare privilege among the several thousand inmates—and the opportunity to consummate his marriage during a 23-hour session with Shirlee in the Combo Area of the penitentiary.

Shirlee divorced Ken in 1993.

In October 1989, our man received a Bachelor of Science in Law degree, and since then he has earned a Juris Doctor degree. At the time of writing, he is a member of the National Bar Association. It could be argued that Bianchi knows as much about the law as anyone, and he does, for, in 1992, Bianchi sued a playing card manufacturer for $8.5 million.

Eclipse Enterprises Inc. of Forestville, California, had launched 10 million of its "True Crime" collector's cards in July the same year. This incurred the wrath of Bianchi, who argued that his face, which was number 106 in the 110 card line up, was causing him irreparable harm, and affecting his appeal process. "They appropriated my face to make money. They breached my copyright," he griped in a letter.

Eclipse fought the case and, in a landmark decision, the judge ruled in their favor. Nevertheless, the cost of defending the action brought

Eclipse to bankruptcy. A former partner in the firm, Katherine Yron-wode, explained to me, "Bianchi was part and parcel of my company's collapse. The cost of defending the case caused the break-up of my marriage, and everything I had worked for 20 years to achieve came to nothing. I cannot say what I think of Bianchi. I just can't say."

In 1995, I saw the Hillside Strangler in the flesh for the last time. He was lying on the bunk of cell number 12 in the Special Housing Unit, where he is kept for his own protection. The very sight of me peering through the bars of his cage infuriated him. He went berserk, and immediately threatened to sue the Department of Corrections for allowing me to violate his civil rights. This threat was not hot air. For a start, it brought down a mountain of paperwork for the DOC to deal with and, with his appeal against the Bellingham convictions—Petition C95-0934—filed on June 11, 1995, in the pipeline, we have not heard the last of Kenneth Bianchi.

Over years of cumulative experience, professionals know that the majority of psychopaths—or "sociopaths" or "antisocial personalities," as they are also called—lie, manipulate, deny and deceive to avoid taking responsibility for their crimes. Dr. Richard Kraus is quoted in the late Jack Olsen's book *The Misbegotten Son* as saying in reference to psychopaths:

> *Their robotic cruelty reflected dehumanization, stunted conscience, and inability to empathize. They are usually smooth, verbose, glossy, neat, artificial—both controlled and controlling. Behind a "mask of insanity," they lived superficial and often destructive lives.*

Kenneth Bianchi is all of these things and more, so one might categorize him as an exploitative, displaced, sadist serial killer. He is exploitative in that his sexual behavior was that of a man always on the prowl for women to exploit sexually, to force women to submit sexually with no care about the victim's welfare. He is displaced in that his sexual behavior was an expression of anger and rage, the cumulative backlog of experienced and imagined insults from the many people he had met over the years, all of which continually chipped away at his self esteem and fragile ego. It was his mother who said, "It seemed that, whenever Ken had a fight with a girlfriend, or had problems, he went out and killed someone."

And, of course, Bianchi was a sexual sadist. With Angelo Buono, another perverted individual cast from the same mold, both men were able to enjoy their sadistic tendencies to the full and this made them extremely dangerous creatures indeed.

It goes without saying that Bianchi did suffer a form of psychological child abuse during his formative years, and there can be no doubt that this damaged him. Many believe, as I do, that this is no mitigation for his heinous crimes. By his own admission, he was having sex with young girls before his teenage years, whom he refers to as "women." It is also known that he masturbates at the thought of having sex with preteen girls and his murder victims even today.

Throughout his life, Ken carried the social stigma of being a bastard, and perhaps there is some truth in the fact that Kenneth Bianchi really wanted to be someone special, to be able to prove his worth, not only to himself, but also to his adoptive mother who had all but drained him of emotion for some 16 years. But therein lies the rub, for everything he set his hand to, with the exception of serial murder and rape, he failed at dismally. Whether it was love or work, he was a born loser.

As for Ken's fake multiple personality disorder, the invention of Steve and Billy, these were really only another two in a long list of alter egos, for, by the time of his arrest in Bellingham, he had already consciously invented several other false identities—Dr. Bianchi, Captain Bianchi, the fake cop, the terminal cancer patient, the phony film producer—all of which he put in place to compensate for his secret but self-acknowledged inadequacies. And, without these phony alter egos propping up his self esteem, he would have crumbled mentally.

But has he learned from all of this? Unfortunately not, for his fascination with alternative identities continues to this day. He has legally adopted a couple of squeaky clean new names, with a good, old-fashioned Italian ring about them: "Anthony D'Amato," meaning "of the beloved," and then "Nicholas Fontana." Of course, we shouldn't forget the "Reverend Kenneth Bianchi."

Like most serial murderers, Bianchi is an excellent example of the antisocial personality. He is a liar through and through. He will deny guilt to suit himself and, when the cards are stacked against him, he will lie again and again at the drop of a hat to suit the circumstances. In fact, one rather gets the impression that Ken does not know the meaning of the word "truth."

Today, as he appeals against his convictions for the murders of Karen Mandic and Diane Wilder, he appears to have forgotten that he gave police details of the murders that only the killer would know. Nevertheless, he even concocted a laughable scenario whereby a former staff member at the Whatcom Security Agency conspired with Karen's two boyfriends, not only to murder the two co-eds, but to shift blame on to himself. Yes, it is true that Kenneth Alessio Bianchi does actually exist in a world where elephants fly.

Angelo Buono died from a heart condition at the Calapatria State Prison on Saturday, September 21, 2002. He was 64.

This chapter is based upon two years' continual correspondence with Kenneth Bianchi, his adoptive mother Frances and Veronica Wallace Compton; unrestricted interview access to Bianchi at WSP Walla Walla by the WDC and the assistance of police and the judiciary in Los Angeles, Rochester, NY and Bellingham, WA.

Other Books from Ulysses Press

Cannibal Serial Killers: Profiles of Depraved Flesh-Eating Murderers
Christopher Berry-Dee, $14.95
Delving deep into the twisted actions of Hannibal Lecter–type murderers, *Cannibal Serial Killers* profiles the depraved individuals who prolong their horrific crimes beyond the thrill of the chase to a perverse ritualized finale.

Serial Killers and Mass Murderers: Profiles of the World's Most Barbaric Criminals
Nigel Cawthorne, $14.95
Serial Killers and Mass Murderers present a fascinating investigation of the dark side.

The Voices of Serial Killers: The World's Most Maniacal Murderers in their Own Words
Christopher Berry-Dee and Victoria Redstall, $14.95
The Voices of Serial Killers provides blow-by-blow accounts of the killers' ruthless actions, and then goes even further to let you hear their own words.

To order these books call 800-377-2542 or 510-601-8301, fax 510-601-8307, e-mail ulysses@ulyssespress.com, or write to Ulysses Press, P.O. Box 3440, Berkeley, CA 94703. All retail orders are shipped free of charge. California residents must include sales tax. Allow two to three weeks for delivery.

About the Author

Christopher Berry-Dee is owner and editor-in-chief of *The New Criminologist*, and is director of the Criminology Research Institute. His books include *Talking with Serial Killers*, *Unmasking Mr. Ripper* (a study of the disappearance of Suzy Lamplugh) and *Dad, Help Me*, the story of Derek Bentley and Christopher Craig (written with Robin Odell). He has also worked extensively on television programs dealing with issues of serious crime.